Joachim Zentes / Dirk Morschett / Hanna Schramm-Kl

Strategic Retail Management

Joachim Zentes / Dirk Morschett
Hanna Schramm-Klein

Strategic Retail Management

Text and International Cases

2nd Edition

GABLER

Bibliographic information published by the Deutsche Nationalbibliothek
The Deutsche Nationalbibliothek lists this publication in the Deutsche Nationalbibliografie;
detailed bibliographic data are available in the Internet at http://dnb.d-nb.de.

Joachim Zentes is Professor of Marketing and Management at the Saarland University, Saarbrü-cken, Germany. He is Director of the Institute for Commerce & International Marketing (H.I.MA.) and Director of the Europa-Institut at the Saarland University. He holds a chair in Business Administration, especially Foreign Trade and International Management, and is also a member of various boards of directors and advisory boards in Germany and abroad.

Dirk Morschett is Professor of International Management at the University of Fribourg, Switzerland. He holds the Liebherr/Richemont Endowed Chair of International Management and is responsible for the Master of Arts in European Business. He is Director of the Centre for European Studies at the University of Fribourg and visiting lecturer in several Master and MBA programmes at universities in Switzerland and abroad.

Hanna Schramm-Klein is Professor of Marketing at the University of Siegen, Germany. She holds a chair in Business Administration, especially Marketing, and is visiting lecturer in several Master and MBA programmes at universities in Germany and abroad.

1st Edition 2007
2nd Edition 2011

Editorial Office: Barbara Roscher

Gabler Verlag is a brand of Springer Fachmedien.
Springer Fachmedien is part of Springer Science+Business Media.
www.gabler.de

Cover design: KünkelLopka Medienentwicklung, Heidelberg
Printing and binding: Ten Brink, Meppel
Printed on acid-free paper
Printed in the Netherlands

ISBN 978-3-8349-2536-7

Preface

Retailing is constantly becoming more important in economic terms. This becomes evident when looking at the development of many individual countries in Europe, America and Asia. In highly developed countries, retailing is assuming more and more of a leadership role in the distribution channel. Expansion strategies, retail branding strategies, innovative solutions for supply chain management etc., all reflect this trend. In transformation countries, such as in Central and Eastern Europe, as well as in emerging countries, such as China or Brazil, fundamental changes in retailing structures are becoming apparent and these may lead to comparable developments. In view of internationalisation, a further profound change can be noticed. Retailing companies that were formerly characterised by a local or national orientation are increasingly developing into global players with worldwide operations.

Book Concept and Overview

The present book is devoted to the dynamic development of retailing. The various strategy concepts adopted by retailing companies and their implementation in practice are at the core of the book. This is not a traditional textbook or collection of case studies; it intends to demonstrate the complex and manifold questions of retail management in the form of 15 lessons that provide a thematic overview of key issues and illustrate them with the help of comprehensive case studies. Internationally known retail companies are used as examples to facilitate an understanding of what is involved in strategic retail management and to present some best practices.

The book is divided into four main parts. Part I introduces "Functions, Formats and Players in Retailing" and comprises Chapters 1 to 6. In Part II, growth, internationalisation and retail branding strategies, as fundamental aspects of "Strategic Marketing in Retailing" are dealt with (Chapter 7 to 9). Part III focuses on the "Marketing Mix in Retailing". Store location, merchandising and category management, pricing, instore marketing and customer relationship management are discussed in Chapters 10 to 14. Finally, Part IV "Buying, Logistics and Performance Measurement" deals with retail purchasing strategies and concepts, the modern concepts of physical distribution and IT-based supply chain management, as well as methods of performance and financial controlling (Chapters 15 to 18).

Teaching and Learning

The book is targeted primarily at students in their third and fourth academic year (undergraduate and graduate level) in the field of Business Administration/Marketing/Management at different institutions, such as universities, academies and business schools. In addition, practitioners in the consumer goods industry and in retailing companies, who wish to obtain compact and practice-oriented information on current retail concepts, will also benefit from reading this book.

Furthermore, the book can be used in education as a basis for working with case studies. For this purpose, the case studies are integrated into the lessons in such a way that they provide additional content and a specific application of the individual lessons. That is, they form part of the main topic, but also lead to suggested discussion subjects and questions in order to deepen the understanding of the topic. Instructors are provided with additional resources. For each case study, a solution draft is provided via the publisher's webpage (www.gabler.de).

Acknowledgements

A case study approach cannot be developed effectively without the active support and cooperation of the selected retailing companies. Thus, we first of all thank the companies and their representatives who have willingly supported us in the development of the case studies.

At Gabler Verlag, we thank Barbara Roscher who accompanied and supported our concept for this book from the beginning.

At the universities where the three authors are teaching and researching, we would particular like to thank Dipl.-Kfm. Matthias Schu (University of Fribourg) for the support with the editorial work. We also acknowledge the assistance of several assistants of the three chairs for the preparation of a number of case studies.

Saarbrücken, Fribourg and Siegen, July 2011

JOACHIM ZENTES   DIRK MORSCHETT   HANNA SCHRAMM-KLEIN

Contents

Introduction

Retailing is one of the world's largest industries. It is in a permanent state of change, and the pace of this change has been accelerating over the past decade. From a marketing perspective, retailers are closer to the consumer than manufacturing companies. Retailers represent the culmination of the marketing process and the contact point between consumers and manufactured products. While retailing has long set buying decisions as its highest priority and was very focussed on the product assortment, it now follows a more holistic approach to management and marketing and is seizing the opportunity to be consumer-oriented, engage in personal contact with customers, gather information on consumer behaviour and exploit insights into consumer behaviour and preferences. What was once a simple way of doing business has been transformed into a highly sophisticated form of management and marketing. Retail marketing consistently features more efficient, more meaningful and more profitable marketing practices (Mulhern 1997, p. 103).

Retailing involves those companies that are engaged primarily in the activity of purchasing products from other organisations with the intent to resell those goods to private households, generally without transformation, and rendering services incidental to the sale of merchandise. The retailing process is the final step in the distribution of merchandise.

A number of developments are responsible for the dynamic change in modern retail management. In most developed countries, retailing has experienced a dramatic increase in the scale of operations and in market concentration. **Large-scale retail chains** have appeared and have taken market share from independently owned small shops. These retail chains first developed into regional groups and then into nationally and even internationally active retail operations. In the past decade, mergers and acquisitions between already large players have intensified this development. Many retailers now have massive turnovers, very large numbers of employees and extensive store networks. The world's largest retailer, *Walmart*, achieves an annual turnover of almost 300 billion EUR, which exceeds the gross domestic product of many smaller countries, and employs about 2 million people. *Carrefour*, the largest European retailer and the no. 2 in the world, operates more than 10,000 stores worldwide.

At the same time, many retailers have developed into international multichannel retailers, that is, they operate in many countries and offer different retail formats for their customers. For example, the French retailer *Carrefour* is now a multi-format group that uses hypermarkets, supermarkets, convenience stores, hard discounters and other formats to sell its assortment to customers in over 30 countries. More than half of its turnover is earned outside its home market. The German *Metro Group* employs food superstores (*Real*), food supermarkets (*extra*), consumer electronics category killers (*Media Markt and Saturn*), cash & carry wholesale stores (*Metro C&C*) and other formats and earns about two thirds of its turnover in markets outside Germany. *Tesco* is expanding rapidly into Eastern European and Asian markets and, in addition to several store-based formats, very successfully operates an e-commerce channel, *Tesco.com*. While the rise of e-commerce in retailing was initially overestimated in the days of Internet hype, it has nonetheless developed slowly but surely and *Tesco* now achieves sales of almost 2 billion EUR with its online-channel.

In most country markets, retailing is also a very concentrated industry. According to the market research company *Planet Retail*, the top five food retailers account for more than 55 % of the market in the UK; in Germany and France, it is even above 70 %. Consequently, a **shift in power** within the distribution channel is one of the most influential developments over recent decades. The power of individual retail organisations is growing; they are now comparable to and, in many cases, even larger than many manufacturers, even for global brand manufacturers such as *Procter & Gamble, Sony* or *Nestlé*. Thus, manufacturers now often depend on a few large retailers for a substantial share of their global turnovers. Hand in hand with this increasing size, retail marketing budgets, IT budgets and budgets for top managers have also been increasing. Furthermore, not only the growing size and concentration, but also the increased sophistication of retail management, combined with the better availability of customer data, has contributed to the power shift. Retailing is currently one of the leading industries in the application of new technologies. Retailer **PoS data** has become more valuable as IT systems have facilitated the collection of data at the checkout. Furthermore, as retailers have grown from regional to national chains, they have been able to accumulate knowledge about consumer trends and the development of product sales, etc., which has enhanced their relevance as gatekeepers for products on their routes to the customer. Customer-specific data that is now increasingly being gathered via **loyalty cards** adds to this knowledge. Where manufacturer brands once used to be all important, the past few years have witnessed the power of **retail brands** challenging the positions of suppliers. Retailers have started to embrace the concept of **strategic marketing**; they use strategic planning and position themselves relative to their competitors. Thus, the enormous buying volume of a retailer is only one source of its power base – albeit certainly the most important – with other developments adding to its power.

Retailers are **intermediaries** in the distribution channel. However, while retailing has long been considered a somewhat passive link in the value chain between manufacturer and consumer, retailers now use their positions to become the **dominant player in the distribution channel**. They develop their own marketing concepts and assume **marketing leadership** in their vertical relationships with manufacturers. Retailers have also developed their own logistics concepts and created central warehouses. Accordingly, while it was the manufacturers who traditionally fulfilled large parts of the logistics function, retailers today also strive towards **logistics leadership** in the distribution channel.

With this book, our objective is to cover the most important aspects of retail management with a comprehensive, yet brief, and innovative approach. We discuss 18 different topics in retail management by first giving a thematic overview of the topic that covers the key issues and explains the most important concepts and then illustrating them with the help of extended case studies. For the case studies, internationally known companies were chosen that can be considered best practice cases in the respective strategy fields.

In Part I, the functions of retailers are first introduced (Chapter 1). Then, formats and players in retailing are discussed. A **retail format** represents a specific configuration of the retail marketing mix (e.g. store size, typical location, merchandise, price and service offered) and it often forms the core of the retail strategy. Different formats are described and there is a discussion of those that are currently gaining market share and those formats that are on the decline. For example, category killers such as *IKEA*, *Media Markt* and *Leroy Merlin* have been growing tremendously over the past few decades. Hard discounters, such as *Aldi*, are certainly one of the most aggressively growing retail formats in food retailing worldwide (Chapters 2 and 3). **E-commerce** has grown into a substantial business in general merchandise retailing. Many pure Internet players, such as *Amazon* and *Ebay*, have reached a considerable scale. At the same time, more and more stationary retailers embrace online-shopping, so Internet shopping is offered more and more often as part of a **multichannel** approach (Chapter 4). At the same time, not only new formats, but also new players are competing with existing retailers. The most important trend explained in this book is the emergence of manufacturers as competitors. To an increasing extent, manufacturers operate in vertical marketing systems, trying to control the distribution of their products to the consumer, either through contractual or even by means of equity-based vertical strategies (Chapter 5). But also, vertically integrated players like *IKEA*, *Zara* or *H&M*, that are simultaneously retailers and manufacturers, have captured major market shares in many retail sectors (Chapter 6).

In Part II, the most important aspects of strategic retail marketing are discussed. Dynamic growth is one of the most important developments in retailing over recent decades and forms the foundation for many other subsequent changes. This growth is being achieved through various different **growth strategies**, such as outlet multiplication, acquisitions and franchising (Chapter 7). In addition, since many industrial countries are characterised by stagnating retail markets, this growth is more and more often achieved by entering foreign markets. The process of **internationalisation** poses a complex task, since the local environments in host countries often differ considerably from the home market (Chapter 8). Growth, whether nationally or internationally, can only be achieved with a sustainable competitive advantage, and retailers are now increasingly trying to develop a clear **positioning** for their companies relative to those of their competitors. One important component of this marketing strategy is to create a strong **retail brand**, with clear and distinct associations in the consumer's mind that support the development of customer loyalty to the company (Chapter 9).

Within the framework of strategic retail marketing, retailers have more options available in their **marketing mix** than do manufacturers, because they are in direct contact with the final consumers, who visit their stores and interact directly with them. Part III of the book examines the marketing mix and takes an in-depth look at a number of retail marketing mix instruments. The **location of the store** is considered a dominant determinant of retailing success, because in store-based retailing, good locations are key elements for attracting customers to the outlets. Also, because of its intrinsically fixed nature, location cannot be changed in the short-term (Chapter 10). Within the store, the retailer offers a **merchandise** assortment to its customers, and one of the primary functions of the retailer is to select the appropriate breadth and depth of the assortment and the specific products (e.g. manufacturer brands or **store brands**) and to tailor the offer to the target customers. A new concept is **category management**, which aims at implementing a more strategic and holistic approach to merchandising (Chapter 11). Closely related to the assortment is the **pricing policy**. Since consumers spend a large share of their incomes on retailing, pricing is considered highly relevant for retail patronage decisions and, within pricing processes, retailers have many strategic and tactical options available to influence purchasing behaviour (Chapter 12). As already mentioned, the customer is also influenced by the store environment. Many buying decisions are made at the point-of-sale, so professional **instore marketing** can increase sales substantially. Store layout and store design can support customer orientation in the store and create a positive store atmosphere (Chapter 13). **Customer relationship management** (CRM) is a relatively new element in the retail marketing mix. A key objective of CRM is to establish enduring relationships with customers, and loyalty programmes are manifestations of CRM in retailing. However, behind the loyalty cards that most consumers now carry are very different methods and concepts with which retailers intend to collect data and tailor their marketing to individual customers (Chapter 14).

While Parts I to III focus on the aspects of retailing that are at least partly visible to the customer, Part IV deals with back-end and internal processes that are necessary to create the offer to the consumer. Retailers need to buy the merchandise they offer to their customers, and they use various, heterogeneous supply sources, ranging from global manufacturers of branded goods to external buying organisations in foreign markets and store brand manufacturers. Relationships with suppliers and new concepts such as **efficient consumer response** have emerged, but the **buying concepts** employed must be closely adapted to the specific supply situation (Chapter 15). The products must be transported along the supply chain – from the factory to the store shelf. More and more frequently, **physical logistics** is considered a core competency of retailers who need to establish the necessary infrastructure and coordinate **product flows** (Chapter 16). Those product flows within the **supply chain** are dependent on **information flows**. It is necessary to establish when a product is sold in a certain store, so as to trigger an order to a warehouse, and subsequently to a supplier. The exact process depends on knowing the available products in stock at the various stages of the supply chain and forecasting consumer demand, etc. To enhance the efficiency of the supply chain, different **collaborative concepts** for achieving efficient replenishment have been developed, and these are based on new enabling technologies (Chapter 17). Finally, the intensive competition in retailing, combined with the price pressure to which most retailers are exposed, make it necessary both to perform well and constantly improve the effectiveness and efficiency of all applied strategies and processes. Adequate **monitoring** of financial and operational performance is, thus, necessary, and retailers have developed sophisticated systems for evaluating the profitability of their store networks, supply chain efficiency and financial performance. New concepts, such as value-based management, have also been quickly embraced by retailers (Chapter 18).

This short overview of the different fields of strategic management in retailing shows that the world of retailing has become complex and challenging. In the following 18 Chapters, we cover the most important aspects and give the reader an insight into the main developments and concepts. Based on the case studies, the reader will also gain an understanding of how the concepts are implemented by successful retail companies around the world.

Part I
Functions, Formats and
Players in Retailing

1   Retail Functions

In this Chapter, the tasks of retailers within the distribution channel are explained and recent trends concerning these functions are discussed. This serves to explain the reasons for the existence of retailers as intermediaries between suppliers and final customers in general as well as the complexity of their activities.

1.1   Introduction

Retailing refers – as the definition states – to the process of purchasing products from other organisations with the intent to resell those goods to the final customer, generally without transformation, and rendering services incidental to the sale of merchandise. This is a rather static and traditional definition. While traditional retail functions are still predominant, retailers have developed into complex and sophisticated companies that often coordinate or even own value chains from the production stages down to sales to the customer.

The retailing process itself is the final step in the distribution of merchandise. It results in an intangible outcome, as do all services. While the value a production company adds is obvious, it is – at first sight – less evident what value is created by a retailer. Therefore, marketing and retail researchers have long tried to explain to students as well as to the general public what added value is provided by retailers.

An early justification of the existence of retailers was given by Butler (1917, p. 14; cited from Rosenbloom 2007): "The middleman is the outstanding figure in modern marketing not because he has consciously set out to make a place for himself, nor because consumers have blindly permitted him to come between them and the manufacturers of the things they buy. It is because he has been forced into existence, on the one hand by the necessities of specialised and large scale industry and, on the other hand by the necessities of consumers equally specialised in their activities and constantly demanding more and more in the way of services which the distant manufacturer must usually rely upon the middleman to give."

A simple explanation for the potential advantage of using intermediaries (such as retailers) in a distribution channel is given by the so-called **Baligh-Richartz effect** (Baligh/Richartz 1967). This effect is based on the fact that the integration of an intermediary in the distribution channel (between m suppliers and n consumers) helps **reduce the number of necessary contacts** between the different actors in the system. If m different manufacturers (e.g. one for meat, one for bread, one for detergents, etc.) were to sell to n different households, then the number of necessary contacts would be m*n. Using, in the extreme case, only a single intermediary in this channel, reduces the number of contacts to m+n.

In more recent economic analyses, **transaction cost theory** has often been used to explain the use of independent intermediaries in a value chain. This theory explains the existence of firms in general and the level of vertical integration with the differing costs of transactions (Williamson 1985). As an example, for highly complex products, the cost of transferring the necessary product knowledge from the manufacturer to an independent retailer may be so high that a vertically integrated solution (i.e. direct selling) could be optimal, but in many other cases using independent intermediaries leads to lower transaction costs.

1.2   Traditional Retail Functions

1.2.1   Purpose of Catalogues of Functions

To answer the fundamental question of why retailers exist, instead of, as an extreme scenario, all manufacturers selling their products and services to all final consumers that want to buy these products directly, different catalogues or lists of retail functions (or "distribution service outputs") have been brought forward (Alderson 1954; Sundhoff 1965; Bucklin 1966; Coughlan et al. 2006; Waterschoot et al. 2010). In the following explanation, we do not follow a specific one of these catalogues but derive a list of functions that retailers usually perform in the value chain between producers and consumers as a synthesis of the above-mentioned sources.

1.2.2   Sorting

One of the benefits that a retailer in the value chain provides is the sorting of goods. This creates value because manufacturers typically produce a large quantity of a limited variety of goods, whereas consumers usually demand only a limited quantity of a wide variety of goods (Coughlan et al. 2006, p. 6). Sorting, in this respect, includes **assorting**, i.e. the building up an assortment, and **breaking bulk**, i.e. offering small lot sizes.

Creating an assortment

Retailers provide the customer with an assortment of products and services and thereby offer him **variety** (Bucklin 1966; Waterschoot et al. 2010). They offer the consumer a selection of products (the merchandise mix or product range), which they preselect from a very broad offer of products offered by existing manufacturers, and retailers bring these products into association with each other (see Chapter 11).

For example, in a supermarket, retailers offer a choice of up to 15,000 items that usually originate from over 500 different suppliers. Thus, while manufacturers can specialise in producing a very limited product range, retailers still make a broad product range available for the consumer. Consumers can choose between different products in one category and can combine their purchases and buy several items in the same store, fulfilling the increasing need for "one-stop-shopping".

In a way, creating an assortment is also a marketing function since it facilitates the search process of the consumer. For example, instead of searching, e.g., a printer from many different manufacturers in different locations, the assortment of a retailer helps the consumer to manage the product complexity, to choose between preselected printer brands and models and to compare them easily in one store. Simultaneously, the retailer facilitates the search for customers by the manufacturer (Coughlan et al. 2006, p. 6).

In Chapter 5, the emerging verticalisation strategies of manufacturers will be presented. Some manufacturers, such as *Dell, Apple, Esprit* or, in a few incidences, even manufacturers of fast-moving consumer goods such as *Nespresso*, operate stores that are dedicated to their brand products only. But it becomes obvious that for many manufacturers this is no option because the consumer prefers to do his shopping for several products in one place and because many manufacturers would not be found by the consumer if the retailer did not present them.

Breaking Bulk

Furthermore, retailers offer the consumer other **lot sizes** than manufacturers usually like to ship (Bucklin 1966). To reduce transportation costs and transaction costs, manufacturers usually have the necessary infrastructure and systems to ship full truckloads, pallets or at least cases of products, while consumers want to buy single packages of a product. So, retailers buy products in large quantities, then break down these large shipments ("break bulk") and offer the consumer quantities that fit typical consumption patterns.

It is noteworthy that the term for this institution, relative to the wholesale level, often refers to exactly this function (**"re-tailor"** vs. **"wholesaler"** in English, "commerce de détail" vs. "commerce de gros" in French, "Einzelhandel" vs. "Großhandel" in German).

1.2.3   Bridging Space and Time

Usually, in the system between manufacturers and consumers, there is a geographic and a temporal gap that needs to be overcome. Closing these gaps is a further function of retailers.

Bridging Space

Manufacturers usually produce a specific product in a central location, while final consumption takes places in households across the country. Retailers help realise this **spatial decentralization** (Waterschoot 2010, p. 6) by offering the products in their stores that are closes to the customer. Large retailers have broad **market coverage** with a network of stores so the consumer can easily reach one of their stores.

Concerning this logistical function, the added value by the retailer has drastically increased over time (see Chapters 16 and 17). Initially, the intermediary advantage was mainly given since the logistics chain of the manufacturer did not have to be extended into every single household but only to a specific retail store. In the past, it was common that stores were either directly delivered to by manufacturers or that small retailers bought their products at wholesale markets, which also helped bridge a geographical gap.

However, with retailers setting up their own distribution centres, they now take responsibility for an even larger part of the distance between the production facilities and the consumer. Recent logistics concepts of retailers even involve picking up products at the manufacturing sites directly so that the full function of bridging space is handled by the retailer. In the interplay with the manufacturers, retailers now often try to take over the **logistics leadership** in the channel.

Furthermore, in recent years, retailers more and more often go one step further downstream. With the increasing use of online retailing, retailers manage the delivery of products to the individual household (as catalogue retailers have long been doing), thereby bridging even the final part of the supply chain.

Bridging Time

In addition, consumers want to be able to buy (and consume) products when they wish, while production is often carried out in batches or at least not immediately before the purchase. This temporal bridge is overcome by retailers **holding inventory**. As a part of the logistics process, retailers stock products in their warehouses, and, eventually, also on their store shelves. This makes products available to the consumer at the time of their demand.

Concerning this function, retailers currently work intensively on minimising the inventory in the supply chain while still ensuring that products are not out-of-stock in the store.

1.2.4   Creating Demand

Another function of retailers is the creation of demand. This includes the analysis of markets, the evaluation and identification of consumer needs and the provision of this information to suppliers (or the use of this information to build adequate assortments), etc.

Furthermore, retailers **present goods** to the consumer in their stores, sometimes only on shelves but often also in different display forms (see Chapter 13). For example, electronics articles such as home cinemas, which can be tested by the consumer including a TV, loudspeakers, certain lighting and so on, or the presentation of a clothing collection on display mannequins, increases demand and would be difficult to realise by manufacturers without stores.

Retailers often have knowledgeable salespeople that give advice to help the customer choose. They carry out promotional activities and conduct many other activities to create demand for the products in their assortments.

A part of this function is sometimes labelled "informational market decentralization" (Bucklin 1966; Waterschoot 2010) since it includes transferring knowledge about products, trends and technology from the specific product manufacturer to the customer.

1.2.5   Carrying out Transactions

Each purchase transaction involves the ordering of, pricing of and payment for goods and services (Sundhoff 1965; Coughlan et al. 2006). Retailers carry out these functions. Typically, they reduce costs in this transaction by offering standardisation and routines. Products are offered in the store for a certain price (including price labels which help avoid price negotiations for every single purchase). Products are paid for at a central checkout and simultaneously the purchasing contract is closed and the possession of a product changes from the retailer to the consumer.

However, full routinisation is not always possible. In certain cases, there are intensive negotiations in the purchasing process, e.g. in car or furniture retailing. Products may need to be tailored to the specific customer; prices need to be fixed individually, etc. This is also part of the retail function.

For higher priced non-food items (such as furniture, cars or home appliances), it is also common that consumers have the option to pay later or pay by instalments. Providing this option enhances demand. For a manufacturer, being far away from the consumer would make it very difficult to provide this option since evaluating the customer is not easy and can sometimes be costly. Thus, this **financing function** is often carried out (or at least coordinated) by the retailer.

1.2.6   Product-related Services

Even though the definition of retailing states that products are resold to the final customer "generally without transformation", retailers in certain sectors have long been involved in the final step of the production process, mainly final assembly. For example, retailers of expensive bicycles often assemble a customised bike for a specific customer (Waterschoot et al. 2010, p. 20) or furniture retailers assemble kitchens in the home of the customer.

While the delivery of goods to the household has been discussed as part of the "bridging space" function, the installation, set-up, maintenance and repair of products are additional functions. Indeed, the provision of such **customer services** by retailers is rising drastically. This can be observed, for example, with PC retailers, who not only deliver the PC to the home but also physically set up the computer system, configure the PC, install software, connect it to external devices and the Internet, transfer data from an old PC and so on. Another example is home improvement retailers, where the trend has moved **from "Do it yourself" to "Do it for me"** and retailers now often provide the customer with craftspeople who build a bathroom or a new garage door that has been bought at the retailer. Again, in food retailing ready-to-cook and ready-to-eat products are prepared by the retailer for take-away.

This function, however, still surrounds products that are bought from a manufacturer and resold by the retailer to a consumer. The mentioned services are related to these products and are often a means to differentiate the retailer's offer from that of a competitor by **complementing the product** with value-added services. A further integration of the retailer in the production function will be discussed in the next section.

1.2.7   Flows in the Value Chain

Instead of catalogues of retail functions, other authors have focused on different channel flows that need to be performed between manufacturers and the consumer (see, e.g., Coughlan et al. 2006, pp. 10-13; Rosenbloom/Larsen Andras 2008). Usually, eight flows that have to be created and managed to link buyers and sellers are mentioned in the literature: ownership, the physical possession of the product, promotion, negotiation, financing, risking, ordering and payment.

Eventually, however, these flows can be associated with the abovementioned retail functions so that the channel flows are just another perspective on the same phenomenon.

1.2.8   Intermediaries Enhancing Efficiency

It has been criticised that catalogues of retail functions merely reflect what functions are currently carried out by retailers but do still not justify the existence of retailers. However, the functions show different activities that usually need to be performed in the system between manufacturers and consumers. Indeed, it does not necessarily mean that they must be performed by a retailer, though. This leads to two considerations:

- Nowadays, retailers usually take many of these activities as a part of their domains. But often, they only manage the process; the execution itself may be carried out via **outsourcing**. For example, the transport function is more and more often in the domain of the retailer (instead of the manufacturer) but retailers often use **third-party logistics service providers** to carry out the transports.

- Manufacturers may carry out these functions themselves. In the verticalisation of manufacturers (Chapter 5), this is the case. However, if the manufacturer decides to eliminate the retailer as a middleman ("disintermediation"), these functions still need to be performed. Considering the retail functions reveals that eliminating the middleman does not lead to an elimination of the costs for the intermediary functions.

From an economic perspective, retailers remain viable participants in the distribution channel as long as they can perform certain distributive functions more efficiently or effectively than other institutions in the channel. Compared with vertical integration, it is likely that different value-added functions (e.g. manufacturing, logistics and store operations) have different optimal output levels (Rosenbloom 2004; Rosenbloom 2007). If this is the case, then vertical disintegration and a specialisation of companies on one of these activities can lead to lower overall production costs. Compared with an internalised type of activity by the manufacturer, the retailer can more easily achieve **economies of scale** for activities with high levels of fixed costs (Rosenbloom 2007), e.g. for providing a store, warehouses or a transport fleet.

Furthermore, **economies of scope** are achieved because offering heterogeneous products from different manufacturers smoothes the demand function. A manufacturer of skiing equipment, for example, faces strong demand for a few months of the year but almost no sales for the rest of the year. This leads to an inefficient utilisation of logistics capacity (such as warehouses) as well as the selling space in a store (and of its salespeople, etc.). For a large part of the year, idle costs would occur. But if a retailer takes over the functions, bundling the products of summer sports manufacturers and winter sports manufacturers in the stores of a sporting goods retailer helps reduce costs through a steady utilisation of the selling space as well as of the logistics infrastructure. Thus, a retailer can more easily compensate for demand fluctuations and generally realise a smoother, more cost-efficient utilisation of capacity.

Finally, bundling the products of many different manufacturers into an assortment by a retailer helps reduce transaction costs for consumers (in particular, search costs).

1.3   Emerging Functions of Retailers

The increasing power of retailers relative to manufacturers has – as has already been mentioned – led to an increasing part of the value chain being controlled by retailers. This partly refers to traditional retail functions in which retailers have taken over additional activities, e.g. in logistics. But it also refers to the emergence of new functions that have traditionally not been carried out by retailers. Increasingly, retailers use **backward integration** and partly or fully take over the production function, a traditional domain of manufacturers.

In recent years, researchers have pointed to the changing value-added systems in the consumer goods sector (e.g. Zentes/Pocsay 2010; Zentes/Bastian 2010; Hertel/Zentes/Schramm-Klein 2011). These changes come as a result of the increasing relevance of store brands (see Chapter 11) as well as the rise of vertical retailers as new competitors (see Chapter 6). The reasons for backward integration are at least three-fold. First, it helps the retailer to differentiate from its competition if the company is involved in product development processes since the company's offer then becomes unique. Second, the coordination of the value chain helps the retailer ensure product quality and product supply, which may become crucial in the case of general supply shortages. Third, it helps the retailer accumulate a larger part of the profit margin in the value chain.

Coordinating the Value Chain

While for manufacturer brands retailers still have a largely "passive" function and the marketing of the products is mainly carried out by the manufacturer that also develops and produces its products, this is different for **store brands**. Here, retailers are involved in R&D activities, mainly product development, including design, packaging and so on. Quality standards are fixed and monitored by the retailer, including the necessary qualities of raw materials. The retailer does not only select from the product offers of different manufacturers but actively coordinates the value chain.

Product specifications are developed by the retailer and the producer (often a specialised private label manufacturer), which is often merely a **contract manufacturer** that provides production capacity for the retailer. The rights on the product, product technology, recipes or construction plans and brand are in the hands of the retailer. Beyond the production coordination, the retailer also has to market these products entirely on its own, i.e. advertising and other marketing functions for these products are carried out by the retailer as well.

An example of far-reaching value-added activities in the production process, in particular the development and design of store brands, is the sporting goods retailer *Decathlon* (see the Case Study in Chapter 11) but other retailers such as *IKEA* or the fashion retailer *Zara* could also be used as examples.

Production Processes

Some retailers go one step further and not only coordinate production processes but instead own the production companies as well. *IKEA* uses **contract manufacturing** but also **owns factories** around the world. This is sometimes also the case in food retailing; for example, the German market leader *EDEKA* owns more than 20 meat factories and more than ten regional bakeries. *Coop* in Switzerland owns a majority stake in Switzerland's largest meat and sausage manufacturer *Bell* as well as many other production companies (Hertel/Zentes/Schramm-Klein 2011, p. 108). *Migros*, a retailer that strongly focuses on store brands, owns the *Migros Industry*, which achieved sales of about 5.3 billion CHF in 2010. From chocolate production to meat production, mineral waters, cheese, detergents and many other product categories, *Migros* produces the products that it sells on its shelves (see the Case Study in Chapter 7). But beyond being a supplier for the *Migros* stores, *Migros Industry* is explicitly seen as a growth pillar of *Migros* and the share of sales to external customers, in particular to those in other countries, is planned to rise in the coming years.

Closed Loop Supply Chains

In recent decades, increasing importance has been attached to environmental protection and sustainable strategies. One consequence of this development is that supply chains are no longer unidirectional, from the manufacturer to the consumer, but that **reverse processes** have become more relevant.

Closed loop supply chains try to close the product flows into a full circle with the objective of reducing waste. Instead of disposing products at the end of their life cycles, sustainable waste management reduces waste by collecting used products (and packaging material), by separating and in some cases disassembling them, by recovering the valuable parts (which can be the entire product, or components or material) and eventually by reusing them through recycling or remanufacturing.

Retailers take over the responsibility of this process. In many countries, retailers have to take back packaging material. In many countries, retailers now also have to take back used products or they do so voluntarily as a customer service. From the trade-in of a used refrigerator or PC to the return of used ink cartridges, from returning a cardboard box to bringing back empty glass or PET bottles, consumers more and more often can dispose of used products and packaging at their retailers. Together with manufacturers and third-party service providers, retailers are increasingly coordinating the accompanying reverse logistics processes.

1.4 Convergence between Manufacturers and Retailers

Retailers that go far beyond their traditional distribution function and that build up own product development and production competence lead to an interesting phenomenon: the distinction between manufacturers and retailers blurs and the characteristics of institutions at both stages in the value chain actually converge.

Migros, Coop or *Decathlon* are traditionally seen as retailers even though their control over the production function is constantly increasing. On the other hand, companies such as *Apple, Esprit* or *Montblanc* are traditionally categorised as manufacturers even though they have long started to integrate the retail function into their own systems and to open stores or at least control stores and other retail channels (see Chapter 5). The extreme cases are so-called verticals such as *Zara, H&M, IKEA, Dell* or *Nespresso,* where a vertically integrated exclusive system from manufacturing to retailing has emerged (see Chapter 6).

1.5 Conclusion and Outlook

Retailers add value to products and services by providing a number of retail functions. While these functions mostly do not create a tangible output and are, thus, not evident for everybody, they are still necessary in the value chain between manufacturers and consumers.

Retailers as specialists for distribution have a number of advantages in providing these functions more effectively and efficiently than can other institutions, e.g. they can often achieve economies of scale and economies of scope in the distribution function. But with increasing size and sophistication, retailers have started to use their position as a gate-keeper to the customer to gain a growing share of the value chain and to increasingly take over functions that were traditionally carried out by manufacturers.

Given the takeover of production functions by retailers and vice versa, of retailing functions by manufacturers, both types of institutions in a way converge. These developments clearly indicate that the classic conceptualisations of retail functions are not comprehensive enough to describe and analyse many modern retailers. It has therefore been proposed to revise the classic conceptualisations and to broaden them (Waterschoot et al. 2010).

▌ Further Reading

Coughlan, A.; Anderson, E.; Stern, L.; El-Ansary, A. (2006): Marketing Channels, 7th ed., Upper Saddle River/NJ.

Rosenbloom, B. (2004): Marketing Channels: A Management View, 7th ed., Mason/OH.

1.6   Case Study: Best Buy[1]

1.6.1   Profile, History and Status Quo

The origins of *Best Buy* go back to 1966, when Richard Schulz and a business partner opened the *Sound of Music* Store in St. Paul, Minnesota. Only a year later, the first acquisitions took place; *Sound of Music* acquired *Kencraft Hi-Fi Company* as well as *Bergo Company*. In 1969, the type of the company was changed into a publicly held company and *Sound of Music* opened three new stores. The following year, *Sound of Music* hit the one million USD mark in annual revenues. The *Sound of Music* company grew steadily, the number of stores multiplied and by the end of 1978, the company operated nine stores in Minnesota.

In 1983, the board of directors of *Sound of Music* approved a new corporate name, *Best Buy Co., Inc.* Furthermore, *Best Buy* opened its first big-box store (a category specialist) in Burnsville, Minnesota. In 1985, *Best Buy's* initial public offering on the *Nasdaq* raised eight million USD. The following years, *Best Buy* forced the successful expansion of its store network. In 1989, pioneered a new "grab-and-go" big-box store concept in a warehouse-style environment. The year 2000 highlighted another great step in *Best Buy's* company history: the entering of the online retailing business by launching the website www.bestbuy.com. Moreover, *Fortune magazine* named *Best Buy* one of the top performing stocks since 1990. One year later, *Best Buy* entered the international marketplace and started its expansion into foreign countries with the acquisition of the Canada-based company *Future Shop*. In 2003,

---

[1] Sources used for this case study include the websites http://www.bestbuy.com, http://www.bby.com and various annual and interim reports as well as investor relations presentations.

Best Buy opened its first global sourcing office in Shanghai. Four years later, in 2007, *Best Buy* celebrated the grand opening of its first retail store in Shanghai, China.

Nowadays, *Best Buy* is the world's largest retailer of technology and entertainment products and services with operations in the United States, Canada, Europe, China, Mexico and Turkey with a strong commitment to growth and innovation. *Best Buy's* corporate vision is "People. Technology. And the pursuit of happiness." and is flanked by the four corporate values: "Have fun while being the best. Learn from challenge and change. Show respect, humility and integrity. Unleash the power of our people." At the end of the fiscal 2010, *Best Buy* employed 180,000 employees and generated more than 49 billion USD in annual revenue under its different retail brands.

1.6.2   Sales and Distribution Network of Best Buy

Best Buy has a widespread store network in order to be close to the customer. The company operates 4,026 stores on three continents with different retail brands. In its home country, the United States, Best Buy is present in 1,192 locations with the retail brands Best Buy (for store count by state see **Figure 1.1**), *Best Buy Mobile*, *Magnolia Audio Video*, *Pacific Sales Kitchen and Bath Centres* as well as *Geek Squad*.

In Canada, the company runs 212 *Future Shop, Best Buy* and *Best Buy Mobile* stores. China is covered through 164 locations with 158 *Five Star Appliance* stores, which were acquired in 2006, and six own-branded *Best Buy* stores. However, at the beginning of 2011, the company announced that it may sell its *Best Buy* stores in China. In Europe, *Best Buy* operates with the retail brands *The Carphone Warehouse* and *The Phone House* in a 50 % venture with a partner, but it has also started the rollout of *Best Buy* stores in the United Kingdom, Spain and Turkey (LZnet 2010).

In general, the stores' merchandise is shipped directly from the manufacturers to *Best Buy's* distribution centres and then distributed in smaller quantities into the stores with contract carriers; the stores are dependent upon the distribution centres for inventory storage and the shipment of most merchandise. An exception is large-screen televisions, which are shipped to satellite warehouses in each major market. *Best Buy* does not make use of wholesalers. In 2010, the merchandise inventories of *Best Buy* totalled 10,064 million USD.

Best Buy also runs its own **online shop.** There, the customer can choose whether they prefer to shop by product category, e.g. mobile phones, or by brand shops, such as *Apple* or *Sony*. In addition, the customer can choose different services, e.g. car and GPS installation services. To address the considerable group of Hispanics in the USA, the *Best Buy* online shop is also available in Spanish. Furthermore, *Best Buy* has taken into account the increasing market of smartphones and has also created a Mobile App. So customers can compare prices and order products on the move, as well as rate products and share them with friends. Another online service of *Best Buy* is the so-called "store pickup". The store pickup allows the customer to buy a product online, but skip the shipping charge and pick it up at least 45 minutes after placing the order in the store that was chosen in the ordering process.

Figure 1.1   The Number of Best Buy Stores in the USA per Federal State

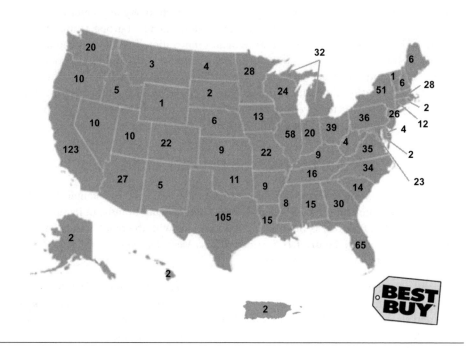

Source: Best Buy 2011.

1.6.3   Manufacturer Brands and Store Brands at Best Buy

Best Buy stores have offerings to the customer in six categories: consumer electronics, home office, entertainment software, appliances, services and others.

Best Buy's strategy depends upon its ability to offer customers a broad selection of **manufacturer brand** products and, therefore, its success is dependent upon satisfactory and stable supplier relationships. In 2010, the 20 largest suppliers of *Best Buy* accounted for approximately 60 % of the purchased merchandise. Therefore, the five main suppliers *Apple, Hewlett Packard, Samsung, Sony* and *Toshiba* represented 35 % of the total merchandise purchased. Other brands available at *Best Buy* stores include *LG, Casio, Microsoft, Fender, Epson, Intel, Panasonic, Whirlpool, Garmin, Dell, Canon* and many more. Altogether, *Best Buy* offers more than 130 brands to its customers. To react better on regional changing customer needs, *Best Buy* stores can offer additional products on a certain level to their customers, which aren't designated at national level. Partially, *Best Buy* uses shop-in-shop solutions to present certain product brands, for example products from *Apple*, but it also provides multi-brand showrooms in certain departments, e.g. for home theatres.

Besides the established manufacturer brands, *Best Buy* also sells its own exclusive **store brands**. With them, *Best Buy* intends to offer high standards of quality at a reasonable price to its customers. **Table 1.1** gives an overview of *Best Buy's* store brands. With this strategy, *Best Buy* pays respect to the increasing relevance of store brands for retailers. This approach is also a sign of the increasing power of retailers in relation to manufacturers and the growing part of the value chain controlled by retailers. Through this backward integration in the supply chain, *Best Buy* can gain a unique position in the consumer's mind and can differentiate from the competitors. Furthermore, through the coordination of the value chain, *Best Buy* can ensure product quality as well as product supply. Moreover, *Best Buy* accumulates a larger part of the profit margin in the value chain.

Table 1.1   The Store Brands of Best Buy

Store brand	Product fields
Insignia	DVD Players/Recorders and DVD Player/VCR Combos, Home Audio Components, Home Theatres, Portable Audio, Speakers, TV`s, 2-Way Radios
Dynex	Audio, Cables/Cords/Adapters, Computer and Entertainment Accessories, Mobile Phones & Office Equipment, Television & Accessories, Video
Init	Media Storage, Equipment Bags, TV Stands and Media Furniture
RocketFish	Computer Accessories, Gaming Accessories, Accessories for Home Theatres, Mobile Audio & Video Products, Mobile Phones & GPS
Platinum Cases	Quality Cases for Smart Phones

Source: Best Buy 2011.

Best Buy is involved in the research & development for its store brands. For example, Best Buy met with designers, printers and manufacturers of packaging and has developed new package designs for its exclusive brands, products that required less plastic, are smaller and use recycled materials when possible. Furthermore, the *Best Buy* packaging team has made a concerted effort to reduce the packaging size if possible. Most of *Best Buy's* exclusive store brands are made in Asia by specialised private label manufacturers (e.g. **contract manufacturing**) Therefore, *Best Buy* develops the product specifications according to its quality standards in cooperation with the producers. The advantage of this approach is the coordination of the value chain through the retailer.

To improve communication with its store brand suppliers, *Best Buy* operates its own **global sourcing office** in China. Nowadays, most of the worldwide consumer electronics has been produced in Asia, especially in China. Therefore, *Best Buy* has a better buying position while purchasing directly from the manufacturer and can also meet new product trends faster.

Moreover, *Best Buy* audits its store brand suppliers every year after certain criteria to ensure that they are managing their businesses in a way that demonstrates respect for the environment and is aligned with the company's sustainability goals. In these factory audits, the contract manufacturers will be ranked by balanced scorecard results and they can receive a rating from A (very good) to D (inadequate). Furthermore, *Best Buy* evaluates its exclusive brand product suppliers on non-compliance factors such as harassment and abuse, health and safety, forced labour, environmental, wage and compensation, discrimination, right to freely seek association, working hours and child labour.

1.6.4   From Products to Solutions

Nowadays, technology is becoming more prominent in consumer's lives, but also increasingly complex. More and more, consumers have problems integrating the technology and realising its full potential. Therefore, *Best Buy* uses its unique culture, global resources and customer-centric approach to help consumers get the most out of their technology purchases. With this approach, *Best Buy* has enlarged its business field, from solely selling hardware towards solution providing (see **Figure 1.2**).

Figure 1.2   The Enlargement of Best Buy's Business Fields

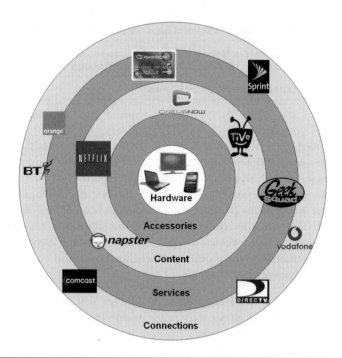

Source: Best Buy 2010.

One of these solutions for the customer is **services**. To provide its customers a great variety of services, *Best Buy* entered in 2002 into joint operation with *Geek Squad*, providing consumers with a 24-hour service operation to help them manage their growing dependence on technology. *Geek Squad* service stations can be found in *Best Buy* stores as well as standalone units. Altogether, 20,000 highly skilled, trained professionals and technicians support customers' needs. *Geek Squad* delivers the products that customers have bought at a *Best Buy* store, if it may be required, e.g. a home theatre. Furthermore *Geek Squad* installs and assembles products at home for the customer. Moreover, *Geek Squad* runs its own repair sites and also has mobile repair teams to make in-home appliance repairs. In fact, it is unimportant whether the customer has bought the products at a *Best Buy* Store or not. Additionally, *Geek Squad* provides do-it-yourself manuals and videos in order to teach and support customers how to use their equipment. Furthermore, it offers prepaid protection plans exclusively at *Best Buy* stores for most appliances a customer can purchase at *Best Buy*.

1.6.5   The Customer-centric Approach

Until the 1980s, *Best Buy* was growing well, but it was not strongly differentiated from its competitors. Like most companies in this sector, it strongly focused on price. Furthermore, such as in many other companies, its salespeople pushed customers strongly to buy its products. Over time, *Best Buy* started to understand that customers did not want to be pushed into purchases but prefer to buy after seeing and understanding their choices. While pushing can increase short-term sales volumes (and manufacturers of premium-priced products certainly depend on salespeople that push their products), it often leads to a negative customer experience. As a consequence, a highly controversial innovation in its sales concept was introduced in 1989, when *Best Buy* stopped paying commissions to its sales staff and instead put them on salaries. Customers liked this **no-pressure atmosphere** in their dialogues with the salespeople (who now took more time to offer real customer advice) and company revenues grew at a high pace for subsequent years, enabling *Best Buy* to outpace its rivals (Boyle 2006; Walden 2006, p. 34).

A more recent innovation, which was first tested in 2003, has since been intensively discussed by retail experts around the world. *Best Buy* decided to abandon its former mass-market approach with standardised stores that all have the same merchandise mix and services and instead developed a unique store approach (Walden 2006, p. 34). More particularly, *Best Buy* started a segmentation approach. The company identified its most important (i.e. most profitable) **customer segments** and then took the time to understand each segment's specific needs. For example, *Best Buy* discovered that more than half of its customers were women and that for the most part they did not enjoy their shopping experience at the retailer. Men look for a specific product at a discount price. Women, according to *Best Buy*, are more interested in buying a product together with other, related products (i.e. a digital camera and a photo printer) and they care less about the price and more about the full solution. Furthermore, they appreciate support for installation, while men often prefer to try to put things together themselves. As a result of this segmentation, *Best Buy* categorised

its customers into five groups. Each segment was given a nickname to facilitate the charac-
terisation and to facilitate day-to-day operations with the segments:

- **Affluent professionals** (nickname "Barry"): typically these are men aged between 30
  and 60, married with children, who earn more than USD 150,000 annually. They are
  shoppers who want the best technology, demand excellent service and price is not a
  constraint.

- **Family men** (nickname "Ray"): they want technology that improves their lives but also
  are sensitive to price and are more likely to check out what *Walmart* is offering.

- **Busy suburban soccer mom** (nickname "Jill"): they want to enrich their children's lives
  with technology and entertainment. Before the segmentation, Jill visited *Best Buy* stores
  to buy CDs and DVDs for her children, but the techno-speak of the salespeople turned
  her off from additional spending.

- **Young, active men** (nickname "Buzz"): this group is tech-savvy and these customers
  want the latest in consumer electronics products. Income and spending power is,
  though, limited.

- **Small business customers** (no nickname): this target group was identified since the
  owners of small business are heavy spenders in the electronics market (e.g. for computers, notebooks, standard software, etc.) but this group had been underserved by
  electronics retailers. This segment needs additional services (such as installation, extended guarantees, 24/7 repair services or replacement products during the repair time),
  is usually more rational in its buying decisions and focuses on other product characteristics (e.g. total cost of ownership).

Based on the **demographics** in the catchment area and an analysis of the existing customer
base of the store, each store was configured to serve the needs of one or two customer segments. Adaptations include the concrete merchandise mix as well as store layout, signage
and the salespeople and their specific training. For example, many stores were redesigned
to target "Barry". These stores all have separate departments with home theatre systems,
expert salespeople for this category and specialists in mobile electronics. Stores that focus
on small business owners have a central information and service counter and the employees at these counters are more formally dressed than they are in other stores. Stores with a
focus on "Jill" offer personal shopping assistants to steer customers through the store and to
the right products. Stores for "Buzz" have broad assortments of video games. In many cases,
this restructuring of the stores required heavy investment. For example, the redesign of a
store to target Barry could cost more than half a million USD (for technical equipment,
fixtures, lighting, etc.).

As another cornerstone of this sales approach, the company intensively trained its employees to focus on specific customer segments and their needs. *Best Buy* decentralised its structure for decision-making regarding targeted customer service initiatives. More autonomy
was given to store managers and salespeople that are in direct customer contact were em-
powered to make their own decisions. Intensive training, including training on key figures

for financial controlling, was given to salespeople to allow them to take more informed decisions. This led to more flexible reactions to changing customer needs. *Best Buy* argues that this has given it a significant competitive edge in this highly competitive retail market (Walden 2006).

1.6.6   Sustainable Supply Chains: Recycling Programmes

In times of commodities running short and increasing prices, sustainability becomes more and more important for industry companies as well as for retailers. Furthermore, sustainability and environmental protection plays an increasing role in consumer's mind and their buying decisions. Therefore, *Best Buy* has launched *Greener Together*, a new approach to help its customers consume less energy and make smart technology decisions. *Greener Together* is a part of *Best Buy's* initiative to reduce the carbon footprint across its operations. The original goal – an 8 % reduction per US retail square foot by 2012 – was reached in 2009. *Best Buy* is currently in the process of developing a new goal and evaluates the measurement capability across all brands and regions, concerning improved store designs, fuel reductions and employee awareness and training.

Best Buy's Green Together initiative consists of two parts: saving energy and reducing waste. To support the saving of energy, *Best Buy* offers a huge selection of energy-efficient *Energy Star*-certified products. Furthermore, *Best Buy's* entire private label brand of *Insignia* LCD TVs holds the *Energy Star* 3.0 rating. The second pillar of *Greener Together* is the reduction of waste through recycling. *Best Buy* plans to expand its recycling and technology trade-in programmes in the United States and around the globe. In 2010, *Best Buy* recycled over 1.4 million customer units in the US. In general, the costs of mining and manufacturing raw materials are higher than are the use of recycled resources. Therefore, *Best Buy* is currently evaluating how the loop in the value chain can be closed by using recycled content in its own products and/or across the industry.

Best Buy offers its customers a couple of options to get rid of old appliances, electrical equipment and portable batteries, as well as ink cartridges, audio and video cables and other devices. Every *Best Buy* store in the USA has free recycling kiosks to drop off inkjet cartridges, rechargeable batteries as well as CDs and DVDs. Furthermore, *Best Buy* offers a so-called *"Tech Trade-In"*: customers can share used video games, musical instruments and selected, used electronics such as *iPods, Zunes*, laptops or mobile phones towards a *Best Buy* gift card. Another recycling service is the *"TV and appliance haul-away"*: *Best Buy* removes old TVs or appliances from a customer`s home for free when a replacement *Best Buy* product is delivered by *Geek Squad* or *Best Buy Home Delivery*. Moreover, *Best Buy* removes for a fee TV units or appliances from a customer's home for recycling. Therefore, it does not matter whether the old product was purchased at a *Best Buy* store or not.

1.6.7   Summary and Outlook

As a retailer, *Best Buy* acts as a bridge between manufacturers and customers. It offers its customers a dense network of retail stores throughout the USA and in other countries. Each store carries a very wide selection of products in different product categories. In the USA, the stores, with regard to the merchandise offered and service provided, are even customised to the needs of specific customer groups.

However, as the description of the activities of *Best Buy* has shown, the activities today go far beyond the "purchasing of products from other organisation with the intent to resell those goods to the final customer, generally without transformation". *Best Buy* has moved from purely selling products to become a coordinator of (international) value chains. It has also developed from selling products to providing solutions to customer problems. Beyond that, *Best Buy* has even started selling multimedia content such as films with *Cinemanow* or music with *Napster*. Therefore, its customers can buy or use the content for their electronic devices, e.g. music for a new *Apple iPod* or films and series for watching on a new home theatre, directly from a subsidiary of *Best Buy*. Moreover, *Best Buy* offers the installation and repair of technical equipment in the customer's home with *Geek Squad*. In a type of backward integration, *Best Buy* has broadly expanded its positions and functions in the value chain and it now offers its own store brands such as *Insignia* or *Dynex* to the customer.

The case of *Best Buy* impressively shows how a retailer can expand its classical functions and exploit further parts of the value chain. Nowadays, this trend, as a counterpart to the takeover of retailing functions by manufacturers, is widespread in retailing. In the future, it is expected that the boundaries between manufacturers and retailers will become even more blurred.

▌ Questions

1. Using the catalogue of retail functions, describe *Best Buy's* activities in terms of these functions.

2. Imagine if *Best Buy* bought its own factories and increased its amount of store label brands. What would this mean for its relationship with manufacturers such as *Apple*, *GE* or *Sony*? Explain.

3. Assume a manufacturer such as *Sony* decided to sell directly to the final consumer. Comparing that to the functions currently executed by retailers such as *Best Buy*, what would *Sony* have to do?

▌ Hints

1. See Chapter 1 for the tasks of retailers within the distribution channel.

2. For a discussion of vertically integrated retailers see Chapter 6.

3. Consider Chapter 5 concerning the vertical strategies of manufacturers.

2   Retail Formats - Food

Retailers have various ways of meeting customer needs through organising and designing their retail outlets. The objective of this Chapter is to describe the different types of food-oriented retail institutions that represent different types of retailer strategies in selling their goods and services.

2.1   Types of Retail Institutions

From a managerial point of view, understanding the different types of **retail institutions** is important because they have a competitive impact on the retail business. Several types of retail institutions mirror retailer business operations. Thus, each type represents a specific retailing strategy.

Several systems of retail classification have been developed by governmental institutions in order to collect and analyse business data more effectively. One of the first classification systems was the **Standard Industrial Classification** (SIC) code, which was developed for the *US Census Bureau* in 1930 and uses special codes (special sets of numbers) to identify types of retailers (Ogden/Ogden 2005, pp. 88-89). This served as the basis for the further development of classification systems that are also applied on an international basis such as the **International Standard Industrial Classification of all Economic Activities** (ISIC) of the *United Nations*, the NAICS (**North American Industrial Classification System**) or the NACE (**Nomenclature statistique des Activités économiques dans la Communauté Européenne**) of the *European Union* (see **Figure 2.1**).

In these classification schemes, retailers are assigned hierarchical codes based on the types of products and services they sell. However, it has to be noted that retailers that sell the same category of merchandise do not necessarily compete directly. These classification schemes, therefore, are mainly used for data collection and statistical analysis to provide insight into the development of the various retail institutions at a national or international level. For retail managers, though, the more strategic aspects of the different types of retail institutions are of primary importance. Therefore, for **strategy development** and competitive analysis, the classification of retail institutions in terms of the characteristics of the strategies that retailers employ in selling goods and services is important. Such types of retail institutions are referred to as **retail formats**. Retail formats are specific configurations of the retail marketing mix that are maintained consistently over time (e.g. type of store design and atmosphere, merchandise offered, services provided, pricing policy, type of location, approach to advertising and promotion, etc.).

Figure 2.1   NACE Codes - Examples

G - Wholesale and retail trade; repair of motor vehicles and motorcycles
G47 - Retail trade, except of motor vehicles and motorcycles

G47.1 - Retail sale in non-specialised stores
G47.1.1 - Retail sale in non-specialised stores with food, beverages or tobacco predominating
G47.1.9 - Other retail sale in non-specialised stores
G47.2 - Retail sale of food, beverages and tobacco in specialised stores
G47.2.1 - Retail sale of fruit and vegetables in specialised stores
G47.2.2 - Retail sale of meat and meat products in specialised stores
G47.2.3 - Retail sale of fish, crustaceans and molluscs in specialised stores
G47.2.4 - Retail sale of bread, cakes, flour confectionery and sugar confectionery in specialised stores
G47.2.5 - Retail sale of beverages in specialised stores
G47.2.6 - Retail sale of tobacco products in specialised stores
G47.2.9 - Other retail sale of food in specialised stores
G47.3 - Retail sale of automotive fuel in specialised stores
G47.3.0 - Retail sale of automotive fuel in specialised stores
G47.4 - Retail sale of information and communication equipment in specialised stores
G47.4.1 - Retail sale of computers, peripheral units and software in specialised stores
G47.4.2 - Retail sale of telecommunications equipment in specialised stores
G47.4.3 - Retail sale of audio and video equipment in specialised stores
G47.5 - Retail sale of other household equipment in specialised stores
G47.5.1 - Retail sale of textiles in specialised stores
G47.5.2 - Retail sale of hardware, paints and glass in specialised stores
G47.5.3 - Retail sale of carpets, rugs, wall and floor coverings in specialised stores
G47.5.4 - Retail sale of electrical household appliances in specialised stores
G47.5.9 - Retail sale of furniture, lighting equipment and other household articles in specialised stores

G47.6 - Retail sale of cultural and recreation goods in specialised stores
G47.6.1 - Retail sale of books in specialised stores
G47.6.2 - Retail sale of newspapers and stationery in specialised stores
G47.6.3 - Retail sale of music and video recordings in specialised stores
G47.6.4 - Retail sale of sporting equipment in specialised stores
G47.6.5 - Retail sale of games and toys in specialised stores
G47.7 - Retail sale of other goods in specialised stores
G47.7.1 - Retail sale of clothing in specialised stores
G47.7.2 - Retail sale of footwear and leather goods in specialised stores
G47.7.3 - Dispensing chemist in specialised stores
G47.7.4 - Retail sale of medical and orthopaedic goods in specialised stores
G47.7.5 - Retail sale of cosmetic and toilet articles in specialised stores
G47.7.6 - Retail sale of flowers, plants, seeds, fertilisers, pet animals and pet food in specialised stores
G47.7.7 - Retail sale of watches and jewellery in specialised stores
G47.7.8 - Other retail sale of new goods in specialised stores
G47.7.9 - Retail sale of second-hand goods in stores
G47.8 - Retail sale via stalls and markets
G47.8.1 - Retail sale via stalls and markets of food, beverages and tobacco products
G47.8.2 - Retail sale via stalls and markets of textiles, clothing and footwear
G47.8.9 - Retail sale via stalls and markets of other goods
G47.9 - Retail trade not in stores, stalls or markets
G47.9.1 - Retail sale via mail order houses or via Internet
G47.9.9 - Other retail sale not in stores, stalls or markets

Source: European Union 2011.

2.2   Theories of Retail Evolution

2.2.1   Overview

A number of theories explain the present structure of the retail industry and predict the future development of current and new retail formats. The **wheel of retailing** and the **retail life cycle** are two particularly important theories.

2.2.2   The Wheel of Retailing

The **wheel of retailing** (McNair 1931) is a well-established framework for explaining developments in retail institutions. The theory suggests that retail institutions go through cycles (see **Figure 2.2**). The rationale is that as low-end retailers upgrade their strategies to increase sales and profit margins, new forms of low-price (discount) retailers take their place in the market.

The **wheel of retailing** consists of three stages (McNair/May 1978; Berman/Evans 2010, pp. 124-126):

■ According to the wheel theory, retail innovators often appear as low-price operators. Thus, the cycle begins with retail institutions starting off with **low prices** and **low service levels**.

■ The second phase is called **"trading up"**. Retailers wishing to expand their businesses and attract more customers, enhance the quantity and quality of merchandise handled, provide more services and open outlets in more convenient locations. This leads to an increase in operating costs and prices and thus offers opportunities for new competitors to enter the market with low-price strategies.

■ The third phase is characterised by an **increase in competition** in services of all kinds and by a convergence in terms of the marketing mix of retailers as they mature. They become vulnerable to new competitors that enter the market with low prices.

Figure 2.2   The Wheel of Retailing

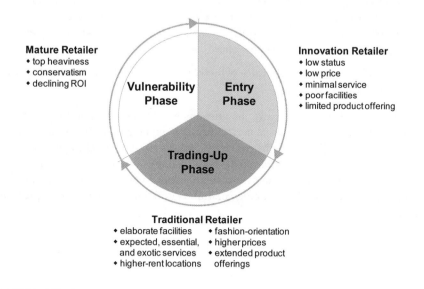

Source: adapted from Brown 1988.

2.2.3   The Retail Life Cycle

The concept of the retail life cycle refers to the succession of identifiable stages a retail format goes through over time (Berman/Evans 2010, pp. 127-129; McGoldrick 2002, pp. 21-23):

- In the **development stage**, the new format is introduced to the market. There is a departure from the strategy mix of existing retail institutions, as at least one element of the marketing mix is altered in the new format.

- In the **introduction phase**, sales and profits are low, but growing. Costs and risks are high because long-run success is not assured at this stage.

- The **growth phase** is characterised by the rapid growth of both sales and profits. Existing companies expand their markets and new competitors with the same retail format enter the market. Towards the end of this stage, growth acceleration begins to decline and cost pressure may emerge.

- The next stage is characterised by the **maturity** of the retail format, which is brought on by market saturation, in turn caused by a high number of firms in this retail format and competition from new formats. Sales growth declines and profit margins may have to be reduced in order to stimulate purchases. Once maturity is reached, the main goal is to prevent the business from declining and to sustain profit as long as possible.

- In the final stage **(decline)**, sales volume declines and prices and profitability diminish. Companies can try to avoid decline, for example, by **repositioning** the retail format, but many companies abandon the format altogether and start introducing new formats to keep their customers or attract new ones.

Figure 2.3 illustrates the characteristics of these five stages and indicates the stages in which present retail formats operate.

In the context of the retail life cycle, the phenomenon of **store erosion** (Berger 1977) is defined as a diminution in the appeal and ability of a retailing company to attract customers over time because of changes in the company's internal and external conditions. As a selection process in a **dynamic environment**, new retailing formats that meet new customer needs render existing retail formats obsolete. In order to avoid decline and survive, retail companies must adapt to the changing conditions in the marketplace and **reposition** their retailing concepts.

Figure 2.3   The Retail Life Cycle

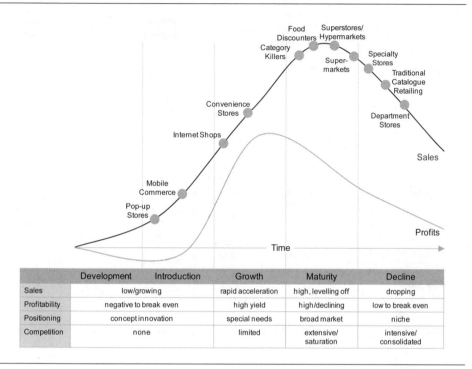

	Development	Introduction	Growth	Maturity	Decline
Sales		low/growing	rapid acceleration	high, levelling off	dropping
Profitability		negative to break even	high yield	high/declining	low to break even
Positioning		concept innovation	special needs	broad market	niche
Competition		none	limited	extensive/ saturation	intensive/ consolidated

Source: adapted from Berman/Evans 2010, p. 128; Zentes/Schramm-Klein/Neidhart 2005, p. 34.

2.3   Formats in Food Retailing

2.3.1   Overview

Over the past few decades, food retailing has undergone substantial changes. **New competitors from general merchandise retailing** have entered the market by expanding their assortments and selling food. But traditional food retailers (in most cases) also carry merchandise outside their traditional lines, i.e. general merchandise, and offer other kinds of services. These developments indicate that it is difficult to precisely allocate retail institutions to either food or general merchandise retail formats. In this part of the book, superettes, conventional supermarkets, superstores, combination stores, hypermarkets and supercentres, convenience stores, food discounters, warehouse clubs and several non-store formats are presented. **Table 2.1** provides an overview of the characteristics of the most important retail formats.

Table 2.1   Selected Characteristics of Store-Based Formats in Food Retailing

	Superettes	Conven-tional Su-permarket	Superstore	Hyper-market	Conven-ience Store	Hard Dis-counter
Size (m²)	100-399	400-1,000	1,000-5,000	5,000-30,000	200-400	500-1,500
SKUs	20,000	20,000-30,000	30,000-40,000	40,000-150,000	1,000-3,000	700-1,500
Merchan-dise	small to medium width and depth of assortment; average quality; manufac-turer and store brands	extensive width and depth of assortment; average quality; manufac-turer and store brands	full assort-ment of supermar-ket items, plus health and beauty aids and general merchan-dise	full selec-tion of supermar-ket and drugstore items, and general merchan-dise; exten-sive width and depth	medium width and low depth of assortment, average quality	medium width and low depth, heavy use of store brands (up to 90 %)
Percentage Food	90 %	75-90 %	60-80 %	60-70 %	90 %	80-90 %
Prices	average/ competitive	average/ competitive	competitive	competitive	average to above aveage/high	very low
Atmosphere and Services	average	aveage/ good	average	average	average	low
Location	city or neighbour-hood	city or neighbour-hood	community shopping centre or isolated sites	community shopping centre or isolated sites	neighbour-hood, city or highly frequented sites	neighbour-hood, traffic-oriented
Promotion	little to moderate	use of newspa-pers, flyers, coupons	heavy use of newspa-pers, flyers, coupons	heavy use of newspa-pers, flyers, coupons	little to moderate	heavy use of newspa-pers and flyers

Source: adapted from Berman/Evans 2010, p. 137; Levy/Weitz 2009, p. 41; Nielsen 2010.

2.3.2   Superettes

As a retail format, superettes, **minimarkets** or **minimarts** have been under pressure for a while, even though they once were the traditional neighbourhood store format in food retailing. However, this very small store format of less than 400 m² that offers a limited assortment of food and related items of daily and short-term requirements remains important in some markets such as in the Asia-Pacific region. To give an example, in **Figure 2.4** the market share of the main retail formats is presented for South Korea and Indonesia.

Figure 2.4   Market Share (in %) of Retail Formats in South Korea and Indonesia

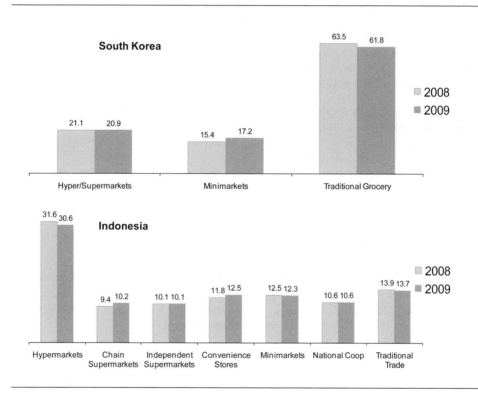

Source: adapted from Nielsen 2010.

Because of its long tradition of losing market share, many retailers in Western markets have written off **superettes** and streamlined their store chains. However, with the efforts of other retail chains such as *EDEKA* or *REWE,* which have supermarkets but also operate superettes, this retail format is undergoing a revitalisation. These retailers have changed the positioning of their small store formats by using trading-up strategies with regard to the retail marketing mix applied in these stores. This strategy of positioning superettes as a form of neighbourhood-oriented proximity retailing – not be mistaken with convenience stores – in **neighbourhood locations** or in the city, with modern instore designs, a revamp of the assortment strategies and usually lower prices, has led to a new relevance for this store format.

Because one of the main problems of superettes in the past was store productivity, many retailers have also changed the **ownership structure**. In most cases, they operate their superettes now as franchise systems or voluntary chains to guarantee their profitability (see Chapter 5).

2.3.3   Conventional Supermarkets

Conventional supermarkets are self-service stores that carry a wide range of **food items** (mainly groceries, meat and produce), including fresh food (e.g. fruits and vegetables) and related items. The share of general merchandise offered in this retail format is limited to between 10 % and 25 %. The format covers, for example, health and beauty aids and products (Berman/Evans 2010, p. 133; Ogden/Ogden 2005, p. 102).

Supermarkets are usually located in city or neighbourhood locations with sizes between approximately 400 m² and 1,000 m². Important players that utilise supermarkets in Europe are, for example, *Sainsbury's*, *EDEKA*, *REWE*, *Ahold's* supermarket *"ah"* or *Intermarché* as well as *Kroger* and *Albertson's* in the USA.

This retail format has been the main format for grocery shopping and has accounted for the majority of sales in food retailing for several decades. Yet, it faces **intense competition** from new formats that offer, for example, more convenient shopping facilities, more product lines and more varied assortments or lower prices as a result of lower operating costs (Weitz/Whitfield 2010).

Companies such as *REWE* or *EDEKA*, for example, have tried to **reposition** their supermarkets and thus improve their competitive positions by emphasising freshness and high quality assortments, introducing medium to higher level store brands and improving store atmosphere in order to provide a better **instore shopping experience**.

2.3.4   Superstores

Food-based **superstores** are larger and more diversified than are conventional supermarkets. Their size varies between 1,000 m² or 1,500 m² and 5,000 m² with expanded services such as a deli, bakery, seafood counter and general merchandise sections (Berman/Evans 2010, pp. 134-135). They are **"true" food stores** with a share of general merchandise ranging from approximately 20 % to 40 %, but offer expanded **one-stop-shopping** possibilities to consumers.

A similar store concept that tends to be larger than superstores (up to 9,500 m²) and offers a higher share of general merchandise (from 25 % to 50 % of sales) is sometimes referred to as **combination store**. These stores combine food and general merchandise, thus offering a higher level of one-stop-shopping for consumers than superstores (Berman/Evans 2010, p. 135).

This combination of food and general merchandise in superstores and combination stores yields operating efficiencies and cost savings. The main reason for this is that non-food items tend to have higher margins. Superstores and combination stores usually follow either a **high-low pricing strategy** (HiLo), which means that they are very promotion-oriented (e.g. intensive advertising or distribution of flyers), or an **everyday-low-price strategy** (EDLP) using few promotions and selling their merchandise permanently at the same – low – price (see Chapter 12). Superstores and combination stores can be located in city or neighbourhood locations as well as in isolated sites or in shopping centres oriented towards customers who drive to the store by car. Important players that operate super-stores or combination stores are, for example, *Intermarché, REWE, Tesco* or *Albertson's*.

2.3.5   Large Retail Formats

Over the past few decades, large retail formats have gained market share in grocery retailing. These large-scale retail formats are also referred to as "big-box retailers" (Levy/Weitz 2010, p. 45).

Whereas the trend towards such large retail formats has developed more or less similarly in the international context, specific types of formats have nonetheless been developed in different countries. Of these, **hypermarkets**, which originated in France, are the largest. Their size ranges from 9,000 m² to 30,000 m² (e.g. *Carrefour* and *Auchan*). The German **"SB-Warenhäuser"** (e.g. *Metro's* format *Real* or *Kaufland*) tend to be smaller with sizes from 5,000 m². Whereas these European formats have a larger share of food items ranging from 60 % to 70 %, in the USA the **"supercenters"** format (e.g. *Walmart, Kmart, Target*) ranges from 14,000 m² to 21,000 m² and carry a broader assortment of general merchandise. Thus, the share of general merchandise is higher, ranging between 60 % and 70 % (Levy/Weitz 2010, p. 45).

These large retail formats usually follow an aggressive, promotion-oriented **low-price strategy**. The stores are generally located in isolated sites or integrated in or close to shopping centres. The architecture is usually cost-oriented with a simple store design and a **functional-oriented** store atmosphere. As these large retail formats offer a broad assortment of food and general merchandise and thus provide **one-stop-shopping** opportunities, customers usually shop bigger shopping baskets. These store formats have a greater market area than do the smaller store formats (e.g. supermarkets), i.e. customers are willing to drive longer distances to visit these types of retail outlets. These stores, therefore, offer substantial parking facilities. Because of their low operating costs and the combination of food with higher margin general merchandise, which allow for an often **aggressive pricing strategy** and shopping convenience (e.g. in terms of a broad and deep assortment), during the past few decades, large retail formats have gained market share mainly at the expense of conventional supermarkets. In some countries, for example in France, though, saturation point seems to have been reached and hypermarket operators are searching for modifications of the concept to maintain their market shares.

2.3.6   Convenience Stores

Convenience stores ("c-stores") are usually situated in locations that are easy to access, such as in heavily frequented areas or urban neighbourhood locations. They open long hours (up to 24 hours, depending on local or national legislation). The stores are small and facilities are limited, with an average atmosphere and average service level. Convenience stores can be operated as stand-alone units (e.g. *Tesco Express, 7-Eleven, Auchan, Coop Pronto*), but are often associated with petrol stations (e.g. *Shell Shops, BP* or *Aral Stores, Esso Shops*).

The **very limited assortment** of these stores is food-oriented. A high proportion of sales consist of impulse purchases, with most in areas such as snack foods, soft drinks, beer and wine, tobacco products or newspapers and magazines. The average transaction in convenience stores is small and prices are usually above average.

Convenience stores focus on **ease of shopping**. They offer fast shopping, thus enabling customers to purchase quickly, picking merchandise in a short time without having to search through a large store or wait in long checkout lines. They also offer "mental convenience", as the assortment is limited, which enables customers to make their choices quickly (Berry/Seiders/Grewal 2002).

2.3.7   Hard Discounters

Hard discounters in food retailing usually follow a very aggressive **every-day-low-price strategy** with prices up to 20 % to 30 % below those of conventional supermarkets. They offer a small selection of items and, therefore, are also referred to as **"limited-line stores"** or **"limited-assortment stores"** (e.g. Ogden/Ogden 2005, p. 106). At *Aldi*, as the best-known example, the typical store carries about 1,000 stock-keeping units (SKUs). The basic assortment consists of food items with a high rate of turnover and few sizes and brands are offered per product category. Other prominent examples of internationally successful hard discounters are the German *Aldi* or *Lidl* and *Carrefour's Dia*.

The stores are characterised by a "no-frills" setting, which means that, for example, there are almost no services available (no helpdesk, no sales staff in attendance, etc.) and store design and atmosphere are very simple and cost-oriented. Often, products are sold out of boxes ("**box stores**") or cut cases and are presented on pallets. Food-based hard discounters often carry only a limited range of manufacturer brands and rely heavily on **low-price store brands**. Thus, prices are less comparable between different retailers.

They often complement their assortments with a weekly or semi-weekly changing selection of **general merchandise,** which is sold at very low prices and heavily promoted by newspaper advertising or the distribution of flyers to households. These items come from a variety of product categories (ranging from personal computers and furniture to home accessories) and often have no association with the regular merchandise carried by the retailer. Such items are offered in order to increase store traffic, and non-food items that, in some cases, are produced exclusively for this purpose usually have a higher margin than do food items.

Hard discounters are usually located in easily accessible **traffic-oriented and cost-oriented locations** with a focus on low occupancy costs, e.g. neighbourhood locations or periphery sites with adequate parking facilities. Because of their aggressive pricing strategies, the convenience dimensions (e.g. "mental convenience" because of the limited assortment and quick shopping because of the small store size) and location strategies, hard discounters have grown consistently over recent decades. They often play an important role in **proximity retailing**.

2.3.8   Warehouse Clubs

Warehouse clubs are a food retail format that is specific to the USA and not prevalent worldwide. Warehouse clubs sell their products both to end users and to small to medium-sized companies. Business members typically represent less than 30 % of the customer base, but account for approximately 70 % of sales (Weitz/Whitfield 2010, p. 90). **Membership** is required and customers are charged an annual fee. The largest warehouse clubs in the USA are *Costco* and *SAM'S CLUB (Walmart)*.

This type of store is characterised by **low prices** for a limited assortment comprising half food and half general merchandise. The stores are very large (9,000 m² or larger) and are located in secondary sites, i.e. in low rent districts. Store architecture and design are very simple and cost-oriented, characterised by a simple interior, concrete floors and wide aisles (Ogden/Ogden 2005, p. 104).

Items are usually presented on pallets. In this type of store, fast moving, high turnover merchandise is offered, thus minimising holding costs. Warehouse clubs concentrate on special purchases from popular brands. Often, products are sold that are sourced on special occasions from manufacturers (e.g. overruns, returns, etc.) (Berman/Evans 2010, p. 142).

The concept of warehouse clubs resembles **cash and carry wholesalers** (e.g. *Metro Cash & Carry*) that also require membership. Even though membership is restricted to companies and these outlets focus on **business-to-business trade**, end users also frequently purchase at these stores.

2.3.9   Non-Store Formats in Food Retailing

The dominant share of food retailing is generated by store formats. Nonetheless, there are several **non-store formats** in which groceries and related products can be purchased by consumers. For example, **remote ordering** channels, such as traditional catalogues or Internet shops, can be used to distribute merchandise. While these formats are generally gaining importance, the share of groceries offered through mail order channels remains rather limited (see Chapter 4).

For fresh merchandise (e.g. farm produce, bakery products, meat or fish), the use of **market stands** or **truck and van sales** is a traditional mode of distribution that, for example, small producers use to reach their customers as a specific form of direct selling. Because of the close and personal contact with their customers, these vendors often have high retention rates among their customer base, but the costs associated with direct selling are very high and, therefore, so are the prices.

Vending machine retailing constitutes yet another alternative. Merchandise such as snacks and soft drinks are stored in a machine and dispensed to customers when they deposit cash or use a credit card. Vending machines are usually placed at convenient locations with high traffic (Levy/Weitz 2009, pp. 58-59). Developments in the field of vending machines are innovative. For example, new types of **kiosk vending machines** provide customers with product displays and information on the merchandise or electronic systems track inventory and cash, thus reducing out-of-stocks or malfunctions.

2.4   Conclusion and Outlook

The food retailing landscape has changed dramatically over the past few decades. **Competition** has increased because of various factors including mergers & acquisitions and the internationalisation of retail companies (Fox/Sethuraman 2010; Dawson 2006). In addition, the main retail formats in this sector have also changed as a result of these developments, **technological progress** and responses to changes in customer behaviour (Weitz/Whitfield 2010).

Even though new non-store retail channels have been developed, because, for example, of new developments in information and communication technology, **bricks-and-mortar store formats** remain the most important channels for selling groceries. Important developments result from new store formats that have been developed and have gained market share. Most important in this context is the increase of discount-oriented retail formats such as large retail formats (e.g. hypermarkets) and small food-based hard discounters. *Convenience stores* are also becoming progressively more important.

In order to remain competitive in the mature business of food retailing, more and more retailers carry merchandise outside their traditional businesses. This phenomenon is referred to as **"category migration"** (Zentes/Schramm-Klein/Neidhart 2005, pp. 52-55) or as the "blurring" of retail formats (Fox/Sethuraman 2010, p. 246; see Chapter 11). For example, food discounters offer general merchandise as special offers in weekly or semi-weekly promotions to generate store traffic and improve profit margins. Another important trend is that food retailers are extending their regular assortment to increase sales and margins.

For instance, hard discounters have extended their basic assortments in recent years by adding fresh meat or frozen food (Zentes/Schramm-Klein/Neidhart 2005, pp. 54-55).

❙ Further Reading

BERRY, L.L. (2001): The Old Pillars of New Retailing, in: Harvard Business Review, Vol. 79, No. 4, pp. 131-137.

BIBA, G.; DES ROSIERS, F.; THERIAULT, M.; VILLENEUVE, P. (2006): Big Boxes versus Traditional Shopping Centres: Looking at Households' Shopping Trip Patterns, in: Journal of Real Estate Literature, Vol. 14, No. 2, pp. 175-202.

MORSCHETT, D.; SWOBODA, B.; FOSCHT, T. (2005): Perception of Store Attributes and Overall Attitude towards Grocery Retailers: The Role of Shopping Motives, in: International Review of Retail, Distribution and Consumer Research, Vol. 15, No. 4, pp. 423-447.

2.5   Case Study: Ahold[1]

2.5.1   Profile, History and Status Quo

Ahold is a major international retailer based in the Netherlands (*Ahold* Europe) and in the United States (*Ahold* USA) with different retail formats (e.g. supermarkets and hypermarkets) and retail brands (e.g. *albert heijn, albert, hypernova, Peapod, MARTIN'S*) in Europe, North America, Latin America and Asia. Today, the group's activities are concentrated mainly on the European and North American market.

Founded in 1887 by Albert Heijn, *Ahold* (*Albert Heijn Hold*ing) became the largest grocery chain in the Netherlands in the 1970s. It remains the largest Dutch retailer with a market share of about 30 %. Its overall mission is "to make the ordinary affordable and the extraordinary attainable" for customers. In 1973, *Ahold* entered the US market by acquiring the *BI-LO* supermarket chain in North and South Carolina, Georgia and Tennessee, and expanded its activities in the Eastern US by the acquisition of *Giant Food Store* with operations in Pennsylvania, New Jersey and New York. Today, *Ahold* is one of the top retailers in the US, evidenced by the no. 8 position in the 2010 "**Top 75 North American Food Retailers**" based on estimated sales of 29.5 billion USD in 2010. In 2010, the company operated more than 2,900 stores with more than 118,000 employees (in full time equivalents) worldwide. Furthermore, *Ahold* is listed on *Euronext Amsterdam*, on the *New York Stock Exchange* as well as on the *Frankfurt Stock Exchange*. **Table 2.2** provides a brief overview of *Ahold's* history.

---

[1] Sources used for this case study include the company's website www.ahold.com, as well as various annual and interim reports, investor relations presentations as well as explicitly cited sources.

Table 2.2   Ahold's History

Year	Activities
1887	Albert Heijn took over his father's small grocery store on his wedding day in 1887. Within ten years, stores had opened in Alkmaar, den Haag and Amsterdam taking the total number to 23.
1911	The first Albert Heijn brand name products – cookies baked by Albert Heijn himself – started to appear on the shelves in 1911.
1948	In 1948 Albert Heijn's company was first listed on the Amsterdam Stock Exchange.
1955	Albert Heijn opens the first self-service supermarket in Rotterdam.
1973	Ahold enters the US market, acquiring the BI-LO supermarket chain.
1981	Ahold acquires its second US supermarket company, Carlisle-based Giant Food Stores.
1987	Queen Beatrix of the Netherlands awarded Ahold the designation 'Royal' on the 100th anniversary of the very first store opening.
1990	The fall of communism enables Ahold to establish a foothold in Central Europe.
1992	Ahold and its Portuguese partner form Jerónimo Martins Retail (JMR). The joint venture operates a supermarket as well as a hypermarket banner under the name Pingo Doce.
1993	Ahold stock trades for the first time on the New York Stock Exchange.
1994	Ahold acquires Red Food Stores' 55 US supermarkets in Tennessee and Georgia. The chain is later merged into BI-LO.
1996	The company acquires Stop & Shop in the US In the summer Albert Heijn introduces a new distribution system, guaranteeing store delivery within 18 hours.
1998	Ahold acquires Landover-based Giant Food Inc. in the US.
1999	The company announces a partnership with ICA Group, Scandinavia's leading food retailer.
2001	Ahold forms a strategic alliance with Amicus Financial, the US division of the Canadian Imperial Bank of Commerce (CIBC), to offer a range of financial services in selected Ahold stores in the USA through telephone call centres, ATM's and the Internet.
2002	In February, Ahold introduces Albert Heijn XL and Albert Heijn to go in the Netherlands.
2003	With the Road to Recovery strategy, Ahold introduces plans to divest non-core businesses and significantly underperforming core business. These included operations in Indonesia and South America, Golden Gallon in the US and two Polish hypermarkets.
2004	Ahold continues consolidation with the divestment of Ahold's remaining 204 convenience stores in the US, the final Asian operations in Thailand and the sale of operations in South America, Poland and Spain. Ahold also announced its intention to divest its Benelux foodservice unit, Deli XL.

2005	In central Europe, Ahold sells three shopping centres and its larger Polish hypermarkets in order to concentrate on supermarkets and the smaller hypermarket format. It completes the sale of Tops convenience stores, BI-LO and Bruno's in the United States, Deli XL in Benelux and further South American interests.
2006	Ahold further restructures its retail portfolio by the divestment of its retail operation in Poland to Carrefour, and acquisitions of the Konmar stores in the Netherlands. With its retail brand Giant Food Stores, Ahold acquires 14 stores from Clemens Markets Inc. of Lansdale, Pennsylvania.
2007	Ahold completes the sale of Tops Markets and announces the sale of US Foodservice.
2008	Ahold's US division Giant Carlisle acquires Ukrop's Super Markets.

Source: Ahold 2011a.

2.5.2   Business Strategy

In general, the company's strategy is designed to accelerate identical sales growth, to improve returns, as well as to strengthen foundations for future expansions and to create shareholder value. To achieve these goals the company continuously innovates products, services and store formats to build **customer loyalty,** especially to achieve **sustainable profitable growth** with prices that are competitive in all channels. *Ahold* operates food retail businesses in the European and North American markets. The company tries to operate its different retail formats in markets where it can identify clear prospects and reach one of the top positions with regard to market share as a basis for sustainable profitable growth. Operating two continental platforms – *Ahold* Europe and *Ahold* USA – with different retail brands in different regions enables the company to balance its local, continental and global decision-making. To achieve the company's growth objective, it has established powerful local **retail brands** through a better understanding of customer behaviour, continuously improving the products and services offered and competitive price levels and cost savings (Ahold 2011b).

2.5.3   International Growth and Retail Brands

Ahold started its worldwide expansion nearly 40 years ago. After acquiring the *BI-LO* supermarket chain in 1973, the company bought the *Red Food Stores'* 55 US supermarkets and merged them into *BI-LO* in 1994. *BI-LO* became *Ahold's* oldest non-Dutch subsidiary until the company announced its plan for restructuring including the intention to divest *BI-LO* in 2004. In the course of this restructuring *BI-LO* was sold to an affiliate of *Lone Star Foods*. In 1981, *Ahold* acquired its second US supermarket company, Carlisle-based *Giant Food Stores* with operations in the Eastern US market. *Stop & Shop* was acquired by *Ahold* in 1996. In 2001, *Stop & Shop* opened its first "low energy" superstore. In the same year, the company entered into a strategic alliance with *Amicus Financial*, the US division of the *Canadian Bank of Commerce* (CIBC), increasing customer service by offering different financial services in selected *Ahold* stores in the US through telephone call centres, ATMs and the Internet. From

2002, however, the *Ahold* group suffered major problems with regard to earnings, sales and debt and had to start a programme of portfolio rationalisation and debt reduction.

Table 2.3 summarises the most important retail brands and retail formats of the *Ahold* group in the North American and European markets.

Table 2.3   Ahold's most important Retail Brands

Brand	Retail formats	Region	Established in	Acquired by Ahold
Ahold Europe				
Albert Heijn	Hypermarkets, supermarkets, convenience stores and online shop	Europe, the Netherlands	1887	
etos	Drugstores	Europe, the Netherlands	1918	1974
Gall Gall	Wine and liquor stores	Europe, the Netherlands	1884	1989
hypernova	Hypermarkets and supermarkets	Czech Republic and Slovakia	1991	1991
ICA	hypermarkets, supermarkets, discount stores	Sweden, Norway and the Baltic States	1917	2000 (joint venture)
pingo doce	Hypermarkets and supermarkets	Portugal	1992	1992
Ahold USA				
Stop&Shop	Supermarkets and super-stores	United States (New England)	1914	1996
Giant	Supermarkets and super-stores	United States (Washington D.C. area)	1936	1998
GIANT Food Stores	Supermarkets and super-stores	United States (East Coast)	1923	1981
Peapod	Online Shop	United States (East Coast)	1989	2000

Source: Ahold 2011b.

Today, after huge efforts regarding the restructuring of the *Ahold* group in the North American market, the company consists of the operating company *Ahold USA Retail* with the retail divisions: *Stop & Shop New England* and *Stop & Shop Metro New York* (conventional supermarkets and superstores), *Giant Landover* and *Giant Carlisle* as well as *MARTIN'S* as a part of *Giant Carlisle* (conventional supermarkets and superstores). In connection with the increasing relevance of the Internet and demand for online shopping, *Peapod.com* – one of America's leading Internet grocers – joined *Ahold* in 2000, providing Internet-based home shopping as well as grocery delivery as an integrated element of the *Stop & Shop* and the *Giant Landover* operating company.

With regard to the European market, *Ahold* started to expand at the beginning of the 1990s. During this period, the fall of communism enabled the company to establish a foothold in Eastern Europe, starting with setting up a holding company in the then Czechoslovakia in 1990. A year later, *Ahold* opened *Mana*, the company's first wholly owned supermarket chain in the region. Today, *Mana* trades under the *Albert* banner. In 1992, *Ahold* and its Portuguese partner formed *Jerónimo Martins Retail* (JMR). This joint venture operates conventional supermarkets and hypermarkets under the label *Pingo Doce*. In 1999, the company announced a partnership with the *ICA Group*, Scandinavia's leading food retailer. In this relationship, *ICA* and *Ahold* formed a joint venture to develop and operate discount stores and hypermarkets in Sweden and Norway.

Today, the company operates stores in a wide range of retail formats, including store and non-store formats, as well as different retail brands offering different kinds of products in the European market: conventional supermarkets (e.g. *albert heijn, albert, ICA*) superstores (e.g. *albert heijn XL*), hypermarkets (e.g. *hypernova, Pingo Doce*) and convenience stores (e.g. *AH to go*) in food retailing; quality wine and liquor stores (*Gall & Gall*); drugstores and health, body and beauty care stores (*etos*); and an online shop and online delivery service (*albert.nl*) as a non-store format. The latter, established in 2001, offers the same products as the *Albert Heijn, etos* and *Gall & Gall* stores, although *albert.nl* products are delivered to customers within 24 hours.

The expansion of *Ahold* into the European and North American markets was the result of a structured approach. Since its first steps in the US market in 1973, the company had focused on the acquisitions of local retailers operating different retail formats in the North American market and, in most cases, following the same strategy as that used to expand into the European market at the beginning of the 1990s. This approach contributed to the rapid international expansion of the group. Furthermore, it enabled *Ahold* to transfer its own retail brands as well as to build up new store formats, while respecting and taking advantage of the development of the retail landscape in a specific region or in an entire country. These processes of transforming local stores into powerful local retail brands were based on the application of deep consumer insights to improve products and services. With regard to the specific requirements and preferences of consumers in the different markets, the company also tried to realise economies of scale and economies of scope by replicating key components for the improvement of each of the different retail brands and retail formats. These key components were:

■ **providing the best choice** every time by improving product quality, assortment and product presentation,

■ **making shopping easy** by providing more convenience-focused products and services and enhancing the overall customer experience to make shopping more convenient.

With regard to the latter, the development and application of a variety of retail formats was an important tool to make shopping more easy for the consumer. Each of *Ahold's* operating companies improved existing retail formats and developed new format concepts using different layouts, sizes, assortments and service models. In this context, the company also strengthened the quality, quantity, variety and form of its marketing communications, inside and outside of its stores.

2.5.4   Retail Formats

2.5.4.1   Hypermarkets

Ahold operates hypermarkets only in the European market. Under the banner *Albert Heijn XL (AH XL)*, the company offers a large choice of between 50,000 up to 60,000 items of food and non-food products as well as additional customer services in the Dutch market. This concept envisions one 'XL' market for every larger town and the surrounding region. Today, the company operates 21 hypermarkets in the largest regional centres in the Netherlands such as Amsterdam, Den Haag, Eindhoven and Rotterdam. In 2009, *Albert Heijn's* XL format was named the best store in the Netherlands.

Hypernova – established in 2001 – is one of *Ahold's* brands in Eastern Europe, operating a hypermarket format offering a similar range of food and non-food products and customer services in Slovakia. At the end of 2009, the company operated 26 markets in Slovakia. Under the labels *ICA* and *Pingo Doce, Ahold* also operates hypermarkets in Sweden, Norway, Portugal and in the Baltic States. With regard to *Ahold's* overall business strategy, the company has decided to increase the attraction of its hypermarkets by strengthening its price image, gaining deep consumer insights to meet customer expectations, preferences and needs, building customer loyalty through powerful local brands and private labels and encouraging sustainable and **socially responsible corporate behaviour**.

Through the combination of a supermarket and a department store, hypermarkets allow customers to satisfy their shopping needs within one shopping trip. They offer a wide range of products under one roof, including a full range of groceries as well as general merchandise. In general, *Ahold* stands for high quality products, but until 2008 it also stood for relatively high prices. In 2008, *Ahold* started a "price war" in the Dutch market by reducing the prices of more than 1,000 branded products, improving its price image significantly. Therefore, its hypermarkets now stand for high quality products at an acceptable price level. This adjustment in price strategy was also applied to the *hypernova* hypermarkets in Slovakia. Prices can be further discounted by using a free customer discount card – the "*Bonuskaart*" – in the Dutch market. Interestingly, in some cases special offer products can only be purchased at the discount price if the customer shows his discount card at the checkout.

Furthermore, the hypermarkets also now stand for a huge variety of products. Owing to the wide range of food and general merchandise offered *Ahold* takes care of customer needs and preferences for big shopping trips as well as for their daily shopping needs and also provides guaranteed parking and broad accessibility. The company has also succeeded in fulfilling customers' demands for high quality products by offering extensive ranges of fresh produce, delicacies and wine. Today, the company inspires consumers with unique products and services (e.g. one-hour photo developing, self-service checkouts) and a range of private label brands developed to meet the needs of specific types of customers.

The company has four private label ranges: *AH Huismerk* (house label), *AH Excellent, AH Biologisch* or *AH puur & eerlijk* (pure & honest, organic food) and *Euro Shopper*. *AH Huismerk* products are designed to fulfil customers' everyday needs at a low price. Prices are kept low by maintaining direct contacts with suppliers and large-scale purchasing. *AH Excellent* products are comparable to products from specialist shops. They offer "a good value – the best money can buy in the culinary world". *AH puur & eerlijk* includes five different product categories providing a variety of responsible products. These categories are organic, fair trade, sustainable catch (fish), free-range meat and ecological cleaning products at a normal price level, thereby improving customer loyalty. Comparable to *AH Huismerk*, the *Euro Shopper* line offers a huge variety of everyday products at low prices. *Euro Shopper* products are not only sold in the *AH XL* hypermarkets but also in other retail formats. Some of the *Euro Shopper* products are purchased in collaboration with other retailers in order to gain economies of scale. Overall, these private labels account for approximately half of sales in the Dutch market. With regard to the *hypernova* hypermarkets, strengthening the brand through an increasing emphasis on private label products is also a key component of the company's strategy in the Slovakian market.

2.5.4.2 Superstores

Under the labels *Stop & Shop, Giant Landover* and *Giant Carlisle, Ahold* operates superstores only in the North American market. These superstores are in general larger and more diversified compared with conventional supermarkets. The size of such superstores varies between 1,000 m^2 and 5,000 m^2 with an expanded customer service, bakery, deli counter, seafood counter and non-food section, e.g. clothery, jewellery, hardware and appliances. *Ahold's* superstores are "true" food stores with a share of non-food products of 30 % on average. Similar to hypermarkets they offer expanded one-stop shopping opportunities to customers.

Stop & Shop pioneered the superstore concept in New England in 1982. Their superstores are sized between 4,000 m^2 and 5,000 m^2. Similar to combination stores, some offer additional customer services such as petrol stations, full-service pharmacies and one-hour photo development. In recent years, *Stop & Shop* has taken the development of this format further, with superstores that not only serve customer needs, but also use less energy according to the overall corporate social responsibility (CSR) strategy of the *Ahold* group by setting up the "low energy superstore project" in 2001. This project was the result of three years of research and development aimed at reducing the energy usage of a single store by 30 %

including significant changes in store design. For example, a number of skylights maximise the use of natural daylight. Coupled with the further use of dimming controls and highly efficient artificial light, these changes should result in approximately a 50 % reduction in energy usage for interior and exterior lighting. An added benefit is that these efforts create a friendlier store atmosphere for customers and employees. Furthermore, state-of-the-art refrigeration systems could reduce related energy consumption by 26 %. Moreover, insulation and reflective paint on the roof contribute to more energy savings in terms of heating and cooling the superstores. In addition, the necessary construction materials were selected with regard to environmental performance and recycled content. Certain innovations of this project are already being incorporated in the *Giant Landover* and *Giant Carlisle* superstore formats as well as in other retail formats of *Ahold's* portfolio.

To persuade customers to visit the superstores more often, *Ahold* differentiates its superstores not only in product quality, product price and a sustainable socially responsible behaviour, but also in product mix. Following the same strategy as in its hypermarkets, *Stop & Shop, Giant Landover and Giant Carlisle Ahold* have built up powerful **private labels** in different product categories. Under the label *Nature's Promise,* natural and organic food is offered at a low price. *Simply enjoy* includes premium snacks, finger foods and desserts available at an everyday affordable price. *CareOne* stands for top quality health & beauty products, vitamins and over-the-counter products. Under the label *Guaranteed Value* the company offers essential everyday items (e.g. juice, ketchup, paper goods). Household, leisure and entertainment products are provided under the label *Smart Living. Pure Power* and *Pure Softness* include cleaning, paper and laundry products. *Companion* stands for high quality nutritional pet foods, treats, toys and litter. Surprisingly, *JaVaNa* coffee could only be found in the *Giant* superstores. In the future, additional efforts in the development and refinement of these private labels as a basis for customer brand loyalty are expected.

2.5.4.3   Conventional Supermarkets

Ahold's conventional supermarkets are integrated into the everyday lives of its customers. This retail format is a great success in the company's portfolio of different retail formats in each country in which it is established. The store concept provides a lot of advantages, namely a high product quality including freshness of products combined with a convenient customer services. With a share of more than 48 % of the company's worldwide store portfolio in 2009, this retail format is the most important to the *Ahold* group. In the Netherlands alone, the company operated 835 supermarkets in 2009. In the same year, 561 supermarkets were being run in the North American market.

Ahold operates its conventional supermarkets under various retail brands in the European market – *AH* (the Netherlands), *Hypernova* and *albert* (the Czech Republic and Slovakia), *ICA* (Sweden, Norway, Baltic States) and *Pingo Doce* (Portugal) – and in the North American market (*Stop & Shop, Giant Landover and Giant Carlisle/MARTIN'S*). Supermarkets play an important role in each of the areas the group is present, fulfilling the daily shopping needs of customers. In most cases, each of the supermarkets is a powerful local retail brand with a strong focus on the requirements and preferences of customers by offering a convenient and innovative shopping experience and a wide range of products, especially healthy choices including private labels. In the Netherlands, *Ahold* is known as the pioneer in the development of a modern supermarket concept, introducing many innovations in the past. These innovations range from the country's first self-service formats and the development of general merchandise as a grocery store category to the introduction of new products on store shelves that have since become mainstays of Dutch consumers. In this context, the organisation responds to the needs of its local customers increasing customer loyalty.

Furthermore, with its supermarkets *Ahold* adapts to the local context by taking into account the needs of different customer types and their shopping habits. In the Netherlands, for example, the *AH* supermarkets are mostly located in the neighbourhoods of its customers. Therefore, they are easy to reach and provide an opportunity for flexible shopping by opening up to 10 pm. In larger Dutch cities (e.g. Amsterdam, Rotterdam), these supermarkets are also open on Sunday. Each store looks at the needs and preferences of local inhabitants and listens to the product demands of customers. This approach leads to higher **customer satisfaction** and increased **customer loyalty**. Following this concept, *Ahold* has become the largest grocer in the neighbourhood, and the largest butcher, baker and greengrocer in the Dutch market as well. Overall, *Ahold* operates more than 700 stores of this type in the Netherlands, of which 200 are franchises. In general, the company benefits from this **franchising strategy** by a faster expansion of its retail brand, lower capital outlay and liability and the realisation of economies of scale.

2.5.4.4 Convenience Stores

In recent years, *Ahold* has responded to the increasing need and preference for easy and convenient shopping by starting to operate convenience stores in the Dutch and North American markets. Compared with conventional supermarkets, convenience stores are characterised by a limited selection of products. In many convenience stores, only one or two choices are available for each product category offered. This enables customers to shop quickly, picking the required products in a short time without long waiting times at checkouts. Typically, prices are higher than they are in supermarkets.

Ahold started its convenience store format *Albert Heijn to go* (*AH to go*) in 2002. These stores are located in places with a high pedestrian flow, especially at train stations, petrol stations and in city centres. These small formats are operated as stand-alone units, but also are associated with petrol stations. They mainly offer products for direct consumption or immediate use at a higher price level compared with other *Ahold* retail formats. The stores offer a wide range of fresh food and drinks. Convenience, quality and freshness are the characteristics of the approximately 1,200 *AH to go* articles, especially the company's private label products. The long opening hours – up to midnight – are a specific characteristic of this retail format.

In the North American market, *Ahold* opened its first standalone convenience store under the label *Giant to Go* in 2009 to expand and broaden its geographic reach. At an average of 400 m², this store concept combines an on-the-go service for busy families with high quality and fresh products, but at a higher price level compared with other *Ahold* retail formats in the US.

2.5.4.5   Online Shopping Formats

With *albert.nl* (established in 2001) in the Netherlands and *Peapod.com* (acquired in 2000) in the US, *Ahold* operates two online shopping formats. In the Netherlands, the online shopping channel offers the same attractive value as do the other retail formats operated by *Ahold*. Through *albert.nl*, a range of about 10,000 products are delivered to customers' kitchens within 24 hours at any chosen time between 8 am and 9 pm Monday to Friday, and between 8 am and 2 pm on Saturdays. Eighty percent of all households in the Netherlands are within the service area of *albert.nl*. The *albert.nl* website is designed to help customers make a quick and easy selection of the products they need. The bonus card, *Ahold's* overall loyalty programme, allows customers to look up previous purchases in order to create a new one at the touch of a button.

Peapod.com works in partnership with the *Ahold* USA retail companies and provides Internet-based home shopping and grocery delivery as an integrated element of the *Stop & Shop* and *Giant Landover* companies. As an element of the company's overall CSR activities, *Peapod* introduced the *NutriFilter* tool in 2009, a virtual nutritionist making shopping easier for people with allergies and dietary restrictions. *NutriFilter* follows the *USDA* guidelines for each nutritional component, providing more information than a cereal box ever could. Customers have the option of using five preset plans (gluten-free, peanut-free, *USDA* good fibre, *USDA* low fat and *USDA* low sodium), but can also customise their own plans. Customers are presented a blank nutrition panel, such as those seen on all packaged food products in the US, and they are able to select as few or as many nutritional criteria as are important to them. One can create a sort of dream label, specifying maximum calories, grams of fat, milligrams of potassium and so on, and then activate that specific filter. Besides its obvious convenience *NutriFilter* offers for people with dietary restrictions, it is also an excellent resource for the health-conscious in general. Moreover, by engaging children in the *Peapod.com* online shopping experience, parents can use the *NutriFilter* option to educate their children on the **nutritional values** they should look for.

In addition, *Peapod.com* offers tools to help customers save money and be a smart shopper. Among the money-saving features, there is a running total of expenditures as shoppers compile their orders, the ability to trim orders if they exceed the shopper's budget and a function that compares the unit prices of similar items. *Peapod's* system also allows shoppers to identify which of their usual purchases are on sale. Furthermore, since *Peapod.com* customers fill their grocery baskets from home or the office, there's less seduction for impulsive shopping and snack purchases, for example while waiting in the checkout aisle.

Recently, *Peapod.com* introduced *PeapodMobile* allowing customers to place grocery orders from their smartphones. Furthermore, the company developed a free *iPad* app as an additional element of *PeapodMobile* to give tablet users a convenient way for online grocery shopping. The different apps provide a search function, weekly specials, a list of previous purchases, a customised list with frequently purchased items and the "optimised views" function, allowing customers to view items in a list or a grid format.

2.5.5   Conclusion and Outlook

This case study has shown *Ahold's* historical development from a small retailer in the Dutch market to an international retail company operating several retail brands and retail formats. After becoming the largest grocery chain in the Netherlands, *Ahold* started its internationalisation strategy by acquiring its first supermarket chain in the North American market in 1973. Today, the company operates different powerful local retail brands providing a wide range of retail formats all over the world, but still focused on the European and North American markets. Together, with its efforts towards sustainable and **social responsible corporate behaviour** as well as introducing innovations that make shopping easier and are in line with the specific needs, preferences and requirements of local customers, this strategy has resulted in it becoming one of the top retail companies worldwide.

| Questions

1. Ahold operates multiple retail formats. What are the typical advantages and disadvantages of each retail format?

2. Ahold's strategy of international growth is mainly based on the acquisition of powerful local retail brands. Discuss critically the challenges and opportunities of introducing the brand Albert Heijn with its specific formats in the international market.

3. Ahold operates online shopping formats in Europe and in North American market. Evaluate the relevance of the company's e-commerce and m-commerce formats for future growth in food retailing.

| Hints

1. See Chapter 8 for internationalisation strategies.

2. See Zhang et al. 2010 for a general outlook on future developments in e-commerce and m-commerce.

3   Retail Formats - General Merchandise

In this Chapter, the main characteristics and empirical relevance of a variety of store formats applied in general merchandise retailing are discussed. The diverse forms of retail stores represent different strategies in selling goods and services and are a result of the diversity of product groups that are embraced by the term "general merchandise".

3.1   Diversity of Retail Formats in General Merchandise Retailing

In general merchandise retailing, a variety of retail formats is used to sell non-food merchandise to consumers. This **diversity** results from the **plurality** of product groups that are characterised as non-food items. Even though product groups also vary within the food sector with regard to consumer shopping behaviour, major differences are seen, particularly between general merchandise and food items. These differences relate to product characteristics such as perishability, specific demand patterns, product value (e.g. in relation to product size or volume) or turnover rate. For example, while food is usually purchased daily or several times per week, general merchandise in most cases is purchased infrequently. Some categories such as cosmetics or household articles are bought more frequently than others are, for instance TV-sets or computers, which usually are purchased only every few years.

While in general merchandise retailing substantial sales are generated by traditional store-based retail formats, non-store formats such as catalogue retailing or electronic channels are also vitally important. New developments in technology and customer behaviour in recent decades have led to a change in the relevance of different retail channels and to the evolution of **new retail formats,** mainly in the field of non-store retailing. Another important trend is that many traditional store-based or catalogue retailers have started to sell their merchandise through several retail formats. By adding additional retail channels, they are evolving into **multichannel retailers** (see Chapter 4).

3.2   Store-based Retail Formats

The major types of store-based retail formats in general merchandise retailing that will be discussed in this Chapter are drugstores, specialty stores, category specialists, department stores, full-line discount stores and variety stores, off-price retail formats and pop-up stores.

3.2.1   Drugstores

Drugstores are specific types of specialty stores that focus on beauty, health and personal grooming merchandise (Levy/Weitz 2009, p. 51). In addition, these stores often sell categories such as food items, magazines or newspapers, stationery, toys or gifts. Depending on governmental health care policies, in some cases **pharmacies** are associated with drugstores and sell prescription pharmaceuticals in addition to ethical or over-the-counter (OTC) medicine. The product categories sold in this store format are similar in some respects to food items, mainly in terms of shopping frequency and purchasing patterns **("near-food items")**. In some statistics, drugstores are therefore classified as food store formats.

Compared with traditional specialty stores, drugstores tend to be more aggressive on price and apply pricing strategies such as every-day-low-price (EDLP) strategies or promotion pricing. Important players include *Boots, Walgreens, A.S. Watson* or *dm-Drogeriemarkt*.

Drugstores are often located in city or shopping centres, but are now found more and more at locations such as neighbourhoods or isolated sites. Thus, they play an important role in **proximity retailing** and usually – because of their location strategies and rather small store sizes with speedy checkout facilities – offer a high degree of **shopping convenience**.

3.2.2   Specialty Stores

Specialty stores specialise in one or very few product types and consequently carry a limited number of products within one or few lines of products (and services). Usually, the merchandise is of average to good or **high quality**. While the width in the assortment is narrow, the depth is usually extensive and specialty stores thus provide a **better selection** in terms of a higher choice variety than do competitors from other retail formats such as department stores (Ogden/Ogden 2005, p. 99). Specialty stores additionally offer a high level of **service** and knowledgeable sales personnel. Typically, the stores are located in city locations or shopping centres, are small and the **instore atmosphere** is pronounced to create a pleasant shopping experience (see Chapter 13).

Limited line specialty stores are a specific type of specialty stores that carry only a very narrow assortment, but offer pronounced depth in this limited sector. Often, these stores offer (very) high quality merchandise and a high level of customer service and instore design, while prices are above average.

The specialty store format is traditionally chosen by retailers that sell merchandise such as clothes (e.g. *Gap* or *Abercrombie & Fitch*), footwear (e.g. *Footlocker*), cosmetics (e.g. *Douglas, The Body Shop* or *Sephora*), books (e.g. *Barnes & Nobles, WHSmith* or *Thalia*) or jewellery (e.g. *Christ*). In many cases, however, specialty stores are run by **independent local retailers**.

The main element of specialty stores' strategies is that they focus on a specific market segment. While this offers many opportunities in terms of tailoring their stores to their **target groups**, it also makes them vulnerable to changes in consumer tastes and preferences. They also suffer from the high costs that result from the **quality-oriented strategy** in terms of store environment, merchandise and service offered to consumers (Levy/Weitz 2009, pp. 48-49). This often results in higher than average prices.

While specialty stores have been the traditional format for non-food shopping, in recent years they have been one of the weakest, slowest growing areas in retailing and have lost market share to other store-based or non-store formats.

However, a specific form of specialty stores has evolved and is growing despite this trend. Mainly in fashion retailing, **fast-fashion chain stores** have emerged as a successful store format. Companies such as *H&M, Zara* or *Mango* use a new approach to specialty retailing by rapidly changing their store assortments with new product introductions several times per month. By doing this, they can guarantee very fashionable and up-to-date products in store.

This approach to quality is also different from traditional specialty retailing. Whereas traditional specialty stores suffer from efficiency problems resulting from their high quality strategies, fast-fashion retailers vary in their approaches to instore environments, products and service quality. While they ensure a minimum quality standard, the general quality of store atmosphere, merchandise and services offered is in many cases lower than average, with an explicit focus on up-to-datedness and short refresh periods. This strategy combined with efficient back-end processes, especially with regard to logistics (see Chapter 6), helps reduce costs and thus enables fast-fashion retailers to establish low or medium price strategies. It is also a strategy to enhance the shopping frequency of customers because of the permanently changing assortments.

3.2.3   Category Specialists

Category specialists, also referred to as **specialist markets**, **category killers** or **power retailers**, are price-oriented stores that offer a broad depth of merchandise in a particular category, usually in large stores. They offer an almost complete assortment in a particular category at **low prices** and thus can "kill" a category of merchandise for other retailers (McGoldrick 2002, p. 158), mainly for specialty stores. The service level offered by category killers is usually kept at a low level. Self-service approaches are generally applied to sell merchandise, but assistance is offered if requested by customers.

Outlets usually are located in out-of-town locations. Exceptions, such as *Saturn*, a German-origin category killer in the field of consumer electronics, focus mainly on city locations or combine both out-of-town and city locations (see case study *IKEA* in this Chapter).

Category killers are aimed mainly at motorised customers and they usually offer extensive parking facilities to their consumers and thus draw them from a **large catchment area**. Store architecture and instore design are kept very simple and offer a shopping experience that is dominated by size and pricing (Wileman/Jary 1997, p. 78). More and more often, category specialists join in specific agglomerations, so-called power centres (see Chapter 10), which provide the consumer with several category specialists in one location.

The strategy of **low operating costs** in terms of rents, personnel costs and low cost designs, sometimes with a warehouse atmosphere, combined with huge buying power usually leads to high asset productivity (e.g. space, stock turnover). This makes category killers one of the retail formats with the highest growth rates over recent years. They have gained market share mainly at the expense of specialty stores, because of the advantages in terms of price and product range. Category killers are now established in many non-food categories such as consumer electronics (e.g. *Curry's, Darty, Media Markt* or *Best Buy*), DIY (e.g. *Leroy Merlin, B&Q* or *Home Depot*), sports (e.g. *Decathlon*), furniture (e.g. *IKEA* or *Conforama*), office products (e.g. *Staples* or *Office Depot*), pets (e.g. *PetsMart, Mille Amis* or *Fressnapf/Maxi Zoo*) and toys and baby products (e.g. *Toys 'R' Us* or *Babies 'R' Us*), and the format is still expanding into new categories.

3.2.4   Department Stores

Department stores are **large retail units** that carry a broad variety of merchandise and offer a deep assortment "under one roof". Often department stores consist of several floors. The term "department store" results from the structuring into separate departments for displaying merchandise in a manner that resembles a collection of specialty stores, i.e. each department acts as a mini store in the store. Each department not only has a specific selling space allocated to it, but also usually has its own point-of-sale terminals and dedicated salespeople to assist customers (Levy/Weitz 2009, p. 47).

The merchandise sold by department stores traditionally comprises a wide range of categories such as clothes, accessories, appliances, home furnishings, jewellery, cosmetics, toys, furniture, sporting goods and consumer electronics. Recently, however, most department stores have been reducing product variety and focus more and more on "soft goods" (e.g. clothes and footwear).

The main locations of department stores are **city centres**, or they often serve as anchor stores in **shopping centres**. Department stores offer a pleasant atmosphere, which creates an enjoyable shopping experience. Instore design and visual merchandising are thus important (see case study *Lafayette* in Chapter 13). Also, the services offered by department stores are diversified and may include, for example, a tailoring service for clothes or home deliveries.

In terms of the merchandise carried and services offered, department stores can be categorised into three tiers (Weitz/Whitfield 2010, p. 91):

- Upscale, **high-fashion** stores with exclusive designer merchandise and excellent customer service; these are often the flagship stores of department store chains (e.g. *Harrods, Selfridges, Jelmoli, Saks Fifth Avenue, KaDeWe, Galeries Lafayette Paris Haussmann*); these are usually located in very large cities such as New York, Berlin, Paris, London or Zurich.

- Modestly priced, **mid-level** merchandise with less customer service (e.g. *Macy's, Manor, Hoopers, Debenhams, Kaufhof, John Lewis*).

- Stores with **lower level** merchandise and prices (e.g. *Sears, JCPenny, Kohl's*).

Most department store chains such as *Galeries Lafayette, Karstadt, El Corte Inglés, House of Fraser* or *Saks* operate department stores in several of these tiers.

In recent years, the overall sales and market share of traditional department stores have declined and – internationally – they face substantial competition from other retail formats such as category killers and discount stores or non-store formats (e.g. Internet retailers). These difficulties mainly result from the problems in retail positioning as an outcome of the **"all under one roof"** approach. Whereas first-tier department stores seem to have a clearly differentiated position and usually produce strong financial results, these difficulties relate mainly to outlets in the second and third tiers, which lack such a clear positioning and are therefore struggling. Furthermore, the overheads and **operating costs** associated with such large retail outlets that are oriented towards ambience, attentive services and a broad variety of products are very high in comparison to the more cost-focused and price-aggressive retail formats. Additionally, these retail formats often have better assortments in the limited lines they carry. The departments in a department store simply cannot offer the same depth (Berman/Evans 2010, p. 139).

Problems may also occur from the mere size of the stores larger than 50,000 m². With regard to shopper convenience, department stores, by contrast, offer the service of one-stop shopping for diverse products or needs with the approach of offering general merchandise all under one roof. Because this strategy results in big stores that have a large amount of SKUs in the store, it makes high demands on customer orientation, time of shopping and so on. Department stores therefore offer little "mental convenience" for customers, and shopping in department stores may be difficult (with regard to the mental processes of choice situations in the store) and time consuming for customers.

Even though department stores are trying to respond to their deteriorating positions in terms of giving a clear profile to stores by, for example, tightening up their assortments, increasing the amount of exclusive merchandise or brands offered, introducing store brand programmes and improving CRM or marketing campaigns to improve their image, this erosion of market share still seems to continue.

3.2.5   Full-line Discount Stores

Full-line discount stores are a specific type of department store that offers a broad variety of merchandise at low prices, from such categories as electronics, furniture and appliances, household goods or gardening tools (Levy/Weitz 2009, p. 49). This store format has its origins in the USA, with *Walmart*, *Kmart* and *Target* as the most important players.

Store architecture and instore design are very simple to keep costs low. Also, the merchandise is usually less fashion-oriented than that in department stores. Full-line discount stores offer both store brands, for example, non-durable goods, and manufacturer brands, such as hard goods (e.g. TVs or household appliances). Usually, customer service is limited. Products are sold via self-service. Customers use **shopping carts** to do their purchases and pay at centralised checkout areas (Berman/Evans 2010, p. 140). Thus, operating costs are kept low. This store format struggles from the lack of a pleasant shopping experience and its similarity to hypermarkets (or supercentres) with respect to general merchandise. Full-line discount stores are therefore faced with strong general competition from hypermarkets and category killers in each specific category. Over the past few years, they have lost market share, which, for example, has led *Walmart* to close some of its full-line discount stores or convert them into supercentres.

3.2.6   Variety Stores and Value Retailers

Variety stores, such as *Woolworths* or *Ben Franklin*, offer a broad assortment of inexpensive and popularly priced merchandise. Categories such as clothes, accessories, jewellery, confectionery and toys are covered. Stores offer limited services and do not carry full product lines (Berman/Evans 2010, p. 140). This store format faces strong competition from retail formats such as category specialists, discount stores and (large) food retailing formats that carry a range of general merchandise of similar product lines.

While the conventional form of variety stores is struggling, several new forms have evolved over the past few years. One form is variety stores with a fast-fashion-like approach to their assortment strategies. These retailers such as *Strauss Innovation* offer more focused assortments than do conventional variety stores and concentrate mainly on the fields of home accessories, household supplies, textiles, occasional furniture and clothes. Products are offered at reasonable, rather low prices. However, these retailers do not stock products permanently in their assortments but frequently change their assortments to offer fashionable and up-to-date products in diverse categories. This strategy aims to enhance the shopping frequency of their customers and the constantly fresh atmosphere combined with the rapid changes in the assortment help develop a "buy it now" shopping behaviour among customers.

Another form of variety stores that has evolved is (extreme) value retailers. These are general merchandise discount stores that target mainly low income customers and they are thus located mainly in low rent, lower income urban or rural areas (Levy/Weitz 2009, p. 53).

The merchandise sold covers similar items to those in conventional variety stores, but prices are much lower.

A specific form of such extreme value retailers are **one-price stores** that offer every product at the same price (e.g. dollar stores or euro stores such as *Family Dollar* and *Dollar Tree* in the US or *EuroShop* and *HEMA* in Europe). These "true" one-price stores offer a wide range of products mainly from categories such as home wares, confectionary, cosmetics, gifts and stationery.

3.2.7   Off-price Stores

Off-price stores sell an inconsistent assortment of merchandise, e.g. soft goods such as clothes, accessories, cosmetics or footwear, at low prices. Some off-price retailers focus on fashion-oriented, brand name or designer labelled items. Off-price stores use a very **aggressive buying strategy** without asking manufacturers for additional services such as return privileges, advertising allowances, markdown adjustments or delayed payments. They often negotiate with manufacturers to discount orders, e.g. for merchandise that is out of season or for **irregular items** that have minor flaws (Ogden/Ogden 2005, pp. 99-100; Berman/Evans 2010, p. 141).

Specific types of off-price stores are, for example, **closeout retailers** that sell a broad assortment of merchandise that is purchased at closeout prices or **outlet stores** that are owned by department stores, specialty stores or manufacturers **("factory outlet stores"**, see Chapter 5). In these stores, excess merchandise, overruns or irregulars are sold, and markdown prices in primary stores can thus be avoided (Levy/Weitz 2009, p. 54).

3.2.8   Pop-up Stores

Very specific new store formats are pop-up stores, also labelled **temporary stores**. This retail format is aimed at creating a **"limited edition"** type of retail atmosphere, as these stores open for a specific time, which can be interpreted as a scarcity strategy by retailers or a "promotion gag". They are temporary retail establishments that are only open for a rather short period of time, e.g. a few days, a few weeks or a few months, and they offer an array of usually seasonal products.

The retail environment of pop-up stores in most cases is highly experiential, transporting brand emotions in an event-oriented type of atmosphere. While pop-up stores can also serve as retail events to sell special offers (e.g. with marked down prices), they often serve as retail venues to present and introduce product innovations or even conduct market tests. Therefore, locations are usually in city centres or the trendy neighbourhoods of big cities. Companies that employ pop-up stores range from very trendy brands such as *Comme des Garçons* to established retailers such as *IKEA* (see **Figure 3.1**), *Walmart, Gap* or *Target*.

Figure 3.1   IKEA Pop-up Store in Manhattan

Source: Trendhunter 2011.

With the strategy of **pop-up stores** being the creation of a climate of scarcity, retailers try to build a higher willingness to pay among their customers because there is no option for price comparison and offers are only available for short periods of time, which can increase **desirability**. In particular, temporary stores that sell special offers are consumption events for the customers and their main objective is to get discounts. In some cases, pop-up stores of this type are used to give special offers to long-term, high value customers. In these events, the scarcity effect is reinforced as there is not only a **temporary limitation** of the offers but also the products are only available for specific customer groups. This form of customer segmentation may be used to deepen customer relationships.

Pop-up stores offer a very high degree of flexibility for retailers. As they are not involved in long-term leases, not only location changes are possible but also the profitability of such business operations is usually rather high. Anyhow, this store format is difficult with regard to customer attraction and communicating the opening of a pop-up store. As they are only open for a limited period of time, the main challenge is to advertise the stores, to gain customer awareness and to become known among target customers. Often, huge communication efforts are necessary to establish successful pop-up stores.

3.3   Non-Store Retail Formats

3.3.1   Overview

Non-store retailing comprises all retail formats that do not use bricks-and-mortar stores. The main principle is **distance retailing**, which means that customers and retailers do not have direct contact. The most important type of non-store retailing is **home delivery**, but there also are other forms. Traditional catalogues and the Internet (see Chapter 4) are non-store formats of major importance in general merchandise retailing. Other channels of less importance in terms of market share are direct selling, TV shopping, vending machines or new forms of mobile retailing (mobile commerce or m-commerce).

3.3.2   Catalogue Retailing

Catalogue retailing is the traditional type of non-store retailing. The merchandise offered is communicated to consumers through a catalogue and customers can generally order by mail, phone or fax.

The two main types of catalogue retailers are **general merchandise catalogue** retailers and **specialty catalogue** retailers (Levy/Weitz 2009, p. 56). While the first type relates to retailers that offer a broad variety of product categories (e.g. *Otto, JCPenny, La Redoute,* or *Freemans*), the latter focus on specific categories of merchandise such as clothes (e.g. *Madeleine, Lands' End*) or sporting goods (e.g. *SportScheck*) with an extensive assortment depth. The assortment policy of general merchandise catalogue retailers is comparable to the strategy of department stores, while specialty catalogue retailers correspond to specialty stores in terms of merchandise strategy. In recent years, many general merchandise catalogue retailers have decreased the duration of the validity of their catalogues and, instead of one annual catalogue, have started to launch two or three general catalogues per year. In addition, general merchandise catalogue retailers also launch several catalogues that focus on specific product or target groups.

Catalogues provide consumers with benefits such as the possibilities to look at merchandise and placing orders at any time from almost everywhere and the information is easily accessible. Even Internet retailers argue that their customers still like to browse catalogues and that this often generates the initial (or the final) buying impulse.

A new trend in catalogue retailing focuses on the layout and content of the catalogues. **Magalogs** have emerged as new form of catalogues that are magazine-like (see **Figure 3.2**). In magalogs, not only merchandise is presented but the catalogues are enriched with editorial content, thus enhancing customers' desires to use, read and leaf through the catalogue.

Figure 3.2	Titus Magalog

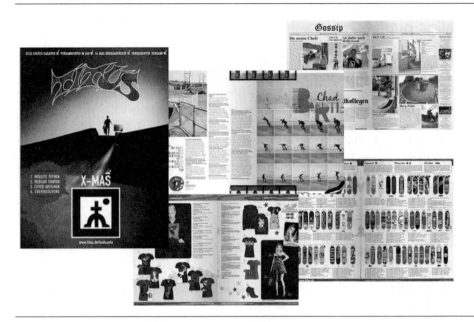

Source: Titus 2011.

Most catalogue retailers, however, do not only offer traditional print catalogues but operate forms of electronic shopping over the Internet. This specific type of non-store retailing will be discussed in detail in Chapter 4.

3.3.3   Direct Selling

Direct selling is a retail format that involves interactive **personal contact** between salespeople and customers at non-store locations. Salespeople can contact customers directly at a convenient location (e.g. customer's home or at work) or they can contact them, for example, via telephone. They demonstrate merchandise, take orders, deliver the products to the consumers or provide them with further information or services (Ogden/Ogden 2005, p. 107). Direct selling channels can be operated by retailers or manufacturers (see Chapters 5 and 6).

The strategy behind direct selling systems that operate with their own salespeople who sell individually to consumers and provide them with a high level of information and, in some cases, extensive demonstrations of products is associated with high operating costs. Therefore, specific forms of direct selling have evolved. The main forms of these are party sales and multilevel marketing systems. **Party sales** are characterised by salespeople encouraging customers to act as hosts and invite friends to a "party" at which the products are presented. In **multilevel selling systems**, master distributors recruit other people to become distributors in their networks (Levy/Weitz 2009, p. 57). Direct selling is applied to product categories such as homewares (e.g. *Tupperware*), cosmetics (e.g. *Avon*) or jewellery (e.g. *Pierre Lang*).

3.3.4 Other Non-Store Shopping Formats

In addition to these main non-store shopping formats, there are also other non-store channels, but they are of less importance in terms of market share. For example, also in general merchandise retailing, **vending machines** can be used for selling books, newspapers, phone cards and CDs or DVDs etc. While the operating costs are relatively low, the main drawbacks of vending machines are logistical, such as filling processes, out-of-stocks or reverse logistics, e.g. in the case of damaged products. Anyhow, several retailers have started vending machine operations such as *Best Buy, Media Markt* and *Saturn* that sell specific items in the field of consumer electronics through vending machines that are positioned at convenient and highly frequented places such as airports or railway stations (see **Figure 3.3**).

Figure 3.3   Vending Machines

Additionally, several non-store retail channels have evolved that are based on specific technologies. For example, in **TV home shopping** products are demonstrated in infomercials and on TV channels dedicated to television shopping or in direct response advertising on TV or radio. Customers usually place their orders via the telephone, but there are also new interactive forms of TV shopping where orders can, for example, be made online (Gilbert

2003, p. 355). TV shopping channels are, for example, operated by *QVC* or *Home Shopping Europe (HSE24)*.

As a result of new developments in information and communication technology, the development of new strategies to sell general merchandise is highly dynamic with regard to non-store retail formats. The most important retail formats that involve new technologies are discussed in Chapter 4.

3.4   Conclusion and Outlook

In general merchandise retailing, traditional retail formats such as department stores, specialty stores or pure catalogue retailers are struggling with competition from new formats such as **price-aggressive store formats** (e.g. category killers, off-price stores), retailers that sell fast-moving non-food items as **special promotions** on a weekly or semi-weekly basis (e.g. *Tchibo*) or **innovative non-store formats** such as Internet shops. This trend towards more price-oriented and flexible formats is predicted to continue in the next few years.

Apart from this trend towards discount-oriented channels, the main developments in general merchandise retail formats result from new developments in **information and communication technologies** that not only lead to the emergence of new retail formats such as mobile commerce, but also offer potential new business models and new modes of communication to customers within the framework of existing retail formats. The new retail channels are not only important as **new competitors**, but many retailers are expanding their existing retail formats by adding such new channels and evolving into multichannel retailers. These developments in retailing are accompanied by changes in consumers' shopping motives and behaviour, such as price or "more-for-less" orientation, convenience orientation and, more sophisticated customers, and can be interpreted as a response to customer needs (Uncles 2010).

▌Further Reading

GANESH, J.; REYNOLDS, K.E.; LUCKETT, M.G. (2007): Retail Patronage Behavior and Shopper Typologies: a Replication and Extension using a Multi-format, Multi-method Approach, in: Journal of the Academy of Marketing Science, Vol. 35, No. 3, pp. 369-381.

LEVY, M.; WEITZ, B.A. (2009): Retailing Management, 7th Ed., Boston et al.

3.5 Case Study: IKEA[1]

3.5.1 Profile, History and Status Quo

This case study illustrates the retail concept of *IKEA*. *IKEA* is particularly suited for a case study on store formats in general merchandise at least for two reasons. First, the company pursues a category killer strategy by offering a broad range of furniture at low prices. Furthermore, *IKEA* uses additional store types (high city stores, catalogue and online retailing as well as pop-up stores) to maintain their success.

With a turnover of 23.1 billion EUR in 2010 and about 127,000 employees, so-called co-workers, *IKEA* is the largest furniture retailer worldwide. With a growth in turnover of 9 % after having reached 21.4 billion EUR in 2009, *IKEA* has consequently enlarged its operative efficiency and reinvested in its businesses by opening new stores during the past few years. During the financial year 2009, *IKEA* opened 15 new stores. With 318 outlets in 38 countries on four continents, *IKEA* is the most internationalised of the furniture retailers. Altogether, 79 % of its turnover is earned in Europe, and the countries with the highest turnover are Germany (15 %), USA (11 %), France (7 %) and Great Britain (6 %).

IKEA aims to be the first choice for home furnishings by enabling people to improve their daily lives. To reach this goal, *IKEA* has lowered its prices by 2-3 % per year on average during the past ten years. In total, 626 million customers visited *IKEA* stores during the financial year 2010. In the financial year 2009, *IKEA* increased EBITA by 8.2 million EUR from 2,831 million EUR to 2,913 million EUR. With growth of 2.8 %, *IKEA* again proved its strength, despite a difficult competitive environment and reached a point of consolidation.

3.5.2 Formation and Development of IKEA

Since its foundation by Ingvar Kamprad in 1943, *IKEA* has become the world's largest furniture retailer, specialising in stylish but inexpensive Scandinavian-designed home furnishings and furniture. Even today, after more than 50 years of business activity, *IKEA* is still strongly associated with Kamprad. In 1943, he founded *IKEA*, selling such items as pens, wallets, jewellery and picture frames. The name *IKEA* is an acronym. *I* and *K* are the founder's initials, *E* stands for Elmtaryd, the name of his parents' farm, and *A* represents Agunnaryd, his hometown in the Southern Swedish province of Småland. A small **mail order catalogue** was established and furniture was introduced into the product range in 1947, which has been the focus since 1951. Owing to customer scepticism towards buying furniture unseen, Kamprad opened a **showroom** in the village of Älmhult in 1953, where customers could examine the products before ordering. In 1955, because of a suppliers' boycott caused by pressure from competitors, *IKEA* started designing its own furniture. One of

---

[1] Sources used for this case study include the websites http://www.IKEA.com and http://www.ikea-group.ikea.com, the "Welcome inside" report 2010 as well as explicitly cited sources.

IKEA's central characteristics, knocked down furniture sold in flat packs, was invented in 1956. In 1958, the first *IKEA* store was opened in Älmhult. Since then, the company has expanded steadily and its first international venture was in 1963, when the first store outside Sweden was opened in Oslo, Norway.

Traditionally, the home furnishings market was very local in orientation, because consumers' tastes vary substantially between regions and because the transportation costs over long distances often render international activities uneconomic. However, the *IKEA* concept has proven itself to be efficient and internationally viable. That is why this retailer currently faces no direct competitors with a comparable global scope.

Despite the retailer's retail brand positioning being thoroughly Swedish, *IKEA* has, ironically, not been Swedish in a "strict legal sense" (The Economist 2006, p. 69) since the early 1980s. This is a result of its complex ownership structure, which is designed to minimise tax and disclosure. Also, the structure renders *IKEA* almost immune to a possible takeover (The Economist 2006, p. 69).

Figure 3.4   Ownership and Organisational Structure

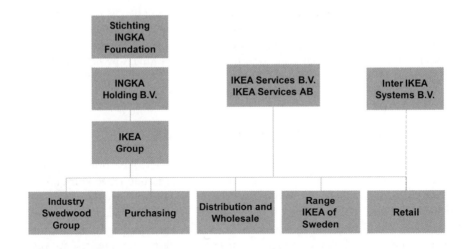

The whole *IKEA* group is owned by the *Stichting INGKA Foundation*, registered in the Netherlands. *INGKA Holding B.V.*, the parent company for all the companies comprising the *IKEA* group, is owned by the foundation. Support for the work within the companies of the *IKEA* group is delivered by nine staff units in the Netherlands (*IKEA Services B.V.*) and Sweden (*IKEA Services AB*). *Inter IKEA Systems B.V.* owns the *IKEA* concept and trademark. It also has franchising agreements with the *IKEA* stores worldwide (see **Figure 3.4** for *IKEA's* ownership structure).

3.5.3   Positioning of IKEA as Modern Category Specialist

The company's official **vision** is "to create a better everyday life for the many people", which is achieved by combining aesthetic and pragmatic furniture design and solid quality with the constant drive to cut costs and pass savings onto customers. This vision is manifested in the business idea "To offer a wide range of well designed, functional home furnishings at prices so low that as many people as possible will be able to afford them".

The cornerstones of the *IKEA* concept, which are the basis for achieving this vision and business concept, are, in many cases, the exact opposite of conventional furniture retailing and these have turned the traditional basis of the furniture business upside down:

- Whereas traditional home furniture stores are located as boutiques in city centres, *IKEA* has developed large, even huge stores on the outskirts.

- Instead of shop assistance, customers serve themselves.

- As opposed to traditional sourcing, the scope of which was always very local, *IKEA* has sourced on a global scale from the very beginning.

- The traditional focus on middle- to upper-middle-aged customers has been shifted to younger people.

- Instead of the assembled furniture being delivered at a relatively high price, customers both transport and assemble the flatpack furniture themselves. This self-service on the part of customers allows *IKEA* to lower its prices tremendously in comparison with traditional home furnishings retailers.

- When *IKEA* started in Sweden, dark and heavy furniture was popular, but *IKEA* introduced its trademark light Scandinavian style, characterised by blonde wood, natural material and modern design (cf. Kling/Goteman 2003, pp. 31-32).

IKEA offers the same product range on an international scale, and adapts the store layouts, presentation of the products, home services offered and prices only where necessary in accordance with national economic and cultural conditions and circumstances. This enables *IKEA* to transfer its profile appropriately worldwide (Miller 2004, p. 37). To cut costs the retailer standardises as much as possible and adapts only what is necessary. There is, for example, only one set of instructions for the assembly of a piece of furniture, regardless of country, because it contains no written language, but only visual instructions (Levy/Weitz 2009, p. 147).

It is widely accepted that if it was not for *IKEA*, most people would have no access to affordable contemporary design (Capell 2005, p. 47). In order to achieve its vision of providing "the many" with excellent value-for-money furniture, which identifies *IKEA* as a **category killer**, *IKEA* is committed to cutting costs wherever possible. Apart from the flatpacked furniture that customers assemble themselves, thus actively participating in making *IKEA's* business model work, the following elements along the value chain also reduce costs:

- **Product range development**: about 9,500 products are in *IKEA's* range, which are sold globally. They are developed by *IKEA of Sweden* according to the principle of target cost pricing, where defining the final selling price of a new product is the first step in the product's manufacturing process. All subsequent steps in the value chain are designed to meet this predefined selling price.

- **Production:** *IKEA's* industrial group *Swedwood*, established in 1991, produces wood-based furniture and wooden components. It has nine production units mostly located in Eastern and Central Europe in order to benefit from low labour costs.

- **Sourcing**: altogether, 29 trading offices are run in 25 countries, managing the mostly long-term relationships with 1,074 suppliers in 55 countries.

- **Distribution**: a total of 27 distribution centres in 16 countries provide for cost-efficient and environmentally conscious distribution.

- **Outlets**: products are bought and transported in bulk; stores are located in inexpensive areas.

It is also widely known that all *IKEA* employees, even top management, always travel as cheaply as possible, proof of how deeply the maxim of cutting costs is rooted in the company's values. This strict **cost-orientation** results in operating profit margins of 16 % to 17 %, which is "phenomenal" in retailing (The Guardian 2004).

3.5.4   Retail Formats at IKEA

IKEA's key target market comprises all customers "just starting out who are in need of relatively cheap, sturdy furniture" (Cook 2003). This includes young, low to middle income families, college students, single households and young urban professionals. This "eclectic mix of customers" (Moon 2005, p. 89) constitutes a whole new customer segment, as opposed to the traditional target market of furniture. *IKEA* itself has described its target market as "young people of all ages" (Martenson 1987, p. 15). The global middle class that *IKEA* targets shares many buying habits (Capell 2005, p. 48), allowing the retailer to transfer its successful business model in an almost standardised manner to foreign markets. This international expansion has worked almost flawlessly, with the exception of the US market, where the retailer struggled after its market entry in 1985. *IKEA's* reluctance to make some necessary adaptations to US habits and preferences, because of the drop in economies of scale, is normally regarded as the reason for these initial problems (Lewis 2005).

The entire retail concept is designed to fit the target group's needs: affordable, yet stylish furniture, in many cases for a couple's first common apartment, one-stop-shopping under one roof, a children's corner called *Småland* where children are taken care of while the parents are shopping and a restaurant inside the store. In 2006, *IKEA* launched its own store brand for groceries. The products are sold at its *Sweden Shops* for groceries inside the outlets and further strengthen the brand image.

IKEA uses large outlets, which are located in out-of-town locations, city located stores, which usually stock fewer products because of their smaller sizes, and pop-up stores, which identify *IKEA* as an innovative retailer (see section "Store-based Retail Formats"). Additionally, *IKEA* deploys non-store formats such as its catalogue and online store.

In its **outlets**, which are usually on the outskirts of urban agglomerations, *IKEA* offers its customers a unique, "360-degree retail experience" (Cook 2003), which speaks to the senses and is largely the same in all parts of the world. The brand logo and outside painting of stores are yellow and blue, the Swedish national colours. Whereas older *IKEA* stores have only few windows, newer ones are built with more glass, which leads into decreasing energy costs as well as a better presentation of the products because of using more natural light. Since 2005, a change of strategy has become apparent from new store openings. *IKEA* store formats are no longer only characterised by large outlets outside the city but also by **high street formats** (Telegraph 2006). Although these new city stores are much smaller than the older outlets are, *IKEA's* high street shoppers are able to get the full range of products in this new format. Furthermore, you can find the typical layout of all *IKEA* stores within the city stores. *IKEA* is able to offer a similar shopping experience for customers at city stores by using traditional concepts adapted to new requirements: the sales area is broken up into several stories and the parking area is located on the roof of the store. Hence, everything is as always just different.

Figure 3.5   Examples of IKEA City Stores (in Queenstown, Singapore (left), and in Hamburg, Germany (right))

Source: Wikipedia 2011; Abendblatt 2011.

As is customary for category killers, *IKEA* offers a wide and deep range of products in furniture and furnishings. To sell them at low prices customers are actively involved in the **shopping experience**. They choose, collect, transport and assemble the products themselves. Because the service level offered by *IKEA* is low and the nuisance of transportation and self-assembly is almost unavoidable, customers usually have to be "educated" (Martenson 2001, p. 32) to understand the *IKEA* concept, and this requires the customer take an active part in the business model in order to have both low prices and modern design. That this has been achieved by *IKEA* becomes apparent by the very loyal customer base, which can be described as a **"solid brand community"** (Cook 2003). It has become common for customers to queue up in front of a new *IKEA* outlet even days before the opening. The fascination with *IKEA* has even been called **"fanaticism"** (Capell 2005, p. 49).

Inside the store, strategically placed bins containing various accessories, paper measuring tapes and pencils provide the shopper with haptic experiences. Customers inside a store follow a marked path to the different showrooms, thus ensuring that all the merchandise is visible. As a result of this fully guided customer flow, the outcome of a typical shopping trip is that the customer purchases various items he did not initially intend to buy or even knew he needed.

A cafeteria where shoppers can rest and refresh is located at the middle of each vast building. This strategically placed cafeteria prevents customers from leaving the store to get something to eat, which would often result in them not coming back to the store at all. In addition, the low prices in the cafeteria are increasingly used to attract customers into the store to have breakfast or lunch.

With *IKEA FAMILY*, a free customer card that provides cardholders automatic club membership with, for example, special promotions and a quarterly magazine with current home furnishings trends and inspirations, *IKEA* has implemented its own **offline-community**. Events and workshops are offered regularly and enhance the retailer's Swedish image, e.g. crayfish meals.

3.5.5   Non-Store Retailing at IKEA

The **catalogue** is the main marketing tool, accounting for 70 % of the marketing budget. From *IKEA's* beginnings, the catalogue has been the primary channel for reaching customers. It demonstrates the breadth of *IKEA's* product range and aims to be a source of inspiration to its readers. With more than 190 million copies printed in 2010, published in 29 different languages, it is also the world's largest free commercial publication. It contains the full product range with some 9,500 stock-keeping units (SKUs). It is also almost completely standardised. The catalogue is designed centrally for all countries. Country subsidiaries can only add between four and 16 pages to this catalogue to focus stronger on certain categories. Furthermore, the central marketing unit can propose more than one possible cover (but usually only about two) and the country subsidiary can choose between them (see **Figure 3.6** for *IKEA* Catalogues from Selected Countries). The catalogue is always valid for one full year, which also means that the prices remain stable for 12 months. Moreover, since prices are the same in the catalogue as they are in stores, the prices in the stores remain stable for at least a year.

Figure 3.6   IKEA Catalogues from Selected Countries

IKEA started its **e-business** activities in 1997 by launching the IKEA website www.IKEA.com. Three years later, it became possible to shop online in Sweden and Denmark, with many other countries following suit. Although the homepage provides an additional distribution channel, the website is primarily used by IKEA to support its stores because of the limited online sales in most countries. The online activity aims primarily at providing information that reinforces *IKEA*'s image for innovative products and low prices as well as to help customers prepare store visits. In addition, the company has started mobile commerce activities with the launch of an iPhone App for its 2010 catalogue. This *IKEA* application has been downloaded more than 200,000 times, and in the first week of its release became the second most downloaded application in *Apple's App Store*. Users can select a piece of furniture from the catalogue and place it anywhere inside the room around them, changing its size to fit the perspective by using the phone's camera.

Despite its use of multiple retail channels, *IKEA* provides customers with a consistent shopping experience across its spectrum of retail channels. Customers are able to get detailed information online about outlets such as opening hours, transport connections or service offers. Additionally, consumers can check out the availability of a product (online and offline) on the homepage for any outlets. They will get information about how many products are still in stock, including an outlook for the next three days. Furthermore, the prices across all channels are identical. The catalogue is visible online and downloadable. In return, the opportunity to shop online is presented in the catalogue as well as an abstract of the outlets. Furthermore, it is possible to return products that were bought online to a store. In conclusion, consumers are able to order and redeem gift vouchers both online and offline and the loyalty programme is the same across all channels.

3.5.6   Summary and Outlook

Since its modest beginnings, *IKEA* is now referred to as a "global cult brand" (Capell 2005, p. 47), complete with genuine *IKEA* fans and their obsession that "has no bounds" (Booth 2005, p. 22). In line with the concept of category killers, *IKEA* positions itself as a price aggressive specialised discounter that keeps product quality high and presents this image to the customer with emotional and polarising advertising campaigns. *IKEA* is "the measure of all things" for furniture in the European market (and soon the world). The high customer involvement and participation at the core of this fascination with the brand is secured along all steps of the buying process as well as the different channels through high integration.

Pre-sale, the retailer actively works to create the need to replace furniture more often on the part of the consumer. As the retailer's most important marketing activity, the catalogue also directly involves the customer who can browse through it and try to picture the proposed designs in his or her own home.

During the sales process, the customer is guided through the different showrooms, which show the products in real-life situations. Since the path through the store is guided (almost forced), the customer sees the store in its entirety and is thus surrounded by all the different situations at home. The children's corner allows parents to fully experience the *IKEA* world without disturbance. Furthermore, the high touch experience during the shopping trip also helps draw the customer in at an emotional level, enhancing his or her involvement.

Post-sale, the direct involvement on the part of the customer becomes apparent when he has to transport and assemble the furniture at home. As *IKEA* pushes the notion of frequent furniture replacement, this three-step process starts again. The *IKEA* philosophy is summarised as "You do your part. We do our part. Together, we save money" by the company itself.

IKEA is one of the most impressive examples of a successful retail concept with high integration across different channels. Every single channel of *IKEA* is a specific, integrated aspect of its overall retail model. All distribution channels work together. The multichannel strategy of *IKEA* becomes apparent by how it integrates the different channels. The way to combine outlets, the catalogue and the Internet by *IKEA* is characterised by maximising the potential of each by communicating in a consistent way to consumers.

By paying a lot of attention to staying lean and keeping a low cost structure, *IKEA* is able to lower its prices every year as well as expanding both within existing and into new markets. For example, after *IKEA* Romania became part of the *IKEA* group in 2010 *IKEA* plans store openings in Serbia and Croatia.

| Questions

1. *IKEA* operates in the same market with three formats: category specialists, online shops and catalogue retailing. What are the typical characteristics and advantages of these retail formats? To what extent do these characteristics and advantages apply to the retail formats used by *IKEA*?

2. The parallel use of different retail formats and/or sales formats is referred to as multichannel retailing. What are the opportunities and risks associated with this concept in general and for *IKEA* in particular?

3. *IKEA* has not yet implemented online shops in every country where it operates. Assess the relevance of this retail format within the framework of the company's future internalisation.

| Hints

1. For a discussion of the advantages and disadvantages, see Chapters 2 and 3 as well as Levy/Weitz 2009.

2. See Chapter 4 on the concept of multichannel retailing. Take into account the website www.ikea.com

3. Check the country-specific websites of *IKEA* and analyse the existing online shops.

4   Online Retailing and Multichannel Retailing

In this Chapter, the main characteristics and empirical relevance of online retailing are discussed. Many retailers sell their merchandise to their consumers through multiple retail formats. This phenomenon, which is referred to as multichannel retailing, is also discussed in this Chapter.

4.1   Online Retailing

4.1.1   Overview

In online retailing or **electronic retailing** (or e-retailing, electronic commerce, e-commerce, Internet retailing), retailers offer their products and services over the **Internet**. Merchandise is thus presented in Internet shops. Customers usually place their orders via **electronic checkouts** or they can use e-mail or traditional modes of communication (e.g. mail, phone and fax).

While, in most cases, customers pay through traditional systems (e.g. credit card, purchasing on account), some Internet shops also offer **electronic payment systems**. In electronic retailing, according to their merchandise strategies, retailers can be divided into general merchandise and specialty retailers.

4.1.2   Scope of Online Retailing

Generally, all kinds of products can be sold over the Internet, but major sales are generated in such categories as books, CDs, DVDs, clothes, computer software, toys and home electronics (see **Figure 4.1**).

The Internet is also of high importance for **digital products** such as software, music and e-books that – unlike physical goods – can literally be transferred through electronic channels. In such cases, the Internet offers additional shopping convenience in terms of the direct and immediate availability of the products purchased ("**transaction convenience**").

The most prominent example of a successful Internet retailer is *Amazon*, which started off as a specialty retailer focussing on books, but has added more and more product categories to its portfolio since, such as music, toys, consumer electronics, pet supplies and even groceries.

Figure 4.1   "What product/services do you intend to purchase online in the next 6 months?" (Global Average)

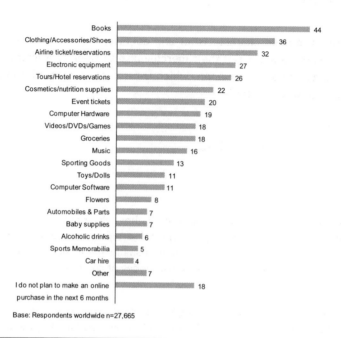

Base: Respondents worldwide n=27,665

Source: Nielsen 2010.

The "hype" that was associated with Internet shopping as a revolutionary retail format in the beginning has receded, and a **market consolidation process** has driven many Internet retailer innovators out of the market. Nonetheless, for several years electronic retailing – internationally – has been the retail format with the fastest growth.

The relevance of the Internet as a shopping channel is prevalent all over the world. In 2010, there were 475 million Internet users in Europe, nearly 270 million in North America, nearly 850 million Internet users in Asia-Pacific and about 170 million Internet users in Africa and the Middle East (Nielsen 2011). While this accounts for a world penetration of about 26 % of the total population, there are strong differences between the developed and developing world (see **Figure 4.2**). The following figures demonstrate the potential of online shopping.

Figure 4.2   World Internet Users by Level of Development 1998-2009

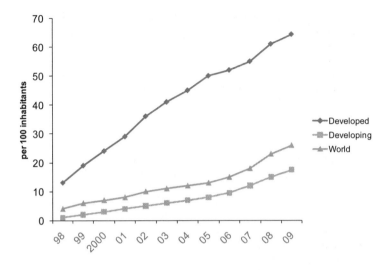

Source: ITU World Telecommunications/ICT Indicators database 2009.

With regard to online shopping, the percentage of people that use the Internet as a shopping channel varies and is as high as 70 % of the Norwegian population, with an average penetration rate of 37 % in Europe (see **Figure 4.3**). In 2010, US online retail sales were as high as 172.9 billion USD, with a predicted growth of about 20 billion USD per year until 2014 (Forrester 2009). This trend of Internet shopping being a retail channel of growing importance seems to be a worldwide trend. For example, online sales in China experienced growth by almost 90 % from 2009 to 2010 to a total of 58 billion EUR.

Figure 4.3   Percentage of Online Consumers 2009[1]

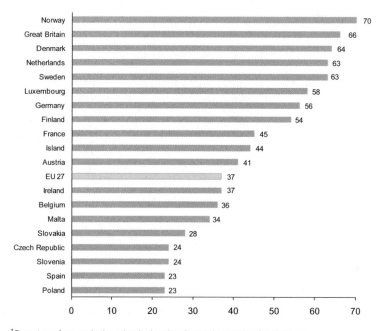

¹ Percentage of persons having ordered or bought online goods or services for private use.
  The persons interviewed are aged between 16 and 74 years.

Source: Nielsen 2010.

However, the relevance of the Internet as a retail channel is still rather low, with a market share of 7 % of all retail sales in North America and 5.5 % in Europe in 2010 (Reuters 2010). This is also reflected in the share of online shopping spending of customers (see **Figure 4.4**). When the Internet was introduced as a shopping channel, there were pessimistic prognoses that predicted that e-commerce would damage traditional bricks-and-mortar stores, but the emerging reality rather proposes that e-commerce has become a **supplementary shopping channel** for customers.

Figure 4.4 Online Shopping Spending Percentage of Total Monthly Spending

What is your online shopping spending percentage of total monthly spending?

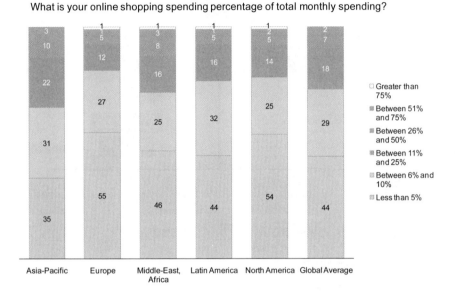

Source: Nielsen 2010.

4.1.3 Shopping Formats in Online Retailing

4.1.3.1 Overview

Because of high dynamics in technological developments, the online channel provides a highly innovative retail environment. As not all online shops follow the same business models, similar to the categorisation of store formats, it is possible to distinguish between diverse **shopping formats in online retailing**. **Figure 4.5** gives an overview of the most important retail formats in online retailing as well as selected examples of each format, categorised by their unique selling propositions (USPs) which poses the main reason why consumers buy at the particular format.

Figure 4.5   Formats in Online Retailing

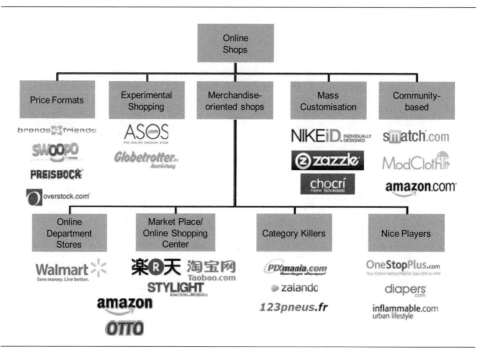

4.1.3.2   Price Formats in Online Retailing

With regard to price formats, the general **price strategies** also can be differentiated in online retailing. For example, there are online discounters that sell products at prices below the average price line and there exist quality-oriented retailers that charge higher prices for more exclusive offers. In online retailing, low price formats such as value retailers, off-price stores and factory outlets also exist that offer products at lower than average prices as well as stock-outs and end of line stock. For example, on sites such as *Overstock.com, Sears Outlet* or *Tesco Outlet*, overstocks, remnants or products from the previous season are offered.

A specific form of online closeout retailers are **private shopping clubs** such as *Gilt Groupe* or *brands4friends* where members can buy popular brands at high discounts. Through this shopping channel, retailers organise time-limited online shopping events in which remnants or liquidation stock in apparel, accessories, homewares or toys are sold only to club members, i.e. registered users. To become a member, consumers need to be invited by other members or they can get waitlisted to get membership. One advantage of the closed membership base is that offers from these online shopping clubs do not appear in price comparison sites, which would hurt the brand image of the offered designer brands.

The emergence of Internet retailing has also led to **new business models** and new forms of retail transactions that are mediated by the computer. With regard to price formats, dynamic pricing models are important. For example, **Internet auctions** have emerged. While in online **Dutch auctions** prices start at a high level and are reduced until the first bidder accepts the price, the most common form of online auctions is the **English auction** where the initial price starts low and the price is bid up by successive bidders. This traditional type of auction is, for example, employed by *eBay*, the most successful online auction platform.

Bids cannot be made for free in all cases. For example, **bidding fee auctions** (also labelled **penny auctions**) have emerged (e.g. *Swoopo*) where bidders must purchase credits to make bids. However, these types of auctions are controversially discussed and have been criticised as being a specific type of gambling.

Another new price format is referred to as **live shopping**. This price format is characterised by a very limited assortment, often only a couple of products, that is available on the live shopping platform for a very low price, often the best online price of the day, but the offer is only available for a very limited time, usually 24 hours. This time limit and the limited availability of the products forces customers to make quick purchasing decisions and often impulse purchases are stimulated. Live shopping is applied by specialised retailers such as *Woot*, *Groupon* or *Daily Deal*, that operate live shopping websites, but traditional retailers such as *Sears* or *Buy.com* also integrate live shopping elements into their online shops.

Other price formats that have been developed are **Internet price comparison** (e.g. *froogle*) or "**name-your-own-price**" systems (e.g. *Priceline.com*), although not all of them are successful.

4.1.3.3   Experiential and Community-based Online Retailing

Technological developments in online communication offer new dimensions in online retailing with regard to **experience shopping**. With the use of videos, avatars, user communities or other interactive measures, many retailing websites have performed a trading-up process. Retailers that follow this approach usually use sophisticated methods to address their customers. Companies such as *ASOS* or *Globetrotter*, for example, provide emotional shopping environments with intensive information on product specifications and usage situations and use product rating systems where customers rate and discuss products, combined with further options to interact with customers as well as topic-related **discussion forums**. Even video shopping is offered where products are featured and can be put into a shopping cart right out of the video.

While in these types of online shops social communities are important but rather peripheral elements of the websites, **community-based retailing** sites have emerged that have been established around a social community or with a social community as an integral element of the retailing concept. For example, on the *Amazon* website, product ratings and discussions between members of the community are integral parts of the retailing concept. *Smatch.com* uses a community as the basis for a product search platform that links products from several retailer websites. Many retailers now use such features but some online shops also now focus on these social interactions in their marketing efforts.

4.1.3.4   Mass Customisation

Online retailing also allows for new business models with regard to the products offered. A specific type of assortment strategy that has emerged mainly in the online environment relates to the **individualisation** of products. In Internet shops that focus on this type of strategy, customers are able to alter product specifications in order to assemble their individual products. Typically, customers can combine different product elements (e.g. form, colour, ingredients, etc.) and create their own, individualised configurations of the product. Usually, retailers provide a standardised set of product elements that is customisable in the hands of the end-user. On retailing sites such as *spreadshirt*, *zazzle* or *chocri*, customers can create or alter the product themselves; the product is then configured "on demand" and shipped to the consumers.

Often, this strategy is applied by manufacturers that use the online channel to directly sell to consumers. Many manufacturers of soft goods such as apparel or shoes use this strategy, e.g. *Nike* with *NIKEID* or *Adidas*. It is also popular in the consumer electronics industry, with companies such as *Apple* or *Dell* providing product individualisation or personalisation options (see Chapter 5). However, mass customisation is also applied in the food industry. For example, on sites such as *Mixmygranola.com* or *mymuesli.com* customers can create their own breakfast cereals.

4.1.3.5   Merchandise-oriented Shops in Online Retailing

Assortment-oriented online retailers provide online shops in which customers primarily search for products. A common type of assortment strategy in online retailing is implemented as **online department stores** that - similar to their stationary pendant - carry a broad variety and a deep assortment. *Amazon* proudly announces that it has the widest possible assortment in most of the categories offered. Companies such as *Otto* or *Walmart* also make a mark in online retailing, mainly with their wide selections of products from a broad number of categories. This strategy corresponds to general merchandise catalogue retailers.

More common in the online environment is **specialty online retailing**. This strategy implies a more focused assortment; thus, retailers concentrate on one or a few specific categories of merchandise. Similar to specialty stores, they offer deep but narrow assortments in specific market segments. Retailers that operate such specialty online shops are *Lands' End* or *Next* in apparel retailing or online bookstores. As a specific form of these specialty retailers, niche players have also emerged that focus on subcategories such as specific styles in apparel, e.g. *Inflammable.com* with a focus on urban lifestyle clothing, baby supplies, e.g. *Diapers.com*, or *OneStopPlus* that offers plus-sized clothing.

Because of the high transparency of prices on the Internet, these online specialty retailers are under high pressure because price aggressive formats are common online. **Online category killers** such as *Microspot* or *Pixmania*, both price aggressive online retailers in consumer electronics, *Zalando* as a price aggressive online retailer in the field of shoes, clothes and accessories or *123pneus*, an online category killer in the field of tyres, offer complete assortments in their categories at low prices.

However, online retailers have challenges with regard to customer attraction and aware-ness. Therefore, high **communication efforts** are often necessary to establish their online shops. Additionally, the operating costs of online shops may be very high, especially if the retailers focus on emotional or experiential shopping environments and want to use indi-vidualisation options on their websites. A method to solve these problems is cooperation between retailers. In this context, platform strategies are common. **Marketplaces** or **online shopping centres** have emerged. On these platforms, a wide and deep selection of products can be accessed by customers. Contrary to traditional online stores that are operated by one retailer, the products on these sites are offered by many retailers. Examples are *Stylight* or *Taobao*, but also *Amazon* or *eBay* serve as electronic marketplaces as they operate platforms for third-party retailers.

4.1.4   Media for Online Retailing

While online shopping is often understood and investigated as purchasing on a retailer's website by personal computer or laptop ("stationary Internet"), new digital devices (e.g. smartphones, tablet PCs or Internet-enabled TVs) provide new possibilities for customers to shop online (see **Figure 4.6**).

Figure 4.6   Forms of Online Retailing

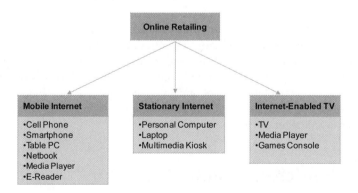

In particular, **mobile commerce** (m-commerce) is rapidly emerging as an alternative form of online shopping. While for a long time m-commerce was mainly associated with mobile phones, portable two-sided digital devices such as tablet PCs or media players are growing in significance for online shopping. Total US m-commerce grew 253 % from 396.3 million

USD in 2008 to 1.4 billion USD in 2009 (ABI Research 2010), as more customers tend to choose mobile shopping over traditional online shopping (see **Figure 4.7**).

Figure 4.7   Mobile overtakes Desktops for Internet Access

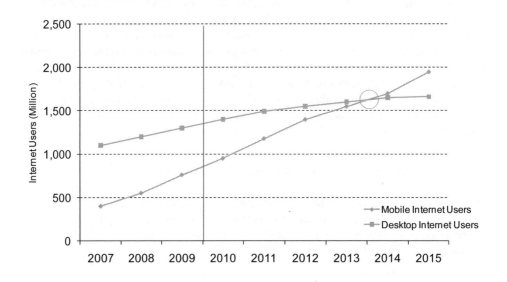

Source: Morgan Stanley Research 2010.

Regarding usage, access to online shopping is spreading from desktops to the living room, supported by the trend of more and more TVs offering Internet access. However, **Internet-enabled TV (IETV) sets** are quickly becoming mainstream, with iSuppli (2010) estimating that global shipments will reach nearly 150 million units by 2014, representing 54 % of the total TV market. Thus, mobile Internet and Internet access via TV obviously differ from stationary Internet, and it is expected that these differences will bring new challenges and opportunities to online retailers.

4.2   Multichannel Retailing

The term multichannel retailing refers to retailers using several retail channels in parallel to sell their merchandise (Schramm-Klein 2003). This strategy has been common for a long time, but has recently become more relevant and topical because of new channels of distribution, in particular the Internet.

A study by Forrester Research (2010) stated that e-commerce sales represent 7 % of all retail sales, but online and **web-influenced offline sales** (e.g. purchasing in a retail store after online price comparison) account for 42 % of total retail sales combined and will continue to grow steadily.

Table 4.1 Relative Attractiveness of Alternative Retail Formats to Consumers

Dimension	Supermarket	Department Store	Category Specialist	Catalogue	Internet Retailer
Providing Alternatives for Consideration					
Number of Categories	medium	medium	low	low	low
Alternatives per Category	medium	low	medium	medium	low
Screening Alternatives to Form Consideration Set					
Selecting Consideration Set	medium	high	medium	low	low
Providing Information for Selecting from Consideration Set					
Quantity	medium	medium	medium	medium	medium
Quality	high	high	high	medium	low
Comparing Alternatives	medium	medium	high	low	low
Ordering and Fulfilment: Transaction Costs					
Delivery Time	immediate	immediate	immediate	days	days
Supplier Delivery Cost	low	low	low	high	high
Customer Transaction Cost	high	high	high	low	high
Supplier Facility Costs	high	high	high	low	low
Locations for Placing Orders	few	few	few	everywhere	many
Other Benefits					
Entertainment	low	high	medium	low	low
Social Interaction	medium	high	medium	low	low
Personal Security	low	low	low	high	high

Source: adapted from Alba et al. 1997, p. 38.

Consequently, many retailers act as **multichannel retailers** and combine several retail formats, such as bricks-and-mortar stores and/or traditional catalogues with Internet retailing. By doing so, companies can exploit the unique benefits of different retail formats and thus increase customer benefits. However, they also have to deal with the specific drawbacks associated with each retail format (see **Table 4.1**).

The main reasons for evolving into multichannel retailers are (Schramm-Klein 2003, pp. 2-3; Levy/Weitz 2009, pp. 83-85; Alba et al. 1997):

■ **Expanding** market presence into new markets (e.g. new target groups, geographically new markets, etc.)

- **Leveraging** skills and assets to increase revenues and profits (e.g. well-known retail brands, supplier relationships, buying power, customer information, supply chain systems, etc.)

- **Overcoming the limitations** of existing formats (e.g. store size, flexibility in pricing and merchandise provision, information-provision modes, etc.)

- **Increasing customer share**/share of wallet (customers' percentage of total purchases with the retailer).

Multichannel retailers applying an **umbrella brand strategy**, which means that all retail formats of the company carry the same retail brand, must provide a consistent image to consumers across all channels. Thus, the integration of retail channels is one of the major issues with which retailers are still struggling (Schramm-Klein 2003, pp. 336-339). The provision of integrated retail channels is important in multichannel retailing, as customers in many cases use several retail channels in combination in their **buying processes**. For example, consumers can (1) gain initial information on brands and product types from the catalogue, (2) inspect the physical aspects (e.g. colours, materials, content) at the store, (3) check prices and (4) availability, (5) complete the transaction in the Internet shop and (6) pick up or (7) return products at or to the store.

Figure 4.8   Types of Multichannel Retailers

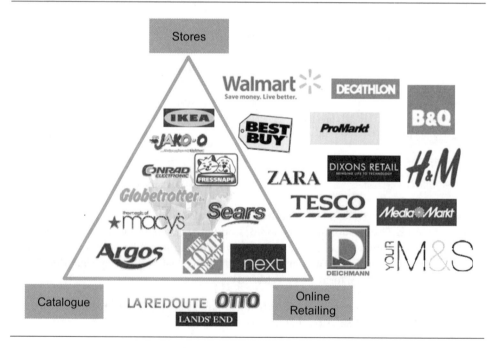

In **Figure 4.8**, the most important types of **multichannel retailing** are presented. Based on the main formats, i.e. stores, catalogues and electronic retailing, diverse combinations of multichannel systems are possible. Successful multichannel retailers include *Otto* (catalogues, stores, Internet shop, mobile commerce and TV shopping), *Lands' End* (catalogues, stores and Internet shop), *Tesco* or *Carrefour* (multiple store formats and Internet shop) and *Douglas* (stores and Internet shop). It is expected that these new developments in online retailing with new forms and situations of online access will bring new challenges and opportunities for multichannel retailers and profoundly reshape the retailing landscape, just as the Internet channel has done to date.

4.3   Conclusion and Outlook

With regard to the retailing landscape, a high share of companies is engaged in multichannel retailing (see **Figure 4.8**). Almost all large retailers that operate stores have opened online shops, and most category specialists, with companies including retailers such as *H&M*, *Deichmann*, *Best Buy* or *Decathlon*, operate multichannel retailing systems. For remote ordering retailers, even though catalogues remain an important means of retailing, online channels are proving vital.

However, many pure players in online retailing such as *Amazon*, *Zalando*, *Pixmania* and many others are among the most successful retailers in their industries, implying that multichannel retailing is not an indispensable strategy a retailer needs to choose.

Thus, even though there are many successful examples of multichannel retailers, multichannel retailing is not appropriate for every retailer. For example, small and medium-sized retailers rarely possess the financial and managerial resources to create seamless multiple channel environments by consolidating disparate retail management systems into one customer-focused system (Levy/Weitz 2009, p. 176). Additionally, the potential **synergies** of a multichannel system are not the same for all retailers.

| Further Reading

LAROCHE, M.; YANG, Z.; MCDOUGALL, G.H.G.; BERGERON, J. (2005): Internet versus Bricks-and-Mortar Retailers: An Investigation into Intangibility and its Consequences, in: Journal of Retailing, Vol. 81, No. 4, pp. 251-267.

SCHRAMM-KLEIN, H. (2010): Integrated Retail Channels in Multichannel Retailing: Do Linkages between Retail Channels Impact Customer Loyalty?, in: Morschett, D.; Rudolph, T.; Schnedlitz, P.; Schramm-Klein, H.; Swoboda, B. (Eds.): European Retail Research, Vol. 24, Issue II, Wiesbaden, pp. 111-128.

WILLIAMS, D.E. (2009): The Evolution of E-tailing, in: The International Review of Retail, Distribution and Consumer Research, Vol. 19, No. 3, pp. 219-249.

4.4   Case Study: Next[1]

4.4.1   Profile, History and Status Quo

NEXT is a UK-based retailer offering fashion and accessories for women, men and children as well as a range of homewares. The *NEXT* brand and retail concept was created in 1982, firstly presenting collections of own-branded womenswear and accessories for women. With the additions of menswear in 1984, home interiors in 1985 and childrenswear in 1987, *NEXT* developed into a **full-line fashion vendor**. In 1988, in addition to its established retail stores, the *NEXT Directory* catalogue was launched. An online version of the *Directory* followed in 1999 at www.next.co.uk. A detailed overview of *NEXT's* history is given in **Table 4.2**.

Table 4.2   Historical Overview

Year	Activities
1982	The first NEXT womenswear store opens on 12th February. There are 70 NEXT stores around the UK by the end of July.
1984	NEXT for Men launches in August. By December there are 52 menswear stores.
1985	Debut of NEXT's first home interiors range.
1987	Launch of NEXT childrenswear.
1988	Launch of NEXT Directory – the brand's new catalogue concept in home shopping.
1993	NEXT announces its brand strategy of "One Brand; Two Ways of Shopping", bringing together the common ranges across both, retail and home shopping formats.
1994	NEXT's 300th store opens. The brand is now trading in 16 countries worldwide.
1999	Launch of shopping on the Internet from the NEXT Directory at www.next.co.uk. This extends NEXT's business strategy to "One Brand; Three Ways of Shopping".
2003	NEXT opens new larger format stores in Nottingham, Birmingham, Dudley and Newcastle Gateshead together with a large home store at Glasgow Braehead.
2009	NEXT extends its home shopping facility to the USA and over 30 other countries worldwide through Nextdirect.com.

Source: NEXT plc 2011a.

In recent years, the Internet has become a significant part of *NEXT's* mail order business. Currently, over 70 % of *NEXT's* home shopping business, which includes more than two

---

[1] Sources used for this case study include the company's website www.next.co.uk, and various annual and interim reports, investor relations presentations as well as explicitly cited sources.

million active *Directory* customers in the UK, is transacted online. In 2010, 64 % of the overall profits were achieved in the *NEXT* retail stores, 11 % by catalogue and a further 25 % online (see **Figure 4.9**).

Figure 4.9   Dispersion of Profits

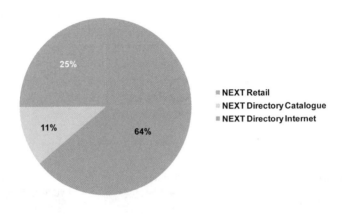

Source: NEXT plc 2010.

Other company businesses include *NEXT Sourcing*, which is responsible for the design, sourcing and buying of *NEXT* branded products; the 2008 acquired brand *Lipsy*, which designs and sells its own-branded younger women's fashion products; and *Ventura*, a business unit that provides customer service management to clients wishing to outsource their customer contact administration and fulfilment activities. The parent company, *NEXT plc*, is listed on the London Stock Exchange. Total revenues for the financial year ending January 2010 were 3.4 billion GBP with profits of 364 million GBP (20 % growth compared with 2009).

4.4.2   Development of NEXT's Business Strategy: "One Brand; Three Ways of Shopping"

When the *NEXT* retail chain launched in 1982, the company was operating as a single channel retailer, distributing via **retail stores**. At that time, the business strategy aimed at a new retail concept in **boutique-style shopping** environments. Over the subsequent years, a full-line lifestyle brand was created by offering a broader range of products. With the *NEXT Directory* catalogue, a hardback book containing 350 pages, a second retail channel was added six years after the first retail store had opened. However, the *NEXT Directory* was not successful in the early years and the company was not able to generate profits with the mail order business. Only after five more years (in 1993) was the relevance and potential of bringing together the common ranges of retail store and home shopping format recognised, and the brand strategy *"One Brand; Two Ways of Shopping"* was announced. By offering the same quality and fashion in the catalogue as well as in the retail stores, commercial success was achieved (Catalogue-Connection 2011). In 1999, an online shop was launched and *NEXT's* business strategy was extended to *"One Brand; Three Ways of Shopping"*. The three distribution channels are illustrated in **Figure 4.10**.

Figure 4.10   NEXT's Retail Channels

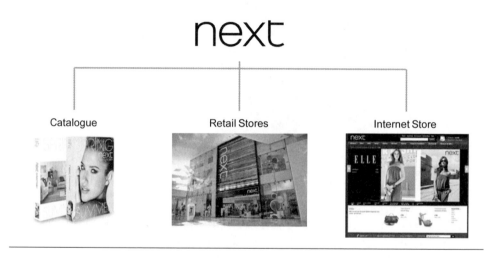

Source: NEXT plc 2011a.

Under the brand *"NEXT"*, the company operates a multichannel retailing system, applying three retail channels:

- *NEXT Retail Stores* has more than 500 stores in the UK and Ireland. With more than 180 stores throughout continental Europe, Scandinavia, Russia, the Middle East, India and Japan, *NEXT* also operates in international markets.

- The *NEXT Directory Catalogue* is a high quality direct mail catalogue with more than 1,300 pages in the Autumn/Winter 2010 book, offering broad and deep collections for men, women and children. Meanwhile, there is an additional catalogue for homewares, which were part of the main catalogue in the past.

- The *NEXT Internet store* is a transactional website that started in 1999 in the domestic market at www.next.co.uk. In 2009, the home shopping facility was extended to the USA and over 30 other countries worldwide at www.nextdirect.com.

Meanwhile, 2.43 million active *NEXT Directory* customers use the possibility of homeshopping by catalogue or online. The proportion of online orders increased from 7 % in 2001 to 70 % in 2010 (Retail Week 2010). With respect to growth, the Internet shop has also outtraded the retail stores for several years. From August to December 2010, *NEXT's* retail store sales went down 3 %, while *NEXT Directory* sales rose nearly 9 % (NEXT plc 2011b).

4.4.3   Channel-specific Advantages and Services

Each of *NEXT's* retail channels offers unique advantages to the customer (Berman/Thelen 2004). For example, the Internet store provides the opportunity for personalised self-service 24 hours a day as well as seven days a week (Payne/Frow 2004).

Table 4.3   Channel-specific Advantages and Services

Channel	Advantages/Services
Retail Store	◆ Ability to touch, try on and test products ◆ Interaction with service personnel ◆ Immediately availability of goods ◆ No shipping costs or delivery time
Internet Store	◆ Extended product range (e.g. electronics, flowers and gifts) ◆ Additional pictures and product information ◆ Customer reviews ◆ 24/7-shopping ◆ "New in" (recent products and prices) ◆ Mini shops (e.g. "As seen in", "NEXT TV", Catwalk Looks) ◆ Search function ◆ Stock status ◆ Personal account (including account summary, balance details, recent online payments, address information) ◆ Fashion editorial ◆ Style blog ◆ Digital customer magazine
Catalogue	◆ Portable and easy to handle ◆ Available for browsing (e.g. in the living room) ◆ Transferable and shareable among customers ◆ 24/7-shopping by phone

Source: adapted from Berman/Thelen 2004, p. 149.

Moreover, consumers are known to have heterogeneous purchase preferences (Alba et al. 1997), and thereby different channels with diverse functions and individual advantages address a broader range of customers and are able to better serve customer-specific needs. An overview of *NEXT's* channel-specific advantages and services is given in **Table 4.3**.

In *NEXT's retail stores*, customers are able to judge the optical and haptic characteristics of goods, e.g. feel the surface or appraise the colours. When customers need additional **guidance,** service personnel is available in the store to give advice or answer questions. Furthermore, products can be purchased immediately, which is important because some customers are impulse buyers or just dislike waiting for delivery or paying shipping costs.

In comparison to the catalogue and retail stores, the *NEXT Internet store* offers an extended product range since there are no space limitations for product presentation. Thus, a wide assortment of consumer electronics (e.g. computing and gaming), flowers or gifts (including wine, champagne and spirits) and even flooring is available only online. Furthermore, *NEXT* presents goods online with additional pictures and further information, which reduces the perceived risk of receiving an inappropriate product. For the same reason, customers are encouraged to write **customer reviews** and let other customers know what they think about a purchased product. The *NEXT* Internet store is always open to place an order or just browse the collections. Another advantage is the timelessness of the online bargain, so recently added products are categorised as "New in" and extend the online overall supply immediately, while the *NEXT Directory* catalogue is updated only once a year. Aside from classical categories, such as clothes, shoes and accessories, *NEXT* has implemented "Mini shops" for specific topics. For example, in the Mini shop *"As Seen In"*, outfits that are shown in recent fashion magazines (e.g. *Elle*, *Vogue* or *Instyle*) can be purchased. Specific goods can also be found by using the search function. By considering the stock status, customers can check the **availability** of a product including colours and sizes. When visitors to the *NEXT* homepage create a personal account, they receive a detailed view of all payments, ordered goods, returns and pending items. To enhance customer value, the Internet store features additional content, such as a fashion editorial, a style blog and a digital fashion, beauty and home magazine.

The advantages of *NEXT's* catalogues are that they are easy to take along, can be used nearly everywhere, e.g. on the "sofa", bus or train, and are easy to handle. In addition, customers can share a catalogue with family and friends. Catalogue orders can be placed, similar to online shopping, 24 hours a day by using *NEXT's* phone order service.

4.4.4   Integration of Channels

Several studies suggest that retailers who offer **multiple channels** have higher customer loyalty and profitability than do single channel retailers (e.g. Neslin/Shankar 2009; Wallace/Giese/Johnson 2004). When using a range of divergent channels, retailers can better satisfy customers' needs by enhancing a channel's individual benefits and overcoming channel-specific weaknesses (Zhang et al. 2010). Thus, the cross-channel use of multichannel systems offers customers more uses and new uses of retail channels (Verhagen/van

Dolen 2009). For example, customers benefit if they can order products online or by phone and pick the purchased goods up from the nearest retail store rather than waiting for shipment. Therefore, the advantageousness of a multichannel system rises with the integration grade of individual channels. This idea conforms to the *complementarity hypothesis*, which indicates that the value of an entire multichannel system is greater than is the sum of its individual channels when channels work synergistically together (Avery et al. 2007). By offering a **seamless integration** of operations and information between channels, customers' purchase intentions can be promoted (Verhagen/van Dolen 2009).

NEXT offers several cross-channel functionalities, which simplify buying processes and should enhance customer satisfaction:

- **Quickshop**: customers can shop in the Internet store by catalogue item numbers. Thus, they can quickly and easily order products that they have found in the catalogue.

- **Order a catalogue online**: a free copy of the *Directory* catalogue can be requested in the Internet store.

- **Find a store**: by entering a city or postcode, the nearest retail store can be found. Next to the address and travel directions, customers can find additional information about opening times, product range and services of the selected store.

- **Free store delivery**: goods can be ordered online and picked up from *NEXT* retail stores. Similarly, ordered and shipped goods can be returned in *NEXT's* retail stores.

- *NEXT* **Directory Card**: with a Directory card, a Directory account can be used in *NEXT* retail stores to purchase, return or exchange goods.

Figure 4.11   Indications for other Retail Channels

Source: NEXT 2011.

NEXT's customers are encouraged to visit and use individual retail channels. Therefore, there are indications in each channel of the existence of other retail channels. When customers shop in the retail stores they find references for the Internet store (next.co.uk) and when they visit the Internet store they can request the catalogue (see **Figure 4.11**).

4.4.5   Conclusion and Outlook

In this case study, *NEXT's* historical development from a single channel retailer to a vendor operating a distribution system with several integrated marketing channels was shown. *NEXT's* first experiences with a second retail channel, the Directory catalogue, reveal that the deployment of separated and self-sufficient channels is not what customers expect from a retailer to fulfil their needs. By applying the new business strategy *"One Brand; Two [and later with the Internet store "Three"] Ways of Shopping"* the potential of an integrated multichannel system was recognised and realised. Aside from the integration of channels *NEXT* promotes the channel-specific advantages and services. For example, the relevance of the Internet store has increased significantly in recent years, and when considering market development *NEXT's* online business will gain even more relevance in the future.

A recent study from Forrester Research projects that overall retail growth will be driven by online retailing (Netimperative 2010). For *NEXT*, in 2010 48 % of UK consumers made an online purchase at least once a month. Until 2014, the absolute number of online shoppers will increase from 31 million to 40 million (two-thirds of the UK's population). In addition, the average yearly amount spent per online shopper is expected to rise from 483 EUR in 2009 to 601 EUR in 2014, while clothing is one of the top three categories purchased online. For multichannel retailers, such as *NEXT*, the soaring relevance of the Internet channel involves the challenge of expanding online appearance and functionality.

Figure 4.12   NEXT's Mobile Shopping App

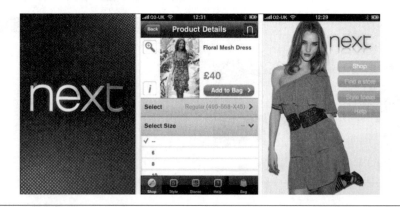

Source: Wheeler 2010.

In addition to continuously expanding the services and functionality of the Internet store, *NEXT* has released a free iPhone app, which allows customers to shop online even when they are on the move (see **Figure 4.12**). The development of mobile commerce per se will be the precondition if *NEXT's* future business strategy has to be extended to *"One Brand; Four Ways of Shopping"*.

▌ Questions

1. In 1999, the business strategy of *NEXT* was extended to *"One Brand; Three ways of shopping"*. Explain the historical development of this process and the necessity for *NEXT* to integrate these different retail channels.

2. A catalogue is an expensive medium since it needs to be printed and distributed to households. If already 70 % of the home shopping orders at *NEXT* come via the online channel, would you recommend *NEXT* to eliminate the catalogue channel from its channel mix in future years? Give arguments for and against this idea. What are the typical advantages and services of the specific retail channels?

3. Which cross-channel functionalities dos *NEXT* offer, and what are advantages of indications between retail channels?

▌ Hints

1. Take into account the website www.nextplc.co.uk for a historical overview of *NEXT's* development. For a discussion of the advantages of integrated channels see Zhang et al. 2010.

2. See Berman/Thelen 2004 for the unique advantages of specific channels.

3. Visit *NEXT's* Internet store and look for indications on other retail channels.

5 New Competitors - Vertical Strategies of Manufacturers

The objectives of this Chapter are to describe the role of controlled and secured distribution systems within the channel strategies of manufacturers and to examine the impact on retail competition. Specifically, suppliers are becoming competitors for their customers and this will lead to a new form of channel conflicts.

5.1 Channel Innovations as Driving Forces of Competition in Retailing

The retail industry is changing rapidly. Some of the most important changes involve the growing diversity of retail formats, including non-store retail formats, as discussed in Chapters 2, 3 and 4, and the new vertical marketing systems or new distribution arrangements of many manufacturers and verticals/vertical retailers (see Chapter 6).

Figure 5.1   Motives/Objectives of Verticalisation

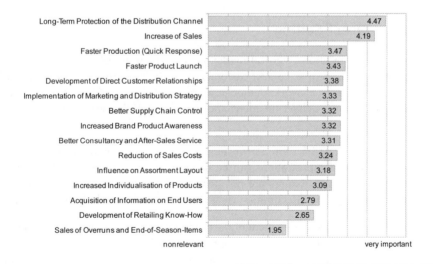

Source: Zentes/Neidhart/Scheer 2006, p. 12.

New players in the world of retailing are, to an increasing extent, manufacturers operating in **secured distribution systems** (fully integrated systems) or **controlled distribution sys-**

tems (contractually-based systems). In both types of vertical marketing systems, the manufacturer can exercise power in the distribution channel (Zentes/Neidhart/Scheer 2006). **Figure 5.1** illustrates the motives or goals of manufacturers implementing vertical marketing systems. The various distribution arrangements with differing degrees of **channel control** are described in this Chapter.

In addition to this **verticalisation** tendency of manufacturers that have operated traditionally with independent wholesalers and/or retailers in **independent systems**, other approaches can be identified. **Verticals** are firms that perform all production and distribution functions right from their founding ("born verticals"). To exploit the competitive advantages of verticals, traditional retailers are modifying their **value chain architectures** by upstream verticalisation (**vertical retailers**). These facets of modern retailing are discussed in Chapter 6.

5.2   Secured Distribution Systems

5.2.1   Overview

In secured distribution systems (fully integrated systems), a manufacturer performs all distribution functions. In addition to traditional direct selling, new kinds of secured distribution systems are emerging, including electronic selling and equity stores.

5.2.2   Direct Selling

Direct selling is a traditional vertical marketing system "in which salespeople, frequently independent businesspeople, contact customers directly in a convenient location, either at the customer's home or at work; demonstrate merchandise benefits and/or explain a service; take an order; and deliver the merchandise or perform the service" (Levy/Weitz 2009, p. 57).

In such a fully integrated system a firm "emphasizes convenient shopping and a personal touch, and detailed demonstrations can be made. [...] direct selling has lower overhead costs because stores and fixtures are not necessary" (Berman/Evans 2010, p. 158). Direct selling is employed by manufacturers such as *Avon, Tupperware* and *Amway*.

Figure 5.2 illustrates the development of the economic importance of direct selling in terms of turnover and sales force. Overall, the worldwide total turnover generated by direct selling has grown by roughly 40 % in the past decade and the total sales force is growing constantly. **Table 5.1** shows the importance of the sales force in direct selling systems of leading manufacturers in this field.

Figure 5.2   Development of Direct Selling (worldwide)

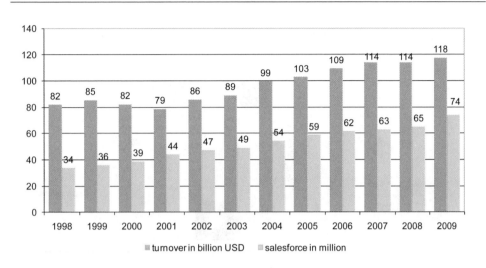

Source: World Federation of Direct Selling Associations 2011.

Table 5.1   Sales Force of Leading Direct Selling Firms

Company	Country (HQ)	Sales People/Partners
Avon Products	USA	6.2 million
Amway	USA	3.0 million
Vorwerk	GER	0.5 million
Mary Kay	USA	2.0 million
Tupperware	USA	2.4 million

Source: Direct Selling News 2010.

5.2.3   Electronic Selling

Electronic selling (through the Internet (e-commerce or m-commerce) or TV shopping) is a technological variant of direct selling. Manufacturers communicate with customers and offer products and services for sale over the Internet or television, for example. The rapid diffusion of Internet access and usage has stimulated not only **bricks-and-mortar retailers** to create Internet shops, but also pure electronic retailers (**pure players**) such as *Amazon*.

Manufacturers have also discovered this distribution channel within the framework of a **multichannel approach** such as *Apple* (see **Figure** 5.3) or as pure players.

Figure 5.3   Multichannel Distribution – Apple

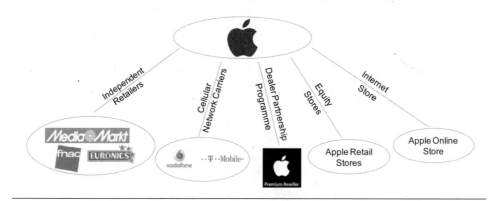

To a growing extent, manufacturers from all industries are "discovering" this form of secured distribution by online selling. A recent example is *Procter & Gamble,* selling its products, e.g. cosmetics, hair care, shaving and home care products on their Internet store (see **Figure** 5.4).

Figure 5.4   Internet Selling Portal of Procter & Gamble

Source: Procter & Gamble 2011c.

5.2.4　　Equity Stores

Equity stores are a bricks-and-mortar approach of secured distribution. The manufacturers operate store retail formats. The major types are concept stores, flagship stores and factory outlets (see **Figure 5.5**).

Manufacturers, especially in the apparel industry, shoe industry, jewellery industry, sports equipment industry, and home equipment industry often operate **monobrand concept stores**. These stores, located usually in traditional shopping streets and shopping centres or malls, can be classified as **monobrand specialty stores** (see Chapter 3), offering the total assortment of a manufacturer by an instore marketing which communicates the "fascination" of the brand. Under the ownership of the manufacturer multiple store units are managed as a **retail chain**. The manufacturers exert strong control, decision-making is centralised, including **price fixing**.

Manufacturers from all industries are "discovering" equity stores. For example, the Swiss company *Nestlé* actually operates about 200 *Nespresso* shops in key cities around the world. These combined retail outlets/coffee shops are exclusively managed as equity stores and they generate approximately 30 % of the company's sales.

In **flagship stores,** manufacturers offer their total production programmes using high quality presentation (lifestyle presentation) in top locations of large metropolitan markets, e.g. *Gucci, Nike* and *Apple*. Kozinets et al. (2002) identified three characteristics of flagship stores:

- They carry only a single brand of product;

- they are company-owned; and

- they operate with the intention of building brand image rather than solely generating profit for the company.

Factory outlets, operated as isolated stores (freestanding retail outlets) or integrated in **factory outlet centres** (FOC), are viewed by manufacturers "as an opportunity to improve their revenues from irregulars, production overruns, and merchandise returned by retailers. Outlet stores also allow manufacturers some control over where their branded merchandise may be sold at discount prices" (Levy/Weitz 2009, p. 54).

As an example of a multichannel distribution system, *Nike* sells its products through different types of channels: independent retailers or retail chains such as *SportScheck* in Germany, *Foot Locker* in the United States, Canada and United Kingdom or *Finish Line* in the United States; flagship stores, as in New York, Miami, San Francisco, London and Berlin; factory outlets, for example in factory outlet centres in Zweibrücken, Herzogenaurach, Metzingen (Germany), Oregon (USA), Queensland (Australia) and Alicante (Spain); and an online shop.

Figure 5.5   Equity Stores of GUCCI

GUCCI Store Hamburg

GUCCI Flagship Store New York

GUCCI Factory Outlet
Leccio-Regello/Florence

5.3 Controlled Distribution Systems

5.3.1 Overview

The structure of controlled distribution systems is extremely diverse and varies from industry to industry. In general, these so-called contractual concepts can be broken down into **contractual dealer systems, franchise systems** and **commercial agent/commission agent systems**.

5.3.2 Contractual Dealer Systems

Contractual dealer systems or **dealer partnership programmes** are (long-term) partnership contracts in which the manufacturer offers a limited support package, including, for example, marketing, advertising, training and IT to participating dealers. "In most of the programmes the dealer also benefits from a common branding. In return, the dealer predominantly markets the brands of the manufacturer. The concepts are often viewed as customer loyalty programmes for independent dealers through which the company can rapidly increase its retail presence" (Uellendahl 2002, p. 208).

There are dealer partnership programmes, for example, in the apparel industry as **shop-in-shop concepts** and **corner concepts** (Zentes/Neidhart/Scheer 2006), or in the tyre business (replacement business) as dealer partner concepts. As an example, the *Goodyear Dunlop Company* runs outlets in Germany through the retail concepts *HMI* and *HMI plus*, in the United Kingdom by *Hi-Q* and in France by *Vulco*. Contractual dealer systems in the fashion or apparel industry include support towards instore marketing, assortment or category/merchandising management as well as supply chain management, as discussed in Chapters 16 and 17, e.g. vendor-managed inventory (VMI).

5.3.3   Franchising

Franchising (see also Chapter 7) involves a contractual arrangement between a franchisor (e.g. a manufacturer) and a (retail) franchisee, "which allows the franchisee to conduct business under an established name and according to a given pattern of business" (Berman/Evans 2010, p. 108). Linked by a common business interest, each partner makes his or her contribution to the cooperation. Thus, both partners (franchisor and franchisee) benefit from the strength of the other. Uellendahl (2002, p. 208) described the structure of the *Goodyear Dunlop* franchise systems (*"Premio"* and *"Quick"*) operating in the German tyre replacement market:

- The franchisor contributes the complete business know-how and organisation (e.g. full support package including marketing, sales promotion, training, IT, autoservice, CRM, national advertising, business counselling, business planning, common branding, financial support, etc.).

- The franchisee contributes his individual effort as an independent businessperson in the local market.

As controlled distribution systems, franchise systems are operated in many industries, for example by car manufacturers (auto/truck dealers), by auto accessory manufacturers (auto accessories stores), by consumer electronics manufacturers (consumer electronics stores), hardware manufacturers (hardware stores) and by apparel manufacturers (specialty stores). Examples in the apparel industry are *Palmers, Rodier, Benetton, Boss* and *Marc O'Polo*.

Figure 5.6 illustrates the differences in the influence of manufacturers on distribution channels in "hard" contractual arrangements (e.g. franchising) and "soft" contractual arrangements (e.g. contractual dealer systems):

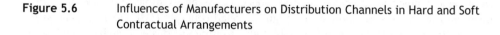

Figure 5.6   Influences of Manufacturers on Distribution Channels in Hard and Soft
                    Contractual Arrangements

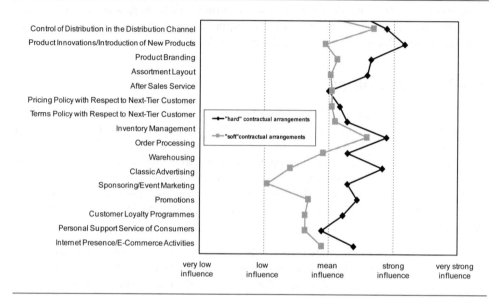

Source: Zentes/Swoboda/Morschett 2005, p. 683.

5.3.4   Commercial Agent/Commission Agent Systems

A third category of contractual arrangements is commercial agent systems and commission agent systems. A retailer operating as a **commercial agent** or a **commercial representative** "is constantly entrusted with the task of arranging transaction on behalf of another business person (i.e. the manufacturer) or concluding such transactions in their name. The arrangement of transactions in the name of a third party distinguishes the commercial representatives from a **merchant** who concludes transactions in his own name for his own account" (Committee for Definitions of Terms in Trade and Distribution 2009, p. 23).

In commercial agent systems, manufacturers are allowed to control the retail prices of their goods and services. In the other forms of controlled distribution, e.g. contractual dealer systems or franchise systems, **vertical price fixing** is not allowed (in the European Union). Besides equity stores, such an agent system is the best way to fix consumer prices.[1]

---

[1] Another possibility is consignment selling, whereby the manufacturer owns the items until they are sold by the retailer. This contractual arrangement can be combined with controlled distribution systems. Empirically, this combination is rare because of legal restrictions (in the EU).

A **commission agent** is a commercial operator who undertakes the sale of goods in his or her own name for the account of the principal. The commission agent bears the risks resulting from the commission contract with the customer (Committee for Definitions of Terms in Trade and Distribution 2009, p. 23).

Commercial agent and commission agent systems are well-known in the oil distribution business as well as in food and non-food retailing. Global oil companies such as *BP*, *Esso* and *Shell* operate with networks of equity stations and petrol stations operated by self-employed commercial agents. Another example is the German company *Tchibo* that operates equity stores and cooperates with retailers and bakeries through commercial agent contracts (see **Table 5.2**).

Table 5.2   Structure of Distribution Network of Tchibo

Sales Channel	Germany	International
Equity Stores	850	300
Commercial Agent Contracts (Depots)	38,000	7,000
E-Commerce (Online-Shops per country)	1	17

Source: Tchibo 2010.

5.3.5   Concession Shops

Concession shops are positioned between secured and controlled distribution systems. "A concession shop refers to a cooperative space concept in the trade in which a concessionaire rents a selling area from a trading company and manages it. As in the case of shop-in-shop concepts, the concession area is separate from the rest of the shop by its own design and corresponding shopfitting elements. The concessionaire sells its goods for its own account, i.e. bears the merchandise risk. A concessionaire normally operates the shops with its own personnel. Marketing activities and merchandise-management processes such as e.g. shop design, assortment planning, price policy or merchandise procurement and control are normally within the area of responsibility of the concessionaire" (Committee for Definitions of Terms in Trade and Distribution 2009, pp. 60-61). The retail company acts as a **lessor**, receiving not only a flat rate to cover the operating costs of its services but also turnover-related remuneration (a **concession fee**). In this way, the retailer bears part of the sales risk, in contrast to purely letting space.

There are two different variants of **shop-in-shop concepts**: concession shops on the one hand and, on the other hand, certain parts of the assortment can be highlighted by a special atmosphere and presentation to profile the collections of leading manufacturers. This variant is a form of contractual dealer systems, in which manufacturers support retailers in assortment planning and instore marketing.

5.4   Advantages and Disadvantages of Secured and Controlled Distribution

Secured, controlled and independent distribution systems are presented in **Figure 5.7**, which characterises these systems in the context of the market-hierarchy paradigm of **transaction cost economics**.

Figure 5.7   Vertical Marketing Systems and Transaction Cost Economics

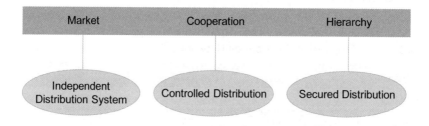

Table 5.3 provides an overview of the main advantages and disadvantages of the different concepts of controlled distribution and secured distribution. The "high degree of control" in secured distribution systems (equity stores) and commercial agent systems includes retail pricing.

Table 5.3   Advantages and Disadvantages of Secured and Controlled Distribution Concepts

	Strengths	Weaknesses
Equity Stores	♦ high degree of control ♦ organisational control ♦ brand/promotional control ♦ guaranteed distribution	♦ high capital costs ♦ huge operational costs
Franchising	♦ limited capital costs ♦ less ownership risk ♦ guaranteed distribution ♦ low fluctuation	♦ limited control
Commercial/Commission Agent Systems	♦ high degree of control ♦ organisational control ♦ brand/promotional control ♦ guaranteed distribution	♦ low capital costs ♦ limited operational costs
Contractual Dealer Systems	♦ relatively low-cost solution ♦ rapid expansion	♦ little control ♦ high risk of losing partners ♦ less stability

Figure 5.8 illustrates the distribution system of the German manufacturer *MUSTANG*, which operates retail partnership concepts, franchising and equity stores. **Figure 5.9** shows the distribution system of the *GERRY WEBER Group*, which managed the turnaround from an apparel manufacturer into a vertical fashion and lifestyle supplier using multiple heterogeneous distribution channels.

Figure 5.8   Controlled and Secured Distribution – MUSTANG

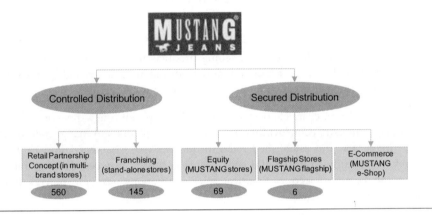

Figure 5.9   Controlled and Secured Distribution – GERRY WEBER

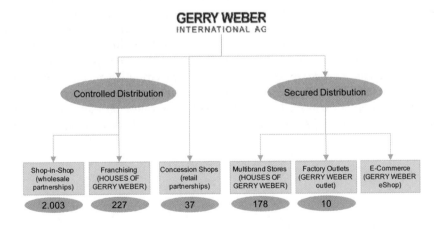

5.5   Channel Conflicts

The development of controlled and secured distribution channels – as possible sales channels for a manufacturer – is a core element in the marketing strategies of many manufacturers (**downstream verticalisation**). While secured distribution used to involve the development of equity chains (owned by the manufacturer), the situation has changed considerably. Over the Internet, a manufacturer can sell directly to consumers without bricks-and-mortar stores, and through contractual dealer systems or dealer partnership programmes and franchising, manufacturers can be engaged in contractual distribution systems, which means cooperating with independent dealers. Technological developments and contractual arrangements enlarge the potential for controlling distribution channels.

The main challenge for manufacturers is to manage the conflict in multichannel distribution systems between independent retailers, selling products from a particular manufacturer, retailers, cooperating in a contractual system with this manufacturer, and equity stores or other direct distribution channels from this manufacturer as competitors.

Conflicts in distribution channels or **channel conflicts** are not a new phenomenon in the consumer goods industry. **Conflict theories** in retailing explain retail change in terms of the rivalry between new and established retail institutions (see Chapters 1 and 2). This approach refers primarily to **horizontal conflicts**, i.e. conflicts between different retail formats, but can be transferred to "vertical retail institutions" as new players (see e.g. McGoldrick 2002, pp. 24-25).

Vertical channel conflicts are the result of **shifts of power**. Traditionally, the distribution of consumer goods was characterised by a manufacturer-centred view of channels: retailing has been a relatively passive link within the channel of distribution from manufacturers to consumers. The abolition of **resale price maintenance**, in 1964 in the UK and 1974 in Germany, the concentration of retail trade, the development of store brands and retail branding have shifted the power from manufacturers to retailers. This development of **retailer power** can be illustrated by the relative weakness of manufacturers in negotiations with these customers. The dependence of suppliers on major retailers has initiated the development of new vertical systems in order to control or even secure distribution, including the intention of building brand image. By verticalisation, manufacturers are rebalancing the power within the distribution channel. This rebalancing by verticalisation leads to a new type of channel conflict. Manufacturers are suppliers of the retailers as well as of their competitors.

5.6   Conclusion and Outlook

Managing multichannel distribution systems and conflicts in distribution channels are the main challenges for manufacturers with regard to the demand side. Upstream, they are also restructuring their value chains by outsourcing production activities and concentrating on "intellectual" activities such as innovation and quality management. Finally, this leads to new **value chain architectures**.

By contrast, retailers are to a growing extent integrating upstream activities into their value chains: developing store brands, produced by contract manufacturers ("controlled production") or by its own production sites ("secured production"). This strategy leads to a higher degree of **upstream verticalisation** ("vertical retailers"; see Chapter 6) and finally means a convergence of the value chain architectures of manufacturers and retailers (see Chapter 1).

▌ Further Reading

COUGHLAN, A.T. et al. (2008): Marketing Channels, 7th ed., New Jersey.

KPMG (Ed.) (2001): Verticalization in the Trade: Effects in the Future Sales Channel Structure, Cologne.

ROSENBLOOM, B. (2004): Marketing Channels: A Management View, 7th ed., Mason.

5.7   Case Study: Nike[1]

5.7.1   Profile, History and Status Quo

Nike is the world's leading designer, marketer and distributor of authentic athletic footwear, apparel, equipment and accessories for a wide variety of sports and fitness activities, including basketball, football, golf and running. The success of the company is built upon a long history of practical experience in running as well as shoe manufacturing and distribution.

Before there was *Nike*, there were Bill Bowerman, *Nike's* future co-founder and legendary track and field coach at the University of Oregon, and Philip H. Knight, a middle distance runner on Bowerman's track team. In the late 1950s, Bowerman was eagerly experimenting

---

[1] Sources used in this case study include the website http://www.nikebiz.com, NIKE Inc.'s annual report 2010, information from http://www.textilwirtschaft.de and statistical data from http://de.statista.com as well as explicitly cited sources.

with shoes: he was convinced that an ounce off a running shoe could be enough to win a race. In 1962, in the process of completing his MBA at Stanford University, Knight asserted in a research paper that the US could recapture the leadership in the athletic shoe industry from Germany by importing high performance, well-crafted, but low priced shoes from Japan. Shortly after graduation Knight went to Japan and persuaded the *Onitsuka Tiger Company*, a Japanese producer of quality athletic shoes, to give him a distributorship for *Tiger* shoes. Returning home, he took samples of the shoes to Bowerman, which laid the foundation for the joint distribution activities with the name *Blue Ribbon Sports (BRS)*.

In 1964, the marketing efforts started unconventionally for that time – by servicing athletes. Knight began to sell imported *Tiger* running shoes out of the back of his car at track meetings, directly to the consumer (**direct selling**). A year later, Jeff Johnson, a former competitor of Knight on the track, agreed to work on commission as *Blue Ribbon Sports'* first employee. This form of controlled distribution complemented the existing secured distribution efforts. It wasn't until 1966 when they expanded their direct selling efforts by opening a retail store.

Knight and Bowerman developed their own shoe in 1972 and, after a dispute with *Onitsuka Tiger*, decided to manufacture it themselves. In 1978, *Blue Ribbon Sports* officially changed its name to *NIKE Inc.* This was the beginning of an era of product innovation, marketing campaigns and the constant extension of the **distribution network**.

What was once only the athletic shoe industry now is an industry expanded far beyond its original focus. The former US-based footwear manufacturer today is a global marketer of athletic footwear, apparel and equipment that is unrivalled in the world. **Figure 5.10** shows the leading position of *Nike* in terms of global turnover.

Figure 5.10   Top 10 International Manufacturers of Sportswear 2009

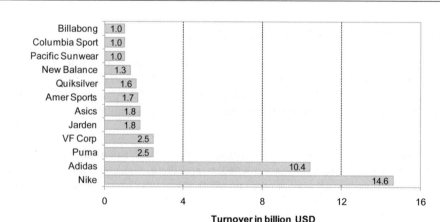

Source: Statista 2010.

In the past decade, *Nike* has established a strong **brand portfolio** with several wholly owned subsidiaries, which are subsumed in the *NIKE Inc.* group, including *Cole Haan*, which designs, markets and distributes luxury shoes, handbags, accessories and coats; *Converse Inc.*, which designs, markets and distributes athletic footwear, apparel and accessories; *Hurley International LLC*, a California-based surf, skate and snowboard apparel brand that designs, markets and distributes action sports and youth lifestyle footwear, apparel and accessories; and *Umbro Ltd.*, a leading United Kingdom-based global football brand. *Umbro*, with over 70 years of experience and heritage, helps expand *Nike's* **global leadership** in football. *Umbro* designs, distributes and licenses athletic and casual footwear, apparel and equipment, primarily for the sport of football. The subsidiaries are operated on their own authority and their distribution activities are mostly autonomous.

For the fiscal year ending May 2010, *NIKE Inc.* reported total revenues of 19,014 million USD (a 1 % drop from 2009) and, therefore, is ranked 124th in the Fortune Top 500, the most prominent annual ranking of America's largest corporations (Fortune 2010). The *Nike* brand accounts for 16,509 million USD in revenues, which is attributable to three major product lines: footwear (63 %), apparel (31 %) and equipment (6 %).

Besides its financial success, *Nike* is one of the most heavily advertised and best-known brands in the world. According to *Interbrand's* "Best Global Brands 2010" ranking, the **brand value** of *Nike* is estimated to be 13,706 million USD and ranks 25th among the world's most valuable brands (Interbrand 2010). By contrast, the German competitor's brand *Adidas* is worth 5,495 million USD.

The *Nike* world headquarters is located in Beaverton, Oregon. So while the Pacific Northwest was the birthplace of *Nike*, today the company operates in more than 170 countries around the globe. Through their suppliers, shippers, retailers and other service providers, *Nike* directly or indirectly employs nearly one million people. That includes approximately 34,400 *Nike* employees across six continents, who all contribute to *Nike's* mission, "to bring inspiration and innovation to every athlete in the world".

In the fiscal year 2009, the company initiated a **reorganisation** of the *Nike* brand into a new model consisting of six geographies. In the fiscal year 2010, the most important geographic segment in terms of revenues was North America (6,696 million USD), which accounted for 42 % of total revenues. Within non-US sales, Western Europe played a key role (3,892 million USD), while Central and Eastern Europe (1,150 million USD) were less relevant in absolute values. The contribution of Japan (882 million USD) was rather volatile and of lower importance. Looking at emerging markets (2,042 million USD) and Greater China (1,742 million USD), these segments, despite a relatively low absolute contribution, have constantly gained in importance over the past two years with sales growth above 25 %. Business in China is profitable in particular with a share of sales of 11 % but an EBIT accounting for 28 % in *Nike's* fiscal 2011 second quarter.

5.7.2   Nike's Multichannel Approach

Today, *Nike* sells products primarily through a combination of independent retailers, through *Nike*-owned retail including different store formats (bricks-and-mortar) and Internet sales and through a mix of independent distributors, franchisees and licensees. Historically, the channel strategy has focused on independent retailers, or **retail accounts** in *Nike's* terminology, which have played an outstanding role in terms of turnover. On the one hand, these activities are complemented by **controlled distribution** in the form of sales to franchisees and licensees. On the other hand, *Nike*-owned retail is at a low level but is constantly gaining in importance. This business comprises the three major types of **store-based secured distribution** (concept stores, flagship stores and factory outlets) as well as an e-commerce division.

All these retail activities result in the multichannel distribution system of *Nike* that contains various different channels:

- *Nike* retail accounts (independent retailers)

- Franchising and license agreements

- *Niketowns* (flagship stores)

- *Nike* stores (monobrand concept stores)

- *Nike* factory store (factory outlets, off-price stores)

- *Nike* online store, *NIKEiD*, *Nike* women online store (Internet stores/e-commerce)

- *NIKEiD* apps (m-commerce).

Independent Retailers

Indirect distribution with the help of independent retailers represents the most important form of distribution, with a share of sales of **more than 85 % of *Nike's* total turnover**. The **retail account** base includes a mix of athletic specialty stores, footwear stores, sporting goods stores, department stores, skate, tennis and golf shops and others. Among the biggest global retail accounts are *Foot Locker*, an American sports and footwear retailer operating in approximately 20 countries worldwide, and *Finish Line*, operating over 600 stores solely in the United States (Bloomberg Businessweek 2007).

As of May 31, 2010, the *NIKE Inc.* group had around 23,000 retail accounts in the United States and approximately 24,000 outside the United States (excluding sales by independent distributors and licensees). Hartley (2009, p. 314) described the relationship to customers, especially the large retailers mentioned, as *Nike's* most controllable success factor within its relevant competitive environment. Additionally, *Nike* utilises 19 sales offices in the US to solicit sales and nine independent sales representatives to sell golf and skateboarding equipment as well as outdoor products.

Controlled Distribution

In addition to the retail account business, *Nike* operates **franchising.** The terms of the franchise contract are handled rather strictly. Therefore, the contractual arrangement allows the company to exert a high influence on the choice of location, for instance. Franchisees have to bear the predominant risks, and only the commodity risk is shared in partnership. However, neither initial payment nor franchise fees are known.

The complex implementation of franchising can be illustrated using the example of the German market. The adaptation of the European franchise concept to German market conditions started in 2001, and it should have been worked out in detail together with potential partners. Owing to a lack of interested parties, the process lasted for two years until the first franchise store was opened in Hamburg. The franchise partner was the newly found *Add Value GmbH & Co. KG*, a partner experienced in both retailing and franchising, who was selected with the intention of stabilising the concept. In the end, despite its cautiousness, the first German franchise was not fruitful. While the store in Hamburg remains operated by *Nike*, in Germany there only exist two franchise agreements in Nuremberg und Munich, both of which were signed in 2007.

Additional potential sales volume (105 million USD) and marketing impact are opened up by **licensing.** *Nike* offers license agreements that permit unaffiliated parties to manufacture and sell certain *Nike*-branded apparel, electronic devices and other equipment designed for sports activities. The licensing business is primarily represented in the global brand division, a segment managed centrally and devoid of operating costs such as those for product development or supply chain operations.

One of the latest examples is a deal that makes *Nike* the sole maker and distributor of National Football League-branded apparel and uniforms. The licensing deal, signed in October 2010, will bring an estimated 300 million USD in additional revenues from 2012 (Bloomberg Businessweek 2011).

Secured Distribution

In recent years, *Nike* has increased its power in distribution through integrating retail activities downstream. This has resulted in strong control over the vertically integrated channels and the flexibility to decide about the concepts of the stores, such as the product offer, in-store marketing and price fixing. Above all, *Nike* can combine its production capabilities as a traditional manufacturer with distribution activities, and thus it is able to create totally new shopping experiences.

Nike operates a great variety of fully integrated secured distribution channels from **factory outlets** on the discount side to standard **stores** and **flagships** on the high end. Even though this form of distribution accounts for a relatively small part of turnover, it is gaining in importance as will be described later in this Chapter. The development of *Nike's* global retail outlet network reveals the constantly growing number of *Nike* factory stores and *Nike* stores outside the United States (see **Table 5.4**).

Table 5.4   Development of Nike Retail Outlets

Retail Outlet		2007	2008	2009	2010
Nike factory stores	US stores	102	121	140	145
	Non-US stores	126	141	184	205
Niketowns	US stores	12	12	11	11
	Non-US stores	3	3	4	2
Nike stores	US stores	14	14	16	12
	Non-US stores	33	46	61	55

Source: Nike Annual Report 2010.

Nike's distribution strategy aims to offer consumers access to engaging, exciting and innovative retail spaces. Flagship stores are most suitable to creating such a retail experience even though huge investments are necessary to build them. *Niketowns* are operated to build brand image rather than solely to generate profit for the company, and they can be categorised as a marketing vehicle transporting the world of sports. The focus is on selling newer and exclusive footwear and apparel and showcasing manufactured products. *Nike* offers a high quality production programme in top locations.

Averaging more than 30,000 square feet of selling space (approx. 2,800 m²), *Niketowns* attract millions of customers every year. The first *Niketown* store opened in 1990 in downtown Portland, Oregon. This first store, with athlete-driven and award-winning design, set the standard for future consumer environments. With regard to non-US retail activities, Germany plays a crucial role as a bridgehead into Europe. This is based on the requisite to set off in a highly competitive market where the strongest competitor *Adidas* is headquartered. Therefore, the first *Niketown* outside the US was built in Berlin in 1999 followed by the second *Niketown* in London.

Nike stores are operated as **monobrand concept stores**, either as equity stores that are owned by *Nike* or as concession shops. In the latter way, *Nike* operates a concession area that is located in a store owned by an independent retailer, which leads to a hybrid structure between controlled and secured distribution. One example is the concession shop at *Peek & Cloppenburg (P&C)* with a separate entry from the main shopping street Zeil in Frankfurt.

In accordance with *Niketowns*, *Nike* stores also focus on top locations in major cities and a total production programme is offered. But, on the contrary, *Nike* stores encompass a smaller selling space and communicate the fascination of the brand in a more conservative way, which leads to lower investments. However, owing to the financial strength of the group, *Nike* is able to open up locations that a single retailer would never be able to finance, such as the *Nike* store on the Champs Elysées in Paris, one of the most expensive shopping streets in the world. Additional *Nike* stores are located in Vienna, Zurich, Hamburg and at the airport in Frankfurt.

Meanwhile, there exist derivative *Nike* store concepts, such as *Nike* women stores that focus on footwear, apparel and equipment especially developed for women's needs. The first one of these stores outside the United States was the 1,200 sq. ft. store in Munich (approx. 120 m²) that opened in 2005.

Factory outlets (**off-price stores**) in general are used to improve revenues from irregularities, production overruns and merchandise returned by retailers. *Nike* factory stores carry primarily overstock and close-out merchandise and they are mainly located in factory outlet centres. Consumers will not find the current product line in *Nike* factory stores. Instead, they sell products left over from last season at discounted prices. The factory stores stock casual apparel as well as products for sports such as running, football, athletics and basketball (Olivarez-Giles 2010). The average size of a *Nike* outlet is about 10,000 sq. ft. (approx. 930 m²) (Olivarez-Giles 2010).

Despite the discount-minded orientation, *Nike* holds opening events to attract customers, with gift cards, giveaways and an autograph and question-and-answer session with well-known athletes.

Electronic Selling

At an early stage *Nike* realised the potential of the Internet and started to communicate and offer products and services for sale over the web in the United States in 1999.

Consumers use the websites of sporting goods manufacturers both as information channels prior to purchase and as channels of purchase. Particularly during major sporting events, a higher attendance of the websites of sporting goods manufacturers can be noticed, making the Internet an important tool for the sporting goods industry (ECC 2010). However, the decision on whether to focus on online sales or bricks-and-mortar stores is of strategic relevance. How this choice differs from the perception of branded sportswear manufacturers was analysed in the ECC-Monitor study in 2010. Whereas *Nike* and *Puma* plan to focus on online direct selling, *Adidas* is rather strengthening its dealer network.

Nike's positioning is built upon the belief that the balance of power between retailers and consumers undergoes a fundamental shift and that consumers are gaining in power. In 2007, the challenge for *Nike* was to find a way to deal with the fast-changing behaviour of their digitally driven consumers.

Given this situation, the European *Nike* online store was launched in January 2007, offering products for sale in 19 European countries plus Switzerland. The store is differentiated by language and country-specific sports preferences, but is identical in structure. Besides the traditional product offer and some online functionality, www.nikestore.com is characterised by an innovative approach.

Figure 5.11   Strategic Focus on Dealer Network vs. Online-Direct-Selling:
Top 10 Manufacturers of Branded Sportswear 2009

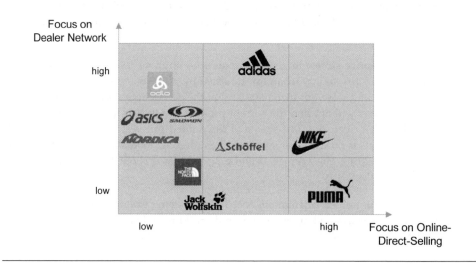

Source: ECC 2010.

Nike combines the company's position as a leading sporting goods manufacturer with its retail activities and offers a **mass customisation concept** called "*NIKEiD*". It is possible to customise products such as shoes or sportswear and decide about on the colour, material and individual size or finish the item off with a personal ID. This concept less targets impulse-driven, price-oriented shoppers but rather untypical, youthful customers that like to wear individual products (Erlinger 2010). Furthermore, the *Nike* women online store offers products created for women's needs and is linked to a women-oriented *NIKEiD*.

The redesigned *NIKEiD* website, www.nikeid.com, is complemented by *NIKEiD* studios, for instance in Beijing, Shanghai, New York and London – instore set-ups where customers can work together with design consultants on designs and discuss the latest trends. This way the border between online and store business is fading.

The latest trend is built upon the enormous diffusion rate of web-compatible smartphones. The development of mobile apps, the *NIKEiD* mobile apps, available for the iPhone, iPod Touch and iPad is the next step in this technology-oriented sales channel.

5.7.3   Nike's Global Growth Strategy

NIKE Inc. introduced its 2015 Global Growth Strategy in 2010. The company announced a revenue target of 27 billion USD for 2015 and plans to expand its global retail activities by opening 250 to 300 new company-owned stores within the next five years. Still, retail accounts are expected to account for more than 80 % of the company's overall business by 2015. *Adidas* counterattacked with its strategic business plan, Route 2015, which aims to provide the basis for taking over leadership in sporting goods manufacturing. The plan is to grow faster than its key competitors can. Herbert Hainer, CEO of *Adidas*, is aiming for a sales growth of 45 % to 50 % in the next five years. With company-owned stores, *Adidas* held a 17 % share of sales in 2008, but it wants to strengthen retail activities by expanding the company-owned store network and e-commerce activities (Adidas Group 2010).

Geographic opportunities for the *Nike* brand exist in all of its six geographies including growth through expansion in its developed regions of North America, Western Europe and Japan. But sporting goods manufacturers are suffering from slowing consumption in the United States and from lower returns in Western Europe because of the weak Euro. So, with the weak market in the US, which is the core market, *Nike* has to look for profitability elsewhere (Bloomberg 2010). Growth potential, targeting low double-digit growth, is seen in the developing markets, especially Brazil, India and China.

Adidas also primarily wants to invest in developing countries, where the network of sporting goods retailers is less close. With regard to geographic importance, *Adidas* has identified North America, China, Russia, Latin America, Japan, the UK and India as important growth markets. Furthermore, the company will expand into focal cities in well-established countries (Adidas Group 2010).

5.7.4   Summary and Outlook

In recent decades, *Nike* has managed to establish the leading position in the sporting goods industry. This success is, to a large extent, supported by company-owned retail activities that strengthen the perception of the brand in the eyes of customers and leverages additional sales potential. Hainer points out that today's competition for **global market leadership** centres on two players (Adidas Group 2010). That is a reason for *Nike* to be aware of *Adidas'* strategic actions. As both companies want to push **vertical integration**, this will lead to increased competition. Future efforts have to be geared towards the exploitation of potentials within the retail channels that can be derived from socio-economic drivers as well as between the different brands of the group.

Questions

1. List the possible motivations for the implementation of secured distribution activities from a manufacturer's perspective and apply the insights to *Nike's* situation in detail.

2. Describe potential channel conflicts for a manufacturer adding a new company-owned retail channel and use *Nike* to illustrate some examples. Please elaborate on ways that are suited to manage channel conflicts.

3. Given the company-owned retail activities of *Nike*, assess the contribution of the current development to the long-term success of the company.

Hints

1. For a general overview of motivations for secured distribution from a manufacturer's perspective see Tsay/Agrawal 2004.

2. Take channel conflicts between a manufacturer's and an independent retailer's channel and between manufacturers' channels into consideration. See the discussion in Bucklin/Thomas-Graham/Webster 2004 for potential channel conflicts and a framework to manage them.

3. Transfer Hauptkorn/Manget/Rasch 2005 on the success factors of verticalisation strategies, for example, to the current situation of *Nike*.

6 New Competitors – Verticals and Vertical Retailers

This Chapter explores the business model of a vertically integrated manufacturer/retailer. This pattern of vertical integration is being more and more adopted by traditional retailers engaging in innovation and quality management and even producing their own products.

6.1 Value Chain Architecture of Verticals

So-called **verticals** perform or at least coordinate all production and distribution functions right from their founding ("born verticals"). Examples of this type can be found in e-business (**electronic retailing**), but also in store formats. *Dell* (www.dell.com), for example, appeals to multiple market segments – from novices to advanced computer users – by selling customised products exclusively over the Internet. *Hennes & Mauritz* (*H&M*), *Mango* and *Zara* are successful examples from the apparel industry, in which verticals are gaining market share. **Table 6.1** provides an overview of the global outlet network of *H&M*.

The value chain architecture of a vertically integrated manufacturer/retailer ("vertical") corresponds to the model of a **producer** or a **coordinator** on the supply-side. Often verticals produce essential shares of their products; a lot of times they even produce all of their products themselves. In these cases, they act as a producer, too (see **Figure 6.1**). *Zara*, for example, a company of the *Inditex Group*, produces around 35 % of its merchandise in manufacturing facilities of its own.

Figure 6.1   Value Chain Architecture of a Producer (Supply-side)

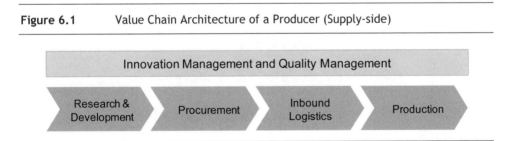

Source: Hertel/Zentes/Schramm-Klein 2011, p. 94.

As a coordinator, verticals control upstream value chain activities such as the procurement, production and logistics of its contract manufacturers through internal innovation and quality management; upstream they concentrate on **intellectual value creation** (see **Figure 6.2**).

Table 6.1   Global Outlet Network of H&M

Countries	Number of Outlets	Countries	Number of Outlets
Austria	66	Luxembourg	10
Belgium	64	Netherlands	112
Canada	55	Norway	101
China	47	Poland	76
Czech Republic	22	Portugal	21
Denmark	87	Russia	11
Finland	43	Slovakia	7
France	151	Slovenia	11
Germany	377	South Korea	2
Great Britain	192	Spain	122
Greece	18	Sweden	168
Hungary	15	Switzerland	75
Ireland	12	Turkey	1
Italy	72	USA	208
Japan	10		

Source: H&M 2011.

Figure 6.2   Value Chain Architecture of a Coordinator (Supply-side)

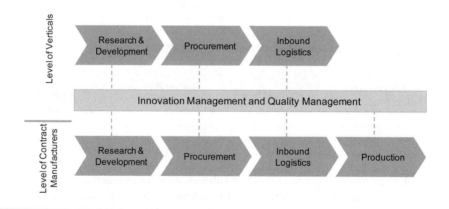

Source: Hertel/Zentes/Schramm-Klein 2011, p. 93.

Looking at the demand side of the value chain architecture, verticals sell their merchandise according to the model of **secured distribution,** meaning through equity stores and other channels such as online shops (see **Figure 6.3**).

Figure 6.3   Value Chain Architecture of Secured Distribution (Demand-side)

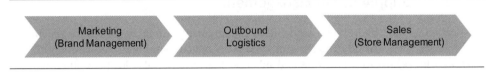

Source: Hertel/Zentes/Schramm-Klein 2011, p. 98.

As an example, **Figure 6.4** shows *H&M*'s distribution channels (multichannel system).

Figure 6.4   Multichannel-System of Hennes & Mauritz

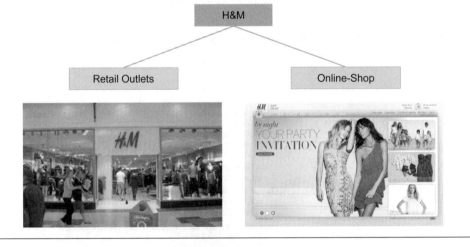

6.2   Competitive Advantages of Verticals

6.2.1   Product Differentiation and Branding

Verticals create essential competitive advantages through their uniform market images. They have direct market access, meaning direct access to the consumer and thus can entirely implement their **retail branding strategies** (see Chapter 9). They control assortment, store layout, merchandise presentation, communication and retail price. This uniform market image guarantees them conveyance of the "fascination" of the retail brand.

Therefore, they create a **unique selling proposition** (USP) in the sense of exclusivity. Products marked by proper, standalone designs and/or specific qualities that are different from competitors' products are solely available in their outlets, where they are offered in a brand compliant manner.

6.2.2   Supply Chain Management

Vertical integration by in-house sourcing or procurement through contract manufacturers not only leads to cost advantages compared with outside suppliers (see Jennings 2001), such as with regard to production and inbound logistics, but also leads to other market-based competitive advantages.

Verticals can create an innovative competitive advantage through a highly efficient supply chain. In this context, "**speed**" becomes a central aspect of the competitive strategies of the so-called **fast-fashion retailers**. *Zara* has essentially influenced this strategic group by optimising its supply chain. As a result of this optimisation, *Zara* has realised the production of a piece of clothing, passing from design through production to delivery and the availability in its worldwide stores within 15 days (see **Figure 6.5**).

Figure 6.5   Optimised Scheduling of Processes for Products with a High-Fashion-Rate Through Verticalisation

---

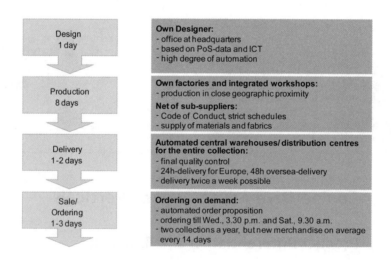

Source: Ferdows/Lewis/Machuca 2005, p. 84.

Figure 6.6 presents the innovative business model of *Inditex*, the Spanish group that *Zara* belongs to.

Figure 6.6   The Five Keys to the Inditex Business Model

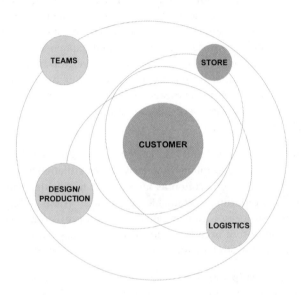

Source: Inditex 2008.

6.2.3   Corporate Social Responsibility and Supply Security

Another competitive advantage of an integrated value chain exists in the consistent control of all processes with regard to complying with ecological and social standards. Questions on **corporate social responsibility** (CSR) and sustainability are increasingly important in public debates, but are also necessary elements of future-oriented corporate strategies. At the same time, social and ecological positioning offers potential for corporate profiling. This in turn requires a holistic **compliance management**.

Hennes & Mauritz (H&M) can be used as an example of **managing sustainability**. "A shared responsibility means that all departments are now individually responsible for integrating sustainable thinking into their business routines, initiating actions and setting targets. All decisions should be taken keeping People, Planet and Profit in mind. To fully integrate sustainability into the different departments will be a step-by-step process. Sustainability issues influencing more than one department are discussed in the decision-making forum called the Green Room. [...] *H&M*'s shared responsibility approach moves us away from having a CSR department that coordinates our sustainability activity, to a CSR support department that guides and advises other departments within *H&M* as they set and move towards their individual sustainability goals" (H&M 2009).

Sustainability in the sense of the social, ecological and economic responsibility of a company (**"people, planet, profit"**) is increasingly complemented with the aspect of **supply security**. Besides the responsible handling of natural resources, e.g. agricultural and metal resources, the question of access to these resources arises on strategic corporate agendas. A growing world population and changing consumption patterns in developing and emerging countries lead to shortages because of an only limited expandable supply, such as of agricultural cultivation areas (see PwC/H.I.Ma. 2010). Thus, **vertical backwards integration** includes not only production but also preliminary stages through to agricultural production, e.g. the cultivation of bio-cotton. Verticals have a competitive advantage over traditional retailers here and (downstream) verticalised manufacturers will exercise the competitive advantage in the same way, too.

For example, companies such as *C&A* and *H&M* can be highlighted. *C&A* emphasises long-term business relationships with suppliers to gain **win-win situations**: "At *C&A* we view the long-term changeover to organic cotton as an essential task within the context of our broader commitment to supporting sustainable agriculture" (C&A 2010, p. 103). These long-term partnerships also include cooperations with **non-profit organisations** (NGOs): "In 2005 we joined the non-profit organisation Organic Exchange, which advised *C&A* on the development of a long-term strategy for organic cotton" (C&A 2010, p. 104).

H&M, too, follows a **partnership approach**: „We work to form close and long-term partnerships with our suppliers as this provides mutual benefits. [...] Working in partnership allows us and our suppliers to plan ahead, to gain knowledge from each other and to develop and grow together. [...] Showing willingness to become such a partner will help suppliers become a key supplier, and include several related benefits, such as long-term order planning and stable orders over time" (H&M 2009, p. 28).

6.3   Verticalisation of Traditional Retailers

Today, retailers as well as the most important **buying groups** of most sectors work with an increasing number of store brands in their assortments (see Chapter 11). "This development will continue, whereby a clearly modified working method in the conception, management and character of these brands will be added. It will further enhance the triumphal procession of exclusive store brand concepts and it will further increase the importance of these concepts on a retailer's profitability" (Janz/Swoboda 2007, p. 301).

These brand concepts lead to an increasing independence of store brands and cause a disappearance of a clear differentiation between store and manufacturer brands. These brand concepts lead to increasing vertical integration as well. Thus, traditional retailers try to catch up with the abovementioned competitive advantages of verticals not only in the field of **product differentiation**, but also in areas such as **supply chain management** and **sustainability management**.

Outside supply for these companies means control over the upstream value chains of their contract manufacturers through their own innovation and quality management (value chain architecture of a **coordinator**). Besides this form of **controlled production** appears the model of **secured production** (in-house sourcing) through company-owned production facilities.

In food retailing, many companies have been verticalised upstream for a long time (e.g. the American company *Kroger* and Swiss *Coop*). Approximately 39 % of the store brand units sold are is produced in *Kroger's* 40 manufacturing plants; the remaining store brand items are produced to *Kroger's* strict specifications by outside manufacturers. **Table 6.2** shows the manufacturing facilities of *Coop* in Switzerland.

Table 6.2   Manufacturing Plants of Coop in Switzerland

Name	Product
Swissmill, Zurich	Switzerland's largest grain mill: baking flours, pasta semolina, flakes, maize, extruder products, flour mixtures
Chocolats Halba, Wallisellen	Chocolate bars, chocolate sticks, assorted chocolates, noisette snacks
Nutrex, Busswil BE	Specialities of vinegar for food retailing (e.g. wine vinegar, cider vinegar, herb-flavoured vinegar), food industry (for cans and sauces) and chemo-technical industry (vinegar for cleaning, decalcifier)
CWK	Manufacturer of chemo-technical and cosmetic products: cosmetics, natural cosmetics, non-aerosols, household cleaning products, organic products, industrial cleaners
Steinfels Cleaning Systems SCS, Winterthur	Products, equipment and services for washing, cleaning and hygiene for bulk consumers and industries
Pasta Gala, Morges	Egg pasta, plain pasta, organic pasta
Reismühle, Brunnen	Organic whole-grain rice, organic risotto, organic perfumed rice, parboiled thai rice, perfumed rice, basmati rice
Sunray, Pratteln	Sourcing, processing and packaging of raw materials such as sugar, edible oils, dried fruit
Bell, Basel	No. 1 Swiss meat-processing company: meat, poultry, fish, seafood, charcuterie, convenience; full-service provider for the retail trade, wholesale trade, the catering trade and the food industry

With the exception of verticals, external production (outside supply) dominates the fashion industry; however, the influence of retailers on the supply chain increases with store brands. To an increasing degree, retailers actively influence the supply chain (see Merkel et al. 2008, p. 32). Retailers create assortments and procure directly. Assortment and procurement sub-processes influenced by retail companies are presented in **Figure 6.7**.

Figure 6.7   Sub-processes of Assortment Planning and Procurement

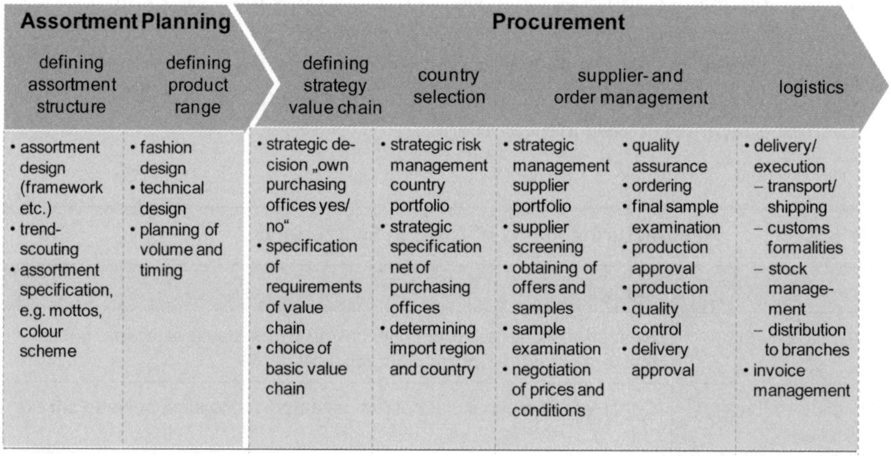

Assortment Planning		Procurement			
defining assortment structure	defining product range	defining strategy value chain	country selection	supplier- and order management	logistics
• assortment design (framework etc.) • trend-scouting • assortment specification, e.g. mottos, colour scheme	• fashion design • technical design • planning of volume and timing	• strategic decision „own purchasing offices yes/no" • specification of requirements of value chain • choice of basic value chain	• strategic risk management country portfolio • strategic specification net of purchasing offices • determining import region and country	• strategic management supplier portfolio • supplier screening • obtaining of offers and samples • sample examination • negotiation of prices and conditions	• quality assurance • ordering • final sample examination • production approval • production • quality control • delivery approval	• delivery/ execution – transport/ shipping – customs formalities – stock management – distribution to branches • invoice management

Source: Merkel et al. 2008, p. 30.

Although the manufacturing of the finished product remains with suppliers, retailers verticalise the process by taking over the procurement and logistics of fabrics and other "ingredients" (yarn, labels, accessories and packaging). Manufacturers are then supplied with these fabrics and other "ingredients" (Merkel et al. 2008, p. 41). This kind of external production is called the **cut-make-trim mode**.

KATAG is an example of a European buying group that, on the one hand, directly influences the marketing of its independent retail partners through an innovative **floor management model** and, on the other hand, influences the production of its contract manufacturers (controlled production) in the Far East by:

■ the internal design of the products,

■ ecological and social/ethical standards and

■ procuring accessories, e.g. buttons.

Figure 6.8 compares the **vertically integrated model** with the **design**, **sourcing** and **distribution model** of the international fashion retail supply chain (see Fernie/Perry 2011).

Figure 6.8   Vertically Integrated Model (VI) Compared to the Design-Sourcing-
Distribution Model (DSD)

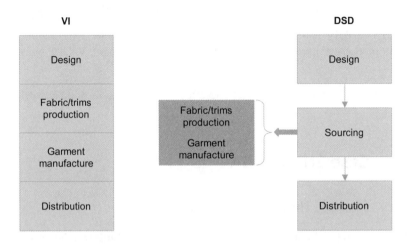

Source: Fernie/Perry 2011, p. 279.

6.4   Conclusion and Outlook

These developments in connection with the explanations from Chapter 5 illustrate that the competitive retail arena is characterised not only by new store formats, online retailing and multichannel retailing (see Chapters 2, 3 and 4), but also by the competition of value chains and value-creating systems. These value-creating systems compete not only in downstream markets but also along the entire supply chain. In this context, the example of the **agile fashion industry** illustrates competitive advantages that a highly performing supply chain management can create in the sense of the **quick response** concept (QR) (see Chapter 17). While the origins of this concept are in the fashion industry, this concept can be applied to other sectors, e.g. the grocery sector.

Value chains or value-creating systems will increasingly be controlled by manufacturers, in the context of their downstream verticalisation (see Chapter 5) or by verticals, leading to vertically integrated manufacturers/retailers. But, to an increasing extent, traditional retailers such as chains and buying groups will approach these value chain architectures.

▌ Further Reading

FERNIE, J.; PERRY, P. (2011): The International Fashion Retail Supply Chain, in: ZENTES, J.; SWOBODA, B.; MORSCHETT, D. (Eds.): Fallstudien zum Internationalen Management: Grundlagen – Praxiserfahrungen – Perspektiven, 4th ed., Wiesbaden, pp. 279-298.

JENNINGS, D. (2001): Thorntons: the Vertically Integrated Retailer, Questioning the Strategy, in: International Journal of Retail & Distribution Management, Vol. 29, No. 4, pp. 176-187.

LANE, C.; PROBERT, J. (2009): National Capitalisms, Global Production Networks, Oxford et al.

6.5   Case Study: C&A[1]

6.5.1   Profile, History and Status Quo

C&A, a privately owned enterprise, is one of the leading clothing retailers in Europe. The company offers the latest fashion at acceptable prices. *C&A* collections include the entire family – women's, men's and children's fashion – and target everyone, no matter what age, size and taste. The company focuses on the customer as the key to its success.

The origins of *C&A* date back to 1841 when Clemens and August Brenninkmeijer opened a textile warehouse in the town of Sneek in the Netherlands. The two brothers from Mettingen in the Münster region of central Germany named the company with their own initials. Originally supplying mainly rural populations with linens and textiles, the brothers came up with an – at that time – innovative business concept. Offering industrially manufactured, made-up products as well as ready-to-wear items of clothing at attractive prices to a broad clientele was revolutionary in 1861. It stood in sharp contrast to the expensive, made-to-order, artisan production of garments typical before then.

The first store proved very successful. This is why the store concept was multiplied in the following years and continued to prosper in its domestic market. International expansion started in 1911 when the first *C&A* store opened its doors in Germany, followed by the first branch opening in England eleven years later. The Second World War temporarily interrupted the company's course of international expansion. In 1945, *C&A* entered the North American market, which marked the beginning of the company's expansion outopean countries. The following years were characterised by rapid expansion with respect both to the number of retail outlets and to their geographical distribution across Europe. *C&A* continuously taps new country markets. The most recent store openings took place in 2005 in Russia, in 2007 in China, Turkey, Slovakia and Slovenia and in Romania, Italy and Croa-

---

[1] Sources used for this case study include the website http://www.c-and-a.com, the C&A Report 2010 as well as explicitly cited sources.

tia in 2009. But *C&A* has also closed stores to streamline its country portfolio. The company exited, for example, the Japanese market in 1993, Great Britain and Denmark in 2000, North America in 2004 and Argentina in 2009. At the beginning of 2011, *C&A Europe* operated 1,490 retail outlets in 19 countries, employing over 36,000 people.

Figure 6.9   C&A's Geographical Expansion (Year of Market Entry/Number of Operated Stores)

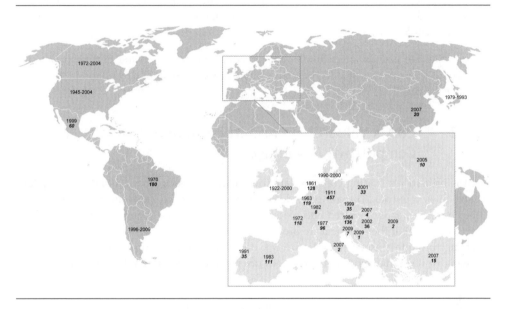

Source: C&A 2010.

C&A offers more than 10,000 different articles in 190 commodity groups. *C&A* has eleven exclusive brands in its portfolio: *Baby Club*, comfortable and high quality fashion for babies; *Canda*, complete range of competitively priced quality basic clothing items; *Clockhouse*, latest fashion addressing young adults from 18 to 25 years old; *Westbury*, attractive quality range of classic men's clothing; *Yessica Pure*, clothing for modern and fashion conscious women; and *Your Sixth Sense*, finest quality and classic styles for elegant women. This reflects *C&A*'s highly complex fashion portfolio and its concept of offering fashionable clothes to everyone.

C&A is organised into a holding structure named *COFRA Holding AG*. *C&A Europe* is one of its subsidiaries. Besides its fashion retail activities, the subsidiary operates a financial services venture named *C&A Money*, offering insurance and financial products to customers in Germany since 2006. In addition to *C&A Europe*, there are *C&A Latin America* and *C&A China*. Both are subsidiaries of *COFRA Holding AG* as well. Each of the organisations operates independently of one another. At the beginning of 2011, *C&A China* had 22 retail outlets in and around Shanghai and Beijing. *C&A Latin America* operated 188 stores in Brazil and 61 more in Mexico at that time. Besides retail activities, the holding company *COFRA Holding AG* encompasses a group of companies located in Europe, Asia, North and Latin America whose activities include real estate, private equity investments and financial services (Cofra Holding AG 2011). The holding structure was introduced in 2001 because of difficulties in the market. "The coming of *H&M* in clothing retailing entailed big difficulties for *C&A* which had to review its marketing, renew its image and restructure its supply chain" (Cliquet 2006, p. 125). Thus, a clear and efficient holding structure was employed to quicken the decision-making process and to make the entire enterprise more transparent (Textilwirtschaft 2001).

Despite difficult economic conditions and a significant decline in the European clothing market, *C&A Europe* was able to generate a stable gross turnover of 6.59 billion EUR during the financial year 2010/11.

6.5.2   C&A's Value Chain Architecture and Competitive Advantages

C&A is primarily a trading company and purchases its goods from around 900 suppliers located in 40 countries. The company does not manufacture any of its merchandise itself. It either purchases manufactured and ready-for-sale merchandise (passive sourcing through contract buying) or the products are produced in accordance to *C&A*'s specifications (active sourcing through contract manufacturing). Both kinds of sourcing comply with a direct sourcing strategy, meaning that *C&A* does not make use of external intermediaries for its sourcing.

The upstream textile supply chain is organised and coordinated by the company's purchasing organisation, *C&A Buying*. The two head offices in Brussels and Düsseldorf employ around 450 buyers, designers and stylists, working to develop and research the latest fashion trends and to buy final products for *C&A*.

One of *C&A*'s channels to directly and actively purchase goods is through *C&A Buying*. This operates eleven buying offices in nine countries. Its employees work directly with *C&A* contractual partners at the local level, visiting the manufacturing facilities and ordering goods on site. The following activities are *C&A Buying's* key tasks:

- Analysis of production markets
- Market analysis of suppliers and production facilities
- Agreeing capacities and production schedules with suppliers and buyers
- Inspection of samples
- Checking workmanship and fit
- Monitoring delivery times

- Quality control and final acceptance

- Coordination of transportation logistics

- Customs formalities.

Another method *C&A* employs to actively purchase its goods is through a subsidiary, the *Canda OHG*. This sourcing strategy can be classified as contract manufacturing because the subsidiary works with *C&A* designers, utilises its production knowledge, procures fabrics and other materials and organises the production and shipment of the goods. *Canda OHG* thus controls the entire upstream textile supply chain. The manufacturing facilities with which *Canda OHG* cooperates are mostly located in Eastern Europe and China. *C&A* obtains around 5 % of its merchandise this way.

C&A also procures goods following a passive sourcing strategy. *C&A Buying* purchases from approximately 500 suppliers located in Europe in the form of contract buying. These suppliers sometimes commission producers who, in turn, may employ the services of sub-contractors. Through this channel *C&A* buys final and ready-for-sale merchandise. The company thus possesses less control of the upstream textile supply chain compared with following an active sourcing strategy.

C&A purchases its merchandise all around the world. **Figure 6.10** presents *C&A*'s supplier origins.

Figure 6.10   Percentage of Production Units in Supply Countries

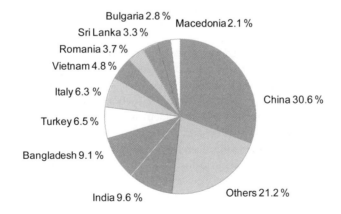

Source: C&A 2010.

After procuring the merchandise, *C&A* transports it from the factories to its 13 distribution centres in Europe. From there goods are distributed to local retail outlets. *C&A* uses a variety of means for long distance transport, mainly in primary distribution. For example, 93 % of manufactured goods are transported by ship, whereas only 7 % are transported by plane. *C&A* only transports merchandise by air if the clothing might miss the season because of late delivery or if the goods concerned are the very latest examples of a fashion trend that has to be served quickly. *C&A* aims to further reduce long distance transport by plane through the proper planning of its two main collections, Autumn/Winter and Spring/Summer. By contrast, *C&A* chooses transportation by rail and truck over short distances, and thus mainly in the context of secondary distribution, to make possible flexible store deliveries on a daily basis possible.

C&A sells its fashion without exception through its proper distribution channels, meaning that no intermediaries are involved in the distribution process. Consequently, *C&A* has direct market access and thus has a direct connection to the customer. Besides its equity stores, *C&A* has expanded into e-commerce as an additional direct distribution channel. An online shop in Germany was launched in 2008 after a successful test had been conducted in the Netherlands. Two new *C&A* online shops, France and Austria, went online in March 2011. Following the successful start-up of its online sales activities, *C&A* plans a roll out to other European countries in the near future.

Because *C&A* assumes full responsibility for its products, good quality management is of great importance. Over recent decades, *C&A* has developed a comprehensive system that ensures the human and ecological integrity and safety of its products. This begins with the manufacture of the fibres, and covers the entire manufacturing chain, concluding with the random sampling of individual products from its stores. The implementation and control of this system is the task of *C&A's Quality Assurance Department*, which operates around the globe and informs suppliers of *C&A's* quality standards. Active and passive purchasing channels are monitored this way.

Considering the multitude of different supply partners and their interests as well as logistics and distribution, managing the textile supply chain is a challenging task. In this context, *C&A* has significantly increased the share of active purchases to make it more transparent. This also permits *C&A* more frequent access to production facilities and allows better control over both capacity management and manufacturing conditions. In 2010, *C&A* procured about 80 % of its merchandise via direct and active sourcing. To further increase the supply chain's transparency, *C&A* is steadily decreasing the number of suppliers. This is not always possible because of its strategy to increase active sourcing for which new contract partners need to be tested.

New business contacts have to undergo a selection process based on commercial criteria, such as the product quality and social and ecological conditions in their production facilities. As mentioned above, *C&A* has clear ethical, social and ecological principles. The company defines safety standards throughout the entire supply chain, from design through production to transport and sales. These standards are binding components of its business relations and are defined in the *C&A* Code of Conduct and in the company's General Delivery Instructions. All suppliers are required to comply with these guidelines before the start of a business relationship.

Once in a business relationship with *C&A*, the company attaches great importance to cultivating long-term, trusting business relationships at all levels: with customers, employees, suppliers and other parties with whom it works together on a daily basis. This can be illustrated by looking at the relationships with contract supply partners, which are of essential importance to the company. More than 40 % of *C&A*'s current suppliers have been cooperating with the company for over 10 years and some of them for over 20 years. *C&A*'s suppliers are regularly evaluated and monitored to guarantee their profitability (Supplier Profitability Report), quality (Supplier Quality Report) and social responsibility (Supplier Compliance Rating). A clear competitive advantage of *C&A*'s integrated value chain exists in the consistent control of all processes. In this context, the company sees it as one of its responsibilities to monitor the consequences of its economic activity, especially in terms of raw materials and energy.

6.5.3   Sustainability at C&A

An ever-increasing price pressure and continuously changing trends in the fashion sector pressure all players in the textile supply chain with regard to costs and timely production. If not managed properly, these factors can affect production conditions. This is why *C&A* made its task to embed the "triple bottom line" principle (people, planet and profit) throughout the entire company. The aim was to obtain greater commitment from each individual and to secure sustainable progress in doing so. To achieve this aim, *C&A* developed a sustainability strategy with the primary purpose to focus the corporation on the socio-political and environmental challenges of the future. The centre of this sustainability strategy is the materiality matrix (see **Figure 6.11**), which combines the *C&A* perspective looking outwards and the *C&A* stakeholder perspective looking inwards. This identifies significant topics of relevance to the company that are capable of contributing to the creation of sustainable development and resource utilisation.

In conformity with its values and standards, *C&A* continually pursues sustainable development. The company emphasises the continuing importance of sustainability as one of the underlying principles behind its business model. For this purpose, *C&A* pursues and supports a large number of sustainable activities and social projects. For example, *C&A* established the *C&A Initiative for Social Development* in the mid-1990s to support sustainable development and to create better long-term prospects for local manufacturers. The company also cooperates with many non-profit organisations such as *Terre des Hommes*, *A Heart for Children*, *Oxfam Ireland* and *Child Helpline International* and *Organic Exchange*. Additionally, *C&A* set up an *Environmental Working Group* in 1989 to address topics such as waste education, recycling and energy saving. Issues such as saving energy in buildings and in logistics, environmental protection in merchandise presentation and waste disposal processes have been addressed by *C&A*.

To fully integrate the concept of sustainability *C&A* bases its corporate culture on clear responsibilities, accountability, trust and transparency in its management structures and procedures. Integrity is the concept *C&A* emphasises most when making business decisions and commercial dealings.

In recent years, *C&A* has established a leading position in selling certified organic cotton and has established *"Cotton Connect"* in partnership with the *Organic Exchange* and the *Shell Foundation*. The aim of the organisation is to transfer its knowledge on the cleaner cultivation of cotton to farmers in *C&A*'s main cotton market of India. This will help them move forward from today's conventional farming methods to the production of more sustainably grown cotton.

C&A's environmental strategy pushes further environmental measures, especially to substantially reduce CO_2 emissions as well as the associated damage of the global climate. The company titles this strategy *"C&Are"* and assumes long-term responsibility. *C&A* intends to become one of the leading five companies in the European retail sector in the fields of product safety, organic cotton, carrier bags, packaging and recycling, renewable energies, eco-store and transport and logistics.

Figure 6.11   C&A Materiality Matrix

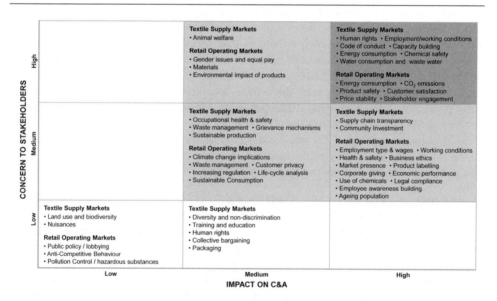

Source: C&A 2010.

6.5.4   Conclusion and Outlook

Because the customer is the company's first priority, C&A will continue to satisfy consumers' wishes, needs and satisfaction and thus it intends to maintain permanent dialogue with them. For this the company uses response forms available in stores or the contact page on its website, which customers can use to give feedback, ideas, comments and criticism. Additionally, the company conducts instore interviews to get in touch with its customers. C&A is especially interested in feedback on the range of offered goods, employee friendliness, smoothness of workflow and furnishings and facilities in the stores. The company utilises this information to steadily enhance its product ranges, services and stores to continuously improve quality and raise the level of customer satisfaction.

Between 2002 and 2008, C&A doubled its number of stores, and the company opened 150 stores in 2008 and 2009 alone. Despite the financial and economic crises of recent years, C&A was able to achieve growth as originally planned. As economies across Europe return to growth, C&A intends to accelerate its expansion in both the existing store base and its Internet business.

▌ Questions

1. C&A can be classified as a "vertical retailer" in the clothing industry. Explain why, taking a closer look at upstream- and downstream-oriented value chain architectures. What are the advantages and disadvantages of being a vertically integrated retailer as opposed to a traditional retailer?

2. In recent years, C&A has significantly increased its share of active sourcing and plans to continue this. Is it advisable for C&A to start manufacturing clothes in its own production facilities and thus exert even more control over the supply chain? Identify the opportunities and risks of clothing retailers becoming producers?

3. C&A pursues many different activities within its sustainability strategy. Explain the concept of sustainability, name the key corporate aspects of the three dimensions of the triple bottom line and classify C&A's different sustainability approaches in these three dimensions.

4. In 2007, C&A decided on a long-term strategy to expand the use of organic cotton for its products. In the context of sustainability, name and explain key drivers for a higher control of the upstream supply chain.

▌ Hints

1. For a discussion of the advantages and disadvantages of verticalisation see for example, Blois 1972, Jennings 2001 and Vickers/Waterson 1991.

2. Consider aspects such as added value in textile production, product life cycles in fashion and dependencies within the supply chain.

3. To name the key corporate aspects of the three dimensions of the triple bottom line see for example the Global Reporting Initiative website. To find additional sustainability approaches check C&A's annual (sustainability) report.

4. Consider corporate drivers on the supply and demand sides.

Part II
Strategic Marketing
in Retailing

7   Growth Strategies

The aim of this Chapter is to introduce the alternative routes to company growth for retailers. Ansoff's matrix, as a strategy tool, is introduced. Outlet multiplication, cooperation and mergers & acquisitions are considered to be the basic alternatives for expanding the retail store network.

7.1   Growth Options

Almost all retailing activities start as independent, single outlet operations. Compared with other business sectors, such as manufacturing, entering into retailing by opening a retail store is relatively easy and does not require high capital resources. The desire to grow business and increase value is often a fundamental objective from the very beginning. For retailers, among other benefits, sales growth provides benefits through purchasing from suppliers in large quantities and from economies of scale in operations (e.g. IT, logistics, and administration) (Ogden/Ogden 2005, p. 92).

Figure 7.1   Alternative Routes to Company Growth - The Ansoff Matrix

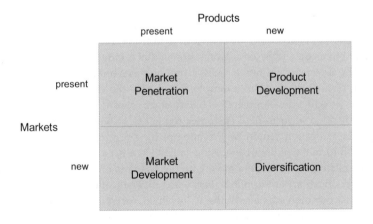

Source: Ansoff 1988, p. 109.

For decades, strategic management has analysed alternative routes to company growth. The Ansoff matrix (also called the product-market matrix) is a well-known categorisation of growth strategies (see **Figure 7.1**). It consists of four separate strategies, depending on **what** products and services are offered and **to whom** they are offered (Ansoff 1988):

- With present products and in present markets, growth can be achieved by **market penetration**. Higher sales from existing markets can either be obtained by attracting current non-customers, who either do not buy products in the offered categories at all or who buy them from competitors. Alternatively, the loyalty of the existing customers of the retailer can be improved and the value of their shopping baskets increased.

- **Product development** is characterised by offering new products to existing markets. This can be done by providing the existing customer base with new product categories in existing stores (see Chapter 11). Apparel stores expanding into selling shoes would be a good example. *Amazon* increasing its product offer from media products into general merchandise such as fashion or even food is another example.
  Considering that the retailer's "products" are its stores (see Chapter 9), product development in retailing often means introducing new retail formats in existing markets (see Chapters 2, 3 and 4). Store retailers starting to offer their products on the Internet or supermarket retailers opening convenience stores are examples of product development.

- A current product offer can be targeted to a new customer segment, often in a new geographic area (**market development**). Regional retailers expanding their traditional store formats into other regions or national retailers expanding into new countries attempt to increase revenue for the company with this strategy. This strategy will be discussed in more detail in the Chapter on internationalisation.

- **Diversification** entails offering new products to new markets. Within diversification, there are a number of strategy sub-types: horizontal diversification, vertical diversification and conglomerate diversification:

    ♦ **Horizontal diversification** refers to diversification into a related business field on the same level of the value chain as before. In the case of a retailer, this is the case if the company opens up stores (or acquires stores) that are dedicated to new product categories. The German food retailer *REWE* that operates home improvement stores (*toom*) is a typical example. This example shows that the distinction between the strategy type "product development" is blurry since offering new products (or new retail formats) often attracts new customer segments as well. Another example of horizontal diversification would be the attempt by *Tesco* to open up a new store format, a small format neighbourhood store called *Fresh & Easy*, in California.

    ♦ **Vertical diversification** refers to a move into the business on the level of customers (forward diversification) or suppliers (backward diversification). Since retailers are usually the last commercial stage in the value chain, forward diversification is seldom. Backward diversification, however, i.e. taking over activities that have traditionally been carried out by the suppliers, is a frequent strategy. As shown in Chapter 1, retailers now often operate manufacturing facilities in which they produce their own products. The case study to this Chapter, *Migros*, is an excellent example of this strategy type.

♦ Finally, **conglomerate diversification** refers to the offering of new products or services to new markets that are unrelated to the core business of the company. A number of retail companies (e.g. *Tesco, Migros, Auchan*) are active in banking. This is not entirely unrelated because customer credit cards, financing, etc. for the retail process can be handled via these banks as well. Some retailers have entered into the travel and tourism market, e.g. the *REWE Group* or *Casino*. Other retailers have entered wholesale markets. For example, the Swiss retail group *Coop* is now Europe's second largest food wholesale company after it acquired a 50 % stake in the *REWE Group,* a large food wholesaler that operates cash & carry markets and delivery services. A prototype of conglomerate diversification is the Virgin Group. Originally started as a record store and owning *Virgin Megastores*, the company now operates *Virgin Airlines, Virgin Finance* and many other unrelated businesses (see Morschett/Schramm-Klein/Zentes 2010).

Because diversification often leads retailers beyond traditional retail markets, the management literature warns of the dangers when the core competence of a company lies in other fields. As the example of *Tesco's Fresh & Easy* – as well as others – has shown, inexperience in two fields – in the market and in the product – often leads to low performance.

In almost all cases (except for the diversification to other levels of the value chain), growth strategies for retailers can take two basic forms:

■ Enhancing sales in existing retail outlets

■ Enhancing sales by enlarging the outlet network.

Most retailers' statistics, therefore, differentiate between revenue changes in existing stores (also called comparable store sales growth or like-for-like) and changes in the scale of operations owing to opening or acquiring new stores. The latter is the focus of this Chapter, because the establishment of new stores is the most important growth route for retailers. For example, *IKEA* entered Poland in 1991 and now operates eight large stores in the country; in 2005. *Federated Department Stores* (now called *Macy's*) added 400 department stores to its store network in the USA, while *Fressnapf,* a Germany-based pet supply retailer, was founded in 1989 and now controls a store network of about 1,150 stores in twelve 12 European countries, thereof almost 800 in Germany. *Inditex* entered Germany in 1998 and now operates 72 outlets under the *Zara* and the *Massimo Dutti* banner in this country. *Tesco* entered Eastern Europe in 1994 and now operates about 730 stores in four countries. These examples also indicate the most important options for outlet growth:

■ Organic growth: *IKEA's* large surface area stores in Poland – as in most other countries – were established through organic growth.

■ Joint ventures: *Inditex's* market entry in Germany was realised in a Joint Venture with the German retail group *Otto*.

■ Franchising: most of *Fressnapf's* growth in Germany comes from attracting new franchise partners, who open outlets under the *Fressnapf* brand.

- Acquisition: *Macy's* growth in 2005 was the result of the acquisition of the *May* company and the conversion of these stores into *Macy's* department stores.

- Mixed strategies: *Tesco* entered most Eastern European markets with small acquisitions, buying a few stores of regional retailers or, as in the case of the Czech Republic and Slovakia, from US retailer *Kmart*. Then, many new stores were opened via organic growth but if the opportunity to purchase additional stores emerged, the company used it, for example in Poland where it acquired the stores of a German retailer who left the country.

7.2   Organic Growth through Outlet Multiplication

The direct establishment of their own new outlets is usually the primary method for retailers to expand their businesses (Zentes/Morschett 2002, p. 173). This is also called organic or internal growth. The resulting chain stores operate multiple retail stores under common ownership and usually engage in some level of centralised decision-making. Large retail chain stores comprise up to several thousand stores.

Advantages of Outlet Multiplication

Opening new branches offers the advantage that the retailer's concept can be transferred to the new store right from the beginning. The location decisions and store layout and all attributes of the new store can be tailored to the existing strategy. Store managers are company employees, which enables activities to be monitored closely and decisions to be made centrally. Risk is limited as expansion is gradual. By opening up outlets, necessary adaptations can be identified early and new outlets can then be modified during the process. Furthermore, financing is sequential, i.e. the existing outlets contribute with their cash flows to the financing of the new outlets.

Constraints of Outlet Multiplication

At the same time, considerable financial resources become successively tied up in the store network. The opening of branches requires substantial capital investment, which is a major constraint to growth. In many markets, organic growth is slow because of zoning restrictions, planning permission, the search for sites, including the acquisition and development of the premises and so on. This entails the risk that the critical mass is not reached fast enough and other retailers with similar concepts, but not similar constraints, expand faster. This problem particularly affects retailers that require large sites for their outlets, e.g. category killers and hypermarkets (see Chapter 10), because approval for these sites is restricted in many countries.

Another drawback is the loss of flexibility over time. Many chain store operations are slower to respond to changes in consumer demand and other situational factors because of bureaucracy and the decreasing motivation of employees that are typical of larger businesses. Tailoring the assortment to the specific local needs is often easier for independent retailers than it is for large chain stores (Ogden/Ogden 2005, p. 93). However, modern retail information systems increasingly allow combining centralised decision-making with locally adapted marketing, including a locally adapted merchandise mix or prices.

7.3   Cooperative Arrangements

7.3.1   Joint Ventures

While the variety of cooperative arrangements is wide, joint ventures are clearly among the most popular forms of alliances. Since joint ventures are not retail-specific, they are only outlined briefly here. A joint venture is formed when two or more parties decide to undertake economic activity together and create a new enterprise as a legal entity in order to pursue a set of agreed goals. The parties agree to contribute equity and share the revenue, expenses and control of the enterprise (Morschett/Schramm-Klein/Zentes 2010, p. 286; Sternquist 1998, pp. 133-139). For example, when the Spanish *Inditex Group* entered Germany in 1998, it did so in a 50:50 joint venture with the German *Otto Group*. The joint venture operated the *Zara* stores in Germany.

Combination of Resources

A major advantage of forming a joint venture is the combination of the resources of two companies. Both companies bring financial and management resources, know-how, store outlets or other assets to the deal. Especially when a retailer enters a new retail or service sector or a culturally distant foreign market, the market knowledge of a joint venture partner is valuable and can facilitate expansion. In the example of *Inditex* and *Otto*, *Inditex* owned the retail brand and had the operating model for fast fashion, while *Otto* had the knowledge of the local market and better insights into location selection in Germany.

Risk Reduction

Another benefit of joint ventures is the reduction of risk for each company by splitting the risk between the participating companies. The larger the retail company, the more likely it is to expand on its own, because it can more easily afford the expenses and absorb the risk in this case.

Coordination Costs

The major drawbacks of joint ventures are the high coordination costs, because two independent partners with potentially conflicting objectives have to work together. Opportunism may emerge if one of the companies can gain a profit at the expense of the other. Thus, managing a joint venture is more complex than is managing a wholly owned company. Full control over the strategy of the joint venture is lacking because all decisions have to consider the interests of all participating companies. As a consequence, the stability of joint ventures is often considered to be rather low.

7.3.2   Franchising

While the fast food chain *McDonald's* is the most often cited example of a franchise system, many well-known retailers also operate as franchise systems. *Benetton, The Body Shop, Fress-napf/Maxi Zoo, OBI* and *7-Eleven* are examples.

Franchising is defined as a contractual agreement between two legally and financially sepa-rate companies, the franchisor and the franchisee. The franchisor, who has established a market-tested business concept, enters into a relationship with a number of franchisees, typically small business owners, who are allowed to use the franchisor's brand and must operate their business according to the franchisor's specified format and processes. The franchisor provides ongoing commercial and technical assistance. In return, the franchisees typically pay an initial fee as well as fees (royalties), which average about 5 % of gross sales, plus some advertising fees (Inma 2005, p. 29).

According to different national franchise associations, the franchising sectors in different country markets have reached considerable sizes. In France, there are about 1,400 franchise systems, in Germany about 960 and in the United Kingdom about 850. On average, each franchise system has between 40 and 50 franchise outlets, but the largest often exceed 1,000. All statistics show that franchising is growing continuously (see, for example, **Figure 7.2**).

Figure 7.2   Franchising in France

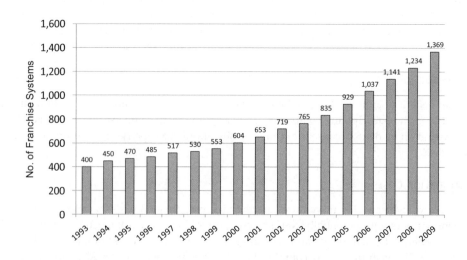

Source: Fédération Française de Franchise 2011.

Division of Tasks

A fundamental characteristic of franchising is that it always involves two separate and independent companies that assume distinct roles and a strict division of tasks in order to achieve a joint objective. Since the franchisee owns its own business, it is entitled to all profits that are generated. Franchising thus combines the benefits of a large, efficient retail system, including economies of scale in procurement, logistics, national advertising, IT systems and administrative activities, with the strength of an independent entrepreneur who manages the outlet, including customer contact and supervising store employees (Zentes/Morschett/Neidhart 2003). The common brand enables all participants in the franchising system to benefit from the advertising and goodwill generated by each outlet. From the consumer's perspective, it is often impossible to detect the difference between franchising and own branches.

Forms of Franchising

There are two main forms of franchising (Sternquist 1998, p. 123):

- Direct unit franchising is the basic form. In a unit franchise, the franchisor grants the franchisee the right to engage in a single franchised business operated at a specified location.

- In a master franchising agreement, the franchisor grants the master franchisee a set territory, and within this territory the master franchisee is allowed to establish unit franchises.

Sources of prospective franchisees can vary:

- Often, start-up entrepreneurs are targeted. Their inexperience makes the franchisor's business package relatively more attractive.

- In **multi-unit** franchising, successful franchisees are allowed to open new branches. This strategy is a type of organic growth within a franchise system. The number of outlets per franchisee, however, is often strictly limited because multiple franchise outlets diminish some of the advantages of franchising.

- **Conversion franchising** occurs when a franchisor adds new franchisees to the system by recruiting existing independent retail businesses (Hoffman/Preble 2003). Store owners may affiliate with the franchise system to take advantage of the brand and other components of the operating system.

Advantages for the Franchisee

For the franchisee, there are a number of benefits compared with a non-franchised independent business. Upon opening the franchise store, the franchisee enjoys instant goodwill in the market because it can use an established brand name, exploit a tried-and-tested business concept and carry out standard operating procedures.

It also receives comprehensive information on the business concept before starting, including information on necessary investment and likely profits. It obtains training and support, and financing is usually easier since belonging to the franchise system provides the franchisee with access to financing that would otherwise not be available as easily. From the perspective of a bank, it is easier to give credit to a franchisee since it can provide a business plan that has been based on the example of existing franchisees.

Advantages for the Franchisor

For the franchisor, as a growth strategy, franchising also has considerable benefits (Berman/Evans 2010, pp. 108-111; Zentes/Morschett/Neidhart 2003):

- Franchising allows for rapid growth of a retailing company. Especially when the success of a concept depends upon rapid market coverage, franchising is a way of multiplying a concept without the usual financial constraints. Franchisees also finance the investment for establishing stores.

- Motivation of franchisees is high, because they manage their own stores.

- Franchisees have knowledge of the local markets; customer and employee contact of franchisees is direct and personal.

- Written franchise agreements require the store owners to keep to stringent operating rules set by the franchisor.

Disadvantages for the Franchisor

One major disadvantage for the franchisor is that it has no direct hierarchical control over the franchisee. The franchisee is an independent contractor, not an employee. Franchisees can harm the overall reputation of the franchise if they do not maintain company standards. Changes in the franchisor's strategy may be slow to implement because franchise contracts usually run for three to five years and substantial changes are only possible through changing the contracts. If competition between different outlets occurs, it leads to conflicts (stronger than in own outlets since the profit is shifted from one franchisee to another). Also, franchisees may join to restrict the influence of the franchisor and attempt to change the rules. Another drawback is that under European law, the franchisor is not allowed to fix the final consumer prices for products. Accordingly, the marketing and management of a franchise system is more complex than it is for a truly uniform and hierarchically managed system of company-owned stores.

Often, the dynamics of the balance between the benefits and drawbacks of franchising leads to a change in the use of this growth strategy during the life cycle of a retailer. The resource scarcity that motivates retailers to embrace franchising as a growth strategy in the expanding stages of their life cycles lessens as the system becomes more established and growth rates decline. The costs associated with managing a complex franchise system gradually outweigh the benefits associated with the resources provided by franchisees. Consequently, over time franchisors tend to buy back franchises and increase the number of company-owned stores (Oxenfeldt/Kelly 1969). However, over the past few years the opposite development has also been occurring. Since, for many chain stores, operating small stores with low turnovers in certain market areas is not profitable in the form of company-owned stores, and the higher motivation in manager-owned stores has often proven capable of making a store profitable, some large chains have started to spin-off certain retail outlets and transform them into franchised stores. Smaller supermarkets and convenience stores are typical objects of such transformations (Zentes/Morschett/Neidhart 2003, p. 227).

Plural-Form Networks

Often, franchising is not used as an exclusive company strategy, but franchisors also own a substantial number of retail outlets themselves. The complexity of managing such plural-form networks is higher than that of managing monolithic systems of own stores or franchises. Synergies can be drawn from applying two different growth strategies simultaneously in the company, such as higher franchisor flexibility when deciding on new store openings. At the same time, the risk of conflict throughout the network is substantially higher and the management culture required to manage a franchise system of independent store owners is often different from the culture needed to manage a chain store (Cliquet 2000).

7.4   Mergers & Acquisitions

Companies also have the option of external growth, namely expanding by acquiring resources from other companies. Expansion through mergers & acquisitions (M&A) involves the consolidation or purchasing of existing retail companies or retail outlets. It can, in the case of diversification, also refer to the purchase of companies in other sectors than retailing. In a **merger**, two companies are combined and at least one of them loses its legal independence. In an **acquisition**, one company acquires a majority interest in another or takes over certain assets (stores) of another company. The term acquisition is often restricted to a full takeover. The legal independence of the acquired company can remain intact (Zentes/Swoboda/Schramm-Klein 2006, pp. 278-281).

M&A have played a major role in structural changes in the retailing sector over recent decades and they constitute a well-established growth mechanism (Burt/Limmack 2001). For example, in 1999 *Carrefour* merged with *Promodès* to form the largest European retail company and the second largest worldwide. In 2005, the merger of *Sears* and *Kmart* into *Sears Holding* created the US's fourth largest retailer. In 2006, the *Metro Group* took over 85 *Walmart* stores in Germany, expanding its own *Real* hypermarket network of 330 stores by a quarter. The Austrian *XXXLutz*, the second largest furniture retailer in the world after *IKEA*, bought five furniture chains in Germany. The largest acquisition, *Mann Mobilia*, added seven stores to the company's network. In 2011, *ASDA* took over the store network of *Netto* (Dansk) in the UK, giving it the possibility to establish a chain of small supermarkets. A list of similar examples would be long.

Advantages of M&A

M&A allow rapid expansion by overcoming the bottleneck created by the difficulty of establishing and developing adequate retail locations, which can take years from site selection to finally opening a store (Burt/Limmack 2001, p. 4). Within a short period of time, an acquisition makes an entire bundle of resources available to a company. Especially when first-mover advantages are pursued in a new market, this can be a critical success factor (Meyer 2001, p. 359). Since the customer base of the acquired retail company may be preserved, market share in a new market is gained quickly. Thus, with M&A a company has a substantial turnover in a new market from the very beginning, which may help pay for the investment.

After an acquisition, either the integration process comprises a change in the brand name of the outlets or the original retail brand of the acquired retail outlets is retained. The latter is often the case, when the acquisition is used to expand into other retail sectors or formats. A food retailer entering the DIY market, or a supermarket company acquiring a discount chain, for example, could be well advised to keep the acquired chain's established retail brand. The acquired company's existing resources – management expertise, personnel, sites and so forth – focus on its established field of business; thus, an objective of an acquisition is to exploit the know-how and dedicated assets of the acquired company.

Disadvantages of M&A

However, integration costs following an acquisition can be high. An incompatibility of company strategies, capabilities, resources and cultures often results in an insufficient exploitation of existing potential for synergies. The takeover and associated cultural change in the acquired company may also result in a brain drain and the loss of significant management skills. Also, in many markets it is difficult to find suitable takeover candidates. Successful retailers are, in most cases, not available for acquisition and less successful retailers often have retail locations, stores and premises that are not attractive enough for acquisition. Adequately evaluating the value of a retail company before an acquisition is, however, not an easy task and the real value and quality of the acquired company can often only be assessed correctly after the acquisition (Burt/Limmack 2001, p. 4). For example, in Germany *Walmart* faced the problem that the store network acquired for market entry was unfavourable and, over time, other targets for takeover were not available on the market. The option of further expansion through acquisition may also be limited by antitrust laws, as the example of *Safeway* in the United Kingdom illustrates. In already highly concentrated markets, the acquisition of other outlet networks by the largest players is often not approved by authorities.

In summary, acquisition is a fast growth strategy when adequate takeover objects are available, but the associated risk is substantially higher than it is with organic growth.

7.5   Minority Investment in Retail Companies

Owing to the difficulties associated with full-scale acquisitions, acquiring a minority stake in another retail company is also a frequently pursued strategy. For example, *Kingfisher* bought a 21 % stake in the German DIY retailer *Hornbach* and supports *Hornbach*'s national and international expansion, for example by providing funds. In 2004, Hong Kong-based *A.S. Watson* purchased a 40 % stake in German drugstore chain *Rossmann*.

Acquiring the partial ownership of another retail company involves similar advantages and disadvantages to the acquisition strategy in general. However, successful retail companies generally prefer another company buying an equity stake in their company to being fully acquired. Equity participation by a larger company can add resources that support its further expansion. Furthermore, the strategy can be useful in situations where full-scale acquisitions are difficult because of the particular market conditions or government control. At the same time, the remaining equity stake of the initial company reduces the risk of a brain drain (Zentes/Morschett 2002, p. 174), since the established management team of the acquired company often retains control, frequently only supplemented by additional management capacity from the acquiring company. The risk of overestimating the value of the acquired company is reduced because the acquiring company achieves full transparency over business processes and results, facilitating a potential full acquisition after a certain period.

7.6   Reduction Strategies and Withdrawal from Markets

While most companies focus on growth, some authors point out that strategic planning and analysis should also include the strategic withdrawal options from certain product or geographical markets. Sometimes closing down or divesting (selling-off) the unprofitable parts of a business or those that do not match the current strategy can help the retail company as a whole (see also Chapter 8).

For example, in 2002 *Fressnapf*, the European market leader in pet food and pet supplies, closed down its online shop (which it reopened in 2010). In 2006, *Walmart* withdrew from Germany after accumulating losses since its market entry in 1997. *Netto Dansk* left the UK in 2011 by selling its outlets to *ASDA*. In 2005, *OBI* sold its DIY stores in China to a competitor *Kingfisher*. Even though *OBI* operates about 500 DIY stores internationally and has sales of more than six billion EUR, it decided strategically that the future investment needed to ensure success in this huge market would be too high. At the same time, the company announced the opening of 100 new stores in Europe over the next five years. It is noteworthy that *Kingfisher* itself announced in 2009 to divest a third of its stores in China because they did not promise to return a profit or because they did not fit the future strategy in the country. In 2010, *Carrefour* announced it intended to sell off all of its hypermarkets in Thailand to *Groupe Casino*. *Saturn*, usually an internationally successful electronics retailer, announced at the beginning of 2011 that it would sell its stores in France to a competitor.

These examples demonstrate that in retailing, growth strategies are closely connected to withdrawal strategies. Withdrawal is not always the result of failure in a country, even though it often is. Other reasons include a change in corporate strategy, a change in external conditions, the necessity to generate cash to strengthen operations in the home country or low future expectations concerning the specific retail format.

Generally, divestment reveals that the retailer expects a better opportunity for investment and growth elsewhere. Retailer portfolios, with respect to their stores, store formats and country markets, are often reassessed, and a strategic withdrawal from one market often provides the starting point for expanding into other markets or for opening additional stores in the remaining markets.

7.7   Conclusion and Outlook

Growth continues to be highly relevant for the success of a retail company but, at the same time, it is more difficult to achieve because of several factors. These include the power of large retailers and the crowding out of independent retailers and small chains as well as the already high and increasing level of concentration in many retail markets combined with market saturation in many product categories.

Flexible growth strategies, therefore, become more important. Retail companies usually do not use these strategies in isolation but in combination, as the example of *Tesco*'s internationalisation or the description of plural form networks illustrated. If a retail company wants to enter a completely new country or establish a new store format (e.g. a food company entering into electronics retailing), then an initial acquisition helps achieve critical mass quickly. From that point on, the company can grow by establishing new sites and opening stores. Furthermore, as has been shown in the context of the increasing concentration in retailing, companies then often make a major step forward by acquiring smaller chains that leave the market.

Larger, divisionalised retail store groups with different retail formats often implement different growth strategies for different formats and/or markets. For example, *Carrefour* operates its hypermarkets in most parts of the world as own outlets, while it franchises its system in the Middle East (United Arab Emirates, Egypt, Saudi Arabia) to the *Majid Al Futtaim Group* that operates a number of large *Carrefour* hypermarkets in the region. The difficult market conditions in this region and the local knowledge of its franchise partner are the probable reasons for this strategy. Most of *Carrefour*'s convenience stores all over the world are franchised, and the expansion of supermarkets stems at least partly from franchised outlets, while there is also a substantial number of own outlets. Concerning the Balkan region, *Carrefour* established a joint venture in 2010 with the Greek company *Mari-*

nopoulos to open stores in Bosnia, Slovenia, Serbia and Croatia and other countries. This is a typical picture of retail companies that use different growth strategies over time and which tailor these strategies to the retail format and specific situation.

▌ Further Reading

HOFFMAN, R.; PREBLE, J. (2003): Convert to Compete: Competitive Advantage through Conversion Franchising, in: Journal of Small Business Management, Vol. 41, No. 2, pp. 187-204.

7.8 Case Study: Migros[1]

7.8.1 Profile, History and Status Quo

The origins of the Swiss retail group *Migros* date back to 1925 when Gottlieb Duttweiler founded *Migros* as a limited company in Zurich, Switzerland. His vision was a sales organisation without intermediate trade, aiming to create a direct **bridge** from manufacturer to customer. At the beginning, he started his company with five Ford T trucks used as mobile retail shops and only six articles of everyday essentials, including coffee, rice and soap. Shortly after the company's founding, the mobile retail shops offered their goods in 293 destinations across Switzerland and the assortment of goods increased. The early success of Duttweiler's corporate strategy was based on his pricing; partially he sold goods with a price reduction of 40 % in comparison with his competitors. This was achieved by focussing mainly on private labels. Only a year later, *Migros* opened its first store in Zurich. In spite of everything, *Migros* struggled for economic survival in its early years. During the Second World War, Duttweiler decided to change *Migros'* limited company structure into regional cooperatives and founded the *Migros* cooperative alliance. Nowadays, the alliance consists of ten cooperatives.

To reduce waiting times and deal with the increasing number of shoppers, *Migros* opened Switzerland's first **self-service store** in 1948. A specific feature of *Migros*, based on the dreams of its founder, are its social values, e.g. social capital, education for everyone and the abandonment of selling alcohol and tobacco.

Nowadays, *Migros* is the biggest retailer in Switzerland, holds a market share of 20.4 % and has approximately 61,700 employees and a group volume of 24.9 billion CHF in 2009. The company concentrates on five business segments: cooperative retail business, trade, industry, wholesaling and travelling. The cooperative retail business with its grocery stores is the core business of *Migros*.

---

[1] Sources used for this case study include the website http://www.migros.ch and various annual and interim reports, investor-relations presentations as well as explicitly cited sources.

In Switzerland, *Migros* operates many different retail formats: supermarkets, hypermarkets, category specialist stores such as *Micasa* and *Ex Libris*, department stores, restaurants and convenience stores. **Figure 7.3** shows the portfolio of the retail business of *Migros*.

Figure 7.3   The Portfolio of the Retail Business of Migros

Source: Migros 2011.

7.8.2   Organic Development in Selected Fields in Recent Years

As shown in this Chapter, organic growth – usually through outlet multiplication – is a primary method for a retailer to expand its business. However, *Migros* forces the renovation and expansion of its consisting branch network as well. This practice can be seen as a form of risk reduction, whereby a proven concept is transferred to new stores. Between 2000 and 2009, the sales area of the company's grocery retail formats (*Migros* MMM stores can be defined as hypermarkets, the MM stores as large supermarkets and the M stores as small supermarkets) increased from 829,174 m² to 1,017,672 m², an increase of 23 %; the selling space of the whole retail business grew from 964,792 m² in 2000 to 1,265,059 m² in 2009, which was equivalent to an increase of 31 % (GfK 2010, pp. 109-114). Since 2000, the total number of grocery retail stores has remained steady during a continuous process of store closures and new store openings. This indicates that the average store size has increased.

It is noteworthy that *Migros'* organic growth in grocery retailing is becoming difficult. While the company increased its sales space by 23 % from 2000 to 2009, sales volume only increased by 7.5 % in the same period, as is evident in **Figure 7.4**. This comparison also reveals that one important productivity measure – sales per square metre – has deteriorated over the past decade. Furthermore, it can be seen that revenues have dwindled since 2009 because of the adverse circumstances in *Migros'* core business, e.g. increased competition. This negative sales trend also has an effect on productivity: the average revenue per square metre is declining in all three supermarket formats (Gfk 2010, pp. 119-121).

Figure 7.4   Revenues and Expansion of Store Areas in the Grocery Retail Formats of Migros (M, MM, and MMM)

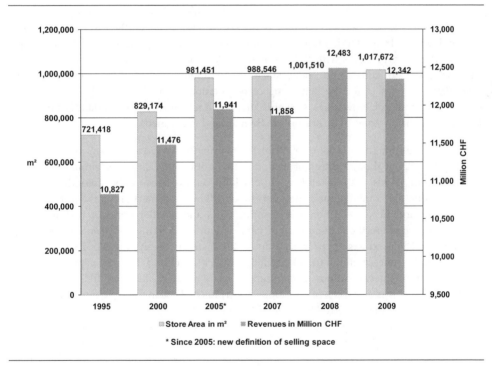

Source: IHA-GfK 2003, p. 87; GfK 2010, p. 113.

7.8.3   Cooperative Growth and Buying Stakes

Cooperation is another growth strategy. The most popular forms of alliances to grow are **joint ventures,** which combine the resources of at least two companies to reduce the business risk for both parties. *Migros* also uses this strategy to grow. In 2008, *Migros* established a joint venture with the mineral oil group *Shell* to run its **convenience stores** in the petrol stations of *Migros* and *Shell* as well as rail stations and to expand the branch network under the revived brand *Migrolino*. In 2009, *Migros* and *Shell* owned 217 convenience stores and the development of this joint venture exceeded expectations. *Migrolino* stores carry a similar assortment to other convenience stores, including alcoholic beverages. They also sell *Migros* store brand products. *Migrolino* and *Shell* remain independent companies and a merger of the particular chains of petrol stations is not planned. An example of the low stability of joint ventures is the failed joint venture *Cevanova* between *Valora* and *Migros*, which was the predecessor of the joint venture with *Shell*. It existed from 2000 to 2008 and operated 95 convenience stores under the retail brand *"avec"* in petrol and rail stations. After the breakup, the shops were divided among the former joint venture partners, but the brand rights stayed with *Valora*.

Another popular form of cooperative arrangements is **franchising,** which involves two separate and independent companies with distinct roles and a strict division of tasks. An example of this type of growth strategy is the partnership between the German DIY chain *OBI* and *Migros*. In Switzerland, *Migros* is the exclusive partner; the regional *Migros* cooperatives run the *OBI* stores with their own staff. *OBI* offers widespread assortments in the category groups of construction materials, DIY, habitation, gardening and pets with more than 80,000 articles. After the beginning of negotiations in 1997, the first *OBI* store was opened 1999 in Basel. Nowadays, *OBI* and *Migros* run ten stores in Switzerland. In the mid-term, an expansion up to 15 to 20 stores in Switzerland is planned.

In 2009, *Migros* bought a stake of 49 % in the German *Gries Deco Company* with its retail brand *Depot*. Even though different in detail, this approach was rather similar, from the perspective of *Migros*, to the establishment of a joint venture because the strengths of different companies are combined and the interests of different partners still have to be considered. The brand *Depot* sells home accessories, gifts and smaller items of furniture. The strengths of *Depot* are the presentation of varying worlds of living and emotional stagings of products. The products are produced under the instructions and ideas of *Depot*. In 2010, *Depot*, with the concept and market knowledge of *Gries Deco* and the fresh capital influx by *Migros*, opened 71 new locations. The volume of trade reached 200 billion EUR, in comparison to 2009, this was a surplus of 70 %, after a surplus of 35 % in the previous year (Bender 2011). *Migros* was the preferred partner of Christian Gries, manager and co-proprietor of *Depot*. Furthermore, both parties expect a long-term relationship with dynamic growth. In 2011, five new stores in Switzerland and 70 new locations in Germany are planned (FAZ 2011). *Migros* also believes that there is a great potential between its own subsidiary firm *Interio* and *Depot*. Both entrepreneurial concepts will be adapted similarly, and synergy effects will be realised. Furthermore, it is notable here that a stake regularly has other aims than M&A. A stake initially appears to be more like a partnership on an eye level, whereas M&A is the assimilation of a company.

Another example of growth by acquiring a stake is the online retail channel *Migros LeShop*. *LeShop* was founded by Christian Wanner and three partners as a start-up in 1997, and it started selling food online in April 1998. *Migros* entered into a strategic alliance with the company in 2003. After a few years of successful cooperation, *Migros* bought 80 % of *LeShop* in 2006, which was later stocked up to 90.5 %. The management team of *LeShop*, in particular the managing director and co-owner, remain in charge and it maintains a high level of autonomy within the *Migros* group.

In 2010, *Migros LeShop* held a market share of 67 % in food online shopping in Switzerland. The online supermarket provides a large assortment of *Migros* private labels and – different from *Migros* grocery stores – also stocks a large selection of manufacturers' brands. It also sells wine, beer and liquor. *Migros LeShop* delivers the products directly to the customer's front door and aims at young families and working mothers, which appreciate the simplicity as well as the saving of time. *Migros LeShop* has about 50,000 regular customers; 91 % of them are repeat buyers. The revenues of *Migros LeShop* are constantly growing **(see Table 7.1)**. Furthermore, a robust growth in online grocery retail for the next years is forecasted (GfK 2010, p. 338).

Table 7.1 Revenues of Migros LeShop between 2000 and 2010 in Million CHF.

Year	2000	2001	2002	2003	2004	2005	2006	2007	2008	2009	2010
Revenues	6	11.5	12.8	15.2	32.6	47.1	64.5	92.3	112	132	151.1

Source: Migros LeShop 2011.

7.8.4   Mergers & Acquisitions

Expanding by acquiring other companies is another option to grow. This enables a company to gain an entire bundle of resources and, furthermore, rapid expansion. *Migros* recently used this strategy to grow. In 2007, it acquired a 70 % stake in the Swiss discounter *Denner*. This stake was bulked up to 100 % in 2009. *Denner* is the number three in the Swiss retail trade and the leading discounter in the country. It is noteworthy that a major part of *Denner*'s sales stems from alcohol and tobacco. In fact, *Denner* stores have often been co-located with *Migros* stores so *Migros* customers that could not buy these products in *Migros* due to the founder's principles could still easily buy them at the same shopping trip, at the *Denner* next door.

The former owner of *Denner*, the Gaydoul family, sold the retailer to save its long-term competitiveness in a market with intensified competition because of the market entry of the German discounters *Aldi* and *Lidl*. *Denner*, a discounter who only sells in Switzerland, would probably not have had the necessary purchasing volume on its own to compete with these two foreign discounters. Despite *Denner*'s expansion plans, the Gaydoul family was afraid that the growth of the retailer would stagnate and decided to sell *Denner* to create a long-term solution for the company. *Migros* took this chance and entered this market segment. Before, *Migros* was not represented in the discount sector with its own stores.

Figure 7.5   Development of Sales of Denner from 1995 to 2009 in Million CHF

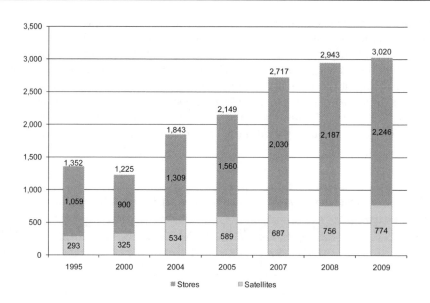

Source: GfK 2010, p. 169.

Following the decision of the Swiss competition commission, *Denner* remains an autonomous company with its own brand presence. After the bulk up of the stake at the end of
2009, the former *Ex-Libris* managing director Peter Bamert became the head of the discounter. In 2009, *Denner* generated revenues of more than three billion CHF, an improvement of 2.6 % in comparison with the previous year. With this growth, *Denner* exceeded the
total retail market, which realised a growth of only 0.5 %. Overall, *Denner* has maintained
its position in a difficult market environment. At the end of 2009, *Denner* ran 752 stores, 437
stores of which were autonomous and the 315 remaining stores are so-called *"Denner-
Satellites"*, which distributes the *Denner* products, but ran by independent merchants (GfK
2010, pp. 166-169). **Figure 7.5** shows the development of the sales of *Denner*.

However, an acquisition has a higher risk than does organic growth: integration costs can
be high and the possibility of incompatible company strategies, resources and cultures is
always there. The **takeover** of *Denner* has also produced hurdles for *Migros*. According to
the competition commission, *Denner* cannot be fully integrated into *Migros* Company, e.g.
both companies cannot buy goods together for resale. Another problem is the frictions
concerning the growth strategy of *Denner*. As a result, the CEO of *Denner*, Peter Bamert left

the company after only one year as CEO even though he had increased revenues and forced the expansion of *Denner* (Tagesanzeiger 2011).

7.8.5   Migros Industry

Migros not only operates as a retailer, but also operates in other fields. This **diversification** initially aimed to reduce the cost of goods sold, to secure supply and to reduce risk. However, it has developed into a central pillar in the strategy of *Migros*. *Migros Industry* delivers primarily to *Migros* channels such as *Migros* grocery stores, *Denner*, *Migrolino* or *Migros LeShop*, as well as third-party customers domestic and abroad.

In previous years, *Migros Industry* expanded its market position. In 2010, *Migros Industry* generated revenues of 5,316 billion CHF, up 2.5 % despite a tough economic context. The focus of business operations was Switzerland but also Germany, England and France. For example, the largest manufacturing companies, *Chocolat Frey* and the cosmetics producer *Mibelle*, produce different store brands for the German retailers *REWE*, *EDEKA* and *dm-Drogeriemarkt*. *Migros Industry* employs 10,049 employees in Switzerland. In 2009, *Migros* reinvested 151 million CHF in projects aimed at the growth and rationalisation the industry sector. The companies of *Migros Industry* are shown in **Table 7.2.**

Table 7.2   The Companies of Migros Industry

Product Field	Company
Meat/Poultry/Fish	Micarna, Mérat, Favorit
Dairy Products/Cheese	Elsa, Mifroma, Dörig, Mifroma France
Bread/Cakes and Pastries/Pasta/Rice/	Jowa, Midor, Riseria, Jowa France
Chocolate/Coffee	Chocolat Frey, Delica
Convenience/Beverage	Bina, Aproz, Gastina
Near-food	Mibelle, Mifa, Hallam Beauty
Wholesale Business	Scana

Source: Migros 2011.

Migros Industry is a driving force of growth within the cooperative. Therefore, *Migros* forces an expansion in the industry sector, domestic and abroad. The focus lays on a strengthening of marketing force in the main markets and on an upgrade of assortments. Furthermore, the dependency of brand manufacturers can be reduced and *Migros* cooperative can obtain more favourable buying conditions.

7.8.6   Summary and Outlook

Company growth is essential for retailers. As shown in this case study, *Migros* does not focus on only one growth strategy, but uses different strategies in combination, depending on the business segment and distribution channel. The most obvious part of the diversification strategy is the backward diversification with *Migros Industry*.

In the grocery channel, *Migros* cooperative makes use of a strategy of organic growth. Instead of increasing the number of outlets (which would be difficult in a rather saturated market with zone restrictions), it does so by growing the outlet sizes of its M, MM and MMM stores. The disadvantage of this strategy is the relatively slow growth, the decreasing productivity of the sales area and a loss of flexibility over time.

Another growth strategy has also been used to realise market entry in the discount sector. In order to gain a strategic size in this market sector, especially against the background of the market entry of German retailers *Aldi and Lidl*, *Migros* decided to buy the Swiss discounter *Denner* to realise a rapid expansion. *Migros* also used the possibility of cooperation to grow, for example by establishing *Migrolino* convenience stores in a joint venture with *Shell*. Similarly, it bought stakes in interesting companies such as the *Gries Deco Company* and *Migros LeShop* to develop new market segments. All these growth strategies can be seen as a part of diversification and risk spreading in different branches. It is noteworthy, however, that the expansion strategy watered down the principles of the founder because *Denner*, *Migrolino* and *Migros LeShop* now sell alcoholic beverages and tobacco products.

In the future, *Migros* will continue its strategy of diversification and growth. Nevertheless, this strategy concentrates on Switzerland with regard to retailing. This geographical restriction on one core market could cause disadvantages concerning international competitors that push into the Swiss market. Only *Migros Industry* has an international position and is likely to increase internationalisation (Morschett et al. 2009).

| Questions

1. Discuss the consequences for a company which arises of a poor organic growth. What are the problems?

2. Which problems can emerge with acquisitions?

3. What are the advantages and disadvantages of joint ventures?

| Hints

1. Consider Chapter 8 concerning the possibility of acquisitions.

2. See Chapter 8 as well concerning the relevance of joint ventures.

8   The Internationalisation of Retailing

The purpose of this Chapter is to discuss the key themes relating to the internationalisation of retailing. The Chapter describes the various facets of international retailing and the scope of retailer internationalisation, considers the basic strategic options, methods and ways of market selection and market entry/market operations and reviews international retail marketing opportunities.

8.1   International Activities

The internationalisation of retailing has two main elements: sourcing and selling. International retail sourcing has a long tradition and is by no means a new phenomenon. "Even if their stores are entirely domestic, many retailers have been buying goods from foreign countries for a long period" (Howard 2004, p. 96). The internationalisation of store operations (**cross-border retailing**) is the form of internationalisation on which this Chapter concentrates: "Cross-border retailing has accelerated dramatically through the last two decades, though of course it began much earlier" (Howard 2004, p. 97). However, it still remains a limited activity for most retailers.

Table 8.1 compares the relative importance of the international activities conducted by the largest food-retailers worldwide in terms of total turnover. In only four cases does turnover outside the domestic market exceed 50 % of total turnover.

8.2   Basic Strategic Options

The major dilemma for international retailing – and for international marketing – is that of **standardisation** vs. **adaptation**: "Some products are global products, meaning they can be sold in foreign markets with virtually no adaptation. This is what is meant by standardisation. Most products, however, need some changes in the product or promotion strategy to fit new markets. This is what is meant by adaptation. In retailing, the product is the retail business" (Sternquist 2007, p. 7).

There are four basic options with regard to standardisation vs. adaptation (Helffrich/Hinfelaar/Kasper 1997; Zentes/Swoboda/Schramm-Klein 2010):

- Domestic market orientation
- Global orientation
- Multinational orientation
- Glocal orientation.

Table 8.1   International Sales of the Largest Food Retail Companies in 2010

Rank	Company	Country	Sales (in billion EUR)	International Turnover as % of Sales
1	Walmart Stores	United States	292	25
2	Carrefour	France	90	61
3	Metro Group	Germany	67	65
4	Tesco	Great Britain	66	32
5	Kroger	United States	59	0
6	Costco	United States	55	21
6	Schwarz Group	Germany	55	55
8	REWE Group	Germany	53	30
9	Aldi Group	Germany	49	52
9	Walgreens	United States	49	0
11	Target	United States	47	0
12	Seven & I	Japan	45	33
12	Aeon	Japan	45	12
14	Groupe Auchan	France	43	54
15	EDEKA	Germany	42	0

Source: Annual Reports; Handelszeitung; LZNet; Statista.

This market-oriented classification corresponds to the **integration/responsiveness-framework** of Bartlett/Ghoshal (1989) in the context of international management (see Morschett/Schramm-Klein/Zentes 2010, pp. 32-35). **Figure 8.1** shows these basic options in the "benefits from local responsiveness/benefits from integration" matrix.

Domestic market orientation means that the retail concept from the home market is transferred to other countries. This approach leads to a unified programme of an ethnocentric kind ("**transference**"). Therefore, a **global orientation** in international retailing does not adapt to differences in local markets. This kind of standardisation is characterised by focussing on exploiting similar markets across the world and benefiting from economies of scale. In contrast to the domestic market approach, the company seeks homogeneous markets worldwide, which are the basis for developing a retail strategy or concept.

Figure 8.1   Four Basic Types of International Retailing

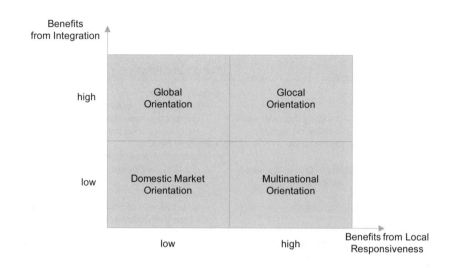

This approach can be described as diametrically opposed to a **multinational orientation**, which is characterised by substantial adaptations or diverse formats/concepts operating in heterogeneous markets. The **glocal orientation** ("think global, act local") seeks the advantages of both: moderate adaptations to heterogeneous markets. The retail company tries to bring together economies of scale ("**efficiency**") and a concentration on country markets ("**effectiveness**").

These four basic kinds of international retailing largely determine the decisions as to market selection and timing, the mode of entry or mode of operations in foreign countries and, of course, the marketing concept itself (site selection, assortment, pricing, communication mix, etc.).

8.3   Market Selection and Timing

8.3.1   Assessment of Potential Markets

The issues of market selection and the assessment of potential markets and timing are closely connected. "Timing is crucial – taking opportunities as they arise, particularly as markets open to foreign investment, and as consumer spending reaches absolute levels and levels of growth that are sufficient to support a new entrant" (Howard 2004, p. 108). These questions of international market appraisal and timing are also closely connected to the basic options of domestic market orientation, global orientation, multinational orientation and glocal orientation.

Table 8.2   International Market Appraisal Checklist

Spending Power	Barriers and Risks

♦ Total GDP
♦ Disposable incomes:
  – spending patterns, spending improvements, seasonal fluctuations, taxes on income, taxes on spending, saving ratios
♦ Population size:
  – age profile, cultural/ethnic groupings, expatriates and tourists, lifestyles, religion
♦ Residential structure:
  – urban vs. rural, housing density, ownership levels
♦ Adjacent markets:
  – cornerstone status, market proximities, market similarities, market accessibilities
	♦ Entry barriers:
	  – tariffs, quotas, development restrictions, competition laws, barriers to foreign entry, religious/cultural barriers
	♦ Political risks:
	  – change of government, nationalisation or controls, war or riot, international embargoes
	♦ Civil risks:
	  – effectiveness of policing, rate of theft, rate of murder/violence, level of organised crime
	♦ Economic risks:
	  – inflation, exchange rate fluctuations, employment structure and stability, taxes on business
	♦ Other risks:
	  – geological, climatic

Costs and Communications	**Competition**

♦ Factor costs:
  – land availability and costs, costs of acquisition targets, taxes on business, energy costs, labour availability and costs, training costs, development costs
♦ Logistics and costs:
  – road networks, rail transport, air freight, sea freight, available carriers, distances between markets, transport safety, transport reliability
♦ Communications and costs:
  – telephone/fax lines, automatic international dialling, available international lines, costs of calls
♦ Marketing communications:
♦ TV/Radio advertising, direct mail agencies, outdoor advertising, print/magazine advertising, cable TV penetration
	♦ Existing retailers: competition
	  – same or similar formats, indirect competition, specialist retailers, other marketing channels, price competitiveness, extent of differentiation
	♦ Existing retailers: cooperation
	  – synergies from partnerships, international alliances, franchising activities, cumulative attraction, acceptance of format
	♦ Saturation levels:
	  – structure of outlets by sector, concentration levels, primary/secondary markets
	♦ Gap analysis:
	  – positioning of competitors, viability/size of gaps, reasons for gaps, age of existing stores
	♦ Competitive potential:
	  – site availability, financial strength of home retailers, attractions to international retailers, opportunities to reposition

Source: McGoldrick/Blair 1995, pp. 169-170.

Retail companies following a global approach, for example, consider to what extent there are shared customer aspirations and similar infrastructures (logistics, media, norms, regulations) in different nations in order to implement a standardised strategy that conforms to these needs. The multinational approach concentrates largely on country markets, developing a specific strategy for each market. For this strategy, the market size or the spending power and competitive environment are primary considerations in market evaluation.

Table 8.2 contains a general checklist for evaluating international markets. This table "is designed to help appraise national opportunities; specific locations must then be evaluated" (McGoldrick/Blair 1995, p. 170).

Table 8.3   Market Assessment Matrix

Country	Regulation	Economy	Society	Culture	Retail Structure	Total	Average
French Hypermarket Retailer							
Bulgaria	4	3	4	2	4	17	3.4
India	1	2	2	1	4	10	2.0
Kenya	2	1	1	1	4	9	1.8
Great Britain	3	4	3	3	1	14	2.8
United States	3	4	3	3	2	15	3.0
French Premium Fashion Retailer							
Bulgaria	4	1	3	2	1	11	2.2
India	3	2	2	1	1	9	1.8
Kenya	2	1	1	1	1	6	1.2
Great Britain	4	4	4	3	4	19	3.8
United States	4	4	4	3	4	19	3.8

Note: 4 = very suitable; 3 = suitable; 2 = unsuitable; 1 = very unsuitable

Source: Alexander/Doherty 2009, p. 236.

Based on a few assessment criteria, **Table 8.3** illustrates a hypothetical market evaluation process of two retailers using a simple **scoring model** (with equal weighting factors). This **market scanning** "allows retailers quickly to assess the relative merits of a wide selection of different markets. It is a relatively inexpensive process and may be termed desk research" (Alexander/Doherty 2009, p. 234). An **in-depth approach** using secondary and primary data is market research, which is more expensive and, therefore, used in a further stage, e.g. after market scanning, analysing only a limited number of markets.

Scanning foreign markets can also be carried out by using not only secondary data but also the results of market research companies or consulting firms. **Table 8.4** shows the actual values of the **Global Retail Development Index** (GRDI), elaborated by A.T. Kearney. Methodically, the index scores are the result of a scoring model using country risk, market attractiveness, market saturation and time pressure as assessment criteria (equal weighting factors: 25 %).

Table 8.4   Global Retail Development Index (GRDI) 2010

Rank 2010	Country	Country risk (25 %)	Market attrac-tiveness (25 %)	Market satura-tion (25 %)	Time pres-sure (25 %)	GRDI score	Change in rank com-pared to 2009
1	China	86	51	33	87	64	+2
2	Kuwait	94	75	56	25	63	N/A
3	India	51	35	62	98	62	-2
4	Saudi Arabia	87	65	51	31	58	+1
5	Brazil	74	74	47	37	58	+3
6	Chile	92	72	28	38	58	+1
7	United Arab Emirates	100	79	19	32	58	-3
8	Uruguay	74	68	59	23	56	N/A
9	Peru	55	43	72	49	55	+9
10	Russia	55	64	32	62	53	-8

Source: A.T. Kearney 2010.

A multi-stage process of market selection based on market scanning and detailed **feasibility studies** using secondary and primary data is illustrated in **Figure 8.2**. This figure shows the market selection process of the *Metro Group*.

Figure 8.2   Market Selection Process of Metro Group

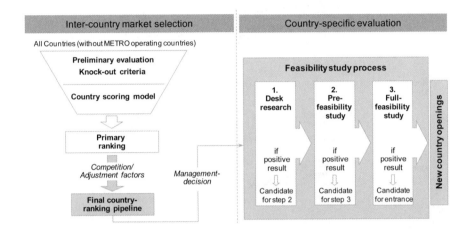

Source: adapted from Swoboda/Schwarz/Hälsig 2007.

8.3.2   Expansion Patterns

Three approaches to the strategic sequencing of foreign-market entry are discussed in the literature (Zentes/Swoboda/Schramm-Klein 2010) (see **Figure 8.3**). Ayal/Zif (1979) proposed a hierarchical approach "that produces a slow sequence of entries to different markets depending on the receptivity. This approach has been dubbed the **waterfall model** to depict the situation where innovations trickle down in a slow-moving cascade from the most to the least technologically advanced country" (Bradley 2005, p. 294). Such a procedure helps the company exploit the experience gained in the various markets. With every additional step, there is an increase in the degree of heterogeneity of foreign markets, which must also be accepted.

Ohmae (1985) recommended an alternative approach. The **sprinkler model** means simultaneously entering all relevant markets in the triad countries (Europe, North America and Japan). The reasons for these internationalisation steps relate to competitive strategies such as reaching a critical mass as fast as possible for products with a short lifetime. This pattern of market entry has practically no relevance with regard to non-store formats in retailing, but is of growing importance in **electronic retailing**. In contrast to the necessary investment in a global network of **bricks-and-mortar stores**, electronic retailers ("e-tailers") can operate worldwide by using multilingual websites and delivering via global logistics service providers.

Figure 8.3   Strategic Sequencing of Market Entry

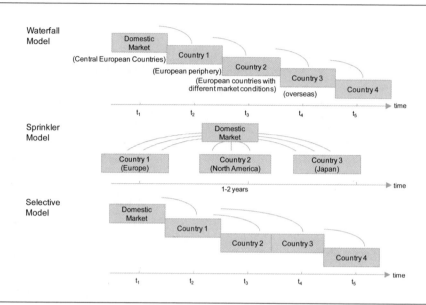

The third approach entails selective action, which can often be observed in reality **(selective model)**. The selective model or ad hoc internationalisation represents a combined procedure. Within the context of this strategy type, a company's resources are concentrated on the development of an adaptation to individual foreign markets. Conversely, other markets are developed simultaneously or successively, depending on the situation, and are treated less intensively. The companies concentrate their resources on selected markets, within which they work intensively (Zentes/Swoboda/Schramm-Klein 2010).

The waterfall model as well as the selective model are expansion patterns by which companies do not change their international activities by leaps and bounds or in a revolutionary manner, but gradually (see e.g. the "**Uppsala concept**" of the internationalisation of the firm over time in Zentes/Swoboda/Schramm-Klein 2010, pp. 7-12). These patterns are typical of retail companies. A second dimension of the expansion pattern refers to the question of where retail companies will be active, i.e. which countries do they enter. Following the concept of **psychic distance**, retail companies do venture at first into countries with which they are familiar, namely those that are psychologically near (see **Figure 8.4**). In the next steps, they approach cautiously countries that are less familiar or considered to be psychologically remote. The strategic sequencing of market entry takes place in the shape of **concentric circles** starting from the home country (Kutschker/Schmid 2011, pp. 466-472). This means that in the initial phase of internationalisation, retailers enter those countries showing little (subjectively felt) psychic distance to the domestic market.

Figure 8.4   Internationalisation along the "Psychic Distance Chain"

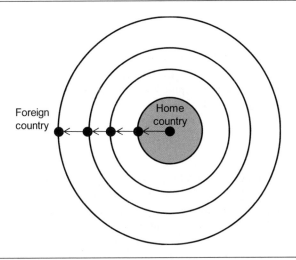

Source: Bäurle 1996, p.90.

As an example, **Figure 8.5** illustrates the international expansion pattern of the *Metro Group*.

Figure 8.5   International Expansion Pattern of Metro Group

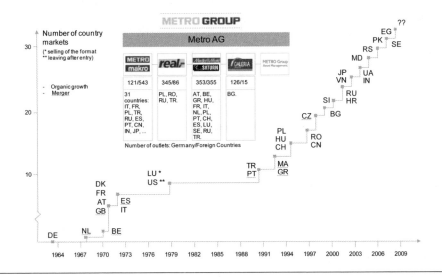

Source: METRO Group 2010.

8.4   Entry and Operating Strategy

8.4.1   Overview

Chapter 7 described and illustrated the growth options of retail companies, namely organic growth through multiplication, cooperative arrangements such as franchising and mergers & acquisitions. This section refers to Chapter 7 and analyses the peculiarities of growth strategies in the context of internationalisation.

8.4.2   Exporting

The choice of market entry mode or operating strategy depends on the basic strategic option, the market position of the firm, market conditions in foreign countries and the amount of resources the retail company can allocate to expansion into foreign markets. "In particular, the selected entry method indicates the level of control that the retailer seeks to exert over their foreign operations, the degree of flexibility required in order to effectively respond to market conditions that their foreign enterprise may face" (Moore/Fernie 2005, p. 16).

Figure 8.6   Entry and Operation Modes in Foreign Markets

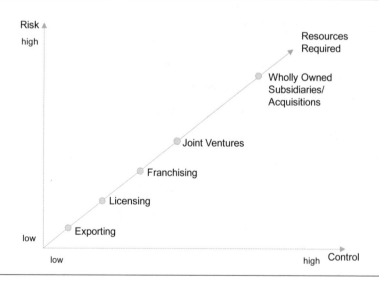

Source: adapted from Bradley 2005, p. 291.

Five basic modes of market entry or modes of operations can be identified within the international retailing literature (see **Figure 8.6**). The lowest level of involvement/commitment and risk is associated with export. This alternative requires fewer resources, but is generally associated with a low degree of control. In retailing, exporting is fairly rare. As an example, exports by (traditional) **mail order companies** or **Internet retailers** (e-commerce) can be mentioned. A foreign consumer can buy goods, e.g. in the American e-shop of *Sears.com*, and have the merchandise delivered by a logistics service provider to his home abroad.

8.4.3   Cooperative Arrangements

The next level of involvement for a retailer is through licensing, which is a **cooperative arrangement**. Such contracts allow a foreign company to use the name or concept of the licensing company (Sternquist 2007, p. 8). For example, *Migros*, the largest Swiss food retailer, licenses its name in Turkey. Another example is *Garant Möbel*, a German cooperation of furniture retailers, which licenses its marketing concept (formats) and name to roughly 3,300 partners in Europe, Asia and the Middle East. Like exporting, licensing arrangements are relatively rare international expansion choices for retailers.

Franchising is a cooperative market entry mode that has led to the rapid expansion of a large number of well-known global retailers (see Chapter 7). Through the franchising arrangement, the **franchisor** gives other companies (franchisees) the right to use the franchisor's (retailer's) name and concept (format, retail marketing). In turn, the franchisor supports the franchisees in running their business (marketing, training, controlling, and logistics). The main forms of international franchising are **direct franchising**, by which foreign franchisees are linked directly to the franchisor, **master franchising**, which means that the franchisor allows the foreign master franchisee to establish unit franchises in a country or a defined territory, and **franchisor-owned foreign subsidiaries** or (equity) **joint ventures** with foreign partners, which operate as the national headquarters of the franchisor (see Chapter 7).

A **joint venture** (equity joint venture) is the next level of cooperative international involvement for a retailer. This entry and operation strategy has become an important aspect of international activity. In most cases, joint ventures involve a local and a foreign (incoming) company. However, there is no reason why two or more retailers should not establish a joint company in order to enter a new market. "Joint ventures provide the incoming retailer with an opportunity to learn about operations in a new market, while at the same time giving indigenous retailers the opportunity to learn from an international player" (Alexander/Doherty 2009, p. 258). The French company *Carrefour*, no. 2 worldwide (see **Table 8.1**), often enters foreign markets with this mode. A good example is the relationship between *Carrefour* and the Arabian *Majid al Futtaim Group*, which operates more than 37 hypermarkets in the Middle East (Saudi Arabia, United Arab Emirates, Egypt, Oman, Bahrain, Kuwait, Jordan, Syria and Qatar).

8.4.4   Organic Growth and M&A

The replication of domestic operations abroad (**outlet multiplication**) through new store development is a growth strategy based on experience (and success) in the domestic market. This strategy means **internal expansion** (Dawson 1994) or **organic growth** by establishing wholly owned subsidiaries (see Chapter 7). Acquiring a foreign retail operation can also be the starting point for transforming existing stores into the domestic or global market concept. This is the case when legal constraints in foreign countries are barriers to developing new stores, for example in large-scale retailing (such as superstores or hypermarkets). **Acquisitions** can also be the appropriate entry and operation mode for implementing a specific country market approach (multinational orientation).

8.5   International Retail Marketing

Retailers that internationalise their operations must define their marketing mixes in domestic and foreign markets with regard to the four basic types of international retailing (as illustrated in **Figure 8.1**). The retail marketing concepts can be roughly characterised by the main elements **format** and **assortment**. With regard to assortment, the strategic or **structural dimension** and the **operational dimension** can be distinguished. The structural dimension refers to the basic categories and the number of SKUs sold, the level of product quality, the price level and the share of store brands, etc. The concrete products offered by a retailer are part of the operational dimension.

Standardised formats, including locations and the mode of instore marketing, and standardised assortments, at a strategic and operational level, are typical for a **domestic** or **global approach** to internationalisation, which can be found e.g. in fashion retailing. *H&M*, *Zara* and *Armani* are typical examples of this type. Characteristically for **glocal orientation** are the adaptation of operational assortments and price/promotion activities that focus on local conditions, e.g. in food retailing to local/regional tastes. *Aldi*, *Lidl*, *Carrefour* and *Tesco* operate like this. Multinational operations imply different formats (i.e. positioning, retail brands) with different assortments and different price/promotion policies in different countries. The international operations of *Ahold*, *Delhaize* and *REWE* correspond to this type.

8.6   International Retail Divestment

Studying retail internationalisation also leads to the question of **divestment**, "considering not only 'what works' but also 'what hasn't worked'" (Burt/Dawson/Sparks 2008, p. 31). Alexander/Quinn/Cairns (2005, p. 8) defined **international retail divestment** as "company actions resulting in a reduced presence in a foreign market. This may take the form of closure of stores, sales of store chain, termination of a business contract/agreement (joint venture/franchising and so on) or organisational restructuring in the form of changing from corporate ownership to a franchising or licensing or distribution agreement. Divestment may or may not involve market exit." In the literature on international marketing, there exists a vast range of terms that are used in this context, such as divestiture, marketing exit, business exit, deinternationalisation, decommitment, failure and business restructuring (see Alexander/Doherty 2009, p. 327; Zentes/Swoboda/ Schramm-Klein 2010, pp. 103-110).

Failure may rise, according to Burt/Dawson/Sparks (2008, p. 33), from different sources:

- **"Market failure**, where the market does not 'behave' as expected and sales do not meet expectations,

- **Competitive failure**, where operational performance does not 'match' that of competitors or regulation impacts upon competitive capabilities,

- **Operational failure**, when a domestic retailer is simply not a good international retailer and domestic competencies do not transfer,

- **Business failure**, when decisions impacting upon the international business are made because of changing domestic circumstances (performance, stakeholder expectations etc.)."

Framing divestment within the context of **organisational restructuring**, according to Palmer (2004), leads to the following sources (Burt/Dawson/Sparks 2008, p. 33):

- **"Financial restructuring**, relating to changes in governance structures and stakeholders expectations,

- **Portfolio restructuring**, arising from merger and acquisition activity and alliances or joint ventures,

- **Organisational restructuring**, reflecting changes in company structure, processes or management,

- **Spatial restructuring**, requiring changes in the geographical scope and scale of activity."

With regard to market exits, **Table 8.5** illustrates the most important reasons from the point of view of international retail companies, especially in the field of food retailing.

Table 8.5   Selected Market Exits

Retail Firms	Country and Year	Key Factors leading to Exit
Marks & Spencer (UK)	US 2006; FR/ES/BE/NL/DE/PT/LU 2001	♦ resource concentration on domestic market ♦ corporate restructuring
Ahold (NL)	AR/BR/BE//ES/CR/ESV/GTM/HN 2005; TH 2004; CL/ID/MY/PY/EC/PE 2003; CNSG 1999	♦ bad forecast and resource realloca-tion ♦ losses, financial irregularities (domestic market)
EDEKA (DE)	CZ 2006; PL 2003	♦ strong competition/no perspective
Auchan (FR)	AR 2005; US 2003; MY 2002; TH 2001	♦ no perspective ♦ no critical mass
Intermarché (FR)	DE 2005; IT 2002	♦ no partner
Dohle (DE)	PL 2002	♦ attractive sales option
Dairy Farm (HK)	AU/NZ 2002; ES/GB/JP 1998	♦ concentration on core competen-cies, reorganisation ♦ strong competition/bad perspective
Reitan (NO)	PL 2003; HU 2002; CZ 1998	♦ competition/bad perspective
Jerónimo Martins (PL)	BR/GB 2002	♦ financial difficulties
Seiyu (JP)	TH 2001	♦ losses and loss of JV-partners
Julius Meinl (AT)	CZ/HU 2005	♦ reorientation
Carrefour (FR)	SK 2008; CH 2007; KR 2006; MX 2005; CL 2004; HK 2000	♦ competition, difficulties in domestic market ♦ hypermarkets with weak perform-ance
Casino (FR)	PL 2006	♦ losses and no perspective
Walmart Stores (US)	GR/KR 2006; ID 1998; HK 1996; DE 2006	♦ losses, difficulties with JV-partner

Source: Swoboda/Foscht/Pennemann 2009, p. 132.

8.7   Concluding Remarks and Future Challenges

The successful operations of retail companies in non-domestic markets revolve around one main principle. Only companies that have proven themselves in a highly competitive do-mestic market have a chance of earning money abroad. An attempt to "escape" into foreign markets because of weaknesses in the domestic market will fail.

One of the greatest challenges facing "cross-border" retailers is the market appraisal of new emerging markets in the BRIC countries (Brazil, Russia, India, China), Eastern European countries that are not members of the European Union and countries in South-East Asia. The right strategic choice in terms of timing and the appropriate mode of entry in these markets are crucial.

Further Reading

BRUCE, M.; MOORE, C.M.; BIRTWISTLE, G. (2005): International Retail Marketing, Amsterdam et al.

DAWSON, J.; USUI, K. (2011): Renewal and Transformation of Value in an International Retailer: Dixons Retail plc, in: ZENTES, J.; SWOBODA, B.; MORSCHETT, D. (Eds.): Fallstudien zum Internationalen Management: Grundlagen – Praxiserfahrungen – Perspektiven, 4th ed., Wiesbaden, pp. 589-610.

8.8   Case Study: A.S. Watson[1]

8.8.1   Profile, History and Status Quo

The forerunner of *A.S. Watson*, a small dispensary named *'the Canton Dispensary'*, opened in 1829 in Guangzhou, China. In 1871, the company changed its name to *A.S. Watson & Company, Limited*. Today, *A.S. Watson* operates 19 retail brands with more than 8,900 retail stores in 36 countries and employs 87,000 people. The company is a subsidiary of *Hutchison Whampoa Ltd.* and is based in Fotan, Hong Kong.

A.S. Watson operates retail stores that offer health & beauty products, perfumeries and cosmetics, food and electronics as well as airport retail stores in Asia and Europe. The company also produces and distributes a range of own-label beverages from distilled water, fruit juices, soft drinks to tea products for retail, office and domestic supplies. Various wine labels are offered through international wine wholesalers and distributors (Bloomberg Businessweek 2010).

8.8.2   Group Structure Hutchison Whampoa Ltd. & Brand Portfolio A.S. Watson

Since 1963, *A.S. Watson* has been part of the Hong Kong-based conglomerate *Hutchison Whampoa Ltd.*, which comprises five core businesses: telecommunications, energy, infra-

---

[1] Sources used for this case study include the website http://www.aswatson.com, all editions of the newsletter WatsOn as well as explicitly cited sources.

structure, investments, retail, property and hotels, ports and related services (Hutchison Whampoa 2011a).

Figure 8.7   Group Structure Hutchison Whampoa

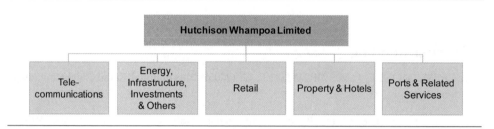

Source: Hutchison Whampoa 2011a.

All retail formats of *Hutchison Whampoa* are run by *A.S. Watson*. In the course of the expansion of the group's operation in Europe, business units have been realigned. As shown in **Figure 8.8**, there is a Health & Beauty Division, a Food, Electronics & General Merchandise Division and a Manufacturing Division.

A.S. Watson consists of several business units and offers a diverse brand portfolio. The category "Health & Beauty" is represented by *Nuance-Watson* and *Watsons Your Personal Store* in Asia (Hong Kong, Mainland China, Taiwan, Macau, Singapore, Malaysia, Thailand, Philippines, Indonesia, Korea and Turkey) and by *Kruidvat* (the Netherlands, Belgium) as well as *Superdrug* (UK), *Rossmann* (Poland, Hungary, Czech Republic, Germany), *Savers* (UK), *Trekpleister* (the Netherlands), *Drogas* (Latvia, Lithuania), *Spektr* (Russia), *Watsons Your Personal Store* (Estonia, Slovenia) and *DC* (Ukraine) in Europe. In addition to the "Health & Beauty" category, *A.S. Watson* is also engaged in "Luxury Perfumeries & Cosmetics". It operates the trade chain *Marionnaud* (France, Austria, Switzerland), *ICI Paris XL* (Netherlands, Belgium, Luxembourg) and *The Perfume Shop* (UK, Ireland).

In Asia, *A.S. Watson* operates groceries retail chains such as *PARKnSHOP supermarket chain* (Hong Kong, Macau, Mainland China), *Great Food Hall* (Hong Kong), *TASTE food galleria* (Hong Kong) and *GOURMET boutique style fine Food Hall* (Hong Kong). Electronics are distributed by *Fortress* (Hong Kong, Macau). The company also owns *Watson's Wine Cellar* (Hong Kong, Mainland China) and distributes wine in Switzerland through the Swiss-based company *Badaracco*. Several airport shops are operated as *Nuance-Watson* airport duty free shops (Hong Kong, Singapore).

In 2010, *A.S. Watson* reported an 8 % growth in total revenue to 123.2 billion HKD (11.1 billion EUR) while EBIT increased 38 % to 7.9 billion HKD compared with 2009. This growth in revenue was driven by the management's strong commitment to improve operating efficiencies, reduce inventory levels, increase centralised purchasing and further expand into high growth markets (Hutchison Whampoa Limited 2011b).

Figure 8.8   Group Structure A.S. Watson

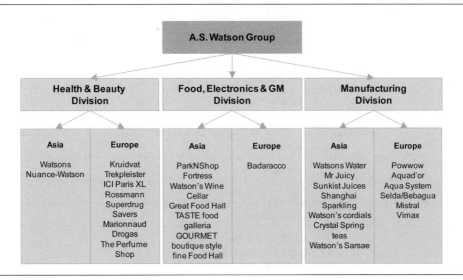

Source: adapted from A.S. Watson 2011.

8.8.3   A.S. Watson's Basic Strategic Internationalisation Decisions

A.S. Watson's declared intention with regard to further growth is the continuing expansion into high growth markets. The company describes its growth strategy as organically expanding into high growth potential markets. Its strategy can be explained as a mix of market penetration (e.g. the extension of the chain store network into existing markets) as well as market development (e.g. through internationalisation in new markets). The international operations of *A.S. Watson* outside of China (incl. Hong Kong) represent a share of about 70 of the company's total revenue, showing the significance of internationalisation for the group's success.

The internationalisation of *A.S. Watson* was initiated by 1883 with market entry into the Philippines. Since 1987, *A.S. Watson* has gradually expanded into other Asian countries before market entries in Europe followed in 2000. **Table 8.6** reviews *A.S. Watson's* foreign commitments since its first foreign market entry. Since 2006, *A.S. Watson* has entered no new foreign markets.

Table 8.6   Foreign Market Entries of A.S. Watson

Year	Country	Total No. of Countries
1828	China	1
1883	Philippines	2
1987	Taiwan, Macau	4
1988	Singapore	5
1994	Malaysia	6
1996	Thailand	7
2000	UK	8
2001	Switzerland	9
2002	Netherlands, Belgium, Luxemburg, Germany, Poland, Czech Republic, Hungary	16
2004	Latvia, Lithuania	18
2005	Austria, France, Italy, Spain, Portugal, Slovakia, Estonia, Romania, Morocco, Turkey, Russia, Israel, Korea	31
2006	Ukraine, Slovenia, Indonesia, Ireland	35

Since 2006 no new foreign market entries

As discussed in section 8.2, the internationalisation of a retailer is influenced by the basic options to either standardise or adapt a "product" (in this case, the retail stores and retail brands) to the foreign market. The strategic decisions, with regard to the internationalisation of *A.S. Watson*, show high local responsiveness. If the company does not pursue growth through building its own branches, *A.S. Watson* acquires existing companies. It is a common strategy for retailers to search for experienced partners to overcome bureaucratic constraints and benefit from the local experiences of the partner in the difficult phases of market entry and market development. Another reason for this strategy is that incumbents often have a dominant position in the foreign markets as many retail operations cannot be easily exported without adaptation. Therefore, they choose partners and retail brands that are already market leaders in their home countries or at least offer a well-known brand in that specific market. After the acquisition, the retail chains are rarely rebranded because of the low level of awareness of the brand *Watson* in Europe. Instead, local brands offer the consumers the familiar shopping experience and symbolise local vicinity. Hence, they are able to operate in heterogeneous markets with diverse formats and concepts and yet still realise economies of scale with an efficient procurement system. Even within China *A.S. Watson* tailors its offers to specific customer demands. Dominic Lai, managing director, puts it this way: "Our offer is different in Shanghai from in the south. This isn't cookie-cutter expansion" (Danaher 2009).

Figure 8.9   Number of Stores Worldwide

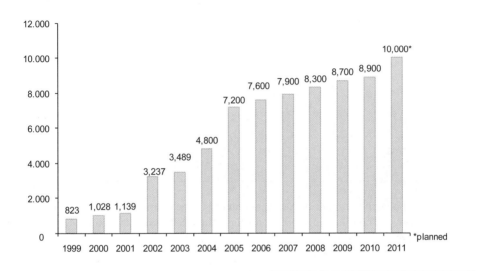

The group's strategy includes a diversified product offering and an expanding customer base owing to new store growth. For its acquisitions *A.S. Watson* chooses partners whose business cultures and operating formats show strong similarities to itself. The advantages realised through mergers outweigh the purely operational level and display strong strategic opportunities. "Organic growth plays a major part in our expansion. We are adding an average of one store every day this year" says Ian F. Wade, former Group Managing Director of *A.S. Watson*. The global expansion plan is to reach 10,000 stores by 2011. **Figure 8.9** shows the development of the number of stores worldwide since 1999.

8.8.4   A.S. Watson's International Expansion Pattern

A.S. Watson pursues an aggressive internationalisation strategy with a gradual expansion from Asia to Europe and with a very high number of new store openings each year. This internationalisation can be grouped roughly into the entry of neighbouring Asian countries in the 1980s and 1990s and a second wave into Europe since 2000.

Figure 8.10   Watson's International Expansion Pattern since 1987

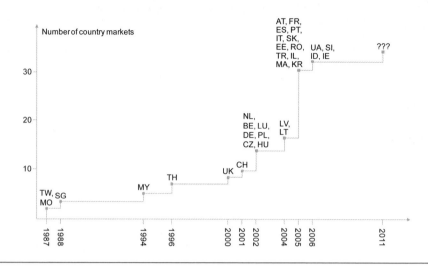

Figure 8.11 shows the number of countries entered in the course of the group's internationalisation process. The following section displays the internationalisation of *A.S. Watson* by geographic areas.

Figure 8.11   Number of Countries entered

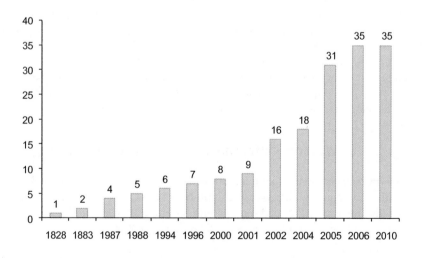

Expansion into Asia

The Philippines were the first foreign market entered by *A.S. Watson* with a pharmacy store. In the course of time, many new *Watsons Your Personal Store* stores (Watson's health & beauty chain) opened. In 1982, *A.S. Watson* became a wholly owned subsidiary of *Hutchison Whampoa Ltd.* and expanded to Taiwan and Macau (1987), Singapore (1988) and Malaysia (1994) with *Watson's the Chemist*.

Since the first outlet opening in Taiwan in 1987, this has become the largest market for *A.S. Watson* in Asia. *A.S. Watson* has a leading position in Taiwan with 400 stores in 2010. Stores include discount shops, drugstores, pharmacies, boutiques and convenience stores. To stay market leader in the Taiwanese market the "New Watsons" programme was launched including process re-engineering and an intensive marketing drive that combined customer service with competitive prices. In 1990, *Fortress* became part of the *A.S. Watson Group* and opened its first store in Taiwan. *Fortress* sells electrical products and provides personal electronics, digital electronics and home appliances to its customers.

In Singapore, the first entry took place in 1988. By now the group had expanded its presence to more than 100 stores. *A.S. Watson* has built strong brand trust, a wide customer base and a leadership position in self-select beauty categories in Singapore. It is no longer just meeting consumers' beauty needs, but also their health needs through pharmacy services.

Expansion into Europe

In 2000, *A.S. Watson* entered its first European market, England, by acquiring *Savers*, a health & beauty chain that offers fast-moving toiletry products. *Savers* operated 176 stores at that time and the discount format was in line with *A.S. Watson's* fast expansion strategy. Now, *Savers* operates over 230 stores in England, Scotland and Wales. *Savers'* retail strategy is a pared down product range, which means that customers can only choose from 3,000 products compared with 10,000 at other key specialists. Its strategy for the future involves opening 50 new stores a year. Since 2002, England's *Superdrug* has been part of *A.S. Watson* as well. *Superdrug* is the second largest health & beauty chain in the UK with over 900 stores nationwide. *Superdrug* offers thousands of own-label products especially tailored to the needs of British customers.

In 2001, *Badaracco* was included into *A.S. Watson's* portfolio, and its wine business was expanded into Europe with the Swiss-based international distributor. Export represents a share of 75 % of total sales, underlining the welcomed international orientation of *A.S. Watson's* partners.

In 2002, *A.S. Watson* acquired the *Kruidvat Group* making *A.S. Watson* the world's third largest beauty retailer. Together with *Kruidvat*, *A.S. Watson* took over *Trekpleister*, *Ici Paris XL* and *Superdrug* and integrated *Rossmann* into the group. *Kruidvat* has a store portfolio of 1,900 stores and operates in the Netherlands, Belgium and Luxembourg. This merger was an important step in their progressive expansion plan in the European market. The merger instantly increased the group's European portfolio to 12 countries. This merger was also an important factor in *A.S. Watson's* expansion strategy as it led to geographical balance for the group's retail business and increased and diversified the group's earnings in Europe. *Kruidvat* was seen as an important door opener for expansion into the Eastern European market, which has high growth potential in terms of GDP and store expansion. In addition to this growth potential, there is also space for an increase in efficiency as the companies have synergies in IT, logistics, accounting, best practices and sales trends. In 2002, *A.S. Watson* also purchased a 40 % stake in the German retail chain *Rossmann* (A.S. Watson 2002). Besides Germany, *Rossmann* is also active in Poland, the Czech Republic and Hungary. Today, *Rossmann* operates 820 stores outside Germany: more than 500 in Poland, nearly 200 in Hungary, about 110 in the Czech Republic, three in Albania and three in Turkey. These stores largely follow the store model developed in Germany and they contributed over one billion euro to *Rossmann's* turnover in 2010. The successful concept will be continued with the opening of more than 100 stores abroad in 2011 (Rossmann 2011).

Drogas was taken over by *A.S. Watson* in 2004. *Drogas* is a well-established health & beauty chain in Latvia and Lithuania. The acquisition was the first step into Eastern Europe where *A.S. Watson* wants to participate from the great potential for economic growth and customer spending. In 2004, *Drogas* operated 85 stores and had a market share of 30 % in the Latvian market. The acquisition was an important strategic factor for the group's expansion: "Latvia and Lithuania is our springboard to the Baltics, the Confederation of Independent States and Nordic markets," says Ian F. Wade.

The acquisition of *Marionnaud* in 2005 made *A.S. Watson* the largest health & beauty retailer as well as luxury & cosmetics retailer in the world. *Marionnaud* is present in France, Austria and Switzerland and adds to *A.S. Watson's* strong family of brands.

Turkey was first entered in 2005 with the acquisition of six stores, which were rebranded the following year under the *Watsons* brand. Now, 35 stores operate in Turkey. Plans are to expand the network to 300 stores by 2016. As a candidate country to join the European Union, Turkey is considered to be a market with huge growth potential.

In 2005, *A.S. Watson* acquired the Russian retail chain *Spektr*, expanding the group's global reach to 34 markets. *Spektr* owns 24 stores in Russia. The first entry to Korea also took place in 2005. Now, the portfolio has expanded to 27 stores.

In 2006, *A.S. Watson* expanded into Slovenia and Indonesia. By acquiring a 65 % stake in *DC*, the Ukraine was also part of the global expansion plan. *DC* is the largest and the only nationwide health & beauty retail chain in the Ukraine with 113 stores. It is operated under the format of a convenience drugstore, offering a comprehensive mix of personal care and toiletry products.

This worldwide expansion of *A.S. Watson* has resulted in a complex group structure with different retail brands and store formats with which a broad target group can be addressed. Despite its worldwide presence, *A.S. Watson* has to offer competitive prices to be successful. Therefore, it attempts to generate synergies in sourcing and selling. In 2004, for example, it standardised its point-of-sale systems in all its subsidiaries and introduced a worldwide uniform electronic point-of-sale system (Wincor Nixdorf 2005).

Further international strategy planning includes business expansion and market penetration across Europe, such as France, Spain, Italy and Scandinavia. However, goals are set to maintain the balance equally between Asian and European business. The group also wants to assess whether the existing European brands and store formats will be suitable for Asian markets.

8.8.5   International Retail Sourcing at A.S. Watson

However, not only is selling important when it comes to international expansion. As stated in section 8.1, the internationalisation of retailing has two main elements: sourcing and selling. Especially for internationally active groups, sourcing is an important component of the internationalisation strategy as, on the one hand, the coordination of buying activities is complex but, on the other hand, it provides high cost saving potential. The extensive network that *A.S. Watson* has established provides many synergies and sourcing opportunities for each retail brand. For this reason, *Watson* established the *ASW International Buying Division*, which centralises and standardises the sourcing practices of the group's global retail operations. Categories of products sourced through international buying include branded goods, own label, general merchandise, food and electricals.

The merger of *A.S. Watson* and *Kruidvat* in 2002 led to synergies with regard to sourcing as many of *Kruidvat's* promotional products and more and more of its standard assortment products are procured in China or other Asian countries. The store formats of the companies were remarkably similar, leading to a combination of *Kruidvat's* extensive European buying network and *A.S. Watson's* unparalleled Asian sourcing capabilities, thereby making possible efficient global sourcing.

A.S. Watson offers an online global procurement management system to bring suppliers and business units together. All business units have access to the procurement system; therefore, chances of multiple purchases and greater volume can be realised. A supplier self-registration area with an international offer base gives suppliers access to a global channel to communicate their offers directly to local *A.S. Watson* subsidiaries. The procedures within the online procurement system are standardised, resulting in less administration and better communication between buyers and suppliers.

Besides this online procurement system, the International Buying Division also holds a large-scale product show, offering a wide range of diversified products that procurement managers from different business units around the world are able to order for their businesses. The goal is to build up group-wide cooperation and harmonisation with regard to international sourcing activities.

The International Buying Division centralises and harmonises the buying practices of the group's global retail operations. It currently works with more than 5,000 suppliers, providing 180,000 individual stock-keeping units (SKUs) to consumers (Global Sources 2011).

8.8.6   Conclusion and Outlook

Over the past 20 years, *A.S. Watson's* speed of expansion has accelerated tremendously. The group now operates retail chains all over Asia and Europe and still plans to continue the strategy of aggressive growth. *A.S. Watson* wishes to benefit from Asia's growth potential by expanding its presence into markets such as China and Singapore. By the end of 2011, it plans to cover more than 100 major and smaller Chinese cities (Bloomberg Businessweek 2010). By contrast, *A.S. Watson* plans to further penetrate European markets to tap into the economic growth in newly developing countries in Eastern Europe.

Because of its international know-how and knowledge of the regional conditions in the target countries it is able to offer exactly the right products and services in order to satisfy customer demand. *A.S. Watson* is meeting the changing demands of consumers, which have grown to be more discerning, demanding greater choices, service, quality, convenience and variety.

❙ Questions

1. The basic internationalisation decision entails the choice between standardisation and adaptation. What strategy does *A.S. Watson* pursue? Comment on the standardisation potential of the health & beauty sector.

2. What are the advantages and disadvantages of capital-intensive market entry strategies in general as well as especially for *A.S. Watson*?

3. In what way does the sequence of *A.S. Watson's* foreign market entries conform to the theoretical concept of psychic distance?

❙ Hints

1. See **Figure 8.1** in this Chapter for the four basic types of international retailing and take into account the culture dependence and standardisation potential of products.

2. See Morschett/Schramm-Klein/Zentes 2010, Sparks 1995, and Lamey 1997 for the general advantages and disadvantages of growth strategies.

3. See Sousa/Bradley 2005 for the concept of psychic distance.

9   Retail Branding and Positioning

The purpose of this Chapter is to explain the concept of retail branding and the advantages of establishing and strengthening the retail brand. The brand architecture of retailers, approaches to measuring brand equity, the concept of brand positioning and principles of successful retail brand management are discussed.

9.1   Emergence of Strategic Retail Marketing

Even though retailing has had the opportunity to be marketing-oriented for a long time because retailers are in closer contact with customers than are manufacturers, mass retailing has been slow to take advantage of this aspect. Higher priority had been placed on buying decisions, operational concerns and short-term objectives than on strategic marketing concepts (Mulhern 1997, p. 104). A lack of a well-defined differentiation between competitors has been a frequently criticised consequence in many retail sectors.

However, this has changed in recent decades. Mainly because of changing industry conditions and increasing management capability in retail companies, a change of attitude towards strategic marketing has been observed. Within the context of strategic marketing, the relevance of establishing a clear-cut and differentiated profile is clearly recognised by retailers, and retail brands are systematically being established and managed (Morschett 2006).

9.2   Retailers as Brands

While in the past the term **brand** has been applied mainly to manufacturer brands (such as *Coca-Cola, Nike* or *Gillette*), the brand concept can be applied to all kind of "products", including retailers.

Some authors define a brand as a name or formal sign. According to the **American Marketing Association**, a brand can be defined as a "name, term, design, symbol, or any other feature that identifies one seller's good or service as distinct from those of other sellers" (www.ama.org). However, separating the brand name from the product or service alters the nature of the brand. If one were to take the *IKEA* logo and link it to a grocery supermarket, it may keep part of its brand strength, but the character of the brand would change with the underlying product. Other definitions therefore encompass the brand name (or brand logo, brand sign) and the branded product to define a brand: "A brand is therefore a product, but one that adds other dimensions that differentiate it in some way from other products designed to satisfy the same need" (Keller 2003, p. 4).

Stores as Branded "Products"

Retail branding is a strategy based on the brand concept that transfers it to a retail company. A retailer's "products" are its stores that can be marketed in a similar way to a branded good. **A retail brand is then a group of the retailer's outlets, which carry a unique name, symbol, logo or combination thereof**. While all retailers constitute brands to some extent, some retail brands are strong, while many are not. Recognition and appreciation by consumers are the essential elements of a strong retail brand (Morschett 2002, p. 108). Retail branding can be understood as a comprehensive and integrated marketing management concept, focussing on building long-term customer loyalty and customer preference.

Retail Brand and Store Brand

The term retail brand has to be distinguished from the term store brand (see Chapter 11). While **retail brand** refers to stores (e.g. *Currys, Lidl, FNAC*), the term **store brand** refers to the product level, and this is used synonymously with private label. While the retail brand is also often used to label store brands, this is not a universal characteristic (Wileman/Jary 1997, p. 17, 134).

Retail Brand Complexity

Retail brands are characterised by enormous complexity, which results from the service attributes of retailers as well as from the multiplicity of brand attributes and consumer-retailer interactions. While manufacturers frequently offer only a few products under one brand and the industrial production process is completed through quality control, customer experience with the retail brand is often shaped by several hundred outlets, with different locations and store designs, thousands of products and dozens of employees in each store, who are also influenced by their moods and emotions. A uniform, consistent and standardised performance and brand message is therefore difficult to convey (Wileman/Jary 1997, pp. 40-42).

Employer Branding and Employee Branding

Two branding themes from other fields are related to retail branding. The term **employer branding** refers to a corporate strategy that uses the branding concept to build an image of the company as a place to work. Thus, the objective is to position the company as an attractive employer and to differentiate it from the competition in the labour market. Given that retailing in general often has reputational problems with highly qualified labour, more and more retail companies have started investing in this type of branding. The term retail branding, however, targets the consumer, not the job candidate.

Employee branding has come up as a recent trend in management literature. The idea is that the experiences of consumers with many organisations, in particular service companies, is dominantly through their employees. In particular for retailers, customers interact with many different store workers at each visit – from salespeople to the cashier. With employee branding, companies try to actively influence the behaviour of their employees so that their behaviour (in their daily work, in particular in their customer interactions) is congruent to their company's brand.

9.3   Advantages of a Retail Brand

Establishing a strong brand can be a key factor to long-term performance (Aaker 1996, p. vii) by providing the retailer with considerable advantages (Keller 2003, pp. 8-12, 59-61; Morschett 2002, pp. 31-41; Bruhn 2005, pp. 27-49):

- An existing retail brand strengthens **brand awareness** and **differentiation** from the competition because it can serve as an anchor for associations with the brand.

- An established brand enhances the **efficiency of marketing measures**. In an age of increasing consumer information overload, established and well-known brands receive more attention than do unknown brands. For example, advertising for strong retail brands is more likely to be perceived and recognised by consumers, resulting in a higher efficiency of marketing budgets.

- From the consumer perspective, strong retail brands **simplify the purchasing process** because there is already some knowledge about the retailer and buyers do not have to search for additional information about assortments, prices, service and so on.

- Strong retail brands also reduce **perceived purchasing risk**. Buying well-known product brands from well-known and trusted retail brands is a purchasing strategy that aims at risk reduction.

- Consequently, strong retail brands may lower the **price sensitivity** of consumers. A well-defined brand profile can establish a preference position that allows a retailer to minimise price competition.

- Strong brands exert **halo effects**. A positive general attitude towards the brand in total positively influences the perception of all specific brand attributes. Considering the impact of these evaluations on the general attitude, a virtuous cycle can develop.

- Strong brands not only represent functional benefits, they can also serve as **symbolic devices**. They represent different values, traits and characteristics. Shopping at a certain retailer might, therefore, allow consumers to project a certain self-image onto themselves and others.

- If a retail company operates in different market segments, **differentiated marketing** with different retail brands facilitates approaching each market segment with a targeted approach. Cannibalisation is easier to avoid and each retail brand can develop its own image – without contradictory image transfers.

- Conversely, a strong brand can be used as a **platform for expansion**. This already occurs when retailers open new outlets, which, from the very start, are loaded with a certain image. Franchising concepts, in which the retail brand is transferred to independent shop owners, clearly illustrate this advantage.

■ A strong retail brand can also facilitate extension into new product ranges. This type of **brand extension** occurs when retailers use their images in one merchandise category to expand into additional categories.

Measurement of Brand Equity

These advantages are enjoyed especially by strong retail brands. However, the measurement of brand equity is not easy, and there is no generally agreed concept. Nonetheless, measurement approaches can generally be classified into two streams, which also differ in their definition of brand equity (Lassar/Mittal/Sharma 1995, p. 12):

■ Financially-oriented, monetary approaches

■ Consumer-oriented approaches.

Monetary Brand Equity

The following definition is typical of the monetary approach: "Brand equity can be thought of as the additional cash flow achieved by associating a brand with the underlying product or service" (Biel 1992, p. RC7). For example, using a complex formula to forecast future revenues for the brand and capitalising them into a present value, the consulting company *Interbrand* estimated that the world's most valuable retail brand in 2010 was *H&M* with a brand equity of about 16.1 billion USD. Other highly valuable global retail brands in the 2010 *Interbrand* ranking were *Amazon.com* (9.665 billion USD), *Dell* (8.88 billion USD) and *Gap* (3.961 billion USD) (www.interbrand.com).

Consumer-oriented Brand Equity

Although in some situations deriving a monetary brand value is important (e.g. for the purpose of selling or licensing the brand), the equity is the result of long-term investment in the brand. For brand management, consumer-oriented brand equity concepts might be more appropriate and sensitive to changes. Keller (1993, p. 1) provided a typical definition: a brand is said to have positive customer-based brand equity when consumers react more favourably to an element of the marketing mix for the brand than they do to the same marketing mix element when it is attributed to a fictitiously named or unnamed version of the product or service. This type of brand equity or brand strength is developed in the mind of the consumer, and the consumer's attitude towards the brand, his associations and experiences with the brand and his evaluation of the brand quality are the most important aspects of measuring brand equity.

Indicators for Retail Brand Equity

Different researchers propose different indicators for measuring consumer-oriented brand strength, which can, aggregated or individually, be considered when managing the brand

and when evaluating the success of certain marketing measures (e.g. Aaker 1996, pp. 7-25, 318-333; Lassar/Mittal/Sharma 1995; Zentes/Morschett 2002, p. 165). Indicators of consumer-oriented retail brand equity are, for instance:

- brand awareness,

- perceived trustworthiness of the brand,

- customer satisfaction with the brand/customer loyalty to the brand,

- brand liking and

- brand differentiation.

Other indicators suggested in the literature for brand equity are not generally appropriate for retail brands. **Price premiums**, for instance, are sometimes used for evaluating brand value. Many successful retailers, however, emphasise their low prices (e.g. *Walmart*, *IKEA*, *Aldi*, *H&M*), and trade off potential price premiums for higher sales volumes or productivity.

9.4   Brand Architecture

As defined above, a retail brand refers to the level of the store group. However, the brand system of a retailer is more complex. **Brand architecture** refers to the internal structuring of the retailer's brands and revolves around how many and what kinds of offers are provided under a certain brand (Ailawadi/Keller 2004, p. 338). Within the **brand hierarchy**, a retailer's brands can be divided into different levels (Keller 2003, pp. 534–565). Retailers have brand names at the level of the retail company as a whole ("corporate brand"), the retail stores, the merchandise (e.g. the store brands) and specific retail services (i.e. banking services or loyalty programmes). Besides the individual branding decision at each level, the interconnection between the levels has to be considered. Branding at the level of the merchandise is discussed in Chapter 11.

As in industrial multi-product companies, retailers with more than one store have to decide whether the stores should carry the same or different brands.

Three general branding strategies can be distinguished at the level of the retail brand (see **Table 9.1** for examples):

- An **umbrella brand strategy**, where all the stores of the company carry the same brand, and in most cases the corporate brand is differentiated by a sub-brand (sometimes this is called an endorsed brand)

- A **family brand strategy**, in which the groups of stores of the retail company (usually different retail formats) carry different brands, i.e. the brands are strictly separated

- A **mixed strategy**, which applies an umbrella brand for some store formats and separates others by using different brand names.

Table 9.1 Branding Strategies of Different Retail Companies

Brand Strategy	Retail Company	(Selected) Retail Brands of the Company
Umbrella Brand	Tesco	Tesco Extra, Tesco (Superstores), Tesco Metro, Tesco Express, Tesco Homeplus, Tesco Lotus
	EDEKA	EDEKA aktiv markt, EDEKA neukauf, E-Center
	Système U	Marché U, Super U, Hyper U, Utile
	Toys 'R' Us	Toys 'R' Us, Babies 'R' Us
Family Brands	Kingfisher	B&Q, Castorama, Brico Dépôt, Screwfix, Koçtas
	Dixons Retail	Currys, dixon.co.uk, PC City, Electro World, Elkjøp
	Metro	Metro Cash & Carry, Real, Kaufhof, Media-Markt, Saturn
	Sears Holding	Sears, Kmart, Land's End
	Inditex	Zara, Pull & Bear, Massimo Dutti, Bershka, Stradivarius
Mixed Strategy	Coop (CH)	Coop, Coop pronto, coop@home, Coop bau+hobby, Coop City, Interdiscount, Fust, Microspot, TopTip, Christ
	Migros	M, MM, MMM, m-electronics, Migros LeShop, Denner, Globus, OBI (as franchise partner in Switzerland), Office World
	Carrefour Group	Carrefour, Carrefour Marché, Carrefour Express, Carrefour City, Dia, Ed
	Groupe Casino	Super Casino, Géant Casino, Petit Casino, Leader Price, Monoprix, Franprix, Cdiscount, Big C, Big C Junior
	GAP, Inc.	Gap, GapKids, babyGap, Gapmaternity, gapbody, Banana Republic, Old Navy, Piperlime, Athleta

The main decision in this context is **brand image transfer vs. brand image separation**. Using an **umbrella brand strategy**, the common brand name leads to a substantial image transfer. Consumers transfer the associations they carry for *Tesco Superstores* at least partly to *Tesco Express* stores. All stores are part of one large brand and have to convey the same message to the consumer, if the brand image is to remain strong and uniform. A **family brand strategy**, by contrast, is usually the result of market segmentation and an unambiguous brand focus with different brand attributes for each store format. *Carrefour* hypermarkets, for example, target a similar customer segment as *Carrefour* supermarkets but they probably appeal to a different group of customers than does *Carrefour*'s discount chain *Dia*. An image transfer would, therefore, probably not benefit either of the stores.

Thus, if a company wants to address different customer segments with different stores that have **different positioning**, then using a family brand strategy is more appropriate. In addition, separate brands facilitate divestments and changes in the portfolio. For example, at the beginning of 2011 *Carrefour* announced it intended to sell the discount chain. Since the chain carries its own name, a new owner can easily maintain the established retail brand, which may enhance the selling price.

A recent trend seems to be a stronger focus on one retail brand and the use of an umbrella brand. For example, *REWE* in Germany traditionally operated supermarkets under the labels *minimal*, *REWE*, *HL* and *Stüssgen*. In a strategic move in 2006, it united all these 3,000 supermarkets overnight under the common retail brand *REWE*. Given that many retail companies are highly diversified, however, and that they used to have family brands, this results in more mixed strategies. For example, *Carrefour* has renamed its supermarkets worldwide from *Champion* to *Carrefour Market*, and many of its convenience stores around the world are now labelled *Carrefour Express* or *Carrefour City*. Similarly, French retailer *Casino* has given an umbrella brand to some of its store formats and now labels its hypermarkets *Géant Casino* (formerly only *Géant*), its supermarkets *Super Casino* (formerly only *Casino*) and its small neighbourhood stores *Petit Casino*. *Macy's Department Stores* in the US comprise many stores that were formerly part of small regional chains and that for a long time maintained their names. But in the past decade, *Macy's* has renamed most of these stores into *Macy's*.

Branding Strategies after Acquisitions

In large retail companies that operate different store formats and different chain store groups, the brand architecture is frequently reviewed. In particular, an acquisition of additional stores or a complete business usually requires the strategic decision on whether to maintain the established retail brand of the acquired chain or to convert it into the acquiring company's retail brand. Given the many incidences of acquisitions in recent decades, there are many examples of either decision. For example, *Walmart* maintained the name *ASDA* in the UK (but added "*by Walmart*"), while it quickly changed the name of *Wertkauf* and *Interspar* in Germany into *Walmart* after the acquisition. *Macy's* converted all *May* department stores into *Macy's* stores and *ASDA* will most likely change the name of the acquired *Netto* stores into *ASDA*. *Migros*, after acquiring the Swiss discounter *Denner*, continues to lead the group under the name *Denner*. The French *Boulanger Group*, who bought the stores of *Saturn* in France, will have to convert the stores into *Boulanger* markets, but when the Swiss retail group *Coop*, which already operated an electronics retail chain under the retail brand *Interdiscount* acquired the competitor *Fust*, it continued to operate both formats under a dual brand strategy.

Generally, the branding decision after an acquisition is similar to the decision in other multi-format retail companies: should there be a strong **image link** between the acquiring company and the acquired retail stores or not. But other aspects have to be considered in addition. For example, the acquiring company has to decide on the **intended future positioning** of the acquired chain. If that is not fully congruent to its own retail brand, it might be wise to maintain the acquired retail brand to be able to clearly separate both company parts (the old store chain and the new store chain). Furthermore, the acquired store chain may have accumulated substantial **brand equity** over time. For instance, consumers in the UK liked shopping at *ASDA* and trusted the brand and, thus, customer loyalty to the brand gave it high brand equity. By eliminating the old brand name, *Walmart* would have risked destroying this brand equity and, consequently, decreasing the value of the acquired stores. Converting store names into the acquiring company's retail brand could also lead to negative customer reactions, protests and maybe even boycotts (e.g. if the acquiring company is seen as a foreign intruder). Finally, a company may not be free in its decision since the buying contract with the former owner may not allow it to continue with the old brand name. For example, when *Carrefour* leaves Thailand, it will not want the new owner *Groupe Casino* using the name *Carrefour* and it will not sell the right to use the retail brand name but only the stores itself.

Retail Branding of Online-Shops

A particularly delicate question is the branding of online shops within a multichannel strategy. This question was discussed in Chapter 4.

Retail Branding in Retailer Cooperatives

A type of retail institution that has strong market relevance in many countries and sectors is retailer cooperatives. These are cooperations between independent retail companies, often between many independent single store operations. Well-known examples of such institutions that are not traditional monolithic companies but rather are networks of retailers that jointly carry out certain central functions are *Intersport*, the worldwide leading sporting goods retailer, *ACE Hardware* in the USA and certain large food retailing groups such as *Leclerc* in France, *REWE* and *EDEKA* in Germany and *Shoprite* in the US. In European electronics retailing, three out of the top 10 are such retailer cooperatives: *Euronics*, *Expert* and *Electronic Partner*.

Initially, most of these cooperatives were founded to provide a centralised purchasing organisation that allows smaller retailers to jointly gain economies of scale. However, their functions often grew over time and, nowadays, many of these cooperatives provide central marketing and they have often established a retail brand together. The abovementioned examples all have their stores linked by a common retail brand, similar to a franchise system. The logo, corporate identity, brand colours and so on are harmonised, which enables the group to have joint marketing, for example in the form of common TV advertising campaigns.

However, comprising many independent retailers, this independence is sometimes also signalled in the retail brand by way of co-branding. For example, retailers that belong to the *Intersport* group often use their own names as well as the group retail brand (e.g. *Intersport Meier*). Electronics stores that belong to the *Electronic Partner* group are usually labelled in a similar way, e.g. *EP: Müller*. Other groups, such as *REWE*, do not use co-branding, but the stores – of different owners – are all labelled *REWE*.

The advantages of each type are evident: while using a completely uniform brand for all stores, regardless of ownership, creates an image of a uniform, very large system that is perceived as one large retail company, the co-branding strategy strengthens the dual character of a retailer cooperative. It emphasises the local ownership of the specific shop and signals to the customer that the store has a strong regional component. This may make it easier to establish local customer loyalty. At the same time, it indicates that the retail store belongs to a large chain, and it can, thus, utilise the synergy effect of national advertising. It may also signal to the customer that the store has the necessary buying power to offer attractive prices.

9.5   Retail Brand Positioning

Strategic brand management starts with a clear understanding of what the brand is to represent and how it should be positioned relative to competitors (Keller 2003, p. 44; Wortzel 1987, p. 47). **Positioning** is the deliberate and proactive process of defining and influencing consumer perceptions of a marketable object, with a strong focus on the competitive position. A product is thus positioned in the minds of consumers (Arnott 1993, p. 24).

Positioning usually applies certain fixed dimensions along which the retail brand defines its position relative to its competitors. Positioning diagrams represent the location of different brands as well as the different target groups' ideal points in a two-dimensional space (see **Figure 9.1**).

Figure 9.1   Differently Positioned Retailers in the Price-quality Space

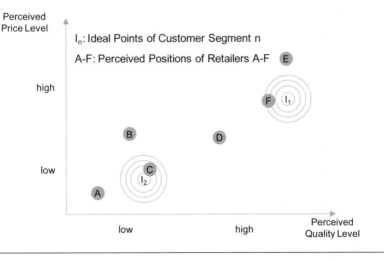

Market Segmentation

Market segmentation is often considered necessary for successful brand positioning. Market segmentation refers to the process of dividing a (heterogeneous) total market by certain attributes into (more homogeneous) partial markets. **Segmentation criteria** can be demographic, socioeconomic, lifestyle, geographic or many others. Segmentation thus includes the selection of one or several market segments and targets marketing towards the purchasing behaviour, motives and expectations of these groups. However, segmentation is often considered difficult for retailers within given catchment areas and those with the need for high customer traffic in their stores, which require appealing to broad customer groups (Wileman/Jary 1997).

Positioning is often based on the two generic competitive strategies of Porter (1980): cost/price leadership vs. differentiation (similar to **Figure 9.1**). While this broad classification can also be applied to retailing, researchers have proposed other frameworks, because retailing reality shows that there are many options for differentiation. The following are among the positioning dimensions most frequently proposed (see e.g. Wortzel 1987, p. 50; Davis 1992, p. 14; Morschett/Swoboda/Schramm-Klein 2006):

- Quality of merchandise

- Variety of merchandise

- Convenience

- Price

- Customer service

- Location

- Store atmosphere.

Successful positioning can be based on any retail activities, and a unique profile along the various dimensions yields a clear position that is the prerequisite of a strong brand. At the same time, the advertising spending of retailers has increased strongly over the past few decades and – as an indicator of the increasing relevance of retail branding – in many countries, retail stores are among the most heavily advertised "products" in terms of media spending.

Retail Brand Image

Retail brand positioning is based on a set of fixed dimensions along which a retailer is perceived to be located. However, the retail brand is broader than is the actual positioning. The total **brand knowledge** that a consumer associates with a brand is relevant to the brand strength.

The **associative network model** views memory as consisting of a network of nodes that represent stored information and connecting links. Any type of information connected to the brand is stored in the memory network, including verbal, visual, abstract and acoustic information. **Retail brand image can be defined as perceptions about a retailer as reflected by the brand associations stored in consumers' memories.** The strength of the brand can be evaluated by analysing the various relevant associations. Their uniqueness, favourability, strength and the certainty with which consumers link the information with the brand are the dimensions to consider (Krishnan 1996; Keller 1993). Retail brand image is complex and it is connected to an array of other images, both at a higher level as well as in the form of sub-images. The retail store format image (i.e. category killer image), shopping centre image, location image, price image, merchandise image and other components of the store or its context are all connected to the retail brand image and are part of the memory network of the consumer. **Figure 9.2** gives an example of a possible associative network that customers typically have of *IKEA*.

Figure 9.2   Consumer's Associative Network of IKEA (Fictitious Example)

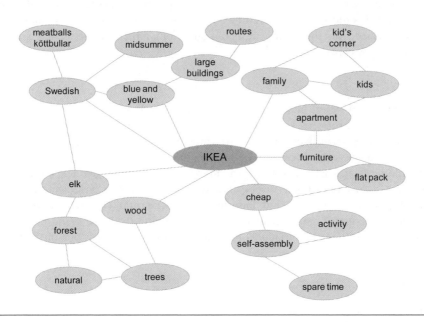

Source: adapted from Morschett 2006, p. 532.

9.6   Principles of Successful Retail Branding

All retail marketing instruments affect the retail brand, as illustrated by the notion of the comprehensive retail brand image, which is made up of a universe of interconnected associations. To develop a strong and successful brand, three basic principles are mentioned in the literature (Morschett 2002, pp. 43-47):

- Differentiation from competitors
- Long-term marketing continuity
- Coherence of different marketing components.

Differentiation

Achieving differentiation (in consumers' minds) is a central characteristic of a brand (Aaker 1996, p. 329), as was pointed out in the discussion on positioning. Higher levels of differentiation from competitors are expected to lead to higher profitability. Only brands that are well distinguished from their competitors can build long-term customer loyalty and avoid store switching by consumers.

Continuity

Establishing a clear brand image is a long-term process. Brands are established through consumer learning processes. Consumers store associations in their memories. Brand associations become stronger over time and they must be reinforced by repeated exposure to the same brand messages because they might otherwise fade away. Past investment in brand building is at least partly lost if the brand marketing changes. Thus, continuity is important. Also, risk reduction is one of a brand's main functions. Consumers trust a brand because it entails a standardised and uniform offer under a certain brand name. Some of the world's most successful brands demonstrate that retaining the same brand message and communication (with slight variations) for years and even decades is one of the key prerequisites of successful branding.

Coherence

The **retail marketing mix** includes all marketing instruments that a retailer can deploy. The term mix indicates that the instruments are not used in isolation, but that they jointly influence the consumer. In order to be successful, all marketing measures must be coordinated to ensure a close fit with one another and that all measures convey the same brand message.

Because inconsistency makes a brand image fragile and consumers strive for internal harmony or congruity in their knowledge and information ("theory of cognitive dissonance"), creating coherence between all the different facets of the retail brand is crucial for success. Considering the complexity of the retail environment, ensuring a fit among the marketing instruments and all brand contact points is challenging. *IKEA, Sephora, dm-drogerie markt,*

The Body Shop, Zara and others are examples of successful brands that manage to project a uniform image with their store atmospheres, merchandise, pricing, communication and service.

9.7   Conclusion and Outlook

Some of the most successful retailers in the world have developed into strong brands without having consciously managed their brands (Wileman/Jary 1997, p. 20). However, while this is true, it is important to note that many successful retailers have developed strong brands by – even though sometimes unconsciously – adopting the abovementioned principles of branding. From the very beginning, *Aldi, IKEA, Tesco, Walmart, Migros* and others have had clear and distinct profiles. They have pursued their own marketing approaches over several decades and, supported by strong corporate cultures, have been coherent in all their activities. Differentiation, continuity and coherence in these cases were often ensured by the founders, who, over the years, developed a clear understanding of what their companies should stand for – and followed that through rigorously.

Brand management gains additional relevance through the internationalisation of retailers (e.g. should retailers use the same name in all countries?), with the ongoing wave of mergers & acquisitions in retailing (e.g. should an acquired retail chain be operated under its old retail brand or be adapted to the acquirer's brand?) and with multichannel retailing. Especially in the case of store retailers expanding their businesses onto the Internet, the strategic decision on using the same retail brand across channels or separating the Internet shop from the store outlets is crucial and far-reaching (see Chapter 4).

In recent years, competition and changing consumer behaviour have increased the relevance of retail branding tremendously. Such branding aims at enhancing differentiation and customer loyalty. Retail brand management includes all components of the retail marketing mix and develops a strategic understanding of the intended positioning of the retail company. Developing a retail branding strategy helps ensure the coherence of all the marketing messages and market appearances of the company. Successful companies change over time, but considering the prerequisites of successful branding, the brand core should remain stable.

❘ Further Reading

AAKER, D. (1996): Building Strong Brands, New York et al.

MORSCHETT, D.; SWOBODA, B.; SCHRAMM-KLEIN, H. (2006): Competitive Strategies in Retailing: An Investigation of the Applicability of Porter's Framework for Food Retailers, in: Journal of Retailing and Consumer Services, Vol. 13, No. 4, pp. 275-287.

WILEMAN, A.; JARY, M. (1997): Retail Power Plays: From Trading to Brand Leadership, New York.

9.8   Case Study: TK Maxx[1]

9.8.1   Profile, History and Status Quo

TK Maxx was launched in Europe in 1994 to introduce the **off-price concept** that had already been successfully operated by the parent company *TJX Companies, Inc.* in the USA for a long time, to the United Kingdom. Today, *TK Maxx* is Europe's leading off-price retailer and the only major one that is operating in several countries. The idea behind the strategy of *TK Maxx* is to offer great value on designer and brand name family apparel ("off-price upscale apparel"), including women's footwear, lingerie, jewellery, accessories, home fashions and other merchandise such as luggage and toys, often with a discount of up to 60 % compared with the original price. This is possible because *TK Maxx* buys opportunistically and countercyclically and often procures excess stocks of designer brands. Still, over 90 % of the goods are from current designer collections (Textilwirtschaft 2010, p. 7).

Nowadays, *TK Maxx Europe* operates more than 300 stores in the United Kingdom, Ireland, Germany and Poland. The first German store was opened 2007 in Lübeck in May 2011, and the company already operates 50 stores there. In future years, *TK Maxx* plans to open up to 300 stores in German cities (Textilwirtschaft 2010, p. 7; Textilwirtschaft 2011, p. 11; Wirtschaftswoche 2009, p. 74). *TK Maxx* prefers store areas of about 3,500 m² in central downtown areas, shopping centres or power centres.

TK Maxx is the European subsidiary of *TJX Companies, Inc.* group, the leading off-price retailer of apparel and home fashions in the United States and the largest in the world. With a family brand strategy, *TJX Companies Inc.* runs the retail brands *T.J. Maxx* – the US role model for *TK Maxx* – as well as *Marshalls, Shoe Megashop by Marshalls* and *HomeGoods* in the USA, *Winners, HomeSense* and *StyleSense* in Canada and *TK Maxx* and *HomeSense* in Europe. All *TJX* chains are specialised in off-price retailing concepts and they use the same business strategy, with a strong focus on family apparel, home, shoes and accessories, depending on the chain.

In 2010, *TJX Companies, Inc.* had revenues of 21.9 billion USD, an 8 % increase over the previous year. The company runs more than 2,700 stores in six countries with approximately 154,000 associates. In Europe, *TJX* generated revenues of 1.8 billion EUR in the accounting year 2010 (Textilwirtschaft 2011, p. 10). The vision of *TJX* is to grow as a global, off-price value company and to exploit the full potential of the existing country markets (see **Fig-**

---

[1] Sources used for this case study include the different websites of the company, various annual and interim reports as well as investor relations presentations and the explicitly cited sources.

ure 9.3). Therefore, the approach to growth is strategic and deliberate, and investments in its existing businesses are prioritised.

Figure 9.3 Number of Stores of TJX in 2010 and Potential for New Openings

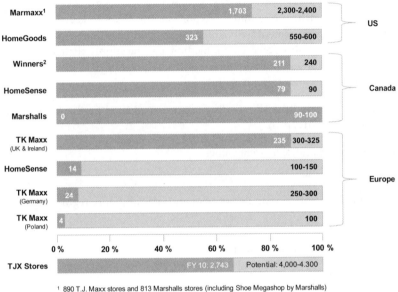

¹ 890 T.J. Maxx stores and 813 Marshalls stores (including Shoe Megashop by Marshalls)
² including Stylesense

Source: TJX Companies, Inc. 2011.

9.8.2 Development and Positioning of the TK Maxx Brand

The prelude to the retail brand *TK Maxx* was the development and launch of *T.J. Maxx* in the United States in 1977. Hitherto, the parent company of *T.J. Maxx* had run the *Zayre* discount department store chain, which was specialised in apparel for the whole family. With the success of *T.J. Maxx*, the company grew and was renamed in *The TJX Companies, Inc.* With the start of the **internationalisation** of *TJX* to the United Kingdom in 1994, the retail brand *TK Maxx* was born. The slight name change for Europe (*TK* instead of *T.J.*) was carried out to avoid confusion with the established British retail chain *TJ Hughes* (which is not associated to *TJX*). *TK Maxx* uses a similar concept as its affiliated company *T.J. Maxx* in the United States, and is the European *TJX* off-price brand pendant in the sector of family apparel.

All *TJX* retail brands make use of the same strategy, namely the utilisation of the off-price concept with no-frills stores. Furthermore, the brand messages are based on the same core statements as well. The philosophy at *TJX Europe*, which is consistently converted at *TK Maxx*, can be described as "labels for less" and contains brand name merchandise at great value. This philosophy rests on the buying power and the **opportunistic buying** strategy of *TJX*. *TJX* employs over 700 people in 12 buying offices in its purchasing organisation, which source from over 60 countries around the world and have a pool of more than 12,000 suppliers. Compared with other retailers, *TJX* acts more like a "global sourcing machinery" (TJX Inc., 2011). The buying power of *TJX* is combined with aggressive inventory management and a low cost structure within the whole supply chain to keep costs down. In this context, the goal is "procurement with added value" and passing the savings onto customers. As a consequence of this procurement method and the supply chain efficiency, *TJX* and its store chain can offer substantially lower prices, which are 20 % to 60 % less compared with department stores and specialty stores.

This off-price concept and the USP of *TK Maxx* are explained by the company as follows (TJX Companies, Inc. 2010, p. 3):

- Brand name merchandise at great values

- Opportunistic buying

- Substantially lower prices than department and specialty store regular prices

- Rapidly changing assortments

- Aggressive inventory management

- Low cost structure.

In the corporate claim, the fact of rapidly changing assortments ("never the same store twice") is outlined as the experience of treasure hunting, which is popular with women (Thompson 2009), and this is used as an argument for frequent store visits since there is a chance of discovering something new every time. Another aspect that underlines the price value of the *TK Maxx* retail brand is the design of its stores, which are designed as no-frills stores to keep costs down. This **low cost design** is also used as a marketing message. For example, the company explains to its customers (via its webpage): "In our stores, we do not have lustres hanging from the ceiling. And there are no expensive leather sofas. ... What we save on that directly benefits the customer" (TK Maxx 2011). Furthermore, the company strongly emphasises that it does not sell "cheap products". It clearly points out to its customers in its advertising that it does not have the cheapest jeans in its assortment but, instead, high quality designer jeans for an unbeatable price.

Although this concept does not address low budget customers, all *TJX* retail chains stand for a unique offer to its customers and are considered as a top store for **smart shoppers**. The typical target customer is female, between 25 and 54 years old and middle or upper-middle income earners. Moreover, the typical target customer is fashion and value conscious and shops regularly in high end department stores and specialty stores. The positioning of *T.J. Maxx/TK Maxx* concerning the perceived price and quality level is illustrated in **Figure 9.4.**

In its positioning, the company is similar to factory outlet centres and thus it manages to occupy an otherwise empty space in the positioning chart: **high quality combined with low prices**. The product offer of TK Maxx is on a higher quality level than that of other mid-price retailers since it comprises designer clothing. The price level for those designer brands, however, is much lower than at the department stores or the speciality stores that carry these designer brands in their permanent assortment. The German magazine *Wirtschaftswoche* titled its article on the company in 2009 with **"Versace, just cheaper"** (Wirtschaftswoche 2009, p. 74). Different from factory outlet centres, though, the brand offer of *TK Maxx* is fast changing so the customer does not know what he or she will find.

Figure 9.4   Price-Quality Positioning of Selected Fashion (Retail) Brands

Obviously, this positioning is "bought" with cost savings in other quality dimensions, such as the uncertainty about the current product offer, the no-frills stores and so on. But these dimensions are – as usual – not easy to illustrate on a positioning chart. Actually, *TK Maxx* even emphasises in its advertising that the focus is on the product, not the surroundings. These other quality facets should, however, be captured when analysing retail brand image.

9.8.3   TK Maxx's Advertising

The main aspects of the brand message of *TK Maxx* are "big brands, small prices" and "up to 60 % less, always" and illustrate the central thread of *TK Maxx*' brand strategy. *TK Maxx* provides its customers a differentiated shopping experience. Through the factors fashion, quality, well-known designer brands and an attractive price structure, *TK Maxx* offers its customers valuable arguments to buy in its stores. Dependent on *TK Maxx* sourcing practice, shopping at *TK Maxx* stands for a kind of treasure hunt, combined with aspects of bargain hunting and entertainment. Through volatile quantities in the buying process, a *TK Maxx* store supplies a unique offer and excellent value on brand name merchandise. These changes are so profound that *TJX* designs its stores without internal walls, which means that the space that is allocated to each product group is flexible, depending on changing market conditions and current sourcing opportunities.

At two different *TK Maxx* stores, the customer will not be able to find the same offer. And during two subsequent visits to the same *TK Maxx* store, this is also not likely the same applies. The strength of *TK Maxx* is its rapid turnover of inventory, which is also the base for strong merchandise margins. As a side effect, the rapidly changing assortment is used to create a sense of urgency and excitement in the customers' minds and encourage them to visit *TK Maxx* stores frequently.

Figure 9.5   Selected Advertising Messages of T.J. Maxx/TK Maxx

Our shoppers mean the world to us

Always up to 60 % less

Step out in style   Love Fashion

Znane marki zawsze do 60% laniey [Well-known brands always up to 60 % less]

Immer neu, immer anders [Always new, always different]

Even more of a bargain

Inspire your inner maxxinista

big labels small prices

real designers. real savings. really.

Loving your style, sister. Fill your basket to the brim, with delicious big labels for less.

We're smart shoppers, just like you.

style savers welcome to big labels

Modnie czy wygodnie? [Fashionable or cosy?]

Never the same store twice

Willkommen im Fashion-Paradies [Welcome to the paradise of fashion]   Love TK Maxx

big brand style, wallet friendly prices.

To communicate these facts to the consumer, *TK Maxx* uses consistent advertising messages. *TK Maxx* and its pendant *T.J. Maxx* in the United States are mindful of this insight and uses a bundle of advertising messages for the retail brand in several countries. Although not always the same slogan, the slogans are around a common theme. **The main** aspects of the brand message of *TK Maxx* are "big brands, small prices" and "up to 60 % less, always" and illustrate the central thread of *TK Maxx'* brand strategy. *TK Maxx* provides its customers a differentiated shopping experience. Through the factors fashion, quality, well-known designer brands and an attractive price structure, *TK Maxx* offers its customers valuable arguments to buy in its stores. Dependent on *TK Maxx* sourcing practice, shopping at *TK Maxx* stands for a kind of treasure hunt, combined with aspects of bargain hunting and entertainment. Through volatile quantities in the buying process, a *TK Maxx* store supplies a unique offer and excellent value on brand name merchandise. These changes are so profound that *TJX* designs its stores without internal walls, which means that the space that is allocated to each product group is flexible, depending on changing market conditions and current sourcing opportunities.

At two different *TK Maxx* stores, the customer will not be able to find the same offer. And during two subsequent visits to the same *TK Maxx* store, this is also not likely the same applies. The strength of *TK Maxx* is its rapid turnover of inventory, which is also the base for strong merchandise margins. As a side effect, the rapidly changing assortment is used to create a sense of urgency and excitement in the customers' minds and encourage them to visit *TK Maxx* stores frequently.

Figure 9.5 shows a selection of *TK Maxx* advertising messages. *TK Maxx* uses its low prices and designer labels at the core of its advertising campaigns with a repeated mentioning of "always up to 60 % less". This advertising slogan functions as a profiling towards other competitors. Consequently, *TK Maxx* distinguishes between the prices of its competitors and attempts to build long-term customer loyalty, beyond the price image, as well. It is noteworthy that the message is homogeneous worldwide; often the slogans are even used in English, not in the host country's language.

To increase customer awareness of the retail brand, *TK Maxx* pursues advertising campaigns on television and in print media. In 2009, *TK Maxx* spent 2.4 million GBP on print campaigns which were in the focus in 2008 and 2009. In 2010, the focus changed towards TV advertising. For example, *TK Maxx* spent about three million GBP on a Christmas television campaign in 2010 (Emap Business Publications 2010). In 2007, *TK Maxx* launched a new homepage in the UK and later also in the other European markets. The Internet becomes, obviously, more and more central in a retailer's marketing strategy. With this new homepage, *TK Maxx* created the possibility of buying gift vouchers online as well as signing up for alerts about new stock. This new homepage was part of *TK Maxx's* media planning, which had a budget of 6.4 million GBP in 2007 (New Media Age 2007, p. 2). In 2009, the homepage was relaunched and supplemented by an **online shop** to exploit new target groups. For *TK Maxx*, this was its entrance into **e-commerce**. The online shop started with selling designer handbags, but the product categories were extended quickly (Thompson 2009). Nowadays, almost the whole assortment of *TK Maxx* is available online in the United Kingdom. There are, though, no online shops in most other European countries.

Recently, the activities of *TK Maxx* in **social media** have been used to strengthen the brand and to bind existing customers. The business concept of *TK Maxx* has a huge potential to create interaction between customers on the Internet, e.g. through viral marketing forms, since "bargain hunting" is well suited to such a phenomenon. During the past two years, the so-called social web has gained in importance through services such as Facebook or Twitter. Therefore, *TK Maxx* decided to contact its customers with this type of media as well. *TK Maxx* operates its own *Twitter* account to provide customers and "followers" with fashion news. Through the active creation of a follower pool, *TK Maxx* can communicate new offers to its target market. Furthermore, a proactive dialogue with the preferred target group, the smart shoppers, is possible. In order to inform bargain hunters that do not use a *Twitter* account, *TK Maxx* uses *RSS feeds* to communicate latest info, for instance about new offers in the shops. It has also launched its own *Facebook* account. Through the creation of a community on this online platform, *TK Maxx* can achieve an individual sales approach and a dialogue for customer acquisition and retention. Furthermore, the draft and implementation of campaigns as well as the control of operations is conceivable. Moreover, the activation of fans and a proactive dialogue with the target group, considering the communication guidelines of the *TK Maxx*, is possible. Through the posting of prize games, special promotions, actual offers and news from the shops, the involvement of the customers will be improved. Another pillar in *TK Maxx's* online appearance is the *TK Maxx* fashion blog, which offers a variety of content on fashion, lifestyle, accessories, shoes, living and much more. The fashion blog has an editorial support and is permanently actualised with new contents, topics and pictures (TWT 2010). *TK Maxx* has coordinated its online activities to bundle the customer approach in the field of social media to generate a uniform image in online users' minds.

9.8.4   TK Maxx' Image

All these activities lead to a clear image of *TK Maxx* in the minds of consumers which can be seen, for example, when browsing through fashion blogs, discussion forums on the Internet and other commentaries on the brand. First, it can be noticed that *TK Maxx* (and, similarly, *TJ Maxx* in the USA) is interesting enough to consumers to discuss the brand on diverse forums. The brand seemingly has high involvement customers and provokes discussions and information exchange about the assortment, prices and bargains. **Figure 9.6** shows a **network of terms** that consumers associate with *TK Maxx* and its stores. This associative network was created on the basis of blog entries and discussions in boards.

Figure 9.6	Consumers' Associative Network of TK Maxx

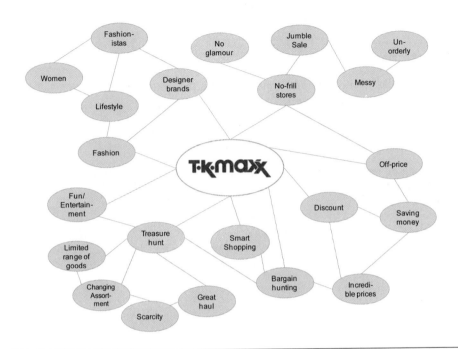

9.8.5   Summary and Outlook

Since 1977, the company has pursued a similar, synergistic off-price concept. The success of *TK Maxx* is based on its flexible, value-oriented business model and its opportunistic buying practice. Over the years, *TK Maxx*, as well as its affiliated firm *T.J. Maxx*, has established itself as a provider of value on family apparel and a creator of purchasing experience and entertainment, evoked through a kind of treasure hunt experience and rapidly changing assortments. Furthermore, *TK Maxx* has a clear understanding of what its strategy stands for and followed it in all countries where *TK Maxx* is present, for example in the United Kingdom as well as in Germany.

TK Maxx exploits a high touch experience in its stores. Through "bargain hunting", the customer is active and highly involved during the whole shopping process. Furthermore, *TK Maxx* also transfers this customer involvement outside its shops. With the online shop in the United Kingdom, fashion blog and Facebook and Twitter accounts, *TK Maxx* carries on the idea of bargain hunting and achieves continuing engagement with its customers.

The off-price concept is an important component in the customer approach and is reflected in all advertising messages of *TK Maxx*. Moreover, the messages are also standardised in different countries to create a consistent image of the company.

| Questions

1. Differentiation, continuity and consistency are three success factors for retail brands. Use these concepts to analyse *TK Maxx's* brand management.

2. Where can you identify discrepancies and potential conflicts between the brand image of *TK Maxx* and its everyday operative practices?

3. Would it be recommendable for *TK Maxx* to use different advertising strategies in different countries? Discuss.

Part III
Marketing Mix
in Retailing

10   Store Location – Trading Area Analysis and Site Selection

Symbolised by the often cited saying that the three most important success factors in retailing are "location, location and location", store location is considered to be one of the most important elements in retail marketing strategy, because it is a long-term decision, associated with long-term capital commitment. Site selection is, therefore, associated with distinct planning processes to solve complex location decisions. In this Chapter, the focus is on bricks-and-mortar retail outlets. The different types of retail locations, the main elements of location decisions and techniques for retail site assessment will be discussed.

10.1   The Importance of Location to Retail Companies

The selection of retail store locations is one of the most significant decisions in retail marketing because in store-based retailing, good locations are key elements for attracting customers to the outlets and sometimes they can even compensate for an otherwise mediocre retail strategy mix. A good location, therefore, can lead to strong competitive advantages, because location is considered one of the elements of the retail marketing mix that is "unique" and thus cannot be imitated by competitors.

Location decisions are highly complex because of the large number of factors that have to be considered, and the costs associated with, for example, opening new stores can be very high. Site selection is, therefore, a **long-term decision** that implies a long-term capital commitment. Once a retail site has been chosen, either for a retailer to build its own store or to sign a long-term retail contract, there is little flexibility, because this decision usually cannot be changed easily without high losses.

Because of its *fixed nature*, location cannot be changed in the short-term contrary to other elements of the retail marketing mix such as price, customer service, product assortment or advertising. These latter factors can be altered if the environment (e.g. consumer behaviour, competition) changes (Wrigley 1988).

The main attention in the context of retail location strategies usually focuses on the opening of new stores. However, location decisions relate to the entire physical structure of retail outlets and are thus more comprehensive. The main types of decisions are (1) the **opening** of new stores, (2) the **extension** of floor space of existing stores, (3) the **relocation** or movement of a store from one place to another within a particular town or area where a better site is available, (4) **rationalisation** decisions, e.g. the closure of individual stores, (5) **repo-**

sitioning of locations, e.g. altering store image by changing the name or appearance, (6) **refurbishment** such as improving or updating the physical environment of an existing outlet and (7) altering the product range and assortment ("**remerchandising**") to tailor the offer more closely to local customers (Hernández/Bennison 2000).

The opening of new stores comprises the most complex type of decision, because it is usually the starting point of activities in a specific geographic area. This section thus focuses on retail location decisions of this type.

10.2   Types of Retail Locations

10.2.1   Overview

Three basic **types of locations** are available for retail stores which will be described in more detail in the following sections: solitary sites, unplanned shopping areas and planned shopping districts. Each of these basic location types has specific advantages and disadvantages (see **Table 10.1**) according to, for example, the size of the catchment area, occupancy costs, pedestrian or vehicle customer traffic, restrictions placed on store operations or convenience of the location.

Apart from these aspects, solitary sites and retail agglomerations such as planned or unplanned shopping districts differ with regard to the possibilities that they offer to consumers in combining shopping purposes. Retail agglomerations offer the advantage that customers may find all their required products in one shopping trip. This is especially important for multi-purpose shopping trips. For example, if customers wish to buy a new clothing outfit, they may prefer to shop at a shopping centre that offers a range of fashion and footwear stores because there is more choice and less risk of not finding a proper combination of clothes, shoes and accessories (Oppewal/Holyoake 2004, p. 61). Also, customers might prefer to combine their shopping for different product categories, e.g. for apparel and for food. While solitary sites usually cannot provide customers with such advantages, retail agglomerations offer the convenience of one-stop shopping for multi-purpose shopping trips.

Table 10.1   Characteristics of the Types of Locations

	Size (1,000 m²)	Trading Area (km)	Shopping Convenience	Pedestrian Travel	Vehicular Traffic	Restrictions on Operations	Typical Format
Unplanned Areas							
Free Standing	varies	5-15	high	low	high	limited	convenience, drug stores, category killers
Urban Locations/ Central Business Districts	varies	varies	low	high	low	limited to medium	specialty stores
Planned Areas							
Neighbourhood/Community Shopping Centres	2.5-30	5-20	high	low	high	medium	supermarkets, discount stores
Power Centres	25-55	5-25	medium	medium	medium	limited	category killers
Enclosed Malls	35-100	5-40	low	high	low	high	department and specialty stores
Lifestyle Centres	15-45	5-25	medium	medium	medium	medium to high	specialty stores and restaurants
Fashion/Specialty Centres	7.5-25	5-25	medium	high	low	high	high-end fashion-oriented specialty stores
Outlet Centres	4.5-40	40-125	low	high	high	limited	off-price stores/ factory outlets
Theme/Festival Centres	7.5-25	N/A	low	high	high	highest	specialty stores and restaurants

Source: adapted from Levy/Weitz 2009, p. 195.

10.2.2   Solitary Sites

This type of location relates to single freestanding outlets that are isolated from other retailers (Gilbert 2003, p. 288). They can, for example, be positioned on roads or near other retailers or shopping centres. Solitary sites usually are characterised by low rental costs or land prices. In most cases, they provide large parking facilities and usually there is no direct competitor in close proximity to the store. However, initial customer attraction might be difficult and might require high advertising expenditure. Such sites are used, for instance, by large store formats in food and general merchandise retailing that offer one-stop shopping convenience or by convenience shops.

10.2.3   Unplanned Shopping Areas

Unplanned shopping areas are retail locations with several outlets in close proximity to each other that have evolved over time. The retail store mix is not the result of long-range planning and for such locations there is no centralised management (Levy/Weitz 2009, p. 195).

Table 10.2   Global Top Ten Retail Strips

Retail Strips	Rent in USD per Square Foot per Year	Change from 2009 to 2010 (in %)
Paris – Champs Élysées	1,225	2.04
New York – Fifth Avenue	1,250	-10.71
Hong Kong – Russell Street, Causeway Bay	1,205	1.30
London – Bond Street	1,174	51.66
Milan – Via Monte Napoleone	929	-1.33
Sydney – Pitt Street Mall	768	71.43
Zurich – Bahnhofstrasse	727	18.57
London – Oxford Street	719	27.69
Rome – Rome City Center	627	-3.85
New York – Madison Avenue	590	-21.33

Source: Colliers International 2010.

The main kinds of unplanned shopping areas are (Berman/Evans 2010, pp. 277-280):

1. **Central business districts (CBDs)** are the traditional "downtown" areas in cities/towns, i.e. "the hub of retailing in a city" (Berman/Evans 2010, p. 277) that offer the greatest density of stores. The rents in CBDs are comparatively high (see **Table 10.2**), even though the popularity of CBDs differs internationally with high popularity in Europe but much lower attractiveness in many US cities.

2. **Secondary business districts (SBD)** are unplanned shopping districts with less wide and deep assortments than in CBDs that are located in larger cities and main streets or high street locations in smaller cities. Larger cities tend to have multiple secondary business districts.

3. **Neighbourhood business districts (NBD)** serve the needs of a single residential area. They typically are situated on major streets and often food retailers are the leading retailers in this kind of location.

4. **Strip** or **string locations ("strip mall")** comprise groups of retail stores that are situated along a street or motorway. For example, car dealership of different brands can often be located next to each other along a major road.

In **Figure 10.1**, the diverse types of retail locations are displayed.

Figure 10.1   Unplanned Business Districts

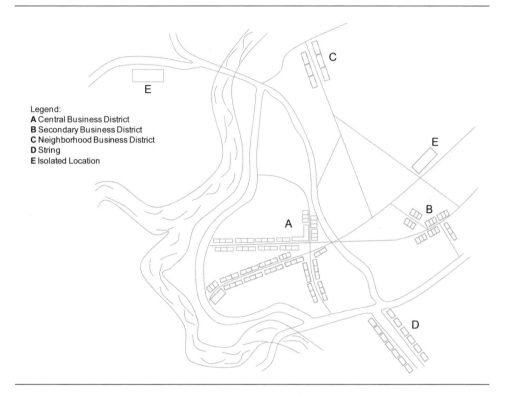

Legend:
A Central Business District
B Secondary Business District
C Neighborhood Business District
D String
E Isolated Location

Source: Berman/Evans 2010, p.281.

10.2.4   Planned Shopping Districts/Shopping Centres

Planned shopping areas are retail locations that have been architecturally planned to provide a unified theme for a number of outlets (Gilbert 2003, p. 288). These sites are developed deliberately and they usually have some large, key retail brand stores ("**anchor stores**") and a number of smaller retailers to add diversity and special interest (Reynolds 1992).

The basic types of shopping centres are (1) **retail parks** that consist of a purpose-built cluster of freestanding retail outlets and (2) **shopping centres** that consist of one large building that is marketed as a unified shopping destination, usually with one name and logo. Both types offer (large) parking facilities but the retail mix in single building shopping centres is different from that in retail parks, as the range of stores is wider and often includes luxury and leisure items as well as clothing, footwear and other typical central location merchandise (Gilbert 2003, pp. 289-290).

Table 10.3   Planned Shopping Area Types

Types		Examples
Intermediate Centres (10,000 - 20,000 m²) *(Centres intercommuneaux, centros intermedios, regionale Shopping-Center)* (at least one anchor, integrated)		
Locational variants	• non-central suburban community • greenfield site, transport node	• Auchan, Torino, Italy • Cameron Toll, Edinburgh, UK
Compositional variants	• hypermarket-anchored • specialty non-food anchored	• Euromarché • BHV, Cergy, France
Regional Shopping Centres (30,000 m²+) *(Centres commerciaux régionaux, grandes centors periféricos, überregionale Shopping-Center)* (two or more anchors)		
Locational variants	• central area in traditional core • central area adjacent to traditional core • non-central suburban growth zone • greenfield site, transport node	• Eldon Square, Newcastle, UK • La Part-Dieu, Lyon, France • CentrO, Oberhausen, Germany • Curno, Bergamo, Italy
Compositional variants	• hypermarket-dominated • department and variety-store dominated • food, non-food and leisure anchors	• A6, Jönköping, Sweden • Lakeside, Thurrock, UK • Parquesur, Madrid, Spain
Retail Parks (5,000 – 20,000 m²) *(parques des entrepôts, parques commerciales, retail warehouse parks, Fachmarktzentren)* (not obviously anchored, not wholly integrated centres)		
Locational variants	• non-central suburban community • greenfield site, transport node	• various • Lakeside Retail Park, UK
Compositional variants	• large retail format tenant mix • factory outlet tenant mix • hybrid tenant mix	• Fairacres Retail Park, Abingdon, UK • Marques Avenue, Troyes, France • Fosse Park, Leicaster, UK
Specialty centres (1,000 m²+) *(Arcades, galeries marchandes, galerias comerciales, Galerien/Passagen)* (fashion-oriented, specialty stores)		
Locational variants	• central area in traditional core • adjacent to traditional core	• Galleria, Hamburg, Germany • Albert Dock, Liverpool, UK
Compositional variants	• non-food specialty stores • department store conversions	• Powerscourt Centre, Dublin, Eire • Karstadt Arkaden, Mühlheim, Germany

Floor space figures are indicative only; centres providing for local or neighbourhood needs are excluded.

Source: adapted from Reynolds 1992, p. 57.

Several specific types of retail parks and shopping centres have been developed (Levy/Weitz 2009, pp. 200–207): (1) **neighbourhood** or **strip/community centres** that are typically anchored by a supermarket, (2) **power centres** that consist primarily of large format retailers, (3) **shopping malls** that are enclosed, climate controlled and lit shopping centres (regional or super regional shopping malls), (4) **lifestyle centres** that encompass an open-air configuration of upscale specialty stores, entertainment and restaurants, (5) **fashion/specialty centres** that comprise mainly upmarket clothing shops and boutiques carrying high quality and price fashion merchandise, (6) **outlet centres** that contain manufacturers' and retailers' outlet stores or off-price retailers (see Chapter 2) and (7) **theme or festival parks** that typically employ a unified theme carried by the retail outlets, their architectural design and their merchandise and can be anchored by restaurants or entertainment facilities. The main types of planned shopping areas are presented in **Table 10.3**.

The decision as to which kind of retail location to select depends on the company's strategy. It is an integral part of the retail location decision process.

10.3   Retail Location Decision Process

10.3.1   Overview

Retail location decisions typically follow a systematic process that starts with a general assessment of geographic areas and leads to a detailed assessment of specific site characteristics.

Figure 10.2   Catchment Area Assessment

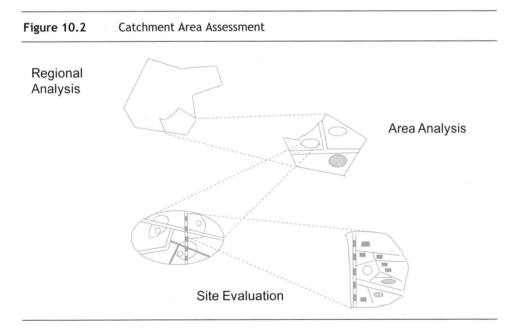

Regional Analysis

Area Analysis

Site Evaluation

Source: adapted from Bienert 1996, p. 115.

This process can broadly be described as a three-step selection process (**see Figure 10.2**; Brown 1992, p. 16):

1. **Market selection**: the first step is the consideration of a region that has potential for a new retail outlet.

2. **Area analysis**: within the chosen region, a potentially optimal area for the store is selected.

3. **Site evaluation**: in the chosen geographical area, the best available site(s) are examined in terms of all features that are relevant to potential store performance. This step concludes with a final decision on the specific site.

10.3.2   Catchment Area

The analysis of the catchment area (**trading area, market area**) of a specific region or a specific site is of high importance in each phase of this retail location decision process. The catchment area is the geographic area that contains the customers of a particular site or region for a company or a group of companies for specific goods or services. Thus, it determines the potential demand at a particular site and, among other factors, influences potential sales and profitability.

Usually, the catchment area is divided into three parts. The **primary trading area** is the zone in which the majority of customers are based. It encompasses 50 % to 80 % of customers. The **secondary trading area** contains about 15 % to 25 % and the **fringe** or **tertiary trading area** includes the remaining customers that shop occasionally at a location as an alternative to local shopping (Berman/Evans 2010, p. 257; Gilbert 2003, p. 280).

These catchment area segments are often described in terms of the **distance** between customers' homes or workplaces and the area or site. Usually, the linear distance (e.g. concentric circles drawn around a site), travel distance (by car or public transport) or time distance measures (by car or public transport) are used to delineate trading area segments. **Mapping techniques** are used to forecast or survey and map such store trading areas (McGoldrick 2002, p. 247).

Geographical information systems (GIS) are important support systems for location research and trading area analysis. These are software systems that combine digitalised mapping with key locational data in order to depict trading area characteristics such as population demographics, customer purchase data and competitor locations.

10.3.3   Location Assessment Techniques

The **appropriateness** of a specific site is based on the retailer's strategy (retail formats, merchandise, pricing strategy, etc.) and is influenced by a substantial number of factors that need to be investigated. A selection of location factors is presented in **Table 10.4**.

Table 10.4   Selected Location Factors

Customers (potential/actual)	Accessibility	Competition	Costs
• numbers by demographics (e.g. population size, age profile, household size) • income level • disposable income per capita • employment by occupation, industry, trends • housing density • housing age/type • neighbourhood classification • home-ownership levels • building/demolition plans • main employers • spending patterns • shopping patterns • population growth, density and trends • lifestyle measures • cultural/ethnic grouping	• site visibility • pedestrian flows • pedestrian entry routes • barriers such as railway tracks, rivers • type of location zone • car ownership level • road network (conditions, driving speeds, congestion, restrictions, plans) • parking (capacity, con-venience, cost, potential) • public transport (types, cost, ease of use, potential) • visibility • access for staff • access for transport and delivery	• existing retail activity (direct competitors, indirect com-petitors, anchor stores, cu-mulative attraction, compatibility) • existing retail specification (selling area, turnover estimates, department/ product analysis, trade areas, age of outlets, standard of design, car parking) • saturation index • competitive potential (outlet expansion, refurbishment, va-cant sites, interception, repositioning, competitor policy) • proximity of key competi-tors, traders, brand leaders	• purchase price • building costs • rent costs • leasing terms • site preparation • building restrictions • development concessions • rates payable • refurbishment needs • maintenance costs • security needs • staff availability • labour rates • delivery costs • insurance costs • promotional media/costs • turnover loss/other branches

Source: adapted from McGoldrick 2002, p. 240; Gilbert 2003, p. 293.

In order to guide retail location decisions and to assess or forecast the potential sales or profitability of retail stores in a specific region, area or at a specific site, a number of techniques have been developed. The techniques range from simple to **Table 10.5**). Either way, most are used to identify and evaluate potential **new sites**, but they can also guide decisions on **existing locations** with respect to extensions, rationalisation, repositioning and so on.

Table 10.5   Location Planning Techniques

Techniques	Subjectivity	Cost	Technical Expertise required	Computing and Data Needs	GIS
Manager's Experience	very high	low	low	low	limited role
Location Evaluation Checklists	medium	low	low	low	limited role
Analogue Method	medium	low	low	low	limited role
Multivariate Statistical Techniques	low	medium	high	medium	information
Spatial Interaction Models (Gravity Modeling)	low	high	very high	high	information, modelling, analysis and modeling
Knowledge-based Techniques (e.g. Expert Systems/Neural Networks)	low	very high	very high	very high	information

Source: adapted from Hernández/Bennison 2000, p. 360.

10.3.3.1   Managers' Experience

Location is a retail function that requires knowledge and expertise. In practice, managerial experience ("retail nose") plays an important role in assessing retail locations. For example, **rules of thumb** are often used as subjective and intuitive guidelines for site assessment. Such rules are developed from the knowledge of the company (Hernández/Bennison 2000).

10.3.3.2   Location Evaluation Checklists

Checklists consist of a number of chosen variables (e.g. location factors) to be considered when evaluating retail locations. One of the first detailed checklist evaluation formats was developed by Nelson (1958).

Companies select factors that they believe influence store performance. While some elements of such checklists are common to all types of retailers, each company is likely to have its own list with factors that reflect its particular strategy and situation (McGoldrick 2002, p. 239). **Figure 10.3** illustrates linkages between retailers' strategic positioning (e.g. focus on price, convenience, variety or proximity), typical locations (e.g. retail parks or high street) and major influences that are considered to be important (e.g. population, competitors, demographics, etc.) and which should be analysed in the context of site assessment.

Figure 10.3   Linkage among Retailer Strategy, Location Factors and Location Types

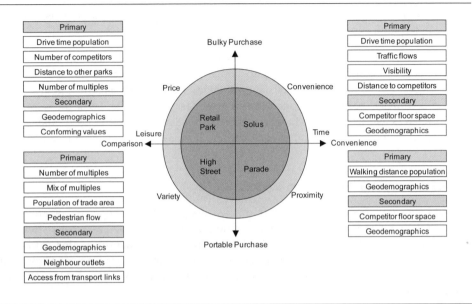

Source: Davies/Clarke 1994, p. 7; CCN Marketing 1993.

10.3.3.3   Analogue Method

The principle behind the **analogue method** (Applebaum 1966) is that new store sites are compared to existing ones that have many features in common with the new store (e.g. store size, merchandise or location characteristics). The likely turnover and profitability of the new store site are estimated on the basis of sales achieved and profits earned by similar stores in existing areas. Such comparisons can be done by **extrapolating** own store data or by comparing the new site with existing competing stores (e.g. stores at the prospective location).

10.3.3.4   Multivariate Statistical Techniques

Given the increasingly complex array of data available for location analysis, multivariate statistical techniques can be used to construct models that harness the predictive power of the available predictor variables for (new) store performance (McGoldrick 2002, p. 257).

Most important techniques are forms of **multiple regression analysis,** which predict store sales and estimate market potential or profit. **Discriminant analysis** can be used to predict category membership. Such sophisticated procedures can identify relationships between store sales and predictor variables such as population in the surrounding area, the spending power of the population, store accessibility, quality of transport links to sites, average distance to population or nearby competition (Moutinho/Curry/Davies 1993).

These techniques provide more objective and systematic insight into the impact and importance of location attributes, and thus they are useful for screening large numbers of locations. However, they require more data than do the simpler methods as well as a higher degree of technical expertise.

Cluster and factor analysis are techniques aimed at grouping data cases or variables in order to segment a portfolio of stores into similar groups (**cluster analysis**) or a range of variables that can be used to predict site profitability (**factor analysis**). The application of these procedures is particularly suited to new store format development or the segmentation of retail networks. These techniques also require a large amount of good quality data as well as a high degree of statistical expertise and business acumen (Hernandéz/Bennison 2000).

10.3.3.5   Spatial Interaction Models

Spatial interaction models are also referred to as "**gravity models**" because they are based on an analogy with the physical law of gravitation. They have evolved as a major stream of development in retail location theory. The basic principle of **spatial interaction** is that the aggregate movements of shoppers are positively related to the attractiveness of a store and negatively related to the distance from the store or other deterrence factors (Craig/Ghosh/ McLafferty 1984).

Gravity models can be used to forecast store performance based on the simultaneous consideration of such factors as store size, store image, distance, population and distribution. One of the earliest models of this type is **Reilly's law of retail gravitation** (Reilly 1929). This law establishes a point of indifference between two towns in order to determine the catchment area of each town. This point of indifference is the breaking point, defined as the point up to which one town dominates and beyond which the other town dominates (see **Figure 10.4**). Thus, it is the point at which consumers are indifferent as to which location they use (Rogers 1992).

Figure 10.4   Reilly's Law of Retail Gravitation

$$d_{01} = \frac{d_{12}}{1+\sqrt{A_2 / A_1}}$$

d_{01} = distance or journey time of the breaking point 0 from town 1
d_{12} = distance or journey time between town 1 and town 2
A_1, A_2 = population of town 1 and town 2

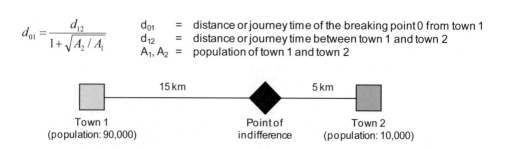

Town 1
(population: 90,000)

Point of indifference

Town 2
(population: 10,000)

Source: adapted from McGoldrick 2002, p. 261; Berman/Evans 2010, p. 261.

This model aids in the delineation of the trading area from which retailers draw customers. However, the model has many limitations (see, e.g., Rogers 1992; Craig/Ghosh/McLafferty 1984). For example, the breaking point formula does not provide estimates above or below the break-even point between the two towns. Also, the model cannot predict the trade areas of more than two towns and the form of the function is not constant for all types of shopping trips. Retailers can offer additional competitive advantages and thus – contrary to the model assumptions – can differ in terms of location attractiveness (McGoldrick 2002, p. 261; Gilbert 2003, p. 295).

In order to overcome these limitations, several refinements and extensions of the model have been developed, including **Huff's law of shopper attraction** (Huff 1964), which is based on the utility that a shopper derives from shopping at a particular store. It describes catchment areas on the basis of the product assortment carried at various shopping locations, travel times and the sensitivity of the kind of shopping to travel time (trip's purpose and type of product sought).

10.3.3.6   Knowledge-based Techniques

Knowledge-based techniques are the most recent models that have been developed to assess retail store locations. The most important techniques are **expert systems** or models developed based on **artificial intelligence**, such as neural networks or computer systems modelling the retail environment and shopper behaviour as "software agents" that simulate store performance at prospective locations. Such systems depend heavily on powerful computer capacities and immense data requirements and are still in the development phase.

10.4   Conclusion and Outlook

Location decisions have a major impact on a retail outlet's success, as location is an important factor in consumers' store choice. The location decision also has a **long-term impact** as it is not very flexible. Thus, location decisions are of critical importance for retailers' competitive advantages. To guide and support retail site assessment, various location assessment techniques have become more and more sophisticated. Such improvements have been triggered largely by advances in computer and software technologies (e.g. artificial intelligence).

It should be noted that retail location decisions consist not only of opening new stores, but that **monitoring existing stores** is of equal importance. This entails, for example, decisions concerning repositioning, relocation or closing outlets. This is important, as retail environments change rapidly (e.g. customer behaviour or competitive structure) and companies must respond in terms of location decisions.

However, retail location decisions cannot be made without taking into account the **retail environment** in terms of the interests of towns/cities or residents. Establishing a retail store can, for example, influence shopping patterns, traffic and pedestrian flows or the retail structure of a town. A major concern of local communities is out-of-town vs. inner-city retail centres. Also important in this context are **business improvement districts** (BID). BIDs, which are **public–private partnerships** (PPP) that comprise property and business owners of a defined area, who try to improve it by collective contributions to the mainte-nance, development and marketing of their commercial districts.

To ensure that the specific objectives are met, retail locations are influenced or constrained by local or **central government planning policies**. Thus, the opening of new stores or even changing or extending existing stores may require planning permission. For example, most European countries have restrictions on setting up **large retail formats** and out-of-town shopping centres. The reason for these interventions is the potentially adverse impact of large stores on small businesses and of new shopping centres on old ones.

However, local authorities do not only restrict retail store settlement. In many **city market-ing** initiatives, an attractive retail mix is known to be one of the key elements of attracting customers to a particular town or city. Local authorities, therefore, try to attract retailers with a good image so that retailers open stores in their towns or cities.

▌ Further Reading

GHOSH, A.; INGENE, C.A. (Eds.) (1991): Spatial Analysis in Marketing: Theory, Methods, and Applications, Greenwich et al.

GUY, C. (1994): The Retail Development Process: Location, Property and Planning, London.

JONES, K.; SIMMONS, J. (1990): The Retail Environment, London.

TELLER, C. (2008): Shopping Streets versus Shopping Malls – Determinants of Agglomera-tion Format Attractiveness from the Consumers' Point of View, in: The International Re-view of Retail, Distribution and Consumer Research, Vol. 18, No. 4, pp. 381–403.

10.5   Case Study: Site Selection at 7-Eleven[1]

10.5.1   Profile, History and Status Quo

This case study illustrates the principles that *7-Eleven* uses for the site selection of *7-Eleven* convenience stores. *7-Eleven* is particularly suited for a case study on site selection for at least two reasons. For one, the company pursues a pronounced expansion strategy in many

---

[1] Sources used for this case study include the company's website www.7-eleven.com as well as various annual and interim reports, investor relations presentations and explicitly cited sources.

geographic regions of the world (Pardy 2009). Second, three different store types (stores with and without motor fuels as well as urban, walk-up stores) require different criteria for site selection.

The Southland Corporation, renamed as *7-Eleven, Inc.* in April 1999, goes back to an idea from 1927: before then, the *Southland Ice Company* in Dallas sold blocks of ice to refrigerate food. Starting in 1927, the company began to sell additional products in their stores, such as milk, bread and eggs when other grocers were closed (7-Eleven 2011a). The success of this idea quickly led to a main assortment no longer being merely blocks of ice, but including conveniently offered foodstuffs.

Today, *7-Eleven, Inc.* is one of the largest operators, franchisors and licensors of convenience stores in the world (7-Eleven 2011a). The company has more than 39,100 stores in 16 countries, 8,300 of which are in North America (Datamonitor 2010). In addition, *7-Eleven* has the largest ATM network of any retailer in the US.

The company pursues a consistent growth strategy: in 2008, they opened more than 150 new *7-Eleven* convenience stores in the USA alone. In the following years, the number of openings also grew rapidly (Mangee 2009; Pacific Epoch 2010).

Since the 1970s, the company has also grown internationally through franchising. The franchising concept was introduced to the company with the acquisitions of 100 *SpeeDee Marts* in California in 1963 (Fundinguniverse 2011). Some *SpeeDee Marts* had successfully been managed within a franchise system for some time. By adopting this system, *7-Eleven* not only achieved faster growth, but also established a decentralised management system of individual markets. Today, the company has convenience stores in Japan, South Korea, China and Hong Kong, Australia, Mexico, Taiwan, Singapore, Indonesia, Canada, the Philippines, Sweden, Denmark, Thailand, Norway, Turkey, Malaysia and the US territory of Puerto Rico (Datamonitor 2010).

Each *7-Eleven* store offers a broad range of products of (convenience) food and beverages. A considerable number of stores also sell petrol. The actual assortment structure varies from country to country (Yahagia/Kar 2009). While petrol generates a major proportion of sales in US stores, Japanese franchises operate generally without selling petrol. Another example is perishable foods that are sold in China but not in Japan.

10.5.2   Market Selection

7-Eleven pursues a consistent **growth strategy**, "new stores are opening daily..." (7-Eleven 2011c). The company names, for example, 25 geographic areas in 15 growing markets within the USA as particularly attractive markets for the opening of *7-Eleven* stores (see **Table 10.6**).

Market selection follows two aims. Firstly, at least in the USA, penetrating existing markets is a declared aim of *7-Eleven*. Daniel Porter, *7-Eleven*'s vice president of real estate, names the existing significant market share of *7-Eleven* as a criterion for market selection (Pardy 2009). He names further criteria to be:

- High population density markets
- Strong store performance of existing *7-Eleven* stores
- Additional demand for 7-Eleven stores.

Table 10.6   Attractive Markets for the Opening of 7-Eleven Stores within the USA

State	Geographic Area
California	Los Angeles, San Diego, Bay Area
Colorado	Denver (The Front Range)
Florida	Dayton, Fort Myers, Orlando, Tampa, Miami
Illinois	Chicago
Michigan	Detroit Metro
New Jersey	Northern New Jersey
Nevada	Las Vegas
New York	Long Island, New York City
Maryland	Baltimore
Oregon	Portland
Virginia	Newport News, Norfolk, Virginia Beach, Metro Washington D.C.
Texas	Dallas/Fort Worth, Austin
Utah	Salt Lake City
Washington	Seattle
Washington, D.C.	D.C. and surrounding Metro

Source: 7-Eleven 2011b.

This way, demand can be better met in markets where *7-Eleven* is already well established. At the same time, *7-Eleven* reduces the financial risk that is associated with establishing new markets. Daniel Porter obviously does not see a danger in market saturation: "People need and want convenience" (quoted from Pardy 2009, p. 1). *7-Eleven*'s public relations director Margaret Chabris added another reason for market selection, in light of the recent difficult economic situation of many smaller dealers in the USA (before 2011), namely that more desirable locations became available owing to the closure of many stores during the recession (quoted from CSDecision.com 2011).

As a second strategic objective, in addition to strengthening the distribution in existing markets, the entering of new markets has been observed, in particular, with large international franchises (Lebensmittel Zeitung 2004). For example, the superstore operator *Ito-Yokado Co. Ltd.*, which already operated 33 general merchandise stores under a different name within the Japanese market, opened the first Japanese *7-Eleven* stores in the early 1970s. In this way, *7-Eleven, Inc.* (at the time still called *Southland*) could open more than 1,200 *7-Eleven* stores in Japan in a relatively short time (until 1981) with *Ito-Yokado's* commitment (Yahagia/Kar 2009). Other market entries, such as in China and Denmark, also go back to the commitment of franchisees, which wanted to enter new markets with the *7-Eleven* brand (cf. Yahagia/Kar 2009, Lebensmittel Zeitung 2004). The franchise approach is the main mode of entry for the internationalisation of *7-Eleven* and related market selection.

10.5.3   Site Selection: Real Estate Requirements[1]

While many operators of convenience stores in the USA limit their selections of sites to freestanding buildings on high traffic corners (Payne 2009), *7-Eleven* does not limit itself to this tight framework. Aside from freestanding buildings, *7-Eleven* also has urban street locations and stores in shopping centres. The variety of locations that *7-Eleven* considers even goes as far as *7-Eleven* actively searching for opportunities to become key tenants in the redevelopment of a centre or revitalisation of a specific area, according to Porter, *7-Eleven*'s vice-president of real estate (Pardy 2009, p. 1).

This great flexibility and consistent growth strategy has led to *7-Eleven* becoming a **popular partner** with landlords. This is even the case when the actual letting is carried out by a franchisee of *7-Eleven* because the company executes all store leases in many cases, even if the stores are run by a franchisee (Pardy 2009). This approach is not necessarily typical but eases negotiations with landlords for *7-Eleven* in the USA. Landlords have "been very receptive to working with us on tenant improvement allowances and finish-out work", reports Porter (quoted from Pardy 2009, p. 2). Thus, landlords often offer *7-Eleven* free rent for a period of time to get the store up and running. *7-Eleven* furthermore aims at **long-term rental agreements** (longer than 10 years), while landlords usually prefer shorter rental agreements.

Despite *7-Eleven*'s abovementioned flexibility towards possible locations for new stores, the company sets narrow site criteria. *7-Eleven* is looking for:

■ Strong retail properties located on signalised intersections with excellent

♦ access

---

[1] The information in these sections is mainly derived from 7-Eleven (2011b).

- ◆ visibility
- ◆ manoeuvrability
- ◆ front parking.

■ 2,000 to 3,000-square-foot retail spaces in

- ◆ strip centres
- ◆ freestanding buildings with front nose-in parking capability (quoted from Pardy 2009 p. 1).

There is also the expectation that it has to be possible to sell beer and wine in the location and that the store can be open 24 hours a day, 7 days a week (7-Eleven 2011c).

These general criteria are accompanied by special requirements for the three store types:

■ Freestanding sites/shopping centres without motor fuels

■ Sites with motor fuels

■ Urban walk-up stores.

The selection criteria can be divided into four groups: (1) trade area demographics, (2) traffic, (3) activity generators and (4) site characteristics.

10.5.3.1   Free-standing Sites/Shopping Centres without Motor Fuels

With regard to trade area demographics, a potential freestanding site or sites within a shopping centre, both without motor fuels, require heavy density within a one-and-a-half mile radius. Five thousand residents or workers per square mile should be in this catchment area. A high density worker population receives particular attention.

With respect to traffic, *7-Eleven* searches for sites in this category that are passed by 25,000 vehicles per day. Sites that have a high pedestrian count are preferred.

In regards to activity generators, sites are expected to have a high density of housing/apartments. A surrounding area that features a good mixture of commercial, office, industrial and university buildings is valued. Additionally, complimentary 24-hour use is expected.

Concerning site characteristics, *7-Eleven* uses these criteria:

■ Corner location with traffic signal – or strip centre end cap

■ Front parking with a minimum of five exclusive spaces

■ A total of 2,000 to 3,000 sq. ft. store size with a minimum of app. 170 m² selling space

■ High visibility and excellent accessibility, far corner preferred, no road medians preferred

■ Ability to sell beer and wine preferred

■ 24-hour operation required.

Figure 10.5 Examples for 7-Eleven Stores in a Free-standing Building (left) and in a Shopping Mall (right)

Source: 7-Eleven 2011b.

10.5.3.2   Sites with Motor Fuels

For sites with motor fuels, *7-Eleven* also attaches importance to a heavy density within a one-and-a-half mile radius. Just as with the sites without motor fuels, 5,000 or more residents/workers per square mile in the trade area are expected. Additionally, these sites are expected not to have any low price petrol brands within a radius of a half mile.

Figure 10.6 Example of a 7-Eleven Store with Motor Fuels

Source: 7-Eleven 2011b.

With regard to traffic characteristics, sites are searched that are passed by at least 25,000 vehicles per day. There is no expectation for pedestrians.

Desired sites are meant to have an adequate mixture of residential, commercial, office and industrial buildings. Sites with freeway orientation and complementary 24-hour use are preferred.

Concerning site characteristics, *7-Eleven* uses these criteria:

- Corner location with traffic signal – or strip centre end cap
- A total of 25,000 to 50,000 sq. ft. space preferred
- High visibility and excellent accessibility with typical petrol station access – far corner and no road medians preferred
- A total of 2,000 to 3,000 sq. ft. store size with a minimum of 1,800 sq. ft. selling space
- Spacious and convenient ingress, egress and in-lot manoeuvrability
- Ability to sell beer and wine preferred and 24-hour operation required.

10.5.3.3   Urban Walk-up Stores

A site that comes into question for urban walk-up stores has to have a very high density within a quarter of a mile. A minimum of 8,000 residents/workers per square mile in the trade area is expected. At the same time, a high density worker population is preferred.

Figure 10.7   Examples for 7-Eleven Walk-up Stores

Source: 7-Eleven 2011b.

With regard to traffic, *7-Eleven* seeks sites for urban walk-up stores that are passed by 25,000 vehicles per day. A prerequisite for the site is a very heavy pedestrian count with at least **10 pedestrians per minute** passing the site.

Concerning site characteristics, *7-Eleven* uses these criteria:

- Street-level corner location preferred

- Minimum 2,000 sq. ft. retail space with 1,600 sq. ft. of selling space

- High visibility and excellent accessibility

- Ability to sell beer and wine preferred

- 24-hour operation

- Ability for standard "tri-stripe" signage, or dedicated street parking spaces preferred.

Finally, two of the three criteria concerning activity generators need to be fulfilled by the site:

- High density housing/apartments/lofts

- Daytime generators such as commercial, office, bus/rail stops

- Evening generators such as restaurants, theatres, bars and convention centres.

10.5.3.4   Site selection and 7-Eleven's Business Conversion Programme

Besides selecting sites, purchasing properties and trying to find franchisees, *7-Eleven's* latest growth vehicle is its business conversion programme, where the company approaches existing businesses to convert them into the national chain and become a part of *7-Eleven's* franchise system. In particular, *7-Eleven* is interested in targeting family-run petrol stations in North America as well as other small businesses. The retail chain invests about 280,000 USD into this programme. By 2009, 110 outlets had been converted into *7-Eleven* stores since the programme started in 2006 (Magee 2009).

7-Eleven has a multi-pronged approach to growth that includes in-line, end cap space in shopping centres, freestanding stores, urban locations in light industrial sites, city residential areas and suburbia. The selection criteria can be divided into four groups: criteria concerning (1) trade area demographics, (2) traffic, (3) activity generators and (4) site characteristics.

Figure 10.8   Example of an Conversion Programme Store in Los Angeles, before (left part) and after (right part) the Conversion

Source: 7-Eleven 2011e.

10.5.4   Summary and Outlook

According to *7-Eleven*, it is the largest chain of convenience stores worldwide (*7-Eleven* 2011c). This results in particular from a strong ongoing expansion course in international markets and within individual markets (Magee 2009, Pacific Epoch 2010). For example, *7-Eleven* plans to double its stores in Manhattan (SCDecisions 2010). In Shanghai, where the convenience store chain currently operates 18 stores, *7-Eleven* plans to open about 150 stores by 2013 (Pacific Epoch 2010). Moreover, *7-Eleven* just expanded its business into Indonesia through a master franchise agreement with *PT.Modern Putraindonesia* (ConvenienceStore-News 2009, Good Indonesia 2010).

Together with this constant expansion, market and site selection within a market play particular roles for *7-Eleven*. Particularly concerning **internationalisation** and the related market selection, the **franchise approach** is the main mode of entry. The initiative for the commitment even started with a franchisee, at least with the largest franchisee of *7-Eleven*, *Ito-Yokado Co. Ltd*, in Japan. Remarkably, after *7-Eleven*'s performance deteriorated markedly in the late 1980s, the *Ito-Yokado group* gained a controlling share of *7-Eleven* in 1991 (Ya-hagia/Kar 2009).

Concerning site selection, *7-Eleven* uses criteria for trade area demographics, traffic, activity generators and site characteristics. These criteria are meant to ensure that sites are large enough to take up the product range, can be regularly frequented, attract a high level of attention and enable convenience shopping (concerning opening times, parking spaces and so on).

Nevertheless, *7-Eleven* is reconsidering some of its site selection criteria (*7-Eleven* 2011d). Based on the in-depth analysis of its current network planning tactics, *7-Eleven* will re-evaluate its current site selection strategy. Furthermore, the results of the project are to reassess ideal store size and configuration as well as impactful product assortment.

| Questions

1. What significance do you attach to the site selection criterion "24 hour operation required"?

2. Which opportunities and risks does *7-Eleven* take when executing all store leases in some cases, even if the stores are run by a franchise?

3. How do you evaluate the strategy to expressly open sites in markets where *7-Eleven* already has a strong market position?

| Hints

1. Bear in mind the *7-Eleven*'s strategic orientation and the associated need satisfaction by the stores.

2. Consider *7-Eleven*'s special expectation regarding the rental agreement duration and evaluate the risks and influence *7-Eleven* has to prevent these risks.

3. Consider the financial risks and expectations of the convenience market.

11 Merchandise and Category Management

The purpose of this Chapter is to explain the different attributes of a retailer's merchandise mix and the aspects to be considered in merchandise planning. The Chapter deals with the merchandise mix, the development and importance of store brands and the integration of merchandise planning into the broader process of category management.

11.1 Merchandise Mix

Product assortment is at the core of the retailing offer. A retailer's total product offering is called its merchandise mix or product range. At a strategic level, merchandise management includes the process of selecting the right items for a store and, at an operational level, ensuring that they are available when customers want to purchase them. The latter function is discussed in more detail in Chapters 16 and 17.

Items in the assortment are organised into groups called **categories. Merchandise planning encompasses selecting the right categories and the items within them.** The selection of the appropriate items for a store refers to the breadth and depth of the assortment, quality levels and the brand portfolio.

The lowest level of detail identifying a product in the retailer's assortment is the **stock-keeping unit** (SKU), which identifies a particular item. For example, a pair of trousers of a certain brand in a particular style, colour and size is one SKU. The number of SKUs at various retailers varies tremendously. While hard discounters often carry around 1,000 SKUs, a supermarket has 10,000-15,000 SKUs. A typical hypermarket assortment reaches around 80,000 SKUs. A DIY store can have around 50,000 SKUs and *IKEA*, as an example of a home accessories and furniture store, has 9,500 SKUs in a store.

Items in the assortment can be grouped by many different criteria. Product life cycle is one important classification criterion (Berman/Evans 2010, p. 392):

- **Staple merchandise** consists of those products that are carried permanently by the retailer and that have relatively stable sales over time. A hammer or a paintbrush at a DIY retailer or jeans and white T-shirts at a department store are examples of staple goods.

- **Fashion merchandise** refers to products that have cyclical sales because of changing tastes and lifestyles. Colours and cuts of clothing change, and fashion products offered this year are usually out of date next year.

- **Seasonal merchandise** consists of products that do not sell equally well over consecutive time periods. Barbecues, skiing equipment, shorts and similar products have very high sales during one season of the year, but they are not sold at all in other seasons.

- **Fad merchandise** generates very high sales for a short time period. Often, toys and games, certain clothing accessories or certain music CDs are fads. *Tamagochis* and *Pokémons*, for instance, were classic fads. Movie merchandise (e.g. *Spiderman* accessories) also constitutes typical fads. Price sensitivity is often very low and ensuring supply, while demand is high, is crucial for success.

The product life cycle of merchandise is relevant because it emphasises that all products in the assortment need to be replaced after a (varying) period of time but that the time span to realise sales also varies. It also has a substantial influence on the ability to forecast demand.

Another frequently used categorisation of products in general is **food, near-food** and **non-food** items. Non-food refers to non-perishable general merchandise such as clothing, electronics, toys and so on. Near-food products are products such as detergents, toothpaste and shampoo, which are not food (e.g. they usually have no expiration date) but which are bought in a similar way to fast-moving consumer goods.

Merchandise can also be considered by **quality level**, which is closely related to **price positioning** (see Chapter 12). Should the retailer focus on premium products and target high income customers, should it offer standard products or focus on lower quality, less expensive items to target mainly (but not only) low income customers? Another strategic option is to cover different quality segments and thereby approach a broader target group. For example, while discount apparel stores (e.g. *KIK* in Germany or the Dutch *Zeeman*) focus on the low quality segment, clothing boutiques focus on the high quality segment and department stores usually cover different quality levels.

The breadth and depth of the assortment are the most commonly used criteria for structuring the merchandise mix:

- The number of product lines (or categories) the retailer offers is referred to as **the breadth (width) of the assortment**. Breadth is generally depicted on a scale from **narrow to wide**. A wide assortment usually has the advantage of appealing to **broad target groups**, and it makes **one-stop shopping** possible, i.e. the customer finds most of the merchandise he or she wants "under one roof". A drawback is that very wide assortments often result in a diffuse, unspecific store image.

- The number of SKUs in a particular category (e.g. brands, colours, tastes, sizes) is called the **depth of the assortment**. Depth is mostly measured on a scale ranging from **shallow to deep**. Deep assortments have the advantage of giving the consumer a good choice within the categories that appeals to customers with high product involvement. Shallow assortments may lead to a weak merchandise image, but a shallow assortment can often focus better on the fast-selling items in a category. Deep assortments often lead to many items with low inventory turns. When a category assortment is deep, it usually covers different quality and price levels.

Specialty stores and category killers are typical examples of retailers that have rather narrow but very deep assortments. Food discounters, by contrast, usually have a rather wide assortment (they cover all relevant food categories, some near-food categories and a few non-food categories) but they are characterised by a very shallow assortment, as illustrated in **Figure 11.1**. Traditional full-line department stores have both: a very wide and a rather deep assortment.

Figure 11.1   The Merchandise Mix: Breadth and Depth of Assortment

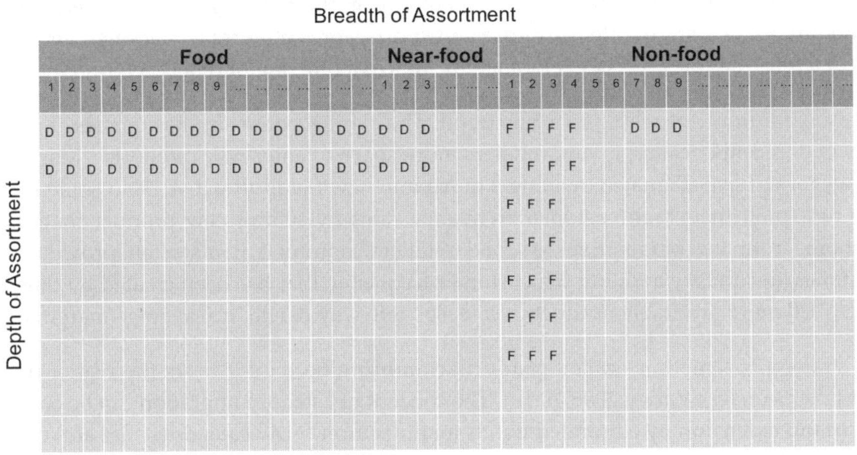

Breadth of Assortment

Food	Near-food	Non-food
1 2 3 4 5 6 7 8 9 … … …	1 2 3 … …	1 2 3 4 5 6 7 8 9 … … … … … …

Depth of Assortment

```
D D D D D D D D D D D D D D D D D D      F F F F      D D D
D D D D D D D D D D D D D D D D D D      F F F F
                                        F F F
                                        F F F
                                        F F F
                                        F F F
                                        F F F
```

D: Discounter (Food), F: Women's Fashion Boutique

However, retailers do not only have a choice between four different strategies, as a combination of these two dimensions (depth/breadth) would imply on first sight. As the example in **Figure 11.1** shows, a women's fashion boutique may carry a deep selection of a few fashion categories (such as evening dresses, blouses and trousers) and, in addition, a small selection of shoes, handbags and accessories.

Complementary Demand

For the assortment decision, demand interrelationships have to be considered in merchandise planning. The consumer usually buys a shopping basket. The demand for certain items is interrelated. This can be the case simply because it is more convenient to do all the food shopping for the week in one store. However, complementary effects within the assortment can also arise because products are used together and thus there are advantages to purchase them together because they can be matched. Shirts and ties or paintbrushes and paint are typical examples of complementary goods.

As a practical consequence, retailers usually try to cross-sell to customers by placing such products next to each other, so that it is more likely that latent demand complementarities manifest in a joint purchase.

Category Migration as a Trend

An increasing number of retailers use a combination of specialist and generalist approaches within their product offers. They are specialists in one or a few categories, but add other categories in which they only offer shallow assortments (Varley 2006, p. 10). Temporarily or permanently, retailers diversify by adding new products to their assortments that do not belong to their traditional merchandise (Zentes/Morschett 2004b). Supermarkets sell non-food products, DIY stores offer furniture and sports stores offer travel packages and food to list just a few examples. This development results in a blurring of retail sector boundaries.

There are a number of reasons for this trend. The average store size has increased continuously over recent decades, giving retailers more space to enter new categories. Many product categories have stagnated, making a move into new fields attractive. And some retailers wish to exploit their high customer frequency rates by selling new product ranges. Furthermore, from the perspectives of food retailers, non-food items often provide higher profit margins; thus, exploiting the customer frequency that has been created by their food offer to sell more profitable products is a reasonable way to enhance average margins.

This strategy is sometimes called **product scrambling** because it bears the risk of diluting the retailer's image (Varley 2006, p. 10). The concept of category migration can be compared with **brand extension** by a branded goods manufacturer. New categories that are related to existing ones, therefore, offer more potential with less image risk. Accordingly, successful category migration usually follows one of two diversification routes (Zentes/Morschett 2004b, p. 163):

- New categories and services are offered that are closely related to the core assortment. Examples include furniture stores that offer accessories, DIY stores that offer garden furniture and sports stores that offer skiing trips or sports nutrition. This even enhances the competence of the retailer in the eyes of the consumer and strengthens its image as a specialist.

- Or retailers diversify the assortment into new categories that appeal to the core target group of the retailer. Clothing retailers for young fashion that add cosmetics or music CDs to their assortments are good examples.

Reduction of Variety as Emerging Trend

Adding new items to the assortment or eliminating items from the assortment is a fundamental and ongoing process for retailers. Studies of retail patronage have found repeatedly that the variety of an assortment is an important determinant of attitude towards the store and store choice, ranking only behind location and price. Shoppers are often looking for specific items. A greater variety and larger assortment increases the probability of finding what they really want. Consumers may also like variety because of a simple desire to purchase different alternatives rather than the same thing each time (Zentes/Morschett 2004b). This has led to many retailers continuously increasing their product assortments.

However, one of the most valuable assets of a retailer, which poses a severe resource limitation, is selling space. Thus, the retailer has to make choices. Furthermore, too much variety in the assortment also has some disadvantages (Hoch/Bradlow/Wansink 1999, p. 528):

■ From the perspective of retail operations, an increasing number of SKUs usually increases retailing costs. Assortment complexity raises various costs, including those of sales, shelf space, planning, advertising, inventory and logistics. Discounters, for example, are very successful with a strictly limited assortment.

■ From the consumer perspective, a large number of alternatives within a category can lead to consumer confusion and make the shopping process more complicated. Often, consumers would, instead, prefer "mental convenience".

Recent studies have shown that even radical reductions in assortment do not necessarily reduce customer visits to the store and sales may remain stable (see the overview by Boatwright/Nunes 2001). It is not the actual number of different products in a category that matters but the consumer's perception of variety that is relevant for store choice behaviour.

The elimination of different but similar versions of the same product in the assortment is often not perceived or evaluated negatively by the consumer. Therefore, many retailers are currently analysing their assortments and rationalising each category by eliminating underperforming items and brands (Zentes/Morschett 2004a, p. 2739).

11.2   Manufacturer Brands and Store Brands

11.2.1   Brand Ownership and Brand Management

In defining their merchandise mixes, retailers also have to decide on the mix of manufacturer brands (e.g. *Ariel, Nestlé, Philips, Ferrero*) and their own brands, so-called **store brands**. While manufacturer brands (in older literature often referred to as **national brands**) are owned, produced, managed and marketed by manufacturers, **store brands** (also called **private labels** or **own brands) encompass all product brands that are owned, managed and marketed by retailers.** The property rights for the brand in this case are held by the retailer.

11.2.2   Functions of Manufacturer Brands in the Assortment

For many retailers, manufacturer brands comprise the main part of their merchandise. *Danone* in food retailing, *Bosch* and *Black & Decker* in DIY retailing, *Adidas* in shoe retailing and *Sony* in consumer electronics are just a few examples. Retailers include manufacturer brands in their assortments for several reasons. The two most important ones are the pull effects and image effects exerted by manufacturer brands (Zentes/Morschett 2004a, pp. 2725-2731):

- **Pull effect:** strong manufacturer brands often enhance customer frequency in stores, because strong brands have loyal customers and their store choice is influenced by the availability of brands. Manufacturer brands are often heavily advertised in the media, so consumers have clear images of them. Brand equity has been built up from which retailers can benefit. Strong manufacturer brands are said to pull customers into the store, so that other selling efforts by the retailer can be reduced.

- **Image transfer:** the images of the manufacturer brands in the assortment influence the retailer's image. A retailer's store image can be improved when it is associated with manufacturer brands that are evaluated positively. The number of available manufacturer brands as well as strong anchor brands in the assortment can affect the retail brand positively (Mulhern 1997, p. 110). Positive effects can be expected to raise the perceived quality level and enhance certain intangible brand features such as brand character. A store carrying a good range of *Camel Active* clothing, *Levi's* and *Timberland* will be associated with other characteristics than will a store carrying mainly *Prada* and *Gucci*.

Furthermore, manufacturer brands are still often **innovation** leaders. Manufacturers invest heavily in R&D and introduce new products into the market. The examples of *Apple*, *Nike* or even low-tech products such as nappies from *Pampers* demonstrate that new product introductions with innovative technologies or features very often still stem from manufacturer brands. However, the suppliers of strong brands are well aware of these benefits and their heavy advertising investment has to pay off. They have a strong negotiation position with retailers, which often results in unfavourable procurement prices for the latter. Therefore, manufacturer brands usually yield rather **low profit margins** for the retailer (Ogden/Ogden 2005, p. 265).

11.2.3   Functions of Store Brands in the Assortment

The proliferation of store brands in many product categories is one of the major developments in retail merchandising strategy (Burt/Davis 1999; Mulhern 1997, pp. 109-110). Once viewed with scepticism by consumers in terms of quality, in most countries store brands are now widely accepted substitutes for manufacturer brands and regarded as being of comparable quality (Varley 2006, p. 82). The store brand market share (by volume) reached almost 50 % in Switzerland, more than 40 % in the United Kingdom and in Germany and more than 30 % in Spain and France (www.plmainternational.com), with an increasing trend.

The major argument of retailers for the introduction of store brands is the profit margins. For example, *Metro* announced in 2009 that one of the most important instruments to increase its profit margin in its hypermarket chain *Real* would be to enhance the sales share of its standard store brand *Real Quality* from 7 % to 14 %.

Differentiation

Beyond the lower profit margins of manufacturer brands, one of the most important disadvantages of a manufacturer brand for a retailer is **ubiquity**, meaning that many other retailers offer these brands. Store brands, by contrast, provide an opportunity for differentiation. They are available at one retailer only and can, therefore, be used to distinguish the retailer from its competitors. The brand image of a store brand must be established by the retailer itself, but the brand can match the retail brand image of the retail company perfectly. The positive effects of store brands on retail image and retail profits have been proven in many studies (see, for example, Dhar/Hoch 1997, Corstjens/Lal 2000).

Enhancing Customer Loyalty

Customer loyalty can more easily be built on store brands than it can on manufacturer brands. If a customer is satisfied with a store brand and intends to repurchase it, he needs to revisit the retailer. Conversely, if he is satisfied with a manufacturer brand, he can still switch stores and buy the product elsewhere. At the same time, store brands are not easily comparable across retailers. Therefore, price competition may be less severe. This factor, combined with lower procurement or production and marketing costs, often results in better profit margins for store brands (Corstjens/Lal 2000, p. 281).

For those retailers that carry manufacturer brands and store brands, a general trend can be observed towards reducing brand selection in order to avoid consumer confusion and enhance efficiency. Only the best manufacturer brands are kept in the assortment, while the others are systematically eliminated or replaced by store brands.

11.2.4   Positioning and Labelling of Store Brands

The first store brands were **generics**, that is very low cost commodity products, with no brand-like labelling, but plain white packages that contained only the name of the product ("sugar" or "milk"). Value store brands such as *Tesco Value* or *M-Budget* today often still have this appeal and clearly signal their no-frills positioning.

However, store brands today exist in all price and quality segments (see **Table 11.1** for examples). Store brands also cover different segments with different attributes, for example, organic food or healthy eating. For value store brands and standard store brands, price still plays a dominant role. The standard store brands are usually positioned as being of as good a quality as is the manufacturer brand, but for a lesser price, and are targeted at the price-conscious customer segment (Dhar/Hoch 1997, p. 211).

Premium store brands, by contrast, are often positioned above the manufacturer brand. Currently, many retailers are establishing a premium store brand segment. While all store brands have an impact on the retail brand, the premium store brands in particular have been introduced to improve the profile of the retailer and shape retail brand image.

Creating Store Brand Portfolios

A recent trend in this field is the increasing segmentation of store brands to address even small target groups by offering several sub-brands that appeal to a wide spectrum of consumer needs. These store brand portfolios then help fulfil the heterogeneous objectives of store brands with a portfolio of different brands. For example, many food retailers now offer store brands for vegetarians (e.g. *Coop Delicorn*), for people with allergies (e.g. *Tesco Free From*) or for children (e.g. *Casino Famili*). Some retailers have introduced store brands that emphasise sustainability (*Tesco Greener Living*).

Table 11.1   Examples of Differently Positioned Store Brands in the Portfolios of Four Retailers

Positioning	Tesco (Food)	Coop (Food)	Castorama (Home Improvement)	Group Casino (Food)
Premium	Tesco Finest	Coop Fine Food	Colours, Form, MacAllister, Soltera, TorQ, Bodner & Mann,	Casino Délices, Casino Désir
Value Added	Tesco Organic, Tesco Free From, Tesco Greener Living	Coop Naturaplan, Coop Naturafarm, Coop Pro Montagna, Coop FreeFrom		Casino Bio, Terre et Saveur, Casino Fairtrade Max Havelaar, Wassila (Halal)
Standard Segmented	Tesco Healthy Living, Tesco Kids, Tesco Carb Control	Coop Delicorn, Coop Weight Watchers, Coop Jamadu, Coop Betty Bossi	Performance Power	Casino Famili
Standard	Tesco	Coop	Casto	Casino
Value/Budget	Tesco Value, Country Barn (cornflakes), Creamfields (cheese), Daisy (washing liquid)	Coop Prix Garantie	1er Prix	Premier Prix Casino

Thus, the portfolio contains store brands whose main task is to improve the margins of the retailer (often the standard store brand), others who have the main task to improve the retailer's image (often the premium brands, the organic products and the fair trade products) and others who mainly should signal the price competitiveness of the retailer (often the value store brands). Others should attract specific target groups and build their loyalty (e.g. gluten-free products). **Table 11.1** shows the store brand portfolios of four selected retailers and **Figure 11.2** illustrates the store brand portfolio of Sainsbury's.

Figure 11.2   Food Store Brand Portfolio of Sainsbury's

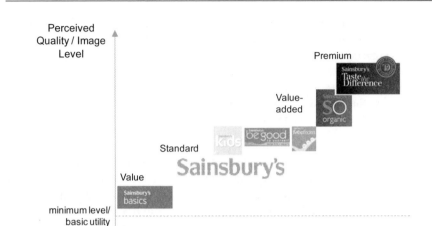

Source: adapted from Zentes/Morschett/Krebs 2008, p. 96.

Castorama, in a strategic restructuring of its store brand portfolio a few years ago, announced its intention to develop a clear three-layered portfolio: *1er Prix* as its budget brand, *Casto* and *Performance Power* as its standard store brands (*Casto* across many categories and *Performance Power* for power tools) and *MacAllister* (power tools), *Colours* (paint and decorative products), *Form* (storage solutions), *Soltera* (garden furniture), *Bodner & Mann* (electrical products, heating, etc.) and *TorQ* (gardening equipment) as its exclusive and upscale store brands. Whether all these brands are, however, perceived by the customer to be premium brands is not clear.

As with every portfolio, it is important that such a portfolio is balanced and that interrelationships are considered. If a portfolio is overfragmented, then cannibalisation may be strong and the critical mass within each different product brand segment may be too low. If the portfolio is too small, there may stay substantial niches that are not addressed.

Choosing a Brand Name for Store Brands

As part of the branding strategy, it also has to be decided how closely the store brand should be associated with the retail brand. Sometimes, the retail brand is used as an umbrella brand for the store brand products (for example, *Tesco* uses *Tesco Finest*, *Tesco Organic*, *Tesco Value*, among others, as store brands), while in other cases the store brand is not directly connected to the retail brand. *Anna's Best*, the store brand for pasta at the Swiss retailer *Migros*, or *Kenmore*, a store brand of Sears for its home appliances, are examples. *Aldi*'s store brands are all of this type.

Considering labelling, there seems to be a clear trend towards using the retail brand as an umbrella brand for the store brands as well. For example, in 2008 *REWE* converted its former store brands *Erlenhof*, *Salto* and *Today* into "*REWE*" products and its ecological line was relabelled from *Füllhorn* to *REWE Bio*. *Carrefour* renamed its value brand line from *Numéro 1* to *Carrefour Discount*. *Migros*, in 2010, followed this trend and announced a new *Migros* store brand *M-Classic* that would comprise many established products that were in the past offered under different store brand names.

The reasons for this trend are evident: no retailer has an advertising budget that would allow establishing store brands alongside manufacturer brands in terms of strength. Fragmentation renders this attempt almost impossible. But by uniting the store brand products under an umbrella brand, the store brand can be strengthened and can be managed similar to a strong manufacturer brand. Furthermore, linking the store brand to the retail brand leads to a cross-fertilisation of both brands. Launching new products under the established brand name is easier and, simultaneously, a successful store brand is much better for the image transfer to the retail brand.

The downside of this strategy is that the image transfer is strong and – as with umbrella brand strategies in general – there is a risk that a single product with quality problems deteriorates the image of the total store brand portfolio. Furthermore, using the retail brand as an umbrella brand for differently positioned store brands may lead to stronger cannibalisation.

In particular for value brands, the optimal strategy is not yet clear. Some retailers link these store brands to the retail brand (such as *Tesco Value*, *Carrefour Discount*, *Coop Prix Garantie*) but others avoid it (such as *REWE*, which just labels these products *Ja!*). In a well-noted move, *Tesco* established a so-called discount brands range in 2008 (besides its *Tesco Value* range) in response to the success of discounters such as *Aldi*. These brands are not branded as *Tesco* but as, for example, *Country Barn* cornflakes, *Daisy* washing up liquid or *Creamfields* cheese. Different from the no-frills value store brand, these products are positioned as (much) cheaper alternatives to manufacturer brands and their packaging is simple but more upscale than that of *Tesco Value*.

Category-specific vs. Cross-category Store Brands

Retailers generally have the choice to establish store brands specifically for each product category or across their total product range. The category brand strategy has the advantage that the brand message can be focused on specific product features and that a clear positioning compared with other product brands in this category is easier, while the second strategy has the advantage – as described above – that advertising spending can be bundled across many different categories.

In food retailing, the trend towards common store brands for different categories has already been described. In non-food retailing, store brands are often focused on specific categories, as the *Castorama* example above showed. *Walmart* and its subsidiary *ASDA*, as a further example, use the store brand *George* for their clothing assortment (separating this brand from, for example, a store brand that is used for yoghurt seems logical). *Sears* has a number of different store brands, among them *Kenmore* that is used for home appliances and which is by far the market leader in the USA, and *Craftsman* that is used for tools and power tools and which is also among the strongest brands in these categories.

11.3   Category Management

In recent years, the merchandising process has often been integrated into a more holistic management approach to retailing, so-called *category management* (see e.g. A.C. Nielsen 2006; ECR Europe 1997). **ECR Europe (1997) defined category management as a retailer/supplier process of managing categories as strategic business units, producing enhanced business results by focussing on delivering consumer value** (www.ecrnet.org). Each category follows a specific strategy, which is embedded in the retailer's overall strategy.

Category management has developed as a stepwise planning process for categories, and was first proposed by the consulting company *The Partnering Group* in the mid-1990s. Over the past decade, it has developed into a standard industry process, which has been promoted by national and international ECR initiatives. Standard processes support an easy knowledge transfer across different retailers and/or suppliers. The basic process is shown in **Figure 11.3**. This is still the most applied process, even though over time simplified processes have also been developed.

The first steps in the **category management process** are the most innovative because they include formulating a clear strategic objective for each category. These first steps distinguish the new process of category management from the traditional, more operational way of merchandising, because they position the retailer by providing a clear profile in its merchandise mix.

Category definition involves determining the specific SKUs that constitute the category, based on which products consumers perceive to be interrelated and/or substitutable. The primary aim is to develop a category definition that is based less on the procurement perspective of the retailer and more on the consumer perspective. Within the category definition, the category is also segmented into sub-categories. This segmentation should be based on the consumers' **decision tree** when purchasing in the category, that is the sequential consumer choice process. For example, the category "wine" could be segmented at the first level by price categories (premium wines, standard wines, budget wines), countries (French wines, Italian wines, German wines), colours (red wine, white wine, rosé) or brands. Another classical example is the question of whether baby lotions should better be placed in a category with other lotions (e.g. for women) or grouped with other baby products into one common category.

Figure 11.3   The Category Management Process

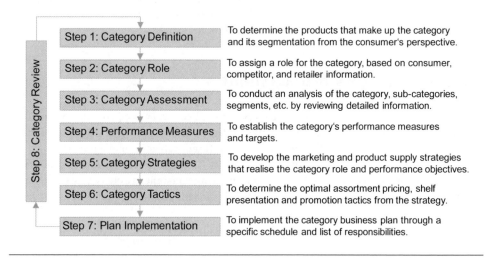

Source: ECR Europe.

In the next step, a **category role** is assigned to each category, namely the purpose of this category for the retailer is identified. Therefore, it is analysed how the category fits into the retailer's company strategy. This facilitates managing categories according to their importance and allocating resources (such as marketing budgets, shelf space and management capacity) optimally. The four roles in the category management approach are shown in. Before assigning a role to a category, the category's importance to the consumer, retailer and competition should be analysed (A.C. Nielsen 2006, pp. 79-93).

After a more thorough analysis of the category and sub-categories (**category assessment**), category targets are set and relevant performance indicators (**category performance measures**) selected because different roles lead to different target indicators. The so-called **fair share** is an important indicator. This is the market share of a retailer in the category compared with its overall market share. This is an indicator of retailer performance in this category relative to overall performance.

Table 11.2   Category Roles

Role	Share of Categories	Role Description
Destination	about 5 % of categories	To be the primary category provider and help define the retailer as the store of choice by delivering consistent, superior consumer value.
Routine	55-60 % of categories	To be one of the preferred category providers and help develop the retailer as the store of choice by delivering consistent, competitive consumer value.
Convenience	15-20 % of categories	To be one of the category providers and help reinforce the retailer as the full-service store of choice by delivering good consumer value (i.e. to support the customers wish for one-stop-shopping).
Occasional / Seasonal	15-20 % of categories	To be a major category provider, help reinforce the retailer as the store of choice by delivering frequent, competitive value.

Source: The Partnering Group.

The next step is to decide on a marketing **strategy** for the category. Many different strategies are possible, including:

■ **Traffic building,** attracting many consumers into the store, for example, by offering price promotions for frequently purchased products

■ **Transaction building,** enhancing the average size of the shopping basket, for example, by exploiting demand interrelationships in space allocation in stores or encouraging impulse purchases

■ **Profit generating,** enhancing the profitability of customers' shopping baskets by offering products with high margins and/or higher inventory turns

■ **Image creating,** improving the retailer's image, e.g. by offering products that are sold uniquely at the retailer or offering an outstanding choice in the category.

At the level of **category tactics,** operational decisions on the assortment, pricing (see Chapter 12), space allocation (see Chapter 13) and other retail marketing instruments are derived from the strategy and the other steps in the process. The final steps of the process are **implementing** the plan and a regular **review** of the category's performance, including plan adaptation

Cooperation of Retailers and Suppliers in Category Management

In such a category management approach, the importance of working together with the suppliers of a category has been emphasised from the beginning. One reason is that manufacturers usually have a deeper knowledge of the peculiarities of their categories because they frequently offer only products in one category and can invest time, efforts and money into gaining intensive consumer insights into it. By contrast, the retailer has knowledge of its customers' behaviour across categories, so that the two can merge their knowledge in the pursuit of mutual goals.

In the initial conceptualisations of category management, a far-reaching idea was that retailers could literally "outsource" the management of categories to specific suppliers, so-called **category captains**. These are leading suppliers in a category that would then manage the category (including their own products as well as competitors' products) on behalf of the retailer for the benefit of both partners. This concept has rarely been used in practice, however, because of the obvious risk that the supplier would strongly prefer its own product sales, even at the expense of its retail partner. However, retailers still often have preferred suppliers in a category, perhaps those that have the best contact with the retailer in terms of providing the retailer with information and making recommendations. These **category consultants** have a stronger influence on the retailer but the final decisions are still taken by the retailer. It is still essential for retailers to maintain (and enhance) the competence to manage their assortments. Retailers and manufacturers may have some common objectives in certain situations but, after all, they are still two independent companies with potentially diverging objectives.

11.4   Conclusion and Outlook

As with many other facets of retail management, merchandising is becoming more strategic and more fact-based because retail information systems provide the necessary data for analysing the effects of merchandise changes. Some trends have emerged in the past few years:

- Retailers are increasingly adding new categories to their merchandise (category migration).

- Retailers are reducing the depth of their assortments in each category, focussing on leading brands and eliminating underperforming manufacturer brands.

- Retailers are increasingly adding store brands to their assortments and store brand portfolios cover all segments, including the premium segment.

- In many cases, merchandising planning is integrated into a category management process, which supports the strategic retail positioning by assigning defined roles to a category and systematically deriving subsequent marketing decisions from the role.

The merchandising process is determined by the retailer's most valuable and limited resource: shelf space. For Internet shops, however, this constraint does not apply. Therefore, merchandise planning for e-commerce is different. Assortments can be larger and structured differently. Products can be placed in more than one category because this does not use shelf space, and constitutes an alternative way of finding the right product. More than one consumer decision tree can be modelled.

Increasingly, Internet shops customise their product offers to specific customers (e.g. *Amazon*). Even though Internet shopping has still not reached considerable market share in most retailing sectors, these merchandising processes could also have an impact on store retailing. Consumer expectations are changing because of the new technology. At the same time, multichannel retailers can use their Internet merchandising to gather knowledge about consumer behaviour (e.g. demand interrelationships) and subsequently use that knowledge to improve the merchandise management in their stores.

❚ Further Reading

A.C. NIELSEN (Ed.) (2006): Consumer-Centric Category Management, Hoboken/NJ.

VARLEY, R. (2006): Retail Product Management, 2nd ed., London et al.

11.5   Case Study: Decathlon[1]

11.5.1   Profile, History and Status Quo

In 1976, Michel Leclerq opened the first *Decathlon* store in Englos near Lille/France. Leclerq was a member of the Mulliez family that controlled retail chains such as *Auchan, Leroy Merlin, Pimkie* and *Boulanger*. However, these retail companies operated independent of each other and they were only linked via ownership. Upon their introduction, *Decathlon* sports stores were innovative and they had a great indoor area in order to test the products sold in the store. Leclerq's idea was to sell a wide assortment of goods under the same roof for nearly every type of sports and sportspeople; independent of age and power stage. The retail brand *"Decathlon"* was used to signal this wide assortment to customers. Furthermore, *Decathlon* had the aim to offer the products at the best possible price.

Only ten years later, *Decathlon* opened its first sports store outside France in Dortmund/Germany. Even though expansion into Germany was not a great success, **internationalisation** was further followed and the company expanded successfully into many different countries. Furthermore, the *Decathlon* **manufacturing company** was founded in 1986 to develop and produce products under the brand *Decathlon*. In 1996, *Decathlon* started its first so-called "passion brands" *Quechua* and *Tribord*.

In 2011, *Decathlon* runs 535 stores with more than 40,000 employees in 17 different countries on four continents. It is among the top three sports retailers in the world. Moreover, *Decathlon* is now part of the *Oxylane* holding. Until 2008, all company activities were under the *Decathlon* brand but then a holding was created. "Oxylane brings together two different activities: creating international sports products and brands, and local and on-line retail" (Oxylane 2010, p. 2). *Oxylane* operates different retail brands. Besides *Decathlon*, which is

---

[1] Sources used for this case study include the websites http://www.decatlon.com, http://www.oxylane.com and various reports, presentations as well as explicitly cited sources.

still by far the most important retail chain of the holding, these comprise *Koodza, Cabesto, Chullanka* and *Terres & Eaux*. *Oxylane* also acts as a producer of sports products and owns the store brands of *Decathlon*.

In 2010, *Oxylane* achieved a turnover of 5.98 billion EUR (excl. VAT), which was an increase of 9.9 % on the previous year. In the five years between 2005 and 2010, the company grew revenues by almost 70 %. Even more impressive is the company's standing in its core market France where it achieves 47 % of its revenues. Here, the company has a market share of 43 % and, at least partially as a result of its store brand strategy, a net margin of 6.3 % which is more than double that of its closest rival.

Figure 11.4   Performance of Decathlon in France

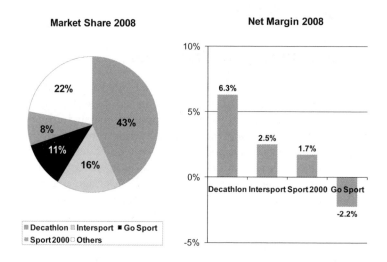

Source: Tanguy 2009, p. 37.

11.5.2   The Structure of Decathlon`s Assortment

In its standard format, **category specialist stores**, *Decathlon* has a sales area of approx. 5,500 m² on average and it offers ca. 35,000 articles. The assortment of *Decathlon* is organised into categories and each category refers to one sport. The categories of *Decathlon* are listed in **Figure 11.5**.

Considering the merchandising in each store, *Decathlon* is highly information-driven and rather centralised. Different from many of its competitors who decentralise such decisions to the store, *Decathlon*'s headquarters carefully analyses the catchment area of each store and based on this the depth of a category and its sub-categories are decided centrally. Those responsible for a specific department in a store then only get to choose a prefixed number of SKUs from a preselected product range. This strongly drives efficiency through a higher level of **standardisation** throughout the store chain, while adapting each store to the specific local context.

Decathlon offers a broad variety of goods at different price and quality levels to its customers. The merchandise mix of *Decathlon* is a mixture of **manufacturer brands**, for example *Adidas, Puma* or *Nike*, and **store brands**, which are now owned and coordinated by the Oxylane holding. Today, more than 60 % of *Decathlon's* sales stem from store brands compared with only 15 % at *Intersport*, its main competitor in France (Magaud 2009).

This strong focus on store brands was initially not the intended strategy of the company. Initially, it tried to sell manufacturer brands but had a problem sourcing them. Since the stores were considered not "chic" enough (Tanguy 2009, p. 38), brand manufacturers did not deliver or delivered late. For example, the renowned bicycle manufacturer *Peugeot* decided not to deliver at all. Thus, the **supply problems** forced *Decathlon*, in 1986, to create its first own brand, "*Décathlon*". At that time, it targeted the low price end of the product range but it took off and within ten years the brand stood already for one-third of *Decathlon's* sales. In 1997, the store brand strategy changed and category-specific store brands (which *Decathlon* calls "**passion brands**") replaced the umbrella brand *Decathlon*. *Quechua* for mountain sports and *Tribord* for water sports were the first of this type of brand. Increasingly, the store brands are pushing manufacturer brands from the retailer's shelves.

Today, the remaining manufacturer brands serve *Decathlon* to take advantage of their pull and image effects towards the customer. Furthermore, customers simply expect global and well-known brands such as *Adidas* or *Nike* in a sports store. They also enhance customer frequency in the stores. The impressive power that manufacturer brands in sports have today can be seen in the annual *Interbrand* ranking, which estimates a global brand value of about 13.7 billion USD for *Nike* and 5.5 billion USD for *Adidas* (Interbrand 2010). However, from the perspective of *Decathlon*, at least two arguments may overcompensate the pull effect of manufacturer brands. First, *Decathlon's* passion brands are not just cheap copies of manufacturer brands but they have developed into "real" brands themselves. Second, at least partly because of the high percentage of store brands in its assortment, *Decathlon* can earn higher profit margins, as **Figure 11.4** clearly shows.

In 1976, Michel Leclerq opened the first Decathlon store in Englos near Lille/France. Leclerq was a member of the Mulliez family that controlled retail chains such as Auchan, Leroy Merlin, Pimkie and Boulanger. However, these retail companies operated independent of each other and they were only linked via ownership. Upon their introduction, Decathlon sports stores were innovative and they had a great indoor area in order to test the products sold in the store. Leclerq's idea was to sell a wide assortment of goods under the same roof for nearly every type of sports and sportspeople; independent of age and power stage. The retail brand "Decathlon" was used to signal this wide assortment to customers. Furthermore, Decathlon had the aim to offer the products at the best possible price.

Only ten years later, Decathlon opened its first sports store outside France in Dortmund/Germany. Even though expansion into Germany was not a great success, internationalisation was further followed and the company expanded successfully into many different countries. Furthermore, the Decathlon manufacturing company was founded in 1986 to develop and produce products under the brand Decathlon. In 1996, Decathlon started its first so-called "passion brands" Quechua and Tribord.

In 2011, Decathlon runs 535 stores with more than 40,000 employees in 17 different countries on four continents. It is among the top three sports retailers in the world. Moreover, Decathlon is now part of the Oxylane holding. Until 2008, all company activities were under the Decathlon brand but then a holding was created. "Oxylane brings together two different activities: creating international sports products and brands, and local and on-line retail" (Oxylane 2010, p. 2). Oxylane operates different retail brands. Besides Decathlon, which is still by far the most important retail chain of the holding, these comprise Koodza, Cabesto, Chullanka and Terres & Eaux. Oxylane also acts as a producer of sports products and owns the store brands of Decathlon.

In 2010, Oxylane achieved a turnover of 5.98 billion EUR (excl. VAT), which was an increase of 9.9 % on the previous year. In the five years between 2005 and 2010, the company grew revenues by almost 70 %. Even more impressive is the company's standing in its core market France where it achieves 47 % of its revenues. Here, the company has a market share of 43 % and, at least partially as a result of its store brand strategy, a net margin of 6.3 % which is more than double that of its closest rival.

11.5.3   The Architecture of Decathlon's Store Brand Portfolio

As mentioned before, *Decathlon* offers a broad variety of store brands to its customers and covers different segments. Different from many other companies that clearly associate their store brands with the company name and that use an umbrella brand strategy across different categories, *Decathlon* has structured its store brands into categories; every single store brand stands for one form of sport and the brands do not overlapping within the assortment. Also different from other retailers, *Decathlon* uses the same store brand to cover different quality and price levels within the category. **Figure 11.5** shows the store brands of *Decathlon* and important manufacturer brands in each of the 17 categories. Each store brand focuses clearly on customer needs in the specific category, as the descriptions of some of the brands nicely illustrate (Oxylane 2009, pp. 13-19):

- "*Quechua* ('Mountain sports for all!'): in the realm of the mountains, *Quechua* couldn't have a more appropriate name than that of the courageous people dwelling amidst the peaks of the Andes in South America. Hikers, skiers, adventure racers, trail runners, climbers, mountaineers. Whatever your discipline, *Quechua* aims to make your mountain sport more enjoyable and safer."

- "*b'Twin* ('The cyclist's favourite brand'): creating a bike, at home on roads and pathways, comfortable, affordable, reliable and enjoyable: an impossible challenge? It would seem not, because this bike already exists and it's called the *b'Twin*! It is also the name of *Oxylane*'s specialist cycling brand, which designs high performance, good-looking and hard wearing products for cyclists of all abilities. What better name to embody the brand's much cherished values: autonomy, passion and pleasure?"

- "*Kalenji* ('Find your rhythm, enjoy your run'): with every stride, an ounce of energy harnessed from the renowned runners of the high Kenyan plains transpires into *Kalenji's* products. The latter are designed to enable runners, whatever their ability, whatever their rhythm and wherever they run (urban or nature) to run free from the constraints associated with the sport, to run with pleasure."

- "*Simond* ('Chamonix – Since 1860'): since 1860, at the foot of Mont Blanc in the Chamonix valley (France), *Simond* has been designing and manufacturing ice picks, crampons and karabiners. These products are safe, ergonomic and enjoyable to use. The brand is a reference in mountaineering circles. It invented the modular blade ice pick for example. *Simond* is the *Oxylane Group*'s latest Passion brand."

The brand *Simond* has to be highlighted since it deviates from *Decathlon*'s usual strategy. In this case, the brand was not created by *Decathlon* but an established manufacturer brand in a specific domain (climbing material) was acquired and turned into a store brand.

Decathlon separates its store brands by using different names for every single brand. Each brand has a clear and distinct **brand personality**. Furthermore, *Decathlon* presents its store brands as a manufacturer would. Often, customers are not even aware that these brands are store brands. This gives them uniqueness but separates them far enough from *Decathlon* that brand-affine consumers that may generally dislike store brands still buy them. By separation, each one can be clearly positioned against the dominant manufacturer brands in the category. For instance, each store brand has its own website.

Figure 11.5   The Categories of Decathlon – Store Brands and Manufacturer Brands

Nutrition	Racket Sports	Cycling
Store Brand:	Store Brand:	Store Brand:
aptonia	ARTENGO	b'Twin
Important Manufacturer Brands:	Important Manufacturer Brands:	Important Manufacturer Brands:
Isostar, Weider	Head, Prince, Wilson	Shimano
Fishing	**Fitness/Competition Dancing/Martial Arts**	**Equestrian sports**
Store Brand:	Store Brand:	Store Brand:
Caperlan	DOMYOS	FOuganza
Important Manufacturer Brands:	Important Manufacturer Brands:	Important Manufacturer Brands:
Rive, Jaf, Havel	Dupont, Tecno	Cherrier
Archery/Dart/Boules	**Golfing**	**Running**
Store brand:	Store brand:	Store brand:
GeOLOGIC	INESIS	Kalenji
Important Manufacturer Brands:	Important Manufacturer Brands:	Important Manufacturer Brands:
-	Callaway, Wilson	Adidas, Asics, Mizuno
Team Sports	**Swimming**	**Walking**
Store brand:	Store brand:	Store brand:
KIPSTA	nabaiji	newfeel
Important Manufacturer Brands:	Important Manufacturer Brands:	Important Manufacturer Brands:
Adidas, Nike	Adidas, Speedo, Arena	Adidas, Kappa, Asics
Roller and Ice Skates	**Alpine Sports**	**Hunting**
Store brand:	Store brand:	Store brand:
oxelo	Quechua	SOLOGNAC
Important Manufacturer Brands:	Important Manufacturer Brands:	Important Manufacturer Brands:
Bauer, Bladerunner, Rollerblade	Petzl, Mammut	Merlet

Aquatic Sports		Snow Sports	
Store brand:		Store brand:	
TRIBORD		Wedze	
Important Manufacturer Brands:		Important Manufacturer Brands:	
Liquid Force, Mares		-	

Overall, *Decathlon* heavily invests in advertising its store brands. In 2008, the company spent about 60 million EUR on advertising its brands, which is six times more than *Adidas'* advertising spend in France (Tanguy 2009, p. 38).

11.5.4   Developing and Producing Decathlon's Store Brands

The *Oxylane* holding controls the entire value chain for its store brands, from the product idea, to design and engineering, testing, production, logistics and sale to final customers through the retail network. To develop its store brands, *Decathlon* created a design department in 2001. This unit today employs 120 designers, recruited from the major international and French design schools. The portfolio of store brands was extended from the ten store brands that existed in 2001 by developing further brands, following the strategy of developing specific competences and lines by *Decathlon*. Furthermore, *Decathlon* created long-term partnerships with sportspeople in specific disciplines to develop and test the respective store brand products against the most advanced requirements of a champion (Pederzoli 2011, pp. 424-425).

One of the critical success factors of *Decathlon's* store brands is the R&D department, which introduces around ten major innovations every year. Its **innovations** are an important way of differentiation for *Decathlon's* store brands (Lecoq 2008, pp. 50-51). Some major innovations over the years have been:

- The "*2 seconds*" *tent* product line, launched under the *Quechua* brand. The tent will deploy in only two seconds when it is thrown into the air

- *Diabolo*, roller skates with an integrated braking system, launched under the *Oxelo* store brand

- *The Kage*, a foldable football goal launched under the *Kipsta* brand

- *Ygolf*, a golf kit to play everywhere, launched under the *Insesis* store brand.

Thus, while store brands are often characterised by lower innovation potential than are manufacturer brands, this is not true for *Decathlon's* brands. For example, *Tribord* spends about 5 % of its sales on R&D. In 2008 alone, *Decathlon* obtained about 15 patents. Since its creation, 44 design prices have been won. The innovations even get imitated and plagiarised. For instance, *Decathlon* noticed 40 copies of the successful *2 seconds tent* (Magaud 2009).

After the turn of the millennium, the management of *Decathlon* decided to **decentralise the R&D activities** and relocate the R&D teams of the particular store brands to locations more specific to the kinds of sports concerned. This choice was motivated by the wish to give the different teams an environment that was more suitable to the specific kinds of sports than the headquarters near Lille/France (Magaud 2009; Pederzoli 2011). The first store brand team that was located away from the headquarters was the team of *Quechua*, which is now based in Domancy in the Mont Blanc valley. This area is the perfect place for designing and testing mountain sports products. The *Quechua* brand employs more than 150 people including 100 who live and work in the Mont Blanc valley. The following activities of *Quechua* are based in the Mont Blanc area: research, prototyping, quality, design, communications, merchandising, finance and administration, textile unit, hardware unit and glacier hiking unit. *Tribord*, the store brand for water sports, is located at Hendayle/France near the

Atlantic sea. A total of 120 team members work there on product creation and design, prototype development and industrial production, in the training centre and the store. *Solognac*, the store brand for hunting, and *Caperlan*, *Decathlon's* store brand for fishing, share a headquarters together in Cestas, close to Bordeaux/France. The Gironde region offers many different fishing and hunting environments. The *Solognac* and *Caperlan* headquarters occupies an 18 ha. site with a 6,000 m² building – including a 3,500 m² store for hunting, fishing and archery goods – a 1.5 ha. lake and 9 ha. of conservation forest. The site of the headquarters invites customers to try out the products. The headquarters hosts the design and supply operations of *Solognac* and the engineering office as well as the quality, design, communication and merchandising, purchasing, finance and administration departments of *Caperlan*.

In 2007, *Decathlon* slightly revised its strategy. Every brand team should still have its own specific location, but whenever possible and adequate for the specific sport, this should be within a radius of 50 km of the central headquarters in order to share synergies concerning competencies of R&D. Furthermore, all store brand headquarters obtained a store, where only the specific brand is sold, as well as spaces for playing sports, open for customers (Pederzoli 2011, p. 426). Following this revised strategy, *Domyos*, the fitness store brand of *Decathlon*, opened its headquarters in 2008 in Marcq-en-Baroeul near Lille/France. The heart of the complex is a fitness centre. The aim was to create an area where a great number of people could practice fitness sports and have fun. Furthermore, the *Domyos* design team can take advantage of the contact with fitness enthusiasts and develop new ideas and products.

These examples show the focus on the optimisation of each store brand. Through the intensive contact with customers and professionals in the appropriate form of sport, the designer and developers of each store brand can better react to consumers' needs and learn what customers really want. Furthermore, the employees in the companies regularly practise the sport of the store brand they are working for.

Most articles of the store brands, more precisely two out of three, are produced in Asia, especially in China, Vietnam and Bangladesh, where *Oxylane* sources from over 250 **contract manufacturers**. This highly efficient production system with low cost locations also allows *Decathlon* to have gross margins of about 25 % for its own brands compared with about 15 % for manufacturer brands such as *Adidas* or *Reebok* (Tanguy 2009, p. 40).

11.5.5   An Innovative Strategy: From Retailing to a Product-centred Company Network

Beyond the store brand-focused merchandising strategy of the *Decathlon* retail stores, there is the highly innovative strategy of the company. In 2008, the *Oxylane* holding was established, which shifted the focus from being a retail company with strong store brands to being a company that creates sports products and brands and sells them via different (own) retail channels. R&D has been defined as its core competence (see **Figure 11.6**). Building on the strong image of the existing store brands and, furthermore, on the strong development competence for products and brands, the company now intends to grow its business around these product brands. Given the enhanced requirements for functional clothing in sports, so-called "component brands" (ingredient brands that label functional materials) provide an additional layer in the competence circle. An example is *Stratermic* for light-weight materials with thermal insulation.

Figure 11.6   The Activities of the Oxylane Holding

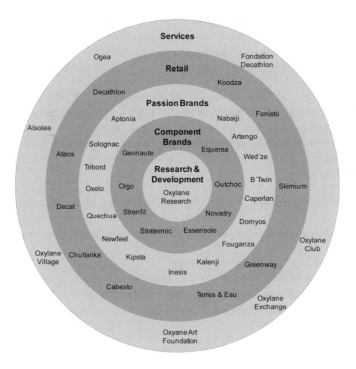

Source: adapted from Oxylane 2010, p. 4.

The store brands that had formerly been exclusively sold at *Decathlon* are now in part of the merchandise mix of the other retail brands of the holding as well. These include *Terres & Eaux*, *Decat'*, *Cabesto* and *Koodza*. *Decat'* is a small format for town centres and shopping malls and the chain offers a 100 % "passion brand" range in a shop-in-shop layout that is build around the different brands. The most successful retail chain of the holding, besides *Decathlon*, is the sports discounter *Koodza* that mainly offers the store brands of the holding and that has 46 stores in eight countries as of January 2011. In addition to physical retail stores, a number of online shops have been created that target different customer segments.

Overall, this enables the company to follow a **multi-format strategy** without the risk of watering down the clear positioning of each retail brand (see Chapter 9).

This development is not at the core of the present case study because it goes far beyond a pure merchandising strategy. As a company strategy, it is probably unique in the world but it clearly confirms the general trend towards verticalisation and towards **retailers as network coordinators** (see Chapters 1 and 6).

11.5.6   Summary and Outlook

Decathlon was forced early in its history to build its strategy around store brands. From an umbrella brand strategy that offered low price products under the name "*Décathlon*", the company switched to category-specific brands and invested heavily to give its store brands real brand appeal. The terminology ("passion brands") indicates the emotional approach.

With its store brands, *Decathlon* covers almost all segments of its assortment and offers a wide range of products at different price points, from beginners right up to professionals, closely related to the aim to offer an appropriate price. More than 60 % of its revenues today stems from store brands. The rest of the assortment is filled with well-known international brands such as *Adidas* or *Nike*, which are still must-haves for a retailer and generate customer frequency.

Obviously, *Decathlon*'s strategy is observed with scepticism by manufacturer brands. The CEO of *Lafuma*, an outdoor brand whose sales at *Decathlon* have fallen from 20 million EUR to 5 million EUR in a few years states: "The stores do nothing to put us forward" (Tanguy 2009, p. 40).

Decathlon indeed has greatly reduced its dependency on manufacturer brands through its store brands. With these store brands, the company has managed to differentiate itself from its competitors and to create added value for its customers while achieving attractive profit margins.

▌ Questions

1. Why do you think, Decathlon has decided against a strategy of cross-category store brands? What would you recommend for the future?

2. What are the advantages and disadvantages of owning factories or coordinating production by contract manufacturing for a retailer? Discuss.

3. Do you think that store brands in the sporting sector are a future-safe strategy? Explain.

12 Pricing

The purpose of this Chapter is to discuss the main aspects of pricing in retailing. The Chapter describes the basic methods of calculating a retail price, the structure of a retailer's prices and the dynamics and psychology of pricing. It concludes with some Internet-related aspects of pricing.

12.1 The Importance of Retail Pricing

Pricing in general, and price promotions in particular, have always been an important marketing instrument in retailing and, up to the present, price has played a very important role in retail marketing. However, it is precisely this focus on price reductions, often based more on belief and intuition on the part of the retailer than on facts and knowledge about its effects, that makes pricing a field of considerable strategic importance today. In many countries, retailer *profit margins* are very low. In food retailing, it is about 1 % of sales, so that a product that is sold for one euro leaves the retailer with an average profit of one cent. This means that by increasing this price by only 1 %, profits could double – if consumers continue to purchase roughly the same amount of this product. Consequently, the profitability potential of pricing is considered to be substantial.

12.2 Methods of Price Setting

12.2.1 Cost-oriented Pricing

There are three major methods for setting product prices in retailing: cost-oriented, competition-oriented and demand-oriented.

The most commonly used method for determining retail prices is the cost-oriented method, also called **cost-plus pricing**. Here, a **mark-up** is added to the cost of products to determine the final retail price. The mark-up percentage is usually calculated as a percentage of the retail price:

(1) $markup\ in\ \%\ (at\ retail\ price) = \frac{retail\ price - merchandise\ costs}{retail\ price}$

Usually, the cost used in the formula is the purchasing price for the retailer, while other variable and fixed costs are estimated in order to calculate the mark-up necessary to cover them. The mark-up percentage also includes the planned profit per unit. Since different product categories lead to different expenses, the markupmark-up is usually different between categories.

Direct Product Profitability

Direct product profitability (DPP) is a sophisticated method for planning variable mark-ups. This technique enables a retailer to find the profitability of each product by computing adjusted per unit gross margins and assigning direct product costs for such expense categories as warehousing, transportation, handling and selling. Based on exact costs per product, appropriate mark-ups can be set (Berman/Evans 2010, p. 476). The major problem, however, is the complexity of assigning costs to specific products, since it is difficult for retailers to allocate overhead expenses with a high degree of accuracy.

While cost-oriented pricing usually does not determine the optimal price, it is the most simplistic method of calculating a price. A retailer has the task of setting prices for merchandise assortments of 10,000 products in a supermarket or more than 100,000 products in a department store. For some items in a supermarket, prices are changed weekly. Obviously, this makes it almost impossible to calculate optimal prices, based on estimated price sensitivity, for all products. Therefore, the cost-oriented method for setting prices is a cost- and time-efficient method for the retailer's planning process.

12.2.2 Competition-oriented Pricing

In competition-oriented pricing, the retailer identifies its main competitors and sets its prices accordingly. Many retailers systematically monitor prices in their competitors' outlets. Depending on the pricing strategy, prices for certain products are then established at or below competitors' prices.

It has even become a common marketing instrument in different retail sectors to give price guarantees, i.e. to guarantee to the customer that he not find the same product cheaper in a competitor's store within a certain distance. While this instrument is often used in non-food retailing for higher priced products (e.g. by the electronics retailer *Media Markt*), food retailers are more and more often using price comparisons for shopping baskets or product ranges in their advertising showing that this shopping basket cannot be bought cheaper elsewhere or explaining that the prices of a certain product range (often the value store brands) are constantly benchmarked against the prices of competitors.

Competition must be considered in many retailing industries because retailing is often characterised by oligopolistic competition. In many countries, a few large retailers account for a very high market share. In this situation, a company has to anticipate the potential reaction of a competitor to its own moves before setting or changing prices. **Game theory** has developed a framework for this kind of analysis, which retailers have applied implicitly for a long time. In Germany, for example, food retailers know that they should not set prices below *Aldi*'s price level for a particular product or *Aldi* will react strongly in order to defend its image as the absolute price leader in the market. Such price wars can result in a generally lower price level in a country, which reduces profits for all retailers.

12.2.3   Demand-oriented Pricing

With demand-oriented pricing, the retailer bases its prices on consumer demand. The sensitivity of consumers to price changes is an important coefficient for setting a demand-oriented price. The **price elasticity** (more precisely: own-price elasticity) of demand is a measure of consumer sensitivity to price. It measures the responsiveness of quantity demanded to a change in price:

$$(2)\ price\ elasticity\ \varepsilon_A = \frac{\%\ change\ in\ quantity\ demanded\ of\ product\ A}{\%\ change\ in\ price\ of\ product\ A} = \frac{\Delta q_A/q_A}{\Delta p_A/p_A}$$

With a price elasticity of $|\varepsilon| > 1$, if the retailer raises prices, total revenue decreases. This is likely when there are many substitute products available. If price elasticity $|\varepsilon| < 1$, that is, demand is relatively price inelastic, a price increase results in a smaller relative reduction in purchasing volume and total revenue increases. For example, late at night, a convenience store usually experiences a relatively price inelastic consumer demand.

Recent studies have shown that there are rather few products about which the consumer is really price sensitive (these are often products that the consumer purchases very frequently and, therefore, has good price knowledge). Indeed, the majority of categories seem to be characterised by rather low price sensitivity, i.e. retailers have the opportunity to improve their profit margins without losing customers (SAP/GfK 2010).

Figure 12.1   Estimation of a Price-Demand Function from Scanner Data

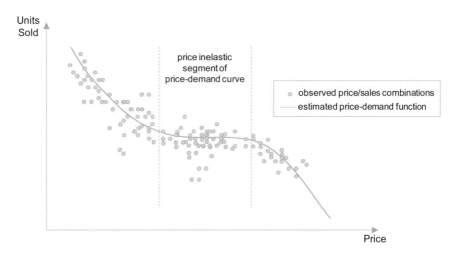

Information on price elasticity can be obtained in different ways. Customers can be surveyed to determine whether they would buy a certain product at a certain price. Experts can estimate sales levels at a certain price based on their knowledge of similar products. For

products that have been in the assortment for a longer period of time, historical data from the retailer's information system (price-volume combinations) can be used and both price elasticity and price-demand functions estimated from these data (see **Figure 12.1** for a ficticious example). Another method is to undertake experiments by using a sample of stores, varying the price systematically while leaving it unchanged for a control group of stores, and observing the changes in demand resulting from the price changes.

The two other methods described above can (and should) be included in demand-oriented pricing. Competitors' prices can be integrated as an influence factor on consumer demand. Since the objective is generally not to maximise sales, but to maximise profit, cost information can be added to determine the optimal level of demand and, subsequently, price

Interdependence of Price-Demand Functions within Assortment

Retailers simultaneously offer a large variety of products to consumers, so that retail pricing is really a multiple product pricing activity. The demand functions of different products are interrelated, and not only the own price elasticity of demand is relevant, but also the various **cross-price elasticities of demand**. The cross-price elasticity measures how the demand for a second product changes if the price of a first product changes. More precisely, it is calculated as follows:

$$(3) \ cross - price \ elasticity \ \varepsilon_{A,B} = \frac{\% \ change \ in \ quantity \ demanded \ of \ product \ B}{\% \ change \ in \ price \ of \ product \ A} = \frac{\Delta q_B / q_B}{\Delta p_A / p_A}$$

Cross-product relations may comprise **substitution effects**. This is often the case between similar products. If, for example, the price for coffee brand A is reduced, then more people will buy coffee brand A instead of coffee brand B. Thus, there is a positive cross-price elasticity. In this case, cannibalisation occurs and the price reduction of one product leads to purchases of this product at the expense of another product. This is often the risk of price promotions. By contrast, demand interrelationships can have **complementary effects**. For example, customers can come into a sports store because the price of skiing boots is reduced and then they buy other skiing equipment as well in this store. In this case, cross-price elasticity is negative. As a basic effect, price reductions create a higher frequency of visits to a store, which may benefit many products. Retail pricing must incorporate such demand interdependencies in order to maximise store profitability. In reality, however, it is not only a pairwise link between products but, potentially, all products in a store have a (stronger or weaker) interrelationship with all other products.

A **mixed calculation**, in which certain products are used to draw customers into the store and to establish a positive price image, while other products are used to make the customers' total purchases profitable for the retailer, is thus a common strategy. Within such a strategy, **loss leaders** are very often used by retailers. Here, a retailer sells selected items in its assortment at less than the usual profit margins or even below marginal costs. Usually these items are heavily advertised. The goal is to increase customer traffic to sell regularly priced goods in addition to the specially priced items. Loss leaders are often frequently purchased products from known brand manufacturers, so that customers are aware of the low prices and can compare them with other stores (Levy/Weitz 2009, p. 435). Selling below costs is regulated or prohibited in many countries by **minimum price laws**. However, calculating the true purchasing costs is difficult, even for the retailer.

12.2.4   Manufacturer's Suggested Retail Price

Whatever price setting method is being used, it is important to note (also when analysing consumer goods marketing) that it is ultimately the retailer who sets the price, not the manufacturer.

While manufacturers are often interested in **resale price maintenance**, i.e. to make sure that a retailer does not sell an item for less than a specific price (Levy/Weitz 2009, p. 404), this is prohibited in many countries. In the European Union, such vertical price fixing is prohibited in most cases since it may reduce competition between retailers. Exceptions are, for example, book prices in Germany or prices for pharmaceuticals, which are, however, often fixed by governments. In the USA, vertical price fixing used to be prohibited but a recent court ruling argued that resale price maintenance is not per se a violation but only if it exerts anti-competitive effects.

Manufacturers may try to publicly advertise so-called "non-binding suggested retail prices", which may act as an upper price threshold (because in practice consumers would not accept a price higher than a signalled suggested price). Suggested retail prices, however, do not usually lead to the intended minimum retail price. In any case, it is important that these price suggestions are "non-binding" and that the manufacturer does not try to exercise any pressure on the retailer to maintain these price levels since this falls under the prohibition of resale price maintenance as well.

Thus, the only legal influence that manufacturers can exert on the retail price is via their own selling price to the retailer. Since – as has been mentioned - selling below costs is prohibited in many countries by minimum price laws, the purchasing price of the retailer usually acts as the lower price threshold.

12.3   Price Positioning and Price Structure

The price image of a retailer is the result of a generalisation process, in which separate price-value impressions created by the different products, departments, and stores of a retailer are aggregated into a total impression of the price level of that retailer in the mind of the consumer. Price images are the result of the fact that consumers are unable and often unwilling to carry out a full and current price comparison for all products offered by a particular retailer (Diller/Anselstetter 2006, pp. 599-600). Certain products are more important for the overall price image than are others (SAP/GfK 2010) and the image-effect of a price reduction may be different from the direct price-elasticity of demand, as the case study in this Chapter illustrates.

Price Structure

With respect to the price structure of a retailer, a differentiation is often made between:

- a value (or budget) price segment,
- a medium (or standard) price segment,
- a premium price segment.

In the premium price segment, retailers attract customers who are less concerned with price than they are with service, merchandise quality, prestige and other store attributes. It does not usually maximise sales, but does achieve high profits per unit. With an aggressive pricing strategy in the budget price segment, a retailer seeks to earn high revenues by setting low prices and selling many units. Profit per unit is low, but total profit may still be high.

Many successful retailers focus on the budget price segment. Hard discounters, such as *Aldi*, full-range discount stores such as *Walmart*, many of the category killers, the dollar stores in the USA, *H&M, IKEA* and many more have gained tremendous market shares with a low or even aggressive pricing strategy. However, offering different price levels (within a merchandise category) allows a retailer to target consumers with a differing willingness to pay for a product. In economic terms, with different price levels, the retailer is able to obtain a larger share of total consumer rent.

Rather than offering merchandise in a category evenly distributed over a continuous price range, many retailers employ **price lining**. This means that they sell merchandise at a limited number of price points. Price lining helps consumers avoid confusion about product differences. Distinct price levels within a category simplify the buying process for customers. For example, the French home improvement retailer *Leroy Merlin* indicates on its shelves in which price line certain products are: "Nos premiers prix" on a yellow sticker shows products for small budgets, "Nos meilleurs rapports qualité/prix" on a green sticker marks products with a standard quality and a good price/quality relationship and "Nos prix haute qualité" on a dark blue sticker marks the best quality products in the category (with a higher price level). Other retailers have copied this approach as well.

12.4   Price Differentiation

Price differentiation means charging different customers different prices for the same product. The extreme case is negotiating the price with each customer individually. In some retailing industries, such as automobiles, such flexible pricing based on negotiations is standard and the prices actually paid vary greatly.

While in the service industry (for example, cinemas), prices for students or senior citizens are often lower, this is not usually implemented by retailers. Here, geographic price differentiation is the most commonly applied approach. Loyalty programmes, another way of price differentiation, are discussed in Chapter 14.

Geographic Price Differentiation

The price sensitivity of a store's customers is – among other factors – a function of the spending power of the clientele and the density and aggressiveness of the competition in the store's catchment area. A store in a poor region next door to a hard discounter might, therefore, use lower prices than another store of the same chain that is located in a rich city with no nearby competitors.

Retailers often use **price zones** as areas (or groups of stores) in which consumers pay uniform prices, while the prices between the zones differ. Such price zones help retailers adapt pricing more effectively to the distinctiveness and competitive environment of a local market area. In large cities, sometimes retailers even have different pricing zones within the same city (Levy/Weitz 2009, p. 431).

While geographic price differentiation usually enhances profits, some retailers follow a **one-price policy**, charging all customers the same price for a certain item, irrespective of store location (Berman/Evans 2010, p. 483). This policy, implemented, for example, by *Coop* in Switzerland, is directed towards consumer trust in the retailer and it is often based on a company mission with a strong corporate social responsibility element.

12.5   Dynamics of Pricing: HiLo vs. EDLP

Two different dynamic pricing strategies can be observed for retailers: EDLP and HiLo (e.g. Hoch/Drèze/Purk 1994; Levy/Weitz 2009, pp. 431-433; Bolton/Shankar/Montoya 2010).

HiLo (High-Low) Policy

With a HiLo pricing strategy, retailers have relatively high regular prices, but use substantial temporary price reductions to advertise their products and draw customers into stores. This philosophy is thus based on the frequent use of price promotions. The effect of such a price promotion is **dynamic** (see **Figure 12.2**), which ultimately makes it difficult to evaluate the overall profit effect. Usually, during the promotion period the volume sold of a product goes up substantially. This immediate effect can be decomposed into the following main sources:

- **Brand switching**: customers in the store that would have bought another brand buy the promoted brand instead.

- **Purchase acceleration**: consumers that would have bought the product or brand later may advance their purchase into the promotion period. In the case of frequently purchased products, this often leads to stockpiling, i.e. the consumer builds an inventory during the reduced price period.

- **Increased consumption**: owing to the reduced prices, consumers may consume more of the product on promotion. This may be linked to stockpiling because the increased availability of a product in a household may lead to enhanced consumption.

- **Store switching:** consumers that usually buy a brand in another store may switch stores to buy the promoted product.

Figure 12.2   Typical Effects of a Price Promotion

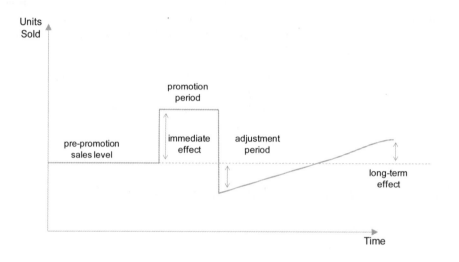

Obviously, not all of these effects are equally desirable from the perspective of the retailer and/or brand manufacturer. Furthermore, in a certain **adjustment period** after the promotion, the sales volume of the brand frequently goes down. This is the result of purchase acceleration, since sales that would normally occur during that period have partly been received during the promotion. The **permanent effect** of the promotion is often an increase in the sales of the promoted brand. Reasons include the brand switching or store switching during the promotion period, which may lead to satisfied customers and a permanent brand or store switch. Again, a store switch is, obviously, much more desirable for a retailer than a mere brand switch is.

How strong the sales increase, the subsequent sales decline and the long-term effect are depend on many variables, among them the relative strength of the abovementioned components. These, in turn, are influenced by aspects such as the usual purchase frequency for a brand, the consumers' price knowledge, the storability vs. perishability of a product, the availability of similar brands in the category and the promotion intensity of other brands. Furthermore, it has to be kept in mind that the retailer's profits stem from all brands within a category and, beyond that, from interdependencies between categories. Thus, to fully evaluate the effect of price promotions, its influence on the sales of other products in the store has to be considered as well.

Many supermarkets use a price promotion strategy. Price promotions can be regarded as a method of price differentiation through customer self-selection (Gedenk/Neslin/Ailawadi 2010). The promotion is offered to all customers, who then decide whether or not to take it up. Less price-sensitive customers buy at regular prices, while more price-sensitive customers wait for a sale and buy then. Price promotions can influence the retailer's price image. Proponents of a HiLo strategy also argue that price promotions create excitement in the store.

However, price reductions pose the danger that they change the customers' **reference price**. While a one-off reduction is considered a bargain, frequent or longer reductions of a product's price reduce the reference price, making it difficult to sell the product at its normal price in the future (Diller/Anselstetter 2006, p. 618). Heavy price promotion activity can also erode consumer confidence in regular prices (Hoch/Drèze/Purk 1994, p. 16).

HiLo pricing is often criticised for encouraging customer disloyalty and appealing to smart shoppers who only buy items at special prices. It may also increase the long-term price-sensitivity of customers. Especially for intensive HiLo strategies, this can lead to reduced profits for the retailer.

EDLP (Every-Day-Low-Price) Policy

The alternative is an EDLP strategy, for which prices remain stable over a long period. This involves offering consistently low prices. *Walmart* or *Aldi* are examples of such a strategy.

EDLP makes the shopping process easier for the customer, and the price continuity enhances his trust in the retailer. Disappointment that consumers of a HiLo store can potentially experience if they see certain products being sold this week at a much lower price than they paid last week can be avoided. Simple and consistent pricing is expected to lead to **price credibility**.

The real advantages of EDLP for the retailer, however, often lie in improving the efficiency of internal processes, thus, in reduced operating costs. While price promotions result in short-term volume volatility (as illustrated in **Figure 12.2**), which leads to increased logistics costs and often increased stock holding, EDLP results in stable sales. Therefore, sales forecasting becomes more reliable. Out-of-stocks can be avoided, and warehousing and transport costs are reduced.

By contrast, EDLP has high price transparency, and thus can only be implemented successfully if the retailer has a very low cost structure. EDLP makes price comparisons much easier for consumers (and competitors) than does a HiLo policy. An EDLP retailer must, therefore, have a very low retail price for most of its products, and only the most efficient retailers will be able to sustain this in the long run (Morschett 2002, p. 249).

EDLP and HiLo both have their advantages. In a survey conducted in the USA, 78 % of customers claimed to prefer EDLP. At the same time, more than one-third stated they would hold out for a price promotion or shop around to get the best deals. This shows why HiLo pricing remains a viable pricing policy, despite the supply chain and trust drawbacks (LeHong 2004).

12.6   Price Reduction Options

Adjustments in product prices are common in retailing, usually in the form of price reductions. **Markdowns** are a permanent reduction of the initial retail price. They are a common pricing tool, for example, in clothing and textiles to sell off merchandise. In the USA, it is estimated that more than 30 % of sales in department and specialty stores are of marked down goods, up from less than 10 % in the 1970s. The main reason is the seasonal character of certain merchandise, which often leads to overstocking at the end of the season, often with products that cannot be sold successfully in future seasons. Markdowns are planned ahead and calculated into the initial mark-up in order to be able to reduce prices as part of a **temporal price differentiation strategy**. Those customers with a higher willingness to pay for new fashion early in the season pay higher prices than do the customers who buy later in the season. However, markdowns are expensive and often after the first, planned markdown, others have to follow to clear off the merchandise. Substantial markdowns are often a signal of poor demand planning or pricing during normal selling phases.

Temporary Price Reductions

The options for temporary price reductions are wider than the above described simple price promotions. In addition, the following forms are common (see Diller/Anselstetter 2006, p. 615):

- **Promotion packs** have some extra content and the price per volume is lower (e.g. "10 % extra for the same price").

- With **BOGOFs** ("buy one, get one free"), a customer receives one unit of a product free of charge, if he buys another one for full price.

- In **multipacks**, several units of the same products are tied together (into a simple price bundle), usually at a lower price than the sum of the individual units.

- With **coupons**, consumers have to show the coupons at the store checkout to get a discount. Coupons can be distributed together with the retailer's advertising or through direct mailings. They can also be distributed by manufacturers' advertising (and be accepted by the retailer, but refunded by the manufacturer), or they can be distributed on the shelf.

- **Store-wide reductions** are another option that applies to the whole assortment. The German DIY chain *Praktiker* regularly offers "20 % off everything instore" for a few days. As these events show, customer traffic in stores increases dramatically during the price promotion period.

However, consumers may get used to drastic price reductions. As the example of *Praktiker* in recent years has confirmed, consumers develop the habit of only shopping during price promotions and deferring purchases in the times in between. This shows that anticipated price reductions are far less effective than are unanticipated price reductions and that there is a danger of overusing these instruments. The advantage of the multitude of price promotion options is that the retailer can vary the instruments and thereby avoid wear-off effects.

12.7   Psychological Pricing

In setting prices, it is not just purely rational economics but also the psychological aspects of prices that have to be considered.

Price-Quality Relationship

Especially when it is difficult for consumers to evaluate a product's quality, price may be used as an **indicator of quality**. Studies regularly show this influence of price on quality perception, and for many retail products, such as clothing, certain food items or technology, consumers often lack the necessary information and ability to judge the merchandise quality accurately.

Price Communication

Even though price seems to be an objective marketing instrument, price perception is – on the contrary – often largely subjective (Hurth 2006, pp. 63-94). Depending on the way a price is communicated, consumers evaluate price-value differently. A red or yellow colour for price stickers, large price signs, crossed out "old" prices, comparisons with recommended retail prices by the manufacturers, and many other communicative measures can lead to perceptions of lower prices. Presenting the price as a major feature in retail communication (i.e. the German retailer *Media Markt*), combined with a heavy advertising budget, often influences price image. Price communication, therefore, can be an important facet of a retailer's pricing strategy.

Odd Prices

Another frequently used approach is that of odd prices, i.e. prices on products that end on an odd number, mostly nine. Consumers are expected to perceive prices slightly below certain thresholds as substantially lower than prices at the threshold. So a product that is priced at 1.99 EUR is often perceived to be much less expensive than a product for 2.00 EUR. Research on the effect of odd prices shows ambiguous results; a positive effect is not really proven. Nevertheless, in most retail sectors, it is common practice.

12.8   Technology and Retail Pricing

While retail pricing has often been based on intuition and simple rules (such as fixed mark-ups), the complexity of the decision and the close interdependency of influence factors, as well as the fact that the prices of many products in the assortment influence the sale of one specific product, make new technology necessary (Russ/Stahmer/Schwaiger 2004; Bolton/Shandar/Montoya 2010).

Price optimisation software (so-called price engines) attempt to predict demand for individual products at a certain price level, based on historical price and sales data, competitors' prices, local demographics, inventory, shelf location and other data. It can be used by retail managers to test and forecast the expected reactions of consumers to changing pricing and promotion tactics in "what-if" scenarios.

An example of such software is the retail simulation suite developed by *Dacos* (www.dacos.com). The price engine, as part of this software, simulates and optimises price changes in the complete assortment. Based on the condensed sales data of several months and on the current purchase prices, it determines a mathematical model of psychological dependencies between retail prices and purchasing probability on the one side and expected gross profit per sold unit on the other. For example, a small price reduction for in a product in which the retailer earns a good profit margin and a small price increase in another product in the same category with a rather low profit margin may lead to a substitution effect and shift consumer demand in a favoured direction. With a price engine, the modifications in buying behaviour following price changes can be simulated and ideal suggestions for price lines automatically created.

With such a procedure, the gross profit in most categories can be increased by simply optimising the permanent prices. Unused potential for price increases can often be found in frequently neglected product lines belonging to the peripheral assortment where the customer has rather low price knowledge (SAP/GfK 2010).

12.9   Pricing and the Internet

All these traditional pricing instruments are also used in e-commerce. In addition, price differentiation is heavily used on the Internet. While store-based retailers usually set fixed prices within one store, auctions, a traditional form of finding the optimal selling price based on a customer's exact willingness to pay, have regained popularity through the Internet, especially on *eBay*.

Multiple price-oriented retail formats have been developed in online shopping, e.g. online shopping clubs or group rebates, as pointed out in Chapter 4.

Another important development is increased price transparency. Comparing prices on the Internet is far simpler and faster than it is by visiting different store outlets. It is therefore carried out more intensively. Certain websites specialise in price comparisons, and these are nowadays even available on smartphones, i.e. while shopping in stores.

Since online shops often price their products aggressively, these prices are used by consumers as reference prices, even when shopping at bricks-and-mortar stores. Since store retailers have to invest in facilities, employees and stock, they have a different cost structure to those of Internet players and matching their prices is not always easy. This price pressure is a problem for traditional store retailers, in particular for multichannel retailers, as pointed out before.

12.10   Conclusion and Outlook

Pricing is a major marketing instrument for retailers. Price is an important element of a consumer's buying decisions, and the right pricing may be a decisive determinant of the profit or loss of a retailer. Certain trends can be observed in retail pricing:

- Increasingly, retailers are setting their prices based on consumer demand and on what the market is willing to pay.

- Many companies have now introduced every-day-low-prices (EDLP). The main reason for this is to improve efficiency in the supply chain, forecast demand more reliably and achieve more consistent sales patterns.

- Even so, many retailers still prefer to reduce their prices as part of a price promotion, with promotional strategies becoming more varied and increasingly complex.

- Regional price differentiation is likely to become even more widespread in the future. It will, however, remain a challenge because, simultaneously, price transparency has increased because of the Internet.

- Prices not only differ from region to region, but also on the basis of different customer profiles. With loyalty programmes, coupons, price promotions, temporaryl and regional price differentiation, customers are becoming increasingly unlikely to pay the same price for an identical shopping basket.

Overall, pricing is becoming more analytical. In the past, pricing decisions were often based on intuition and rough rules of thumb. Today, retailers have far more sophisticated tools at their disposal and they can increasingly analyse how price changes affect the buying behaviour of individual customers, including cross-product price sensitivity and competitors' prices into their calculations. Pricing software also enables retailers to consider more and more the influence factors that determine optimal price. Revenue benefits from more flexible pricing can be expected, but price pressure is likely to remain strong.

| Further Reading

HOCH, S.; DRÉZE, X.; PURK, M. (1994): EDLP, Hi-Lo, and Margin Arithmetic, in: Journal of Marketing, Vol. 58, No. 4, pp. 16-27.

SIMON, H.; GATHEN, A.; DAUS, P. (2010): Retail Pricing – Higher Profits through Improved Pricing Processes, in: KRAFFT, M.; MANTRALA, M. (Eds.): Retailing in the 21st century, 2nd ed., Berlin et al., pp. 301-318.

12.11   Case Study: Carrefour[1]

12.11.1   Profile, History and Status Quo

The roots of *Carrefour* date back to 1959 when the Fournier and Defforey families founded the company. Only a year later, the first supermarket was opened in Annecy, Haute-Savoie. The shops were all located on thoroughfares; hence, the name "*Carrefour*". In other words, the name signifies that the location makes it convenient to shop there (Lhermie 2001). In 1963, *Carrefour* invented a new store concept: the **hypermarket**. Boasting 400 parking spaces and 2,500 m² of sales floor area, the first hypermarket opened in Sainte Geneviève-des-Bois, just south of Paris. The basic principle of this entirely new concept was "everything under one roof" in a self-service environment, which was an overwhelming success. Therefore, *Carrefour* carried on with this new business model. In 1970, *Carrefour* decided to go public, and shares were listed on the Paris Stock Exchange.

Furthermore, from the 1970s onwards, *Carrefour* forced its expansion and set out to conquer foreign markets, first in Europe, and then later in emerging markets such as Brazil in 1975. A year later, *Carrefour* introduced the so-called "produits libres", which are unbranded products but "just as good, but cheaper". In the late 1970s, the company started the development of hard discounting and created in 1979 the *Ed* chain in France. In 1985, *Carrefour* introduced its own store brand; products were labelled with the brand name *Carrefour*.

With the opening of the first hypermarket in Taiwan/Asia, *Carrefour* started 1989 a new wave of **internationalisation** and new stores were opened all over the world. In 1999, *Carrefour* and the French retailer *Promodès* merged to create the largest European food retailing group. After this merger, all hypermarkets of the two partners became *Carrefour* stores, and in France, all supermarkets were labelled with the former *Promodès* brand name *Champion*. In 2008, the *Carrefour Group* adopted a new governance structure, leading to a more fluid and effective operation. *Carrefour* changed its brand strategy (cf. Chapter 9) and used the *Carrefour* brand more widely, e.g. the supermarkets in France were relabelled *Carrefour Market*.

---

[1] Sources used for this case study include the websites http://www.carrefour.fr and http://www.carrefour.com, and various annual and interim reports as well as investor-relations presentations.

Nowadays, *Carrefour*, as the largest private European employer and the seventh world-wide, has emerged to an **international multi-format group** and the world's second largest retailer. *Carrefour* offers its customers almost every type of retail shopping – hypermarkets, supermarkets, hard discounters, convenience stores, cash & carry and online shopping – and adapts these store concepts to every location and lifestyle, in cities as well as in suburban and rural areas. *Carrefour* runs 16,784 stores with over 475,000 employees in Europe, South America and Asia. The sales of the *Carrefour Group* grew by 5.8 % to 101 billion EUR in 2010. Despite this worldwide growth, the development of *Carrefour's* French domestic market gave little satisfaction. Therefore, *Carrefour* decided to reassess its strategic direction. In early 2011, the company decided to spin-off its discount chain *Dia*. In the core business, the company had decided a few years ago to work on its price image.

12.11.2   The Price Image of Carrefour

After the overwhelming success of the hypermarkets in France, which has found a lot of imitators, the concept of *Carrefour* seemed to be getting on, especially regarding the price image of the company. One main goal of *Carrefour* is to be the **price image leader** in the relevant markets.

Figure 12.3   The Price Perception of Carrefour vs. Key Hypermarket Competitors in France

Source: Carrefour 2009.

Unfortunately, in France, the domestic market of the company, the price perception of *Carrefour* has changed in customers' minds. Competitors, especially other hypermarkets such as *Leclerc*, were perceived as cheaper than was *Carrefour* and thus they gained market share at the expense of *Carrefour*. Consequently, *Carrefour*'s domestic earnings decreased (LZnet 2010).

This example illustrates the importance for a retailer to influence the consumer's subjective price perception and shows that the consumer's price perception does not necessarily correspond with the objective price position. In the case of *Carrefour*, there was a significant gap between perception and reality (see **Figure 12.3**).

For *Carrefour*, the objective is to close this gap and improve its competitive price positioning. To do so, it is making use of the following instruments:

- Changes in assortment

- Changes in price communication

- Competition-oriented and consumer-oriented pricing.

12.11.3   Changes in Assortment

Against the backdrop of the mentioned market share losses and the impacts of the global economic crisis, rising unemployment and declining consumption, purchasing power has become a main concern for French households. Purchasing behaviour has changed radically as consumers have adapted their needs, changed their spending priorities and begun to make budgetary decisions that push them more towards essential products. Therefore, a change in thinking about the assortment design of *Carrefour* was necessary.

One effort of *Carrefour* to optimise its assortment was the establishment of effective price lining. **Price lining** means that a retailer sells merchandise at a limited number of price points, thereby avoiding consumer confusion about product differences. Distinct price levels within a category simplify the buying process for customers and clearly signal to the customer that products are available at budget prices, standard prices and premium prices. *Carrefour* has combined the strategy of line pricing with a competitor analysis of products and prices in its different categories. The aim was to identify gaps in competitor price lines, which offers the possibility of creating unique features in terms of price and differentiating *Carrefour* from competitors.

In 2005, the company decided to give its *Carrefour* store brand a complete overhaul by clarifying the store brand portfolio and entering profitable grocery sectors such as fair trade products, nutritional, organic and children's food with own brands (all associated with the name *Carrefour*). Two years later, the brand was extended into non-grocery and service sectors, e.g. decor with *Carrefour Home* or mobile telephone services with *Carrefour Mobile*.

In 2009, *Carrefour* launched the store brand *Carrefour Discount,* which replaced the store brand *Numéro 1,* which was not linked to the *Carrefour* brand. The goal was to offer consumers a selection of everyday essentials at very low prices that meet the *Carrefour* brand's quality standards of quality, innovation and price. This discount product line rounds off the existing brand portfolio and offers a greater choice to customers. The new store brand covers over 400 food and non-food items, including household goods and personal care products, covering the essential needs of everyday life. *Carrefour Discount* consists of 83 % food products such as coffee, tea, cereals, prepared dishes, yoghurt, cheese, fruit juice and bottled water. The remaining 17 % are household goods and personal care products such as cleaning products, shampoo, nappies or tissue paper. *Carrefour Discount* is displayed alongside national brands as well as the other *Carrefour* product lines and offers shoppers access to the full pricing range within one store. The *Carrefour Discount* brand, proposing the best price and quality for all the 400 reference items, fits within the tradition of *Carrefour* brands, but it is aligned with the prices of hard discounters.

Figure 12.4   The Price Perception of Carrefour in France

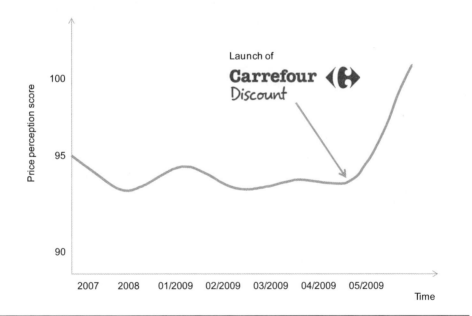

Source: Carrefour 2009.

The *Carrefour Discount* product line is liable to the quality commitments of the *Carrefour Charter*:

■ Products are made by *Carrefour*-certified suppliers in compliance with precise, rigorous specifications, which notably specify the origins of selected raw materials

- Products contain no GMOs

- Food irradiation is not permitted (no radiation treatments for better conservation)

- Products are tested and analysed to verify quality compliance

- Before marketing, products are tested by external consumer panels to guarantee organoleptic quality.

The brand package of the *Carrefour Discount* products is geared towards simplicity and high memorability, combined with a modern, plain logo that is easy to identify. The packaging of the discount line is simple and easy to spot on the shelf. The product is pictured without frills against a white background, which increases its visibility on the shelf and reinforces the common idea of an essential product. Furthermore, nutritional information based on the French National Food Health Plan is displayed on the back of the packing to guide customers when making purchases.

Carrefour Discount complements as a budget brand the other brands of *Carrefour*: the core brand *Carrefour* combines a full range of everyday products with the best price/quality trade-off and it is perfectly adapted to all the needs and expectations of consumers through a great variety of product themes. The premium brand *Carrefour Selection* responds to the exceptional needs of customers and offers over 150 high quality food products that combine refinement, original recipes and affordable prices to gourmet and gourmand consumers. *Carrefour Agir* responds to the sustainable development commitments of customers by combining *Carrefour's* quality standards with responsible consumption. The *Carrefour Agir* line is divided into four topics: *Bio* with organic food products, *Eco Planète* with environmentally friendly products that help preserve the planet, *Solidaire* with fair trade products and *Nutrition* with healthy food.

As *Carrefour* revealed, the effect of this introduction on the company's price image has been clear and positive (see **Figure 12.4**). Critics have argued, however, that the company partly cannibalised its standard level store brand since quality differences between the standard store brand *Carrefour* and the budget brand *Carrefour Discount* were not sufficient and, in some cases, former *Carrefour* products were simply now used for the budget line.

12.11.4 Changes in Price Communication

To improve price image in consumers' minds, *Carrefour* decided to improve price communication. The price image of *Carrefour* was built on a three-pillar-system of everyday prices: everyday low prices, promotions and loyalty. *Carrefour* has a clear understanding of how these instruments affect price image (see **Figure 12.5**). The aim is to optimise the mix of these three elements and create a positive, long-term impact on price image without neglecting the short-term stimuli of promotions.

Figure 12.5   Carrefour's Assumptions about Impacts on Price Image

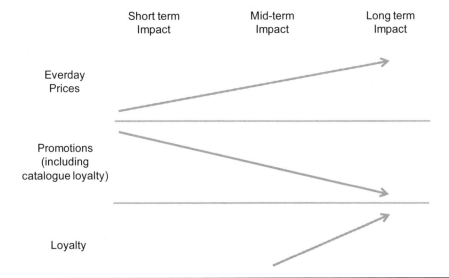

Source: Carrefour 2009.

Through an emphasised price signalling, such as more and larger signs, instore prices were better communicated. In fast-moving consumer goods, e.g. cookies, the labelling now contains detailed information about the product, a recognisable price dominating the label, the weight of the product and the price for one kilogram of the product for a better comparison between different packaging sizes. Price labels for promotions are in signal colours to catch the consumer's eye. Furthermore, consistent low prices, so-called everyday prices, were launched and continuously communicated to create a long-term impact in the customer's mind. Additionally, the number of promotions was reduced.

Moreover, *Carrefour* invested in consistent advertising campaigns such as leaflets with clear price messages to sharpen its price competitiveness. Additionally, catalogues were simplified. Furthermore, it tried to replace manufacturers' brands with its own store brands in consumers' baskets and increased the visibility of *Carrefour* brand products.

12.11.5   Competition-oriented Pricing and Consumer-oriented Pricing

Pricing plays an important role in retail marketing. *Carrefour* uses a kind of competition-oriented pricing, with a strong local focus on competitors. To emphasise the importance of competitive pricing, *Carrefour* introduced the "**Price Alert Line**" in 2006. This scheme encourages customers to alert *Carrefour* via a special phone line if they find the same product at a lower price at a competitor's store within a 30 km radius. As a result, the *Carrefour* store will lower the price of the product within 24 hours. Therefore, *Carrefour* focuses on localised pricing.

Figure 12.6   Impact of Price Changes in Different Product Categories

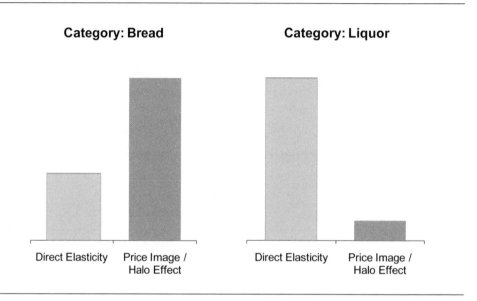

Source: Carrefour 2009.

As an advancement of this general practice, *Carrefour* developed CCP, **Carrefour Competitive Pricing** to achieve an improved price image versus competitors. Ahead of the rollout in France, the concept was tested and later established in Spain, where the market share in the hypermarket channel grew by 1.2 %. The intensity of the price competition between retailers in a region depends on the height of the competitive intensity. *Carrefour* analyses carefully the competitors in the area of its stores. As a result, the prices of goods in *Carrefour* hypermarkets can differ by region and the number of competitors.

Nevertheless, it is necessary to consider that the subjective price-sensitiveness of customers is not only based on the pricing of competitors. The sensitivity of consumers to price changes is an important coefficient, too. This sensitivity to price is measured with price elasticity and also considered in the CCP-concept of *Carrefour*. Depending on the product category, the leverage of the price differs, and changes in the selling prices of different goods have a different effect of the price image and its maturity. **Figure 12.6** illustrates this using the examples of bread and spirits. The change in the selling price of bread has only a small effect on the direct elasticity (i.e. sales of bread do not increase strongly when the price is decreased), but a considerable effect on price image. A change in the price of spirits has the reverse effect. Customers buy it in larger quantity when it is on promotion, but it does not improve the general price image of the retailer. With this knowledge of the price elasticities of product categories, product choice for promotions can be improved. Furthermore, *Carrefour* has achieved better cumulative margins and sales of its promotions.

12.11.6   Summary and Outlook

For a retailer such as *Carrefour*, pricing is an important element to influence consumers' buying decisions. With the right pricing strategy, the profit of a retailer can be significantly increased. Over recent years, *Carrefour* has improved its price strategy to tighten the position of its hypermarkets in a highly competitive environment and to regain market share. As a method to improve price image, *Carrefour* enforces everyday low prices and it has introduced its discount brand *Carrefour Discount*. As a side effect, *Carrefour* can also gain better margins with its own store brands. Furthermore, it focuses on **regional price differentiation** for two reasons: on the one hand, to react to the prices of competitors, whereas, on the other hand, to take advantage of consumer demand and the different levels of willingness to pay. However, *Carrefour* has to deal with the challenge of increasing price transparency because of the Internet.

Carrefour has recognised the strategic relevance of pricing for retail business. To achieve better results, the retailer focuses on the analytical aspects of pricing and uses **pricing software** to optimise promotional campaigns as well as the ordinary pricing in hypermarkets. The example of *Carrefour* shows how much effort a retailer can invest in its price strategy and which instruments are commonly used to realise a price strategy. However, price image is a consumer attitude with great inertia. So, whether *Carrefour's* image really improves strongly and quickly as a result of its strategy remains to be seen.

| Questions

1.   What are the advantages and disadvantages of the store brand *Carrefour Discount* to improve the price image? Explain.

2.   What are the long-term consequences of *Carrefour's* efforts to improve price image?

3.   Everyday low prices are useful to improve price image in the long run but a rather weak instrument in the short run. Promotions have a good immediate impact on sales but may deteriorate the long-term price image of a retailer. Discuss this dilemma and potential solutions to it from the perspective of *Carrefour*.

| Hints

2.   Check the *Carrefour Group* website http://www.carrefour.com/cdc/group/ for further information about the efforts of *Carrefour* to improve the price image.

13 Instore Marketing

The purpose of this Chapter is to highlight the importance of the store environment as part of the retail marketing mix. Options for store layout, the determinants and influence of store atmosphere and the allocation of space to merchandise are described.

13.1 Relevance of Instore Marketing

For all forms of retailing – store retailing as well as non-store retailing such as Internet shops – the store environment is among the most important determinants of **store choice** by customers. It also exerts a very strong influence on shopping behaviour in the store. Many buying decisions are made at the point-of-sale, to the point that professional marketing in the store can increase sales tremendously, for example, by pushing impulse purchases. Instore marketing refers to the use of information and communication-related retail marketing instruments within the outlets of a retailer. It includes the structure of the store and its basic layout, the presentation of goods and allocation of space to the merchandise, as well as all measures for influencing store atmosphere, including instore events (Gröppel-Klein 2006, p. 673). *Visual merchandising* is a term frequently used in the context of instore marketing. It refers to the way products are presented in a retail outlet. While this expression has been used with a focus on merchandise display (e.g. the choice of fixtures to be used and the method of product presentation), it relates to overall store design, store layout and other facets of the store environment (Varley 2006, pp. 182-183). Therefore, it is often used synonymously with the design component of instore marketing.

Two basic objectives of instore marketing are:

■ to facilitate the search process for customers, i.e. to design the store for **easy internal orientation** and

■ to create a positive **store atmosphere**, i.e. to evoke a positive emotional state of mind in consumers while visiting the store.

Both aspects are important to different degrees in different stores and for different consumer segments. A distinction can be made between two different types of shopping processes and motives (Kaltcheva/Weitz 2006; Babin/Darden/Griffin 1994):

■ **Task completion**, i.e. the motive to buy items that are needed (utilitarian motives)

■ **Recreational shopping**, i.e. spending leisure time shopping and browsing through stores (hedonic motives).

When targeting task completion, the retailer's focus is mainly on easy orientation and supporting the consumer search process. When approaching recreational shoppers, however, efforts are shifted towards store atmosphere. Instore marketing always has to consider both aspects. Even in everyday routine shopping for task completion, store atmosphere is important because it can positively influence the customer's mood. In recreational shopping, easy orientation also plays a role because consumers should not be confused, but feel secure and self-confident in the shopping situation.

13.2   Instore Marketing and Consumer Behaviour

The model most frequently used to explain the influence of store environment on customer behaviour was developed by Donovan/Rossiter (1982), based on earlier contributions in **environmental psychology**. They concluded that the stimuli presented in the store and the personality variables of the customers act together to influence the affective and cognitive responses of customers to the store environment. They found that two main dimensions have to be considered as intermediating variables when evaluating the effects of store environment:

- **Pleasure** (which refers to the level of positive emotions)

- **Arousal** (which refers to the feelings of excitement and stimulation).

Together, these two dimensions affect the response behaviour of the customer, that is, the degree of **approach behaviour** or **avoidance behaviour**. Studies have frequently shown that with increasing **pleasure**, the duration of a store visit, amount of unplanned purchasing, willingness to talk to store employees and revisit intentions rise. **Arousal** is a construct with optimal levels. Very low levels of arousal result in a lack of interest, whereas very high levels of arousal can lead to "panic" and lead a consumer to avoid a store or to leave a store as fast as possible. While this seldom occurs in marketing, crowded situations as in summer-end sales or on opening days may create this level of arousal. Thus, the interior design of the store environment should evoke an optimum level of customer arousal. It has frequently been shown that moderate levels of arousal (if the store environment is perceived as pleasant) correspond positively with **approaching behaviour**, i.e. a positive response of the customer to the environment (Gröppel-Klein/Baun 2001, pp. 412-413).

The level of arousal is determined largely by the **information rate** of the store, that is, the novelty (the unexpected, surprising, unfamiliar in an environment) and complexity (the number of elements, changes in the setting, etc.) (Mehrabian/Russel 1974) of the overall store environment. Arousal theory implies that optimal information rates contain some novelty and some complexity that activate the consumer, but also include calming elements. In other words, complexity and novelty are attenuated by giving the consumer familiar cues and signs.

13.3   Store Design and Store Layout

13.3.1   Overview

A store should be planned to (consciously or unconsciously) direct customer flow in specific patterns, which ensure that customers visit certain important merchandise areas. This should achieve optimum sales-space productivity and stimulate impulse purchases. With respect to the consumer's orientation process, the retail layout must be easily comprehensible so that customers quickly understand and assimilate the route through the merchandise (Gilbert 2003, p. 129).

One core component of the store environment design is the macrostructure of elements in the store, i.e. the **store layout**. This layout is represented internally in consumers' minds in so-called **mental maps** of a store. Clear and well-arranged mental maps of a store and knowledge of the locations of specific products, categories, checkouts and so on have been found to positively influence the customer's perceived shopping convenience (Gröppel-Klein 2006, pp. 680-681; Foxall/Hackett 1992, pp. 313-314). For the creation of strong mental maps, i.e. the extent to which a store is easily cognitively organised by a consumer, use is made of orientation points and areas in the store. The design of paths and crossings of paths, appropriate signage, different colours for different sections, escalators, floor material and so forth can act as clues for customers. Some retailers (e.g. *Toys 'R' Us* or *XXXLutz*) support the development of cognitive maps by providing real store maps to visitors in which departments and paths are represented visually.

In designing the store layout, the retailer has two basic options, which can also be mixed (see **Figure 13.1**; Gilbert 2003, pp. 124-125; Varley 2006, pp. 189-190; Levy/Weitz 2009, pp. 512-515):

- A **grid store layout** is characterised by long parallel aisles, with merchandise on shelves on both sides. This layout channels customer flow and, although it is often not very stimulating, it is well suited for shopping trips in which customers need to easily locate certain products and move through the entire store. Self-service is rather easy, and the shopping process for customers is fast and efficient. Space is utilised to a large extent. Supermarkets, drugstores and other retailers of fast-moving consumer goods normally adopt this layout.

- A **free-form layout** (also called **free-flow layout**) follows an irregular pattern that allows customers a free choice of movement in certain areas of the store and along certain paths. It allows for more relaxed and unregimented shopping. However, it may require salespeople to aid the customer to find certain products. This style is found in many clothing stores.

There are a number of variations of these basic types. For example, a **loop layout** (also called a **racetrack layout**) provides a major aisle that loops around the store to guide customer traffic around different departments (Levy/Weitz 2009, pp. 513-514). Within the departments, there is usually a free-form pattern. In an extreme case, a racetrack layout can force a **fully guided customer flow**. This principle is often applied by *IKEA*, where customers have to follow one major path through the entire store, with few possibilities for shortcuts.

Figure 13.1   Two Basic Types of Store Layouts

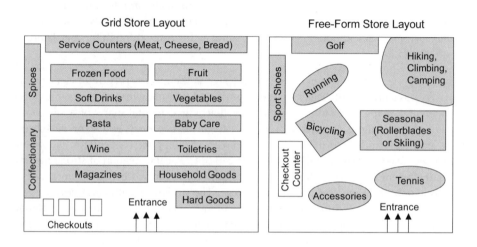

Source: adapted from Gilbert 2003, pp. 125-127.

In combination with certain store layouts, the fixtures used also vary. The most important fixture types are gondolas (shelves), round fixtures (e.g. for hanging clothes), tables (for stacked clothes), dump bins, baskets (for vegetables) and closed counters (e.g. for jewellery). While the grid layout employs mainly gondolas, free-form layouts usually have a mix of many different types of fixtures.

13.3.2   Grouping of Store Offerings

Within the store layout, merchandise is grouped together in sections, departments or aisles. Three principle types of groupings are commonly used by retailers: item-oriented presentation, theme-oriented presentation and brand-oriented presentation.

With an **item-oriented presentation**, the most traditional way of displaying merchandise, products are organised by types of items, such as, for a fashion retailer, one area for shoes, one area for trousers and one area for shirts. A DIY retailer might have a shelf for paintbrushes, one for paint, one for wallpapers and so on. While products are easily found with such a concept, demand interrelationships are not considered and, therefore, not exploited fully.

With a **theme-oriented presentation**, merchandise is displayed together according to a specific theme, such as "living in your home" (e.g. furniture, lamps, rugs and accessories), "outdoor" (e.g. backpacks, outdoor clothes, tents, barbecue grills and special food products) or "office" (e.g. suits, shirts and executive briefcases). Sometimes, a theme-orientation can follow a certain **lifestyle** and display all the fashion in one area that is associated with a common lifestyle such as hip-hop, sophisticated career woman and casual and denim style. Short-term or seasonal themes such as Halloween, Christmas, Olympic Games or the FIFA World Cup can influence the decoration in all parts of the store but can also be used to group certain merchandise together temporarily, often in a special feature area. Theme-based presentations promote cross-selling and they can support the **solution selling** of retailers in which products and services are bundled to provide a full solution for customers. Therefore, in some cases they are implemented as parts of category management strategies (see Chapter 11). Examples are tools, materials, delivery services and even trade services in a DIY store. Skis, ski shoes, services such as waxing and edge sharpening, skiing lessons, skiing clothes and travel arrangements in a sports store are another good example.

With a **brand-oriented** presentation, products from a certain (manufacturer) brand are merchandised together in **monobrand** store areas. In a fashion store, different products such as shoes, suits, shirts and neckties from *Boss* could be grouped together in one area and the equivalent items from *Armani* in another. Often, a brand-oriented presentation takes the form of a **shop-in-shop** (or **store-in-the-store**), a concept in which the merchandise of one brand is clearly separated from the rest of the store in a boutique-like manner. This type of **boutique layout** is sometimes considered a variation of the free-form store layout (McGoldrick 2002, p. 468). Frequently, this takes the form of **leased space** or a so-called **concession store**, in which an external company (often the brand manufacturer) operates this dedicated selling space, including the coordination of merchandise mix and inventory, with separate checkout and specialist staff (see also Chapter 5). Brand manufacturers often design their entire product ranges to match.

Brand loyal customers buy different products from the same brand to wear or consume together. A brand-oriented grouping facilitates such buying behaviour. Large department stores, such as *Saks Fifth Avenue* or *Selfridges*, have traditionally employed concession stores for such products as cosmetics, fashion and other brand-dominated categories. In this way, they act as a **house of brands**. The concept of a shop-in-shop has recently expanded into other retail sectors, such as *Tchibo* stores in supermarkets, *T-Mobile* concession stores in electronics stores, *Starbucks* in bookstores or *Bosch* stores within DIY stores.

13.3.3   Store Design and Store Atmosphere

Store atmosphere refers to the emotional responses of customers to the store interior. It is this emotional state of mind that influences shopping enjoyment and subsequent shopping behaviour (Berman/Evans 2010, p. 508; Varley 2006, p. 166).

While the layout of the store and the arrangement type for the goods are the core components, store atmosphere is created by many more elements. The atmosphere created by the store environment is influenced by all modalities; the consumer perceives the store environment through all his senses. These include (Gilbert 2003, p. 128; McGoldrick 2002, pp. 460-467):

- **Visual** elements (such as colour, brightness, sizes and shapes of fixtures and goods, floors, look of salespeople, etc.)

- **Aural** elements (such as background music, audio advertising on the instore radio or noises from other people)

- **Olfactory** elements (i.e. the scent in the store, e.g. perfumes used in clothing stores or the smell of a bakery department in a supermarket)

- **Tactile** elements (such as the material used for floors or the sensation of touching products)

- **Gustatory** elements (such as food samples in a supermarket, coffee served in a bookstore or champagne served in an elite boutique).

Visual elements, in particular, have been used systematically for influencing consumers, especially colours. **Colour psychology** is applied to the store design. Examples of the different psychological effects of colour include (Varley 2006, pp. 166-167; Hurth 2006, pp. 140-141):

- White and blue appear calm, cool and clean

- Red (similarly orange and yellow) has been shown to be stimulating and arousing and it evokes sensations of warmth, action and sometimes even aggression

- Green is regarded as restful and stimulates associations with life and nature.

Some retailers use a specific colour in their instore branding that they also use extensively in the store. For instance, *The Body Shop* uses green (which emphasises its environmental claim), *Saturn* uses a blue and orange combination (to stress its price aggressive positioning), *Boots* has blue and white (which strengthens its image as a chemist) and *Douglas* uses turquoise (to communicate a luxury image). By contrast, many retailers prefer to use colours only sparsely instore because they could conflict with the colour of the goods sold, which often change with seasons and fashions, as in the case of a clothing retailer.

Other sensual modalities are planned to some extent, but their effects are seldom considered systematically. However, **sound** and **aromas** have been shown to influence customer behaviour and mood, thereby exerting an influence on purchasing behaviour. Slow music, for instance, encourages people to move slowly and spend more time in the store (Berman/Evans 2010, p. 513), while fast music causes more arousal and feelings of excitement, which might lead to more vivid memories of the store and a more active shopping behaviour.

13.3.4   Experiential Retailing

Store atmosphere becomes even more important with the trend towards experiential retailing. This refers to creating a retail environment that offers a unique and memorable sensory experience in order to convert shopping into an interactive, enjoyable and exciting experience for the customer (Schmitt 1999), and provides a coherent overall emotional profile of the store. The atmosphere aims to appeal to the consumer trends of seeking exciting events, pursuing stimulation in shopping and spending leisure time going shopping.

Figure 13.2   Experiential Shopping at REI

Source: Rei 2011.

This kind of "entertailing" or "shoppertainment" (Buzz 1997) is focused on consumers that demand pleasurable experiences in their shopping activities. Both in general merchandise retailing with retailers such as *REI*, *Globetrotter*, *Sephora* or *Douglas* and food retailing with retailers such as *Trader Joe's, Coop (Switzerland), EDEKA* or *REWE*, retailers invest in impressive retail environments to create extraordinary experiences for shoppers (see **Figure 13.2**).

However, the creation of entertaining store atmospheres does not fit all consumer shopping tasks. If shoppers pursue task-oriented shopping goals, they often prefer simpler environments that do not distract them from fulfilling their shopping tasks. By contrast, those consumers that go shopping for fun might prefer exciting store atmospheres. Retailers thus have to keep in mind the typical shopping goals of their target customers when designing their stores. For example, if their customers typically regard food shopping as an unpleasant task, it might make sense to design supermarkets in soothing colours with simpler atmospheres. Conversely, shopping for clothes is often viewed as fun. Thus, fashion retailers can influence shoppers positively when they create exciting atmospheres (Levy/Weitz 2009, p. 532). Anyhow, retailers can vary the level of entertainment and excitement across their stores and can create low arousal environments for categories that are typically purchased in a task-oriented way and high arousal zones for categories that usually are purchased within pleasure-seeking shopping contexts.

While the *Disney Store* or *Warner Brothers' Store*, department stores such as *Galeries Lafayette* (see case study in this Chapter) and urban entertainment centres might be considered prototypes of experiential retailing, elements of this trend are important for every retailer.

These trends show that the retail store's potential to provide pleasure is achieved not only through the static physical facilities of the store, but also through events in the store that can be used as an "experience stage". The store is thus transformed into an interactive "**retail theatre**"(McGoldrick 2002, p. 453). Possible **events** that contribute to pleasant and entertaining instore marketing include cooking lessons in supermarkets, beauty treatments in department stores, fashion shows at apparel retailers, live appearances of artists in music stores or football tournaments in front of a sports store. However, the effects of such events on consumer behaviour depend on the level of innovation and adequacy of the events, i.e. the fit of the event to the retailer, its store and its merchandise (Leischnigg/Schwertfeger/Geigenmüller 2010).

13.3.5   Store Design and the Environment

Operating stores, especially when creating pleasant and exciting store environments with atmospheres such as lightning or sound, requires a high use of energy. Increasing **energy costs** and the importance of the **environment** as one of the main issues for retailers cause them to rethink their strategies with respect to store design, store maintenance and the exterior and interior facilities of the stores.

Coupled with an increasing awareness of customers and the greater society these issues, many retailers are implementing ecologically, environmentally friendly and energy-efficient store buildings and store strategies that are brought forward under terms such as "**green retailing**" or "**greentailing**". The basic principles of these greentailing strategies with respect to store design are the reduction of energy use and the use of renewable resources.

Companies such as *Coop, Marks & Spencer, C&A, Tesco, B&Q,* the *Metro Group, Walmart* and *Zara* have all emphasised the protection of the environment in their retail strategies. One element of these strategies is the establishment of "**green stores**" (or at least "greener" stores). With these green stores, retailers try to make their stores more energy-efficient and environmentally friendly using, for example, renewable resources (e.g. solar or wind power or total energy units), geothermal heating or cooling and energy-efficient refrigeration and lightning. They try to reduce the carbon footprints of the merchandise offered with respect to buying and logistics (see Chapter 12) and install advanced recycling programmes.

13.3.6 Store Design and Retail Branding

Store design can be an important element of a retail branding strategy since it exerts an all-embracing influence on the customer. The memory associations of consumers that comprise the **store image** can be influenced by a direct brand experience (during a store visit), in addition to indirect experiences, such as advertising (Krishnan 1996, p. 394). Because a retailer can offer customers a more extensive and direct physical experience than can the manufacturer of a product, a retailer is better able to relate directly to consumers, trigger intensive emotions and build vivid memories.

This effect on the **retail brand** is especially strong when store design is aimed at not only evoking positive emotions and an appealing store atmosphere, leading to a pleasant shopping experience, but also when it represents the **core of the retail brand** and when it is used to differentiate the retailer from its competitors (Morschett 2006, pp. 537-538). The application of colour has already been discussed, and the concept will be developed further here. The unique store designs of *REI* in the USA, *The Body Shop, Sephora, Old Navy, Boots* and *Lush* can serve as conventional examples, but the flagship stores of manufacturers (see Chapter 5), such as *Niketown, Nokia* stores, *Apple* stores and *The House of Villeroy & Boch,* the prime objective of which is to strengthen the brand, illustrate the effective use of this strategy even more cogently.

However, not only stores following the approach of experiential retailing can use their store designs to convey a brand message to their customers. Hard discounters such as *Aldi* and *Lidl* or wholesale clubs such as *Costco* follow the same principle. Simple, basic stores reduced to the essentials, floors and shelves with an inexpensive appeal presenting the goods in cut cardboard boxes and on pallets, with no unnecessary decoration elements as well as modest and pragmatic exterior design communicate these retailers' main competitive advantages very clearly to the customer.

13.4   Space Allocation

13.4.1   Overview

Space within stores and on the shelves and fixtures is a **scarce resource**. The allocation of store space to merchandise categories as well as allocating shelf space to different products is, therefore, a crucial process for retailers. Store space requires heavy investment. Appropriately allocated merchandise is an important determinant of the productivity of the relevant assets. **Space productivity** is a coefficient that is thus measured by most retailers as part of their operational controls (see Chapter 18). It is typically measured in sales per square metre or sales per linear metre. The retailers that display most of their merchandise on freestanding fixtures usually use square metres, while retailers that display most of their merchandise on shelves prefer to use length, i.e. sales per linear metre, to assess space productivity (Levy/Weitz 2009, p. 522).

13.4.2   Determinants of Space Allocation

The decision on how much space to allocate to a certain product or category is influenced by a number of variables. A simple rule of thumb is that share of space is allocated according to share of sales. However, other determinants such as product profitability, potential to enhance store traffic, demand interrelationships, retail brand positioning, category role (e.g. destination categories vs. routine categories), display needs (e.g. physical characteristics of the products, such as watches vs. bicycles) and inventory turnover (owing to restocking considerations) are also considered frequently.

An important coefficient for determining space allocation is **space elasticity of demand** (similar to the frequently used coefficient price elasticity; see Chapter 12). Space elasticity of demand measures the responsiveness of customer demand to a change in sales space. It is defined as the ratio of the relative change in unit sales (or change in turnover) to the relative change in shelf space. Average space elasticity has been found to be about 0.2, so that doubling the space allocated to a product would increase sales by 20 %. However, the rate of change is different for different products. Figures between 0.6 at the high end (e.g. for fruit and vegetables) and close to zero at the low end (for many fashion products, maybe because of a negative impact on exclusiveness by increasing sales space) have been reported. As with many output/input ratios, a declining marginal return on additional space is likely (McGoldrick 2002, pp. 478-479).

However, profit has to be maximised; hence, **space elasticity of profit**, defined as the relative change in profit in relation to the relative change in space allocated, could serve as an efficiency-enhancing coefficient. In order to obtain an optimum, the space allocated to all products or categories must lead to the same marginal space elasticity of profits. Otherwise, allocating more space to a product with higher marginal space elasticity of profits at the expense of a product with a lower coefficient would increase total store profits. By contrast, with category management (see Chapter 8) the consumer perspective is emphasised more, and allocating space with only short-term profit maximisation in mind might not influence customer satisfaction and customer loyalty positively, i.e. the needs of the customer also have to be considered (Varley 2006, p. 152).

Space allocation also needs to be based on the quality of space. Areas in a store are not trafficked equally by customers, the speed with which customers pass through different areas varies and certain areas of the store (or on a shelf) draw more attention than do others. Accordingly, placement has a profound impact on sales success. Some examples of valuable store and shelf areas are (Varley 2006, p. 185, p. 191, pp. 147-148; Levy/Weitz 2009, pp. 512-515; Berman/Evans 2010, pp. 512-514; Hurth 2006, pp. 122-129):

- Areas at the entrance of the store, especially the first shelf or other fixtures that customers face immediately after entering the store

- Ground-level space compared with other floors, which even results in different levels of rent for different floors;

- End caps of gondolas, which are usually highly visible – even for people who do not enter into an aisle

- Feature displays/special displays (e.g. off-shelf displays in a supermarket), which exert an additional impact and are employed to highlight certain products, especially new product introductions

- The checkout area, since all customers have to pass through it and may have to queue at the till (which makes this a preferred space for impulse items)

- Eye level on shelves, the centre of the shelf and – since customers in Western cultures usually look at items from the left to the right – shelf space at the right side of the shelf compared with that on the left.

13.4.3   Space Allocation Software

The task of space allocation is often based on simple rules of thumb and experience. Yet, the complexity of influencing factors has made it a field in which optimisation software was developed decades ago. With the rise of retail information systems, scanner data at checkouts and even personalised loyalty card data, these systems can now store an immense amount of data.

Space optimisation software uses information on specific products (e.g. product costs, size of product, variations), general information on space productivity in different areas of the store and on the shelf or the specific market (e.g. demographics in the catchment area). It calculates effect metrics (such as space elasticity) and demand interdependencies from past sales data, or the tools integrate estimations (e.g. from experiments). Company strategy (such as category role or inventory targets) is also considered and all variables are applied in a multivariate model to generate suggestions for an optimal store space and shelf space allocation.

Two of the most commonly used software tools for the optimisation of space allocation are *Spaceman* from *A.C. Nielsen* and *Apollo* from *Information Resources Inc. (IRI)*. Typically, the optimisation results are displayed in a **planogram**, which is a visual representation of a store or a shelf that illustrates how many products of a specific SKU should be stocked and where they should be placed. Planograms are also useful for store employees setting up and restocking the shelves because they help them comply with the planned space allocation

13.5   Conclusion and Outlook

Most of the various aspects of store design, store layout and space allocation discussed in this Chapter apply not only to store retailing, but also – at least to some degree – to all types of retailers, including mail order retailers and Internet stores. Space is also precious in the mail order business because square metres in stores are analogous to space on the pages of catalogues. While catalogues cannot offer all that "instore" marketing can achieve, because they only display two-dimensional, static pictures, Internet shops can now employ methods and approaches that are similar to instore marketing. Even though products cannot be touched in Internet shops, the medium has other benefits. Internet stores can be customised for specific users, space is only limited by the duration of the customer's visit and virtual reality means that consumers can be provided with different paths to find the same product and the grouping of store offerings can follow several types of groupings simultaneously (e.g. brand-oriented and theme-oriented). With digital salespeople (potentially customised), three-dimensional views on products, videos, virtual trials, sound effects and modern monitors, Internet shops have many instruments available for creating an exciting and pleasant store atmosphere (see Chapter 4).

However, the main motives for shopping on the Internet are ease and convenience. Therefore, Internet shops should not be designed purely from a technical perspective, but from the consumer perspective. The aim should not be to employ all technical possibilities to excite the customer, but rather to reduce the effort of buying products (e.g. by providing shopping lists from prior purchases), and support the customer. In other words, technology should be used to facilitate shopping.

If a retailer employs different retail channels, **coherence** between store atmospheres in all channels is important. Similarity within the appearance of a **multichannel retailer** has been found to have a positive influence on consumer attitudes towards the retailer (Schramm-Klein 2003, pp. 227-245). Considering the influence of store atmosphere on the retail brand, similarities between the different retail formats of one retailer seem to be an important factor.

Further Reading

SCHMITT, B. (1999): Experiential Marketing: How to Get Customers to Sense, Feel, Think, Act, New York.

ASHLEY, CH.; LIGAS, M.; CHAUDHURI, A. (2010): Can Hedonic Store Environments help Retailers Overcome low Store Accessibility?, in: Journal of Marketing Theory and Practice, Vol. 18, No. 3, pp. 249–262.

13.6   Case Study: Galeries Lafayette[1]

13.6.1   History, Profile and Status Quo

In 1893, Théophile Bader founded *Galeries Lafayette* and in 1912, the famous flagship department store ("**grand magasin**") on Boulevard Haussmann in Paris was opened. It is the largest of the twelve major department stores in Paris. The *Galeries Lafayette* group presently operates in five business segments (see **Figure 13.3**).

Figure 13.3   Galeries Lafayette Group

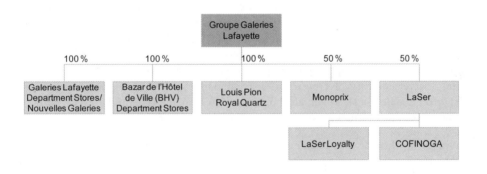

In 2009, group revenue totalled 7,069 million USD (Stores 2010). Around 35,000 employees work in the group's 659 stores and 60 affiliates. *Galeries Lafayette's* total surface area of nearly 500,000 m^2 includes a number of outstanding features, such as the famous neo-Byzantine dome built in the 19th century atop the building on Boulevard Haussmann.

---

[1]   Sources used for this case study include the websites http://www.galerieslafayette.fr, http//www.groupgalerieslafayette.fr, http://www. laser.fr, http://www.galeries-lafayette.de, various press releases, presentations and annual reports as well as explicitly cited sources.

The stores outside Paris are centrally located in major cities across the country. A breakdown of the group's turnover by business segment is as follows: *Galeries Lafayette:* 33 %, *Bazar de l'Hôtel de Ville:* 8.5 %, *Monoprix:* 36 %, *LaSer:* 20 % and *Louis Pion – Royal Quartz* 2.5 %.

In accordance with its former advertising slogan "Il se passe toujours quelque chose aux Galeries Lafayette!" ("Something is always happening at Galeries Lafayette!"), a number of *Galeries Lafayette* **sub-brands** have been created in Paris, which support the strength of the original brand:

- *Lafayette Homme* (2001) – men's apparel

- *Lafayette Gourmet* (2002) – food

- *Lafayette Maison* (2004) – decoration and home improvement

- *Lafayette V.O.* (2004) – children and teenagers

- *Lafayette Shoes* (2009) – women's shoe department.

In Paris, the so-called *Haussmann, Homme, Gourmet, Maison* and *Shoes* stores cover a combined total of 68,000 m² – the Western world's largest retail outlet and Europe's biggest store in terms of sales.

Despite the **withdrawal** from operations in Tokyo, Moscow, Singapore, Bangkok and New York, *Galeries Lafayette* department stores are still based in Berlin, with its famous glass-front architecture on Berlin Friedrichstraße, which was opened in 1996, in Dubai (*Lafayette Gourmet-Store*), which was opened in 2010, in Casablanca (2011) and in Beijing, which will open in 2013. The new stores have sales areas of 3,000 m² (Dubai) and 18,000 m² (Beijing). Ten years after the store opening in Berlin, 250 employees worked at *Galeries Lafayette Berlin*, the "secret embassy of France", as it is sometimes called. The sales area comprises 8,000 m² on five floors. However, after the launch in 1996, the Galeries Lafayette Berlin was not able to operate profitably until ten years after its foundation.

Besides the worldwide introductions of new *Galeries Lafayette* stores, the last big evolution for the group was in July 2009 with the opening of the biggest women's shoes department in the world at Paris *Haussmann*. The department was a staggering 3,200 m². Besides the offer of 150 brands, of which 75 are exclusive, *Galeries Lafayette* launched its own shoe brand, "Galeries Lafayette Paris", with an annual sales target of 100,000 pairs.

After quarrels between the former major shareholder families Meyer and Moulin, the latter and the French bank *BNP Paribas* bought all remaining public shares of the group. As a result, *Galeries Lafayette* shares have not been traded on the Paris Stock Exchange since July 2005. In 2009, *Galeries Lafayette* bought back the share of the company. *BNP Paribas* still owns 50 % of *LaSer* (TextilWirtschaft 2009).

Despite these changes in ownership structure, the group's strategy remains based on the following foundations:

- Department stores (*Galeries Lafayette, BHV*)

- City centre supermarkets (*Monoprix*)

- Consumer credit and customer loyalty programmes (*LaSer*).

13.6.2   Instore Marketing Strategy at Galeries Lafayette – "Theme Worlds"

When *Marks & Spencer* closed its Paris store in 2001, *Galeries Lafayette* bought the site and built its home furnishings department store *Lafayette Maison* there. This left the basement, the former home furnishings floor at the *Haussmann* empty, where *Lafayette V.O.* (for "version originale"), a shopping world for 12-25 year olds, was established. *Lafayette V.O.* has led to a major rethink in the way the rest of the store is merchandised. *Galeries Lafayette* has always been a **"house of brands"** and a **"temple of fashion"**, but has also always been perceived as a place for the high end shopper. To an extent, this is reinforced by the flagship store's belle époque architecture with its stained-glass dome, which has led to the impression of *Galeries Lafayette* being the "grande dame of Paris retailing" (Ryan 2005). Since 2001, however, the **"retail renaissance"** (Costello 2005, p. 21) of *Galeries Lafayette* has been implemented, aiming to create different shopping worlds in a real-life experience instead of traditional departments. *Galeries Lafayette* is trying to evolve from a department store into a **multi-concept store**, with different specialised concepts under one roof (Roulleau 2006, p. 9). This holistic instore marketing concept is based on the following pillars:

- Offering comprehensive "shopping worlds" revolving around a central theme including a large number of brands, instead of conventional departments

- Events to enhance the shopping experience

- A high level of dynamics in terms of new products and short-term offers.

Since this metamorphosis, customers no longer really enter a shop, but several distinct worlds that allow them to experience real-life sensations. This is what the company calls its **"new spaces"**. It is a world customers visit not only to buy goods, but one in which they can take part in a real-life experiences.

On its seven floors (including the patio on the seventh floor), the *Haussmann* store presents its so-called "universes" of fashion, beauty, food and leisure. In 2005, after four years of work, the flagship store's facelift worth 96.5 million USD was completed. **Figure 13.4** shows the store's current divisions.

Apart from the three floors covering an entire world of women's apparel for different income levels and for different shopping occasions, examples of other theme worlds include

Lafayette Enfant, the store's baby and children world, the *Beauty* world and the fourth floor, which is home to raincoats, luggage, furs and leathers and thus provides "everything you need for your holiday in England" (Ryan 2005). These worlds are characterised by the grouping of a large variety of complementary products, often contradicting conventional department store divisions. In the course of the store's remodelling, the walkways have been widened, something that characterises each of the floors and creates the impression of more space, which improves the shopping atmosphere. Instore navigational signage, other than at the escalators, is largely redundant owing to the clarity of the shopping worlds' layout, which groups complementary products logically (Ryan 2005).

Figure 13.4   „Shopping Worlds" at the Different Floors of Galeries Lafayette Hauss-mann

7	Terrace
6	Lafayette Mariage/Souvenirs de Paris/TV&Hi-fi
5	Lafayette Enfant
4	Luggage/Coats
3	Women's – "mode séduction"
2	Women's – "mode tendance"
1	Women's – "mode créative"
0	Beauty
-1	Lafayette V.O.

In the 1970s, *Galeries Lafayette* evolved from a general merchandise department store into a department store specialising in fashion. This vocation for fashion has been demonstrated regularly since 1980, when the first *"Festival de la Mode"*, a runway fashion show free of charge and a renowned tourist attraction, was held. This successful event has also been replicated at the Berlin store (Gebauer 2003, pp. 43-44).

13.6.3   Long-term Instore Marketing: Basic Layout

13.6.3.1   Overview

The bases of *Galeries Lafayette's* holistic approach to instore marketing are the different shopping worlds, whether integrated on the different floors, such as *Lafayette Enfant* or *Lafayette V.O.,* or in the case of freestanding buildings, such as *Lafayette Maison* or *Lafayette Homme.* Designed for a longer timeframe to indulge customers in, they are nonetheless subject to change to respond to current trends. The basis for this specialised approach is a detailed analysis of **customer lifestyles**. The focal point is no longer the product, but the customer and the full variety of his potential needs with respect to a particular aspect of life. Examples of the current status quo are described below.

13.6.3.2   Lafayette V.O.

Lafayette V.O., situated in the basement at the *Haussmann* store, offers a complete shopping universe for 12-25 year olds. It mixes fashion, music and interior decoration into a permanent happening according to the motto: "All the store's a stage" (Faithfull 2005). Before the official opening in 2004, the group created a faux website (www.street-challenge.com) seemingly dealing with urban fashion battles, without revealing its identity in order to communicate with the clientele. This **viral marketing strategy** was necessary because the young customer segment had not so far been attracted to the department store of their parents' generation (Leveque 2004). The concept has proven a great success with its clientele. Filled with music and marketed for the tastes of the teenage generation, *Lafayette V.O.* and its salespeople, who are of the same age and dressed like their customers, "could make you almost forget you're in a department store" (Faithfull 2005).

Throughout its 4,000 m² space, the assortment is ultra customised to meet the tastes of 12-25 year olds. Colour-coded walls divide the floor space into four sections themed around youth lifestyle. Besides fashion, which accounts for 80 % of the assortment, *V.O.* sells cosmetics, cell phones, video games, CDs, vinyl, books, Manga art and stationery. About 150 international brands are sold, appealing to teenagers from all cultural backgrounds. The real-life experience is also conveyed via a multifunctional area devoted to emerging product lines such as those using sustainable materials, and also including small exhibitions, installations by local associations and a nearby D.J. booth where rotating musicians perform live and contribute to the club-like atmosphere (Faithfull 2005). Other attractions include XXL fitting rooms equipped with soft drinks vending machines, displays that whirl clothing around on conveyor belts, impromptu shows for up-and-coming artists and graphic designers and a restaurant and recreation area (Marsh 2004, p. 29). The concept is forever changing to adapt to the fast-moving lifestyles of its clientele and it aims to provide constant novelty, lively emotions and surprise.

13.6.3.3   Lafayette Enfant

On the fifth floor of *Galeries Lafayette's* flagship store, an entire concept store dedicated to children from ages 0-12 was created in 2005, shortly after the realisation of *Lafayette V.O.* Thus, *Lafayette Enfant* fills what had been an age gap. It is also the first concept store of its kind dedicated entirely to children.

The 5,000 m² space offers an assortment covering all customer needs, appealing and appropriate visual merchandising as well as different activities, all aimed at creating a strong real-life experience. The assortment includes the following product categories: apparel for newborns, trendy fashion for boys and girls, apparel for pregnant women, decorative items for children's rooms, "boutique naissance" (equipment for newborns) and toys.

Since *Lafayette Enfant* strongly emphasises the variety of its assortment, more than 85 brands can be purchased, ranging from classic baby and children brands (e.g. *Petit Bateau*) to trendy fashion labels and luxury brands such as *Dior* or *Lacroix*. At the "boutique naissance", shoppers can also create a gift list, for example, for a baptism. The list is comparable to a wedding list and can also be accessed and managed online.

In order to keep customers' shopping experiences up-to-date, the assortment is revised constantly and new brands are added. Furthermore, at "le labo" (short for laboratory), children's apparel created by young designers is sold exclusively at *Lafayette Enfant*.

The shopping ambiance is designed to be fun and lively in order to please the specific target group. The three-metre high giant rocket at the entrance is especially appealing to young children. Since *Lafayette Enfant* seeks to please not only the offspring but also their parents, facilities are provided to occupy the children for a limited period under the supervision of qualified employees, e.g. a *Lego* atelier (Mottez 2005).

On *Lafayette Enfant's* first anniversary, new apparel brands were introduced to stress the newness of the **concept store,** and a number of special events were held to complete the shopping experience. Examples of the special anniversary events included treasure hunts, make-up and customised T-shirt workshops and a children's menu formulated so that children could create their own sandwiches. Additionally, items for children's birthday parties, such as garlands, party favours and balloons, have been added to the basic assortment.

13.6.3.4   Souvenirs Boutique

In 2006, *Galeries Lafayette* launched a new 400 m² space, located on the sixth floor and dedicated entirely to souvenirs. Each year, the *Haussmann* store sells more than 320,000 souvenir products (including 10,000 Eiffel Tower models, 8,000 fridge magnets and 5,000 snowstorm globes) In reaction to this enormous demand for souvenir items, *Galeries Lafayette* has created a whole world of souvenirs for the tourist to indulge in, including detailed visual merchandising to create the desired atmosphere. All the windows are wide open to the dome. A panoramic cloth, showing the roofs of Paris, covers a wall on which shelves are suspended. The roofs-of-Paris scenery is also used as a theme throughout the boutique. After climbing the stairs, customers discover the amazing panoramic view from the terrace and have lunch at the restaurant, enjoying an outstanding 360° view. In order to satisfy the many customer demands and requirements and to offer the best visibility possible, the following eight large product categories share the boutique: *Galeries Lafayette* Paris (e.g. a *Galeries Lafayette* collection of classical tourist souvenirs such as T-shirts or caps), Paris Mode (e.g. textile products branded with various Paris themes), Paris Patrimoine (products reflecting the French way of life ("savoir vivre"), e.g. soap from Marseille or *Perrier* and *Orangina* bottles), Paris Collector (e.g. mugs, flag-shaped keyrings or pens), Paris Metro (e.g. plates printed with Metro stations or street names), Paris Luxe (e.g. Limoges porcelain), Paris Culturel (e.g. typical French books, music, cards) and Paris Gourmand (e.g. wine or foie gras).

13.6.3.5   Lafayette Maison

Just as teenagers have their own shopping world at *Lafayette V.O.*, the equivalent for their parents is *Lafayette Maison,* which used to be integrated in the *Haussmann* store's basement. As trends such as **cocooning** have emerged, it has grown in importance and it has now been outsourced into its own building. The 10,000 m², five-level annex dedicated to home fashions was opened in March 2004 and is also situated on Boulevard Haussmann, across from the main store. It was the first department store to open on Boulevard Haussmann in more than 30 years. The concept underlying *Lafayette Maison* is that when entering, customers do not feel as though they are going into a retail store, but rather into a huge house instead. Accordingly, the selling floors are arranged according to residential activity by "living space" (Sloan 2004, p. 6). Cooking is on the lower level, personal expression items and gifts on the ground floor, dining products on the first floor, relaxation products in the lounge on the second floor and the sleep shop and bath shop are on the third floor (see **Figure 13.5**). The offer ranges from upscale lines to affordable gifts and accessories.

Figure 13.5   Departments at Lafayette Maison

3	Bed and Bath
2	Living Room
1	Dining Room
0	Presents/Decoration Articles
-1	Kitchen

Lafayette Maison offers the complete range of interior decoration and "art de vivre" under one roof in an exclusive atmosphere. Creating this required a 20-month construction period. Only the facade of the former *Marks & Spencer* site remained unchanged. The building now has a central atrium containing eight escalators above which a glass ceiling was installed, allowing natural light to illuminate the interior.

The concept of merchandising through living space also implies a different arrangement of products than those at conventional department stores. For instance, unlike traditional department stores mattresses are offered on the bed and bath floor, which is a logical move in terms of the underlying concept (Sloan 2004, p. 6). This rearrangement of departments, along with clear signage, which is a key element to ensuring effectiveness, helps the customer find the right products. However, it also ensures that customers linger and take their time, which encourages impulse purchases (Baum 2006, p. 67). Furthermore, so-called surprise elements are designed to stop and amuse the browsing customer. The huge candle wax bathtub situated on the bed and bath floor is a good example (Sloan 2004, p. 6).

Brands and designer boutiques are considered essential for creating a holistic, upmarket shopping experience. Therefore, brands are highlighted throughout the store and in the same way in order to achieve a consistent layout.

In order to enhance the shopping experience and event-like character of shopping at *Lafayette Maison*, a number of **instore exhibitions** have been held, such as cooking courses, launches for several product collections, a designer's day and raising awareness for fair trade. There are also country themes where a particular culture, Brazil, India or Japan for example, is represented across various areas including food (Baum 2006, p. 67).

Furthermore, in the kitchen department, chefs regularly demonstrate their cooking skills in front of the clientele. Cocktail tasting is also offered on a regular basis. The aim of these initiatives is to provide an authentic, real-life experience for customers. In order to keep customers coming back, the store is keen to give shoppers something new every time they visit. New products are highlighted throughout the store with "nouveau" signs. Furthermore, in the middle of each floor area, there is a presentation of current trends in home furnishings to inspire customers (Stores and Shops 2004, p. 8). In the 18-month existence of *Lafayette Maison*, twelve major adaptations and changes have been implemented in order to achieve ongoing innovation and newness (Roulleau 2006, p. 10).

Lafayette Maison represents a 24.6 million USD investment for *Galeries Lafayette*, which allowed the retailer to reinvent itself as an event shopping destination and has also made a considerable contribution to the group's performance. In 2004, sales rose 7.4 %, thanks to *Lafayette Maison* (Baum 2006, p. 68). Two years after its launch, the concept has proven a success and been introduced into ten other French cities so far as single floors in existing *Galeries Lafayette* stores (Baum 2006, p. 67). This success has been achieved mainly through the real-life experience concept, which "dramatically breaks away from conventional retailing" (Sloan 2004, p. 1).

13.6.3.6 Lighting

As a major element of visual merchandising, lighting is crucial to creating the appropriate atmosphere for the respective clientele, and this is used in all *Galeries Lafayette* stores. The flagship store on Boulevard Haussmann stands out as the prime example. When the lingerie department on the third floor was redesigned, the aim was to reinforce the Paris theme, as a courtesy to the foreigners shopping at *Galeries Lafayette* who strongly associate the store with the French capital. To accomplish this, a 20-metre stylised replica of the Eiffel Tower was suspended under the building's cupola. In order to achieve a dramatic effect, canvas was stretched between double rows of the open balconies at the top two levels, illuminated with projected images. The floors beneath *Galeries Lafayette's* dome are equipped with coloured lighting that continually shifts in tone and adds to the visual effect.

At *Lafayette Maison*, light plays a crucial role in creating the desired modern and sophisticated atmosphere (Sloan 2004, p. 1), including both natural light pouring through the glass ceiling and artificial lighting. Transparent panels that have been turned into a lighting design feature wrap around the staircase on each floor. Customers riding on the escalators and shopping in the departments facing the atrium can see vistas enhanced by colourful LED-illuminated visual creations. The daylight pouring onto all the selling floors through 150 windows allows customers to examine their selections in both natural and artificial light. Feature lighting for displays is supplied by adjustable-head track and individual surface-mounted luminaries. Multi-head flush-mounted fixtures provide additional ambient illumination in such areas as store directories (Display and Design Ideas 2004).

13.6.3.7   Women's Shoes Department

The women's shoes section is a rapidly growing market and it has become the most sought-after item ahead of sunglasses and bags. *Galeries Lafayette* expects sales of 4.5 billion EUR. The new department store is organised into five themed areas (see **Figure 13.6**).

Figure 13.6   Departments at Lafayette Shoes

3	Upmarket
2	Luxury
1	Urban
0	Contemporary
-1	Fashion

Located on the first floor of the domed department store is a **showcase** for footwear, which aims to offer its customers a unique shopping experience. An entire women's shoes department marked by luxury, innovation, design and fashion can be explored by customers in a "lounge" atmosphere. They are able to enjoy exclusive services such as tailored advice, a genuine closed fitting room to try shoes on in total privacy, a pedicure beauty salon, a skilled cobbler and a restaurant.

In 2009, five **pilot stores** opened outside Paris, and the plan for 2010 and 2011 was to implement between 15 and 18 new showrooms per year. *Galeries Lafayette* is aiming to be the leader in footwear in every city. In September 2009, a new private label was launched under the name "*Galeries Lafayette Paris*" that offers private label shoes for men and women at high quality and competitive prices.

13.6.4   Short-term Instore Marketing: Regularly Varying Mottos

In order to continuously refresh the customer shopping experience at *Galeries Lafayette*, different shopping areas focussing on one central motto are introduced for a limited period. This approach stresses the event-like character of shopping at the department store, and it is expected to keep customers coming back because of their desire to indulge constantly in new shopping experiences. The installation of a new shopping theme is always accompanied by press releases and advertising in various media.

An example of a short-term motto was the three weeks in April 2006 dedicated to the theme of *Los Angeles Fashion*. The entire store was dedicated and redecorated to fit the Los Angeles theme. This ranged from fake nails in the beauty department and typically American brands such as *Tupperware* or *Kitchen Aid* showcasing the "American Way of Life" at *Lafayette Maison* to the women's floors and *Lafayette Homme* offering a large variety of L.A. lifestyle brands such as *Guess, American Apparel* or *Rock & Republic*. Furthermore, numerous activities supported the retailer's attempt to create a real-life Los Angeles atmosphere, such as:

- An exhibition of *Fender* guitars accompanied by free masterclass sessions

- A "Little White Wedding Chapel" at the wedding boutique

- Beauty makeovers and a tanning centre

- A motorcycle tour on a *Harley Davidson*.

The event was rounded off by cheerleaders and marching bands in front of the store (Foreman 2006, p. 10).

Another example of short-term instore marketing is Valentine's Day, before which *Galeries Lafayette* regularly offers a number of related products and services to attract customers: Valentine's Day cards, beauty treatments or a themed dinner "Casanova" at *Lafayette Gourmet*, accompanied by a theatre performance.

13.6.5   Summary and Outlook

In 2004, *Galeries Lafayette* defined its challenges for achieving the performance needed to play a dominant role in the expected consolidation process of Europe's department stores: the clear positioning of retail brands and formats, proactive selling strategy, planned closure of structurally loss-making stores, strategies for improving cost structures, optimisation of capital employed and cohesive management. According to Philippe Houzé, the Chairman of the Executive Management Board of *Galeries Lafayette*, two conditions are necessary to guarantee the positive future development of department stores.

In general, stores have suffered severely from customer price sensitivity and new formats such as category killers. These factors have created the need for a critical mass and the need to reinvent and innovate constantly. That is why the group makes every effort to react constantly to the latest market trends and to adapt its concepts accordingly (Houzé 2006). To achieve growth in the future, *Galeries Lafayette* will continue its strategy of transforming itself into a specialised, **multi-concept store** under one roof by applying the **concept of experiential shopping**. Possible new worlds include sports, leisure and accessories/jewellery.

| Questions

1. In the case study, numerous examples of holistic instore marketing were discussed. What elements exactly constitute a holistic instore marketing approach?

2. For a department store, there are three basic ways to organise its floors. It can be structured either as a classic item-oriented area with traditional categories (such as trousers, books, or kitchenware), as a brand-oriented shop-in-shop concept or by means of different theme worlds such as at *Galeries Lafayette*. Describe the various advantages and disadvantages of these concepts.

3. Why it is it attractive for a retailer such as a department store to apply an upmarket and expensive holistic instore marketing approach, whereas discounters and category killers keep on gaining market share with an extremely simple and reduced store layout?

| Hints

1. See the section "Grouping of Store Offerings" in this Chapter.

2. See Chapters 2, 3 and 4 as well as Berman/Evans 2010 for a discussion of retail formats.

14 Customer Relationship Management

Building enduring relationships with customers has become a prime strategic objective of retail marketing. The purpose of this Chapter is to explain the new paradigm of relationship marketing and to introduce the underlying principles of customer value, the relationship life cycle and the constructs of customer loyalty and customer satisfaction. In retailing, loyalty programmes are manifestations of customer relationship management.

14.1 Relationship Marketing as a New Paradigm

Traditionally, marketing has focussed on attracting new customers for a company. Today, however, companies recognise the importance of retaining current customers by forming relationships with them (Kotler et al. 2002, p. 405). This focus on relationships is built on the premise that it is less expensive to market to existing customers than it is to acquire new ones (Reichheld/Sasser 1990). **Relationship marketing,** a term usually used synonymously with **CRM, involves establishing, maintaining and enhancing long-term relationships with customers** (Morgan/Hunt 1994).

From this perspective, a manager's primary task is to identify profitable and non-profitable customers, focus efforts on the former and balance the cost of acquiring and retaining customers with the current and potential revenue from those customers (Bechwati/Eshghi 2005, p. 88).

In retailing, advances in IT and the spread of loyalty cards have provided a means for retailers to identify a particular customer and to collect customer-specific data, thus enabling individualised marketing. Compared with other industries, retailing has tremendous advantages in CRM since it is in direct contact with the consumer (Hansiota/Rukstales 2002, p. 260).

Principles of CRM

Even though the methods proposed for CRM are heterogeneous, some common and underlying principles have emerged (Homburg/Werner 1998):

■ **Customer information**: companies must gather reliable and detailed information on their existing and potential customers, usually stored in an IT-based customer database.

■ **Individualisation/segmentation**: strong customer orientation leads to a targeted approach to individual customers or customer segments, instead of a standardised mass market approach to retail marketing.

- **Profit orientation**: not all customers are treated equally. Rather, they are classified and prioritised in terms of their profit potential for the company. Investment in customers is undertaken based on their profitability.

- **Customer interaction and integration**: instead of one-directional communication (such as traditional advertising), the aim is to achieve bidirectional interaction with the customer, including a stronger integration in the value-added process.

14.2   Customer Value

In the context of long-term customer relationships, loyal customers can be seen as an enduring **asset** for the retailer (Shugan 2005, p. 191). Customers spend money on certain product categories not just once, but generally regularly (weekly, monthly, yearly) for the rest of their lives. Since the purchasing relationship might extend over many years, the future revenue stream should be discounted to arrive at the net present value of future cash flow. If a single customer spends 400 EUR on clothing every six months, the net present value accrues to about 15,000 EUR between the ages of 15 and 75 (at a discount rate of 5 %).

Customer lifetime value (CLV), the quantified value of a customer, has become a prominent concept with the rise of CRM. CLV is the difference between what it costs to acquire, service and retain a customer and the revenue generated by that customer over the total duration of the relationship with him (Bechwati/Eshghi 2005, p. 88). The formula for CLV in its simplest form is:

$$(1)\ CLV = \sum_{t=1}^{n} \frac{(R_t - C_t)}{(1+i)^t}$$

with R_t = revenue earned from a particular customer in year t, C_t = customer-specific cost in year t, i = discount rate and n = duration of relationship (in years). The same formula can be used to either calculate an average CLV of the existing customer base or the potential CLV if the relationship duration can be extended.

However, the most challenging aspect of estimating CLV is not applying a formula, but projecting future revenues and costs. While this was complicated in the past, it has since become a more manageable task because historical purchasing data for a specific customer, based on loyalty card data, is available and can form a better base for projection.

CLV can be used to develop a profile of high value customers, which can then be applied to focus customer acquisition efforts on similar consumers. CLV can also be employed to categorise the existing customer base into high, medium, and low value customers, which allows a differentiation of product offers and services according to expected customer value and also provides an objective basis for directing retention efforts towards higher value customers. If, for example, handling a customer complaint costs 500 EUR and the lifetime revenue value of this customer is 5,000 EUR, it may be worth investing the money, while for a customer with a value of 300 EUR, it might not be (Bechwati/Eshghi 2005, p. 89).

Monetary Effects of Loyalty

The monetary value of customer loyalty originates from different components. A higher commitment to a company often leads to enhanced purchasing frequency (i.e. more frequent store visits), larger shopping baskets, lower customer price sensitivity and stronger resistance to counter offers from competitors.

Loyal customers search less for competing product and service offers. Lower marketing costs are also assumed, since targeted marketing is possible, and the company acquires substantial knowledge about the consumer, making marketing more efficient. Other advantages of loyalty include **cross-selling**, where the customer buys additional products from the company, and **up-selling**, where the company manages to sell higher value products to the customer.

Accordingly, the marketing focus has shifted from market share in specific product categories to increased **share-of-wallet** for a particular customer (Uncles/Dowling/Hammond 2003).

Non-monetary Effects of Loyalty

In addition, non-monetary benefits also accrue. Loyal customers are expected to recommend the retailer to friends and relatives, and this **word-of-mouth** constitutes effective and efficient marketing communication. They also have an **information value** for the company, since they more often complain when its performance deteriorates. They communicate with the retailer, thereby contributing to maintaining and enhancing the overall quality of the company (Reichheld/Sasser 1990, p. 108).

14.3   Customer Relationship Life Cycle

Pursuing the notion that customers are potential sources of profit over their entire lifetimes, the relationship between customer and retailer can also be regarded as a life cycle. The relationship thus has a clear beginning, a growth stage and a maturity stage, after which a decline and potential termination could occur (see **Figure 14.1**).

The customer relationship life cycle describes regularly observed patterns in the longitudinal development of customer relationships with a company. However, the model is **not deterministic**, i.e. not all stages have to occur in a relationship. Rather, the durations of the stages differ, and a retailer can influence the shape of the curve by, for example, effective counter-measures in the endangerment stage.

Different stages in the relationship require different marketing approaches (Bruhn 2001, pp. 4751). In the early stages, emphasis is on **customer acquisition**. In the growth stage and through maturity, the company needs to strengthen relationships and exploit the full sales potential (**customer retention**). In the later stages of the relationship cycle, it is important to know which customers are at risk of defecting and to employ **customer recovery** measures.

Even after customers have been lost, it may be possible to reactivate them. While identifying the causes of such defections can help win a customer back, it can also help avoid the same mistakes with others. Sending lost customers a special offer or calling them in order to allow them to complain about mistakes might bring them back into the relationship. Through data analysis, defection behaviour can be predicted, and those customers with the highest propensity to discontinue the relationship with the retailer can be targeted proactively (Brown/Gulycz 2002, p. 124).

Figure 14.1   Stages in the Customer Relationship Life Cycle

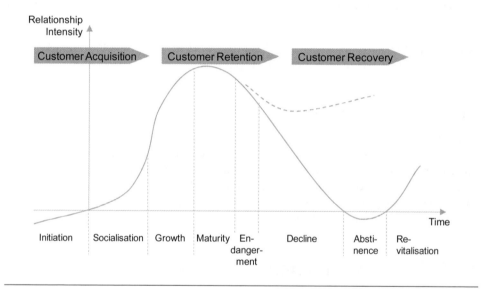

Source: adapted from Bruhn 2001, pp. 46-52.

14.4   Customer Loyalty and Customer Satisfaction

While loyalty has become more important as a marketing objective within CRM, there is no universally agreed definition of loyalty. Two basic approaches to conceptualise loyalty can be identified (Dick/Basu 1994, pp. 99-100; Uncles/Dowling/Hammonds 2003):

■ Often, loyalty is defined with reference to a pattern of purchases. **Behavioural loyalty** is measured in terms of repeat patronage, percentage of budget allocation in a category to a store, amount of switching or purchase likelihood.

■ Many researchers argue that there must be strong commitment to a company for true loyalty to exist. **Commitment** refers to an emotional or psychological attachment to a company. **Trust**, which entails confidence in the retailer's reliability and integrity, is often seen as closely connected to it (Morgan/Hunt 1994). **Attitudinal loyalty** can be measured by asking consumers if they like and trust the store, whether they feel committed to it and whether they would recommend it to others.

Figure 14.2   Types of Loyalty

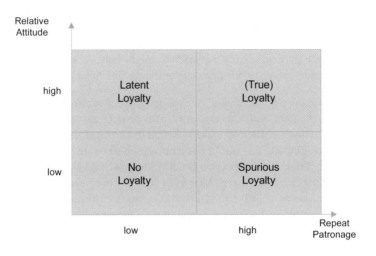

Source: Dick/Basu 1994, p. 101.

Both dimensions are important for evaluating the type of loyalty (see **Figure 14.2**):

- **Spurious loyalty** refers to a situation where repeat patronage is observed, but is not based on a strong positive attitude towards the retailer. For example, a lack of alternatives in the region can result in repeated store patronage. Habitual purchasing behaviour might have the same effect. Therefore, behavioural loyalty may merely reflect situational influences, but it is permanently at risk if situational conditions change, such as rivals entering the market (McGoldrick 2002, p. 114).

- While a positive attitude is an important objective, attitude does not necessarily correspond with behaviour and **latent loyalty** can occur. Situational influences can form a barrier between attitude and behaviour. For example, people can have a very positive attitude towards *Tiffany's*, but not be able to buy there. Alternatively, they may feel very positively towards *Harrods* in London, but live hundreds of miles away. Ultimately, retailers do not target a positive attitude of consumers, but aim at increasing their sales.

- **True loyalty**, the most favourable position, is signified by repeat patronage based on a strong relative attitude towards the retailer (Dick/Basu 1994, p. 102). Most definitions of loyalty now include both dimensions, i.e. behavioural loyalty corresponding with attitudinal loyalty.

Customer Satisfaction

Satisfaction is considered to be a primary prerequisite for loyalty, and loyalty is expected to rise with increasing levels of satisfaction. **Satisfaction (or dissatisfaction) is a consumer's post-purchase response to a product, which results from a comparison of (pre-purchase) expectations and perceived performance** (Dick/Basu 1994, p. 104). It should be noted, though, that the association between satisfaction and loyalty is moderated by a large number of variables. If, for example, the customer is a variety seeker, or social pressure acts against purchasing at a particular store, satisfaction might only be weakly linked to loyalty. However, dissatisfaction usually leads to a substantial decline in loyalty.

A customer's satisfaction with a retailer derives from the overall evaluation of all prior experience with this retailer, and thus not only with respect to a specific transaction. Increasing customer satisfaction, therefore, is important in all stages of the customer purchasing process, while traditionally marketing has emphasised **pre-sale** and **sale activities** (Kotler et al. 2002, p. 405). From the perspective of CRM, the **post-sale stage** is simultaneously a pre-sale stage, since the customer is regarded as being in a continuous buying cycle. Retailers providing their customers with friendly and courteous customer service departments, fair handling of complaints and so on try to enhance customer satisfaction after a purchase, with the intention of increasing the repurchase likelihood.

One challenge associated with customer satisfaction is that results derive from a comparison of performance with expectations – and expectations change over time. Consequently, constantly meeting or even exceeding customer expectations leads to increasing expectations over time. Service levels that enthused the customer when he or she first experienced them can become standard and they can then form a new minimum expectation level. Thus, maintaining stable levels of customer satisfaction is only possible with steadily increasing levels of service quality.

14.5   Loyalty Marketing of Retailers

14.5.1   Loyalty Schemes and Customer Clubs

In retailing, CRM is closely connected to the **loyalty schemes** that are usually based on **loyalty cards**. The pioneers in Europe were *Tesco* in the United Kingdom (see case study in this Chapter) and *Albert Heijn* in the Netherlands (Ziliani/Bellini 2004, p. 9). Many retailers now employ some form of loyalty scheme. Typically, loyalty programmes offer delayed, accumulated economic benefits to consumers based on repeat purchases. Usually, this takes the form of points that can be exchanged for gifts or vouchers. The discount value of points generally ranges between 1 % and 4 % of sales. The option of giving discounts in different "currencies" (e.g. cash, stamps, miles, reward points) can also offer perceptual advantages, e.g. for the retailer's price image (Cuthbertson/Laine 2004, p. 296; Shugan 2005, p. 190).

Most frequently, the ability to accrue benefits in the form of discounts on purchases, as well as the promotional offers connected to the loyalty programme, are the principal motivation for consumers for joining a loyalty scheme. However, emotional bonding and psychological relationship awards might also be important. **Self-actualisation** is considered a basic human need, and loyalty programmes can provide recognition to selected customers by giving them an evaluated status and the feeling of being special. In some loyalty programmes, the sense of being a member of a community is considered more important than are the financial rewards (Shugan 2005, p. 190; Reinartz 2010).

Loyalty programme rewards depend on the cumulative spending by customers at the retailer. There are two basic reward accumulation functions. If the **relative rewards remain constant** even though cumulative spending increases (e.g. one point per EUR spent as in most programmes), this function might lead a consumer distributing his or her spending between different retailers (without a loss for the customer). Only if the **relative rewards increase** with cumulative spending (e.g. one point per EUR when spending is below 100 EUR, three points per EUR when spending is above 100 EUR) does the programme become more attractive for customers who spend more with one retailer. This gives customers a real reward to concentrate their spending at one retailer. This supports a company strategy that aims to focus retention efforts on a small group of high value customers (Reinartz 2010). Sometimes, such a measure is implemented with different types of loyalty cards, such as normal cards, gold cards or platinum cards. **Switching costs** for customers are thereby increased since accumulated assets can be seen as customer investment in the relationship with the retailer, which should in turn enhance loyalty.

Single-Company vs. Multi-Partner Loyalty Programmes

In terms of sponsorship, two types of loyalty programme exist:

- Single-company loyalty programmes

- Multi-partner programmes (or coalition schemes).

Single-company loyalty programmes are run by an individual retailer. Examples are the programmes of *Boots*, *Auchan*, *Esprit* and *Peek & Cloppenburg*. Usually, the loyalty card carries the retail brand, and points can be accumulated at this retailer only.

A benefit of **multi-partner programmes** is that customers can use their loyalty cards more often, collect points faster and qualify for certain premiums or prizes faster (Zentes/Morschett/Schramm-Klein 2006, pp. 615-616). The penetration of the programme in the population is often higher than that for single-company programmes. Especially for retailers with a low purchasing frequency (e.g. DIY stores or consumer electronics retailers), for whom attracting customers in a proprietary programme would be difficult, participating in a coalition programme can be beneficial. While single-company programmes only have data on the current customers of a particular retailer, multi-partner programmes have access to far more data about shopping habits, so that the retailer can also target profitable consumers who are not yet part of its customer base (Cuthbertson/Laine 2004, p. 302). This facilitates analysing customer behaviour on a much broader base (within the limits of privacy regulations and customer acceptance). At the same time, the high cost of a loyalty programme can be distributed among participating retailers. The disadvantage of a multi-partner programme is that loyalty is often focussed on the coalition programme rather than on any particular retailer (Cuthbertson/Laine 2004, p. 298). In addition, the loyalty scheme (e.g. rewards, accumulation function) is not designed to meet a specific retailer's strategy, but rather has to appeal to a group of retailers as a whole. One of the most successful multi-partner programmes in Europe is the German *Payback* system with more than 30 million customer members, in which many large retail companies, such as *Real, dm-drogerie markt, Aral* and *Apollo Optik,* participate. The British multi-partner programme *Nectar* has companies such as *Sainsbury's, Debenhams, Homebase, BP* and *Hertz* as partners. In France, *S'Miles* offers bonus points for purchases with the supermarkets and hypermarkets of *Group Casino, Galeries Lafayette, BHV* and others.

Customer Clubs

In some cases, loyalty programmes are simply called "clubs". However, the focus of customer clubs is more on the emotional bond between customer and retailer. With club memberships, preferred service, newsletters, online forums, telephone helplines and other measures, **two-way communication** is established so that customers can interact with the company and get to know it better (Rowley 2004, pp. 126-127). For example, some retailers have a "baby club" for which customers can register. They identify from their customer base (based on the loyalty cards) if customers start buying baby products and then directly address them with an invitation to register. In the *Babybonus* programme of *dm-drogerie markt* in Germany, the focus is less on earning points and more on a welcome pack (including many test products), information for young parents and so forth. In the *Family Club* of *Coop* Switzerland, which is basically an extended loyalty card scheme, interaction with club members is intensified. For example, club members can use the online forum and can vote on special promotions for a certain period.

14.5.2   Analysing Customer Data

In CRM, data mining techniques are used to analyse customer information. Since the results of the analysis and the forecasting of customer responses can be used to develop marketing measures and the subsequent behaviour of specific customers can be tracked and evaluated, a learning system can be created that studies the specific behaviour of each customer and can also detect changes in behaviour over time (Zentes/Morschett/Schramm-Klein 2006, p. 600).

An important potential advantage of CRM is that the success and profitability of marketing measures can be evaluated in an experimental approach, by comparing the purchasing behaviour of the targeted customer group with a control group, based on incremental sales or contribution margin (Hansiota/Rukstales 2002, pp. 262-263). However, up to the present, the huge amount of data collected through loyalty cards (often millions of datasets daily) has thus far resulted in inadequate usage because IT capacity and methods of data analysis have developed at a slower pace than data availability.

Customer Segmentation

Customer segmentation is a core task of data analysis. In theory, retailers employing loyalty programmes can segment their customer bases down to individual customers, but in practice, the number of segments used is generally limited to between 10 and 30. Potential **segmentation criteria** include purchasing volumes, demographic characteristics, shopping motives, attitudes and lifestyles.

The options start with simple segmentation criteria. **ABC analysis** is used to categorise customers by their **annual purchases**. Very often, a 20/80 rule is assumed that argues that 20 % of the customers ("**A customers**") account for about 80 % of retail sales volume. Even though the ratio is rarely so extreme, it has frequently been shown that the relevance of different customers for a retailer indeed varies considerably. While customer purchase behaviour is a backwards-oriented criterion, **total customer lifetime value** can serve as a sophisticated basis for segmentation. Such customer value-oriented segmentation shows **which** customer groups a retailer should focus on, but it does not show **how** to approach customers.

Segmentations based on such consumer behaviour as **shopping motives** or **attitudes** are better suited to developing tailored marketing campaigns. Many different customer clusters have been proposed in the literature. For instance, customers can be clustered into "price-oriented", "quality-oriented" and "service-oriented", or fashion customers into "fashion enthusiast", "style seekers", "classics" and "timids and uninvolved" (McGoldrick 2002, p. 112). Furthermore, customers' stages in the **family cycle** (e.g. young singles, young couples, couples with young children, older, retired couples) are usually a good predictor of purchasing behaviour.

Based on their own customer data, retailers can, however, use a combination of methods to establish customer segments that are tailored to the retailer's specific needs.

14.5.3   Using Customer Data

Individual customer information provides insights into consumer behaviour that can be used to bring about a general change in a retailer's marketing. In such a case, customer data are used to change the **macro-variables** of retail marketing, such as the merchandise mix, pricing, promotion or location decisions (**micro-macro approach;** Zilliani/Bellini 2004, pp. 12-13). For example, before a product is delisted because of low sales, an analysis can be conducted to determine who still buys it. If, for example, only 20 % of customers purchase the product, but those are the most valuable customers in the store, keeping this product in stock is important for retaining these profitable customers (Cuthbertson/Laine 2004, p. 301).

CRM, by contrast, emphasises **micro-marketing** (or one-to-one-marketing), which targets specific consumers or consumer segments based on the knowledge of their individual behaviour. The retail service (such as the merchandise offered in advertising, promotions, services offered) is then tailored to certain segments and rather seldom individual customers. Since the store itself is still standardised for all visitors, CRM often does not take place in the store offer, but through marketing communication with specific customers. Measures include the following (Zentes/Morschett/Schramm-Klein 2006, pp. 604-609):

- **Addressed direct mailings**: customised direct mailings to customers' homes are used in almost all retailer loyalty programmes. The prime communication channel in loyalty programmes is some kind of (tailored or segmented) product catalogue, often with targeted promotions.

- **E-mail marketing**: direct customer mailings have increased tremendously with the advent of e-mail, which is used to distribute customised advertising and newsletters to customers. Distribution costs are much lower and customising more flexible and cheaper.

- **Instore multimedia kiosks**: similar to the Internet, multimedia kiosks in retail stores can be used to communicate with each customer individually (Swoboda 1996). At electronic point-of-sale terminals, loyalty cardholders can (among other functions) check their points balances, order rewards and print value cheques with which they can pay for their future purchases.

- **Mobile marketing**: some retailers already use customers' mobile phones as communication devices, for example of providing coupons by SMS or MMS.

- **Personal shopping assistants**: digital shopping assistants that a customer can carry or attach to the shopping cart are still in the testing stage. Based on his loyalty card, such a device can guide the customer interactively through the shopping process in real time. Shopping lists can be displayed, the customer led to certain products or recipes recommended, including the necessary ingredients and their locations in the store.

14.6   Loyalty Marketing and the Internet

A higher level of CRM and one-to-one marketing can be employed in Internet shopping. In addition to the purchases, total purchasing behaviour can be observed with **web usage mining**. Over and above the data that can be collected with loyalty cards in store retailing, an electronic retailer can track the date and duration of each visit to its website, the time a customer spends looking at a specific product, products viewed but not purchased, the sequence in which products were viewed or websites browsed (Hansiota/Rukstales 2002, p. 261). In contrast to stores, the individual data can be employed to tailor the entire retail marketing process to a specific customer, from the basic merchandise offer, prices and promotions to store design.

The most successful example, *Amazon*, shows how individualised **product recommendations** are derived from connecting the profile of an individual customer (established from his or her purchase history) to the profiles of other customers. Demand interrelationships are detected systematically. Even the recency of purchases is considered, because purchasing behaviour can change over time. Cookies are placed or the customers log in with a password and the customer is addressed with a **personal store**.

Furthermore, **web 2.0** has brought about new options for loyalty marketing. Here, loyalty is developed by stimulating the interaction between customers. For example, some retailers have started online forums where users discuss with each other and give each other advice. Home improvement retailers around the world (such as *Home Depot*) and pet stores (such as *Fressnapf/Maxi Zoo*) have been among the first to adopt this idea. Fashion retailers (such as *Zara, GAP and H&M*) almost all now have a presence on Facebook where they provide their "fans" with information and where they can truly interact with their customers. These types of **social media** have brought new opportunities for retailers to get in closer contact with their customers and to build loyalty. The negative side is, obviously, that electronic word-of-mouth which is stimulated by these instruments is not fully under the control of the company, different from traditional mass advertising. However, the positive messages distributed by customers to their friends are usually much more effective than is traditional advertising by retailers.

Customer Relationship Management in MultiChannel Systems

Consumers nowadays interact with retailers in many different ways: instore, via the retailer's webpage, via e-mail or on the phone call, via smartphones and/or via social media such as Facebook and many other channels provide a multitude of options for a consumer. The term **"converged retailing"** refers to a strategy in which these multi-consumer interactions are structured and organised in a way that allows the consumer to easily communicate with the retailer via the channels of their choosing (Webster 2010).

Retailers that sell via different channels increasingly try to combine these channels to approach the consumer in a homogeneous and consistent way. For example, the loyalty cards of a retailer can usually be used to collect points in the retailer's online shop as well.

In multichannel systems, customer relationship management faces the challenge that information about the buying behaviour of a specific customer in different channels (e.g. in the physical store and in the online shop) needs to be collected and integrated to get a full picture of the customer. Thus, in multichannel retail systems different sources of customer information can be used to gain consumer insights.

Furthermore, retailers can leverage the assets that they have in these multiple channels by directing the consumer to a specific channel. Instore advertising can be used to attract the consumer to the company's online shop. Visits to the webshop can be used to recommend the customer visit the store. Furthermore, as was discussed in Chapter 4, retailers that operate multiple channels increasingly offer cross-channel buying processes. Consumers are invited to search for information on the website and then buy in the store or vice versa.

Retailers such as *REI* in the USA, *Globetrotter* in Germany and *Interdiscount* in Switzerland bring the offer of the online store into the store, and consumers can even order from the online shop while in the store. This can enhance convenience for the customer. Likewise, many retailers now offer the store pick-up of products that are ordered via the Internet. This does not only bring the benefit of reduced logistics costs. The main advantage is that the customer picks up products in the store and then experiences the physical store and the product assortment there. This often leads to additional purchases and to a more intensive exposure to the retailer, which usually enhances loyalty.

Many ideas on integrating multiple channels to enhance customer loyalty are currently emerging and these are being implemented by retailers. While it is not yet clear which concepts may develop and which are sustainable, it seems obvious that a closer link between stationary stores and the online channel will be a strong trend in future years.

14.7   Conclusion and Outlook

Over the past decade, many retailers have shifted their focus to CRM and introduced loyalty card programmes as a tool. The costs of such programmes are often substantial, regarding rewards, IT systems and administration of the programme (McGoldrick 2002, p. 120). Some researchers are critical of the success of such programmes, claiming that "loyalty programs do not create loyalty" (Reinartz 2010, p. 410). This points to the fact that loyalty programmes have to be monitored closely and that loyalty cards alone are not enough to establish loyalty, but have to be employed as part of the overall retail marketing approach. While some researchers state that it is difficult to judge the ultimate profitability of a loyalty programme, this is true for marketing in general. Nevertheless, the success of loyalty marketing campaigns can usually be measured more accurately than can those of traditional marketing campaigns (Cuthbertson/Laine 2004, p. 299).

CRM must, however, be compatible with the company's broader strategy. If a primary goal is to achieve market leadership by gaining customers from its main competitors and growing rapidly, the maximum number of customers should be attracted. A focus on only the most profitable customers will, in this case, not be appropriate to meet the company's strategic objectives (Bechwati/Eshghi 2005, p. 96). This example illustrates that customer relationship marketing is an increasingly relevant marketing approach in retailing. However, as with all functional strategies, alignment with the overall company strategy is crucial. Some retailers, such as *ASDA*, *Aldi* or and *Lidl*, believe that adhering to their core strategies is more important for establishing and building loyal customers than is creating a loyalty programme. While this is certainly true for them, for many other retailers CRM offers a universe of options for interacting with their customers. Overall, the potential gains of analysing detailed customer data and targeting consumers, especially with new media that lower the communication costs of tailored marketing communication, still seems enormous.

▌ Further Reading

REICHHELD, F.; SASSER, W. (1990): Zero Defections: Quality Comes to Services, in: Harvard Business Review, Vol. 68, No. 5, pp. 105-113.

GRÖNROOS, C. (1994): From Marketing Mix to Relationship Marketing: Towards a Paradigm Shift in Marketing, in: Management Decision, Vol. 32, No. 2, pp. 4-20.

14.8 Case Study: Tesco[1]

14.8.1 Profile, History and Status Quo

The origins of *Tesco Plc* date back to 1919 when Sir Jack Cohen started to sell groceries from a market stall in the East End of London. The name *Tesco* is derived from TES (from *TE Stockell*, a tea supplier Jack Cohen used) and CO (Cohen). By the 1960s, the company had established its self-service model and had developed a reputation as a value-for-money retailer, according to its founder's "pile it high and sell it cheap" motto. However, during the 1970s, the company constantly lost market share to competitors, especially *Sainsbury's*. But by 1995, *Tesco* passed *Sainsbury's* and became the United Kingdom's market leader in food retailing, thanks to a more upmarket strategy since 1977. In 2010, it had a sales revenue of 42.3 billion GBP in the United Kingdom and employed approximately 287,000 people in over 2,500 stores throughout the United Kingdom. *Tesco* now operates four different store formats: *Express* stores with a shop area below 3,000 square feet in busy city centres and petrol stations, *Metro* stores with an area up to 15,000 square feet in high streets and large city centres, *Superstores* with a shop area up to 50,000 square feet and *Extra* stores with greater than 60,000 square feet in city suburbs (Coriolis 2004, p. 37).

The company currently operates in 14 countries outside the United Kingdom across Europe, the United States and Asia. Over 184,000 employees work in the international operations, generating a sales revenue of 20.2 billion GBP in 2,463 stores. Currently, it is the world's third largest food retailer. The company pursues a long-term growth strategy based on four key features (see **Figure 14.3**).

---

[1] Sources used for this case study include the websites http://www.tesco.com and http://www.tescocorporate.com and various annual and interim reports as well as investor relations presentations.

Figure 14.3   Key Features of Tesco's Growth Strategy

Core United Kingdom	International
• market leader	• 13 markets
• multi-format	• multi-format
• Clubcard	• local offer
• increase choice for customers	• flexibility

Non-Food	Retailing Services
• value creation	• www.tesco.com
• private label brands	• Tesco Personal Finance
• extending range	• Tesco Telecoms
• efficiency	

Source: Tesco 2011.

14.8.2   Tesco Clubcard

14.8.2.1   Market Conditions before the Introduction of Tesco Clubcard

At the beginning of the 1990s, *Tesco* faced difficult market conditions. Population growth was low and so was food market growth. The supermarket segment in the United Kingdom was already well developed and relatively saturated, and getting planning permission for large greenfield sites was becoming increasingly difficult. There were also three strong competitors (*Sainsbury's, ASDA* and *Safeway*) in the national market; *Tesco* was the no. 2 in the market with a share of 16.7 % traditional supermarkets were being challenged by the arrival of new formats such as hard discounters such as *Aldi* (Coriolis 2004, p. 3). In order to tackle these difficulties, *Tesco* decided to implement an entirely **customer-focused initiative** based on the customer loyalty card *Tesco Clubcard*. In a saturated market such as the United Kingdom, the goal of the initiative was not only to gain new customers in order to increase market share, but also to enhance existing customer loyalty in order to secure a greater share of their total shopping baskets.

14.8.2.2   Implementation

This programme was developed and implemented with the help of the agency *dunnhumby*, which joined *Tesco* in their marketing efforts. In a trial and error approach, the loyalty scheme was trialled in 12 selected stores in 1994.

In February 1995, the *Tesco Clubcard* was launched nationwide. Responsible was the then marketing director, Terry Leahy, who later became CEO of *Tesco* (Dawson 2011, p. 33). The core purpose of the CRM strategy was "to create value for customers to earn their lifetime loyalty", which was expressed in two key values "No one tries harder for customers" and "Treating people how we like to be treated" (Tesco 2006, p. 1). Thus, the *Clubcard* is more than an "average" loyalty card, and it constitutes a central part of the company's philosophy. The explicit goal of *Tesco*'s CRM strategy is to reward individual customers for their loyalty (Beckett/Nayak 2005, p. 8). Consequently, the focus shifted away from the average to the individual customer. By using the individual customer as the focus, the aim was to create a modern "corner store" (Wylie 2005). This **customer-centric strategy** was also reflected in the pivotal role of *Tesco* employees who deliver the brand promise and customer experience and thus become "brand ambassadors" (Seiler 2005, p. 21) for the company. To ensure the initiative's success, staff training, which included an educational video informing the employees of the functioning and goal of the programme, was crucial.

Even though *Tesco* had tested the loyalty scheme in a limited number of stores, the United Kingdom's first supermarket loyalty programme took the grocery industry by surprise (Rafiq 1997, p. 43). Furthermore, it was not taken seriously by many competitors for historical reasons. Between 1963 and 1977, *Tesco*, among other UK retailers, had used a trading stamps scheme, Green Shield Stamps. These stamps were given to customers when purchasing groceries or other items (in proportion to expenditure), collected in books and could be redeemed for cash or gifts (Rafiq 1997, p. 44). Thus, when *Tesco* launched the *Clubcard* in 1995, Lord Sainsbury famously dismissed the idea as nothing more than "electronic Green Shield Stamps" (Humby/Hunt/Phillips 2007, p. 63). However, *Tesco Clubcard* has proven a roaring success since its introduction, despite the cost of about 300 million GBP over the first three years. These costs included an update in point-of-sale technology, the supporting computer system needed to handle the *Clubcard* data and a call centre with a hotline. However, owing to *Clubcard*'s success, *Tesco* has covered the costs of running its loyalty programme by a sales increase "directly attributable to the promotions that have been created by Clubcard" (Humby/Hunt/Phillips 2007, p. 6. According to many experts, the key ingredient that helped *Tesco* overtake *Sainsbury's* to become the United Kingdom's leading retailer was the implementation of the CRM strategy based on *Tesco Clubcard* (Beckett/Nayak 2005, p. 8). To secure access to *dunnhumby's* know-how in the future, *Tesco* bought a stake in *dunnhumby*. In 2006, this stake was enlarged to 84 %. Even though majority owned by *Tesco*, *dunnhumby* acts as a consultant company to other companies in retail, manufacturing, consumer markets and media. For example, it provides CRM knowledge for the US retail company *Kroger*, the French retail group *Casino* as well as *Danone* and *Coca Cola*. In 2010, *dunnhumby* served other retailers and manufacturers in 26 international markets.

14.8.2.3 Collecting Points

The *Clubcard* scheme starts like other loyalty card schemes: customers receive their own card in exchange for personal details such as name, address, date of birth, family composition, dietary requirements and product preferences. *Clubcard* holders can then present their card at the check out each time they go shopping and earn one *Clubcard* point (which is worth a penny) for every 1 GBP spent. Points can be earned either by shopping instore, at *Tesco petrol* or at *Tesco.com*. Once customers have purchased items worth at least 150 GBP, they can either cash them in at the next shopping trip or redeem them for numerous offers. Each quarter, the accumulated points are transferred into vouchers and mailed to the customers, as well as additional coupons which can be redeemed for specific products (Reynolds 2004a, p. 312). Apart from spending the vouchers at a *Tesco* store or for online purchases, the customer can also transfer them into *British Airways AirMiles*. For example, a 2.50 GBP *Clubcard* voucher is worth 60 *AirMiles*. Also, vouchers can be spent on so-called *Clubcard Deals* such as fun parks, museums, or restaurants. When used to order one of these *Deals*, the value of the voucher quadruples. Along with the customer's statement, the *Clubcard Magazine* is sent out four times a year. Even though delivering the vouchers and magazines by mail is more expensive for the company than e-mail, *Tesco* still uses postal service because of the "bigger uplift" (Spethlift 2004, p. 34) it entails for the company.

The vouchers are valid through one year, which is considered long enough for customers not to feel coerced into spending the vouchers before they want to, but also short enough so that *Tesco* does not build up excessive financial exposure, as it is the case with many airlines, where millions of unredeemed flyer miles accumulate as a growing liability. Since *Tesco* tries to stress the characteristics of a club, vouchers represent the club membership dividend (Humby/Hunt/Phillips 2007, p. 72).

Currently, about 15 million British shoppers receive a statement from *Tesco* every three months (this equals about 35 % of UK homes in every mailing). The annual nominal amount of vouchers redeemed by customers is about 200 million GBP which corresponds to a redemption rate of about 20 %. This is an extraordinarily high number, compared to the industry average of about 0.5 %. This success was achieved to a great extent through a detailed analysis of the data acquired via the *Clubcard* (Spethlift 2004, pp. 33-34).

14.8.2.4   Use of Data

The *Clubcard* programme is not only a loyalty card, but also a comprehensive corporate philosophy and a complete business system. The data the *Clubcard* scheme provides to *Tesco* are used to drive crucial business decisions. Furthermore, this process is estimated to have made *Tesco* into the "most sophisticated marketer in the world" (Spethlift 2004, p. 34). In 1995, however, the company was faced with the limitations of IT technology at that time. Merely transmitting the data between *Tesco*'s IT department, where it was used to run the points accounting database, to *dunnhumby*, where it was analysed for marketing and business information use, took 30 hours, using the highest bandwidth connection then available (Stone 2003, p. 186). In the first three months, data from more than 50 million shopping trips, comprising more than 2,000 million purchased items by more than five million *Clubcard* members, were collected.

Whereas today the capacity for taking the information from every single shopping basket processed through the checkouts and analysing it is readily available, in 1995 only 10 % of the weekly data was analysed and the findings were extrapolated to the other 90 % (Humby/Hunt/Phillips 2007, p. 92). State-of-the-art **data mining techniques** were used to manage and analyse the created database. This analysis enabled *Tesco* to accurately pin-point the time when purchases were made, the amount that was spent and the kinds of products purchased.

Tesco uses the data to segment its customers via the so-called **rolling ball method**, which is based on the notion that a person's shopping basket reveals much about the person's char-acteristics: "You are what you eat" (Reynolds 2004a, p. 317). Furthermore, a unique DNA profile for every single *Tesco Clubcard* user is created based on the correlations and classifi-cations of products in shopping baskets (Hayward 2009, p. 18). In order to understand why customers purchase certain products, interpreting these goods through a "psychological lens" is necessary to reveal the "hidden" desires, aspirations and fears expressed in the purchase of products (Beckett/Nayak 2005, p. 9; Humby/Hunt/Phillips 2007, pp. 142-144). For this purpose, about 50 products were classified by rating about 20 characteristics on a two-tailed Likert scale. These product attributes included "low fat" against "high fat", "needs preparation" vs. "ready-to-eat" or "low price" against "high price", but also "ad-venturous", "exotic" or "fresh" (Humby/Hunt/Phillips 2007, pp. 139-141). This **profiling method** generates a map of the connotations of the goods. Since rating every product in the store by hand is an almost impossible task, 50 "obvious" products that clearly possessed the attribute or quality *Tesco* wanted to measure, such as pineapple for "exotic" or extra virgin olive oil for "adventurous", were chosen as a basis and a computer algorithm programme then took over.

The next step was looking at what other items customers who purchased these products bought, discarding common items such as eggs or milk. Based on the customer's behaviour, different consumer clusters could be identified. The combination of the rated products provides information about the customer's lifestyle and thus helps segment all customers. These groupings must be large enough to be cost-efficient, but "with a richness of common interest to be truly meaningful" (Spethman 2004, p. 34). Accordingly, *Tesco* was able to segment its customers into the categories of *Finer Foods, Healthy, Traditional, Mainstream, Convenience* and *Price Sensitive* (see **Figure 14.4**). The company then launched store brands targeting the identified segments (Humby/Hunt/Phillips 2007, pp. 143-146). Currently, such store brands account for about 45 % of the company's total assortment.

The potential to use and exploit data from the *Clubcard* programme is substantial. By com-paring an individual's shopping behaviour with the average for that specific customer segment, variances can be identified. This analysis highlights not only undershopped de-partments, but also shows which products the individual is likely to want in the future in order to exploit *can-selling* opportunities (Beckett/Nayak 2005, p. 10).

Marketing activities, and most importantly vouchers and coupons, are thus a mixture of gifts and rewards for past and continued behaviour as well as enticements for future behav-iour (Reynolds 2004a, p. 315).

Tesco's data warehouse allows for considerable mass customisation. Although there are **150,000 variations of the Clubcard magazine** alone, based on life stages such as young families, empty nesters and so on (Spethmann 2004, p. 39), the complete quarterly statement, with personalised letter, vouchers and coupons, is so carefully tailored for each recipient that *Tesco* sends out around **four million variations** (Spethmann 2004, p. 33). For example, a significantly decreased amount of grocery shopping is a strong indicator of a forthcoming holiday; *Tesco* can now send the customer coupons for sunscreen lotions. The identified 5,000 "customer needs" sub-groups allow for this personalised "rifle shot" approach.

Figure 14.4   Customer Segmentation

Category	Classification	Characteristics	Store Brands
Up-Market	Finer Foods	time poor, money rich, everyday luxury items	Tesco Finest, Tesco Fair Trade
	Healthy	fruits and vegetables, weight watchers, diabetic etc.	Tesco Organic, Tesco Healthy Living, Tesco Free From
Mid-Market	Convenience	people on the go, no time or inclination for cooking	Tesco
	Traditional	time to buy and prepare meals	Tesco
Cost Conscious	Mainstream	family type meals, kids products, popular brands	Tesco Kids, Tesco
	Price Sensitive	less affluent, tend to buy cheapest or advertised bargains	Tesco Value

Source: adapted from Coriolis 2004, pp. 13-14.

Tesco strives to make its **personalised customer communication** as relevant for the individual as possible. Another finding from the analysis was that in every single store, the top spending 100 customers were as valuable as the bottom 4,000. This led to the decision to run **invitation-only Clubcard events** in major stores as a way of thanking the most loyal customers (Stone 2003, p. 186). A number of **clubs** have also been created based on *Tesco's* unique insight into the shopping habits of its customers:

- *Food Club*
- *Baby & Toddler Club*
- *Wine Club*
- *Healthy Living Club.*

These clubs are free to all *Clubcard* holders and provide benefits such as free magazines, advice, coupons and special offers. Currently, about 800,000 people have become members and voluntarily offer more personal data and preferences.

The *Clubcard* data have also helped *Tesco* identify areas where customers are positively inclined towards online shopping and launched *Tesco.com* in 1997. In 2010, the sales of Tesco.com increased by 26 % to 2.1 billion GBP. Besides the food assortment which that is orderable online, *Tesco* offers more than 15,500 non-food products via the Internet. Furthermore, it is the third most visited website in the United Kingdom. Since 2006, *Clubcard* vouchers can also be used for online shopping at *Tesco.com*.

Furthermore, the company has leveraged the customer data obtained from its loyalty programme to diversify into non-food service offers (in a **micro-macro approach**):

- Financial and banking services such as *Tesco Personal Finance* (TPF)

- *Tesco Telecoms*.

Tesco Personal Finance was created as a 50:50 joint venture between *Tesco* and the *Royal Bank of Scotland* in 1997 (Coriolis 2004, p. 28). Using information derived from *Tesco*'s loyalty card programme and blending it with externally generated demographic data, the company conducted targeted research and developed profiles of customers who would be most interested in basic banking services or other options. *Tesco* found that it could acquire a financial services customer for less than half of what it costs a bank. During the course of the worldwide financial crisis, *Tesco* decided to acquire the remaining 50 % of *Tesco Personal Finance* from the *Royal Bank of Scotland*, becoming a full-service retail bank at the end of 2008. *Tesco Personal Finance* offers a broad variety of financial products and services, such as a credit card in combination with the *Clubcard*, loans, mortgages, car breakdown cover, savings, travel money, car insurance, travel insurance, life insurance and pet insurance. It is also the biggest online car insurer in the United Kingdom. In 2009, *Tesco Personal Finance* exceeded the threshold of million customer accounts and generated a profit of 250 million GBP in 2010. In the same year, it was renamed *Tesco Bank*.

Since 2003, the retailer has also offered a wide range of telecommunication services, such as mobile (in a 50:50 joint venture with *O2*), home phone, broadband, dial-up Internet access and Internet phone. More than 2 million customers make use of the services of *Tesco Telecoms*, which is the number one for customer satisfaction in the United Kingdom (Tesco 2010, p. 26). At the end of 2009, *Tesco Mobile*, a division of *Tesco Telecoms*, broadened its appeal by becoming the third UK operator to offer the *iPhone*. Furthermore, *Tesco Telecoms* forced the expansion of its instore phone shops and runs over 100 shops in the United Kingdom.

Tesco's retailing services are a key feature of its growth strategy (see **Figure 14.3**), and their successful implementation has been achieved through *Clubcard* data. Customers can also collect *Clubcard* points from selected services, e.g. when paying with a *Tesco Personal Finance* credit card for mobile, home phone and broadband services.

14.8.2.5   The Impact of Tesco's Clubcard

For many experts, *Tesco Clubcard* has been the driving force behind the company's transformation from its "pile it high and sell it cheap" to a customer value strategy that has
helped the company become the world's third largest food retailer (McKelvey 2005, p. 13).
Experts agree that because of the *Clubcard*, *Tesco* today knows more about its customers and
their needs than does any competitor (Dawson 2011, p. 33).

Only two months after the introduction of the loyalty scheme, *Tesco* became the UK market
leader. One year after the launch of the loyalty scheme, *Clubcard* holders were spending
28 % more at *Tesco* and 16 less at *Tesco*'s archrival *Sainsbury's*. In 1998, *Tesco* and its agency
dunnhumby received the silver IDM Business Performance Award for the *Tesco Clubcard*
campaign (Marketing Week 1998, p. 77).

However, a main characteristic of the *Clubcard* loyalty scheme is its dynamic nature. As
customer habits change, so do *Tesco*'s business decisions, which are based on ongoing *Clubcard* data. This implies the need for constant innovations such as the *Christmas Savers Club*,
which was launched in 2005 and which allows customers to save their *Clubcard* vouchers to
help with their Christmas shopping. Owing to a decline in *Clubcard* use of 2 % at the end of
2003, *Tesco* decided to relaunch its loyalty scheme in May 2004 (Marketing Week 2005,
p. 89). The company introduced smaller, personalised *Clubcards*, which could be attached to
a key ring, making it easier for customers to remember their cards. Furthermore, the new
cards have a barcode in order to provide customers with a quicker and more convenient
way of collecting their points (Tesco 2006, p. 8). Reportedly, the barcoded cards allow for
quicker scanning by checkout staff; the resulting increase in productivity is supposed to be
worth nine million GBP a year (Marketing Week 2005, p. 89). Moreover, *Tesco* reacted to the
increasing number of smartphones and designed its own *Clubcard* app in 2010. This app
provides the *Clubcard* on a smartphone in the form of a scannable barcode that can be used
in place of the *Clubcard*. Furthermore, customers can check their current points balances in
this way.

Following the relaunch of the *Clubcard* programme in 2010, the company heavily increased
its investment in the *Clubcard* by issuing double points for spending. *Clubcard* users now
receive two points per pound spent. Moreover, customers receive a broader variety of
vouchers for some products in *Tesco* stores or they can trade them for rewards such as days
out and restaurant dining. Furthermore, new partners were added to the rewards scheme,
for example *The London Eye* and *Disneyland Paris*, where *Clubcard* vouchers can be redeemed. These improvements have encouraged even more customers to sign up, and the
Clubcard is now used with a higher proportion of transactions than before with 18 % more
UK households having redeemed vouchers in 2010 compared with 2009 (Tesco 2010, p. 16).

14.8.2.6   Summary and Outlook

Even though many competitors have tried to introduce similar customer loyalty schemes,
such as *Sainsbury's Nectar Card* (introduced in 2002 as the *Reward Card* successor), *Safeway's
Added Bonus Card* (which was abandoned by the company in 2000), *ASDA's Style Card* and

Boots' Advantage Card, Tesco Clubcard remains the frontrunner, as McKelvey (2005, p. 13) realised in 2005. Nowadays, this position seems to be secured. Numerous indicators illustrate the *Clubcard*'s success. One of the most impressive is that while *Tesco*'s floor space in the United Kingdom has only risen by 15 % since the introduction of the loyalty scheme in 1995, market share is up by 52 % (Reinartz 2010, p. 420). The strong customer focus has proven a successful concept in creating value for the customer and profit for *Tesco*. As a result, *Tesco* has cemented its leading position at the top of the market in the United Kingdom. *Tesco* has also started adopting the *Clubcard* programme in several of its international markets in recent years. In 2010, for the first time, there were more *Clubcard* holders overseas than there were in the UK (Tesco 2010, p. 16).

However, *Tesco* lost its position once as UK market leader to *Sainsbury's* in the 1970s and it regained it in the mid-1990s. By withstanding the challenge of the numerous followers in loyalty schemes, *Tesco* has proven that it indeed offers more value to its clientele and in a sustainable manner during the 15 years since the introduction of the *Clubcard* loyalty programme.

| Questions

1. How could data be gathered via the *Clubcard* and then be used? Give some detailed examples.

2. Do you think it is possible for Tesco to replicate the success of its customer loyalty programme in the home market to other countries? Discuss critically.

3. Do loyalty cards enhance loyalty? Discuss.

| Hints

1. See Humby/Hunt/Phillips 2007, pp. 91-107, for details of the exploitation of Clubcard data for marketing purposes.

2. See, for example, Alexander 1997, pp. 29-37, on the limits of the internationalisation of retailing.

3. See Humby/Hunt/Phillips 2007, pp. 19-32.

Part IV
Buying, Logistics and
Performance Measurement

15   Buying – Strategy and Concepts

The objectives of this Chapter are to look at the external environment and the characteristics and instruments of retail buying, to discuss traditional and non-traditional forms of buying and to contrast different buying situations.

15.1   External Environment

15.1.1   Trade Liberalisation and Regional Integration

Retail buying is considerably influenced by the development of external factors. Among these, the following play a predominant role:

- Political-legal factors
- Socio-economic factors
- Technological factors.

From a political-legal point of view, global trade liberalisation as a part of the activities of the *World Trade Organisation* (WTO) needs to be emphasised because it has opened new sourcing markets in almost all regions of the world. An emphasis is also placed on the importance of China and other South-East Asian countries as sourcing markets. As early as in 2007, the HandelsMonitor predicted an increase in **direct foreign procurement volume** of German-speaking retailing from around 15 % to 22 % in 2015 (Zentes/Hilt/Domma 2007, p. 88).

Besides this global trade liberalisation, new sourcing markets are being tapped by increasing **regional integration**, for example through the expansion of the European Union to 27 member states and the intensification of cooperation within the **common market**. For example, more than 50 % of each EU member state's exported goods is are directed to the other 26 states. Similarly, bilateral agreements are opening up new sourcing markets, for instance the one between the EU and Switzerland. The Cassis-de-Dijon principle came into force in Switzerland in July 2010. According to the principle, products may be merchandised in the Swiss market automatically if they are produced and officially accepted for circulation in any EU member state.

15.1.2   Sustainability and Supply Security

With regard to socio-economic developments, the increasing public awareness of the ecological and social responsibility of companies and consumers is emphasised. This results in higher ecological and social standards (e.g. **Social Accountability 8000** (SA 8000)) regarding production in developing countries, such as the prohibition of child labour, the limitation of working hours and so on (see Morschett/Schramm-Klein/Zentes 2010, pp. 221-230). Retail companies embed these standards into their sustainability strategies or in their **corporate social responsibility** (CSR) concepts. In this context, **international codes of conduct** gain in importance. As an example, the **Business Social Compliance Initiative** (BSCI) of the **Foreign Trade Association** (FTA) can be mentioned.

Taking the aspect of **sustainability** into consideration, **supply security** shifts increasingly into focus. This results from an explosively expanding worldwide demand for resources, energy and agricultural products. Driving forces are the rapid growth in population on the one hand and changing consumption patterns in increasingly wealthy emerging countries, such as China, on the other. Consequently, the world's population will grow from 6.7 billion in 2007 to 8.3 billion in 2030 (UNDESA 2009). In East Asia alone, the meat consumption per capita is expected to double by 2050. These developments challenge the mid- to long-term supply and thus encourage long-term contracts (**contract buying**) (see e.g. PwC/H.I.Ma. 2010).

15.1.3   Electronic Marketplaces

One of the most innovative and potentially useful developments because of retailers' growing levels of sophistication with the Internet is retail exchanges. "**Retail exchanges** are providers of Internet-solutions and services for retailers. One of their functions is similar to a trade show, except that they are virtual and, as such, available 24/7. In addition to providing a virtual meeting place for buyers and vendors, they offer software and services to help retailers, manufacturers, and their trading partners reduce costs and improve efficiency by streamlining and automating sourcing and supply chain processes. They provide an opportunity for vendors and retailers to interact electronically rather than meet face-to-face- in a physical market" (Levy/Weitz 2009, p. 396).

15.2   Merchandising Philosophy, Changing Buyer-Seller Relationships and Buying Strategy

The buying strategy of retailers is influenced by the merchandising philosophy and intended relationship between the retail company and manufacturers (suppliers). "A **merchandising philosophy** sets the guiding principles for all the merchandise decisions that a retailer makes. It must reflect target market desires, the retailer's institutional type, the marketplace positioning, the defined value chain, supplier capabilities, costs, competitors, product trends, and other factors. The retail merchandising philosophy drives every product decision, from what product lines to carry to the shelf space allotted to different products to inventory turnover to pricing – and more" (Berman/Evans 2010, p. 384). The merchandising philosophy determines the breadth of the assortment (narrow or wide) and the depth of the assortment (deep or shallow) within each category. In addition, retailers "must select the quality of the items within the assortment – high or low, national brands or store brands. They need to decide on their pricing policies, across categories and within. Finally, retailers must decide if assortments should generally be stable over time or whether there should be surprises, specials, or customisation in assortments" (Kahn 1999, p. 289). These issues were discussed in Chapter 11.

The nature of relationships in the supply chain is another important factor for buying or **sourcing decisions**. The relationships between retailers and manufacturers are changing: from adversarial to **collaborative relationships**. This leads to a shift from short-term buying to long-term buying, from a price focus to a total cost focus, including all costs within the buying process. This represents a major paradigm shift in buying away from the traditional transactional view of exchange (Fernie 2009). This collaborative relationship approach is discussed in Chapter 17 in the context of **efficient consumer response (ECR) initiatives**.

These changing relationships in the supply chain have also transformed the interface between manufacturers and retailers (see **Figure 15.1**). Traditionally, there has been a bilateral interaction between the buyer from the retail side and the key account manager (vendor) from the manufacturer side. Nowadays, multifunctional teams from both sides interact with one another. Key account managers and category managers, responsible for **supplier development**, also coordinate or orchestrate these activities, which leads to new **supplier relationship management**.

Figure 15.1   Transformation of the Interface between Manufacturer and Retailer

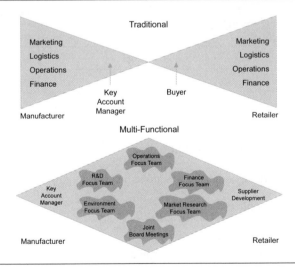

Source: Fernie 2009, p. 52.

In addition to this tendency, a traditional **transaction focus** still exists. Interestingly, the process of closely connecting with vendors and cooperation runs parallel with transactional exchanges, for example through **Internet exchanges**.

15.3   Sourcing Toolbox

15.3.1   Overview

Diverse buying decisions can be systematised by the so-called sourcing toolbox **(see Table 15.1)**. This box describes the strategic options and concepts using several dimensions.

Table 15.1   Sourcing Toolbox

Buying Decisions	Options		
Source	company-owned	outside supplier	
Interacting with Merchandising Source	active	passive	
Supplier Relationships	transactional	collaborative	
Scope of Suppliers	single	multiple	
Stocking Merchandise	stock	stock reduced	stockless
Geographical Market	local/national	international/global	
Mode of Buying	individual	cooperative	
Organisational Form	internal	external	
Technological Form	traditional	electronic (web-based)	

Source: adapted from Arnold 1998.

15.3.2   Merchandise Sources

With regard to merchandise sources, there are two major options:

- Company-owned suppliers
- Outside suppliers.

Company-owned (or internal) means that a retailer owns a manufacturing and/or wholesaling facility. **Outside suppliers** (also called external suppliers) are not owned by the retailer. Manufacturing has a long tradition in food retailing with regard to fresh food such as bread, cakes and pastries and meat products. To a growing extent, retail companies are producing products in other fields, too. The development of **store brands** is a key driver of this insourcing tendency *("up-stream verticalisation")*. Another driver comes from the challenge to secure mid- and long-term supply. Company-owned suppliers refer in this context not only to production sites but also to agricultural sites, i.e. farms (see PwC/H.I.Ma. 2010).

Two basic kinds of outside suppliers can be identified: regularly used suppliers and new suppliers. In the case of a **regular supplier**, the retailer knows the quality of merchandise and the reliability of the supplier. In the case of a **new supplier**, the retailer is unfamiliar with the quality and reliability. The types of outside suppliers are described in **Table 15.2**.

Table 15.2   Outside Sources of Supply

Source	Characteristics
1. Manufacturer	Physically produces goods, may provide shipping and credit.
2. Full-Service Merchant Wholesaler	Buys goods from manufacturers, performs many services for retailer (shipping, storing, credit, information etc.).
a. General Merchandise	Carries a very wide assortment.
b. Specialty Merchandise	Carries a very deep assortment.
c. Rack Jobber	Brings and sets up own displays, usually deals with non-food items in supermarkets and other stores, may be paid after merchandise is sold, convenient for store.
3. Limited-Service Merchant Wholesaler	Same as full service, except that fewer retailer services are provided and costs are lower.
a. Drop Shipper	Buys and sells via the telephone (never physically handles the merchandise), major task is connecting buyer and seller.
b. Mail Order	Catalogue sales to small retailers.
c. Cash-and-Carry	Store where small retailers buy and take merchandise.
4. Agents and Brokers	Do not take title to goods (ownership remains with manufacturer), provide a variety of functions for a fee or commission. Included are auction companies, salespeople, and selling agents.

Source: adapted from Berman/Evans 2010, p. 415.

15.3.3   Interacting with Merchandising Sources, Supplier Relationships and the Scope of Suppliers

Through **active sourcing**, the retailer exerts an influence on outside sources with regard to product development and product improvement, including packaging. **Passive sourcing** means that the retailer buys goods from manufacturers and/or wholesalers that have been developed and produced independently. This situation is typical of the buying process for manufacturer brands (national brands or global brands).

Store brands are products that have been developed and designed by a retailer and that are available for sale only from this retailer. The retailer exerts the greatest influence with respect to these products. Developing store brands also means modifying the value chain architecture from a traditional "buyer", which is characteristic of passive sourcing, to a "coordinator" or even a "producer" (see Chapter 6; Morschett/Schramm-Klein/Zentes 2010, pp. 264-266). Store brands are produced by company-owned manufacturing facilities (value chain architecture "producer") or by outside (contract) manufacturers (store brand manufacturers or private label manufacturers) (value chain architecture "coordinator"). Developing and frequently producing store brands have an outstanding importance in the field of **vertical retailers**, which are discussed in Chapter 6.

Transactional relations are typical in short-term buying, for example, in buying commodities. Electronic marketplaces are modern platforms to run these transactions. In such a situation, the price (given a stipulated quality) is the dominant factor in selecting suppliers. **Collaborative relationships** exist with store brand manufacturers in terms of marketing and logistics and, to a growing extent, with brand manufacturers, and use is made here of the ECR concepts of category management and supply chain management. Collaborative relationships in the form of mid-term and long-term contracts are of growing importance in order to secure supply, e.g. by **contract farming**.

Single sourcing refers to a buying situation in which a product is delivered by only one manufacturer or wholesaler/distributor. This strategy means bundling purchasing volume, which reduces transaction costs but causes risks such as an overdependence on suppliers. **Multiple sourcing** is a counter-strategy whereby several suppliers are included for one product. In order to balance supplier risks, primarily with regard to long-term **supply security**, multiple sourcing will grow in importance, according to the already mentioned study of PwC/H.I.Ma. (2010).

15.3.4   Stocking Merchandise

With regard to logistics and supply chain management, three types of sourcing can be described. **Stockless** means that the manufacturer delivers to the outlets of a retailer and/or a transit terminal/cross-docking terminal of a retailer according to the **just-in-time** philosophy. This implies collaborative relationships using, for example, **electronic data interchange** (EDI) for replenishment (see Chapters 16 and 17). **Stock** characterises a kind of sourcing for which products are stored in one central or in several regional warehouses. This situation is typical for commodities bought in foreign countries at huge quantities for low prices.

Stock reduced lies in between the two extremes. Using the modern concepts of supply chain management, such as **vendor-managed inventory** (VMI), stock volume decreases but the service level remains constant or even increases ("never out-of-stock").

15.3.5 Geographical Market

An important decision is to determine where the merchandise is produced and/or bought: local/national vs. international/global sourcing.

International or **global sourcing** can currently be characterised as a megatrend in retailing. An important reason for sourcing globally rather than domestically is to save money. Drivers of this tendency are the already mentioned tariff reductions on manufactured goods pushed by the *World Trade Organisation* (WTO) in the context of the liberalisation of trade and the establishment of free trade zones such as the *North American Free Trade Agreement* (NAFTA) or common markets like the *European Union* (EU). Retailers involved in the foreign sourcing of merchandise can benefit from the cessation of tariffs in such zones. However, international sourcing costs must be calculated thoroughly: "To counterbalance the lower acquisition costs, however, there are other expenses that can increase the costs of sourcing (private-label) merchandise from other countries" (Levy/Weitz 2009, p. 394).

Figure 15.2   Costs and Benefits of Global Sourcing

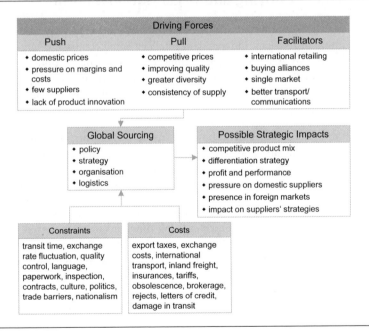

Source: Liu/McGoldrick 1995, p. 102.

A retail company chooses either an individual or a cooperative buying mode. In **cooperative buying,** a group of retailers (independent retailers, small chains and large chains) bundle their purchasing volumes to obtain volume discounts from suppliers. Besides bulk buying, nationwide or European-wide label offering, sales promotion campaigns, launches of new products and product ranges are tasks of **buying alliances** (see the case study on *Coopernic* in this Chapter).

Retailers must also choose whether to have an **inside buying organisation** or an **outside buying organisation**. This decision is closely connected to the mode of buying. In cooperative buying, the office of the buying group is involved in trend identification, product design and development, product sourcing, quality assurance, order tracking and delivery.

However, an outside buying organisation can also be hired in the case of individual buying. For example, within a category all merchandising functions are transferred to a specialist who operates as a **full-service supplier** (e.g. a rack jobber). Another example relates to **outside organisations** specialised in global sourcing. They have buying offices worldwide and thus a better sense of foreign markets and merchandise sources. An outstanding example is the Hong Kong headquartered company *Li&Fung* that operates as a "network orchestrator" (Fung/Fung/Wind 2008).

15.3.6   Mode of Buying and Organisational Form

A retail company chooses either an individual or a cooperative buying mode. In **cooperative buying** a group of retailers (independent retailers, small chains and large chains) bundle their purchasing volumes to obtain volume discounts from suppliers. Besides bulk buying, nationwide or European-wide label offering, sales promotion campaigns, launches of new products and product ranges are tasks of **buying alliances** (see the case study on *Coopernic* in this Chapter).

Retailers must also choose whether to have an **inside buying organisation** or an **outside buying organisation**. This decision is closely connected to the mode of buying. In cooperative buying, the office of the buying group is involved in trend identification, product design and development, product sourcing, quality assurance, order tracking and delivery.

However, an outside buying organisation can also be hired in the case of individual buying. For example, within a category all merchandising functions are transferred to a specialist who operates as a **full-service supplier** (e.g. a rack jobber). Another example relates to **outside organisations** specialised in global sourcing. They have buying offices worldwide and thus a better sense of foreign markets and merchandise sources. An outstanding example is the Hong Kong headquartered company *Li&Fung* that operates as a "network orchestrator" (Fung/Fung/Wind 2008).

15.3.7   Technological Form

Closely connected to the organisational form of buying is the question of whether to choose the Internet as the basic platform for transactions or traditional modes. **Web-based buying** means that an electronic platform or an **electronic marketplace** is used to negotiate the purchase and terms (delivery date, quantity purchased, price and payment agreements, discounts, form of delivery, etc.), to run (**reverse**) **auctions** and to place orders.

Regular connections with suppliers through **electronic data interchange** (via the Internet or direct PC connections and other means) to transmit order data or to receive invoice data in the context of order processing and fulfilment is also used in **traditional buying**. In this case, the Internet (or another technology) is the basis for **operational data interchange**, but not for the selection of suppliers and business negotiations. This remains a face-to-face process.

As an example, *vLinx* (www.vlinx.com) delivers a **global sourcing platform** that facilitates the sourcing and development of private labels/store brands for retailers and their networks of suppliers, agents and service providers. The *vLinx Global Sourcing Platform* includes (www.vlinx.com):

- open collaboration channels between suppliers, sourcing companies, buyers, internal support groups and external third parties,

- coordinated workflow and scheduling, with automated alerts,

- dynamic price translation in multiple currencies,

- hierarchical information management and controls based on organisational structure,

- specification, price and terms management,

- private and public supplier product catalogues,

- product life cycle management (PLM), namely product management from concept to delivery and

- seamless information management exchange with legacy and **enterprise resource planning (ERP)** systems.

15.4   Sourcing Situations

15.4.1   Overview

The manifold instruments of retail sourcing are not applied in a standardised way for the complete product assortment, but rather they depend on the situation and are subject to the requirements of the supply and sales markets. For the sourcing of some product ranges, it makes sense to use electronic platforms, but for others, there is no virtue in doing so because, for example, there are no product standards. In addition, the question arises of whether a product should be purchased nationally or internationally when using electronic marketplaces. Requirements such as product quality and supplier reliability are important for this decision.

The decision about cooperative sourcing also cannot be made unanimously over the entire product range of a company. Whereas this seems to make sense in many cases, e.g. for bundling demand or for using joint logistics services, cooperative sourcing may in fact be counterproductive and lead to price increases, for example in markets with an extremely low supply or the emergence of surplus demand, e.g. in high end fashion assortments.

The sourcing conditions in retailing are characterised by an enormous number of articles and a high assortment dynamic. Nevertheless, these manifold situations can be categorised into four sourcing situations.

15.4.2   Sourcing Situation 1: Branded Products

Sourcing situation 1 is characterised by the dominance of branded products (national or global brands) and by low complexity as far as the supply market is concerned, in the food sector as well as in the near- and non-food sectors (e.g. fashion, electronics). This situation is typical for many branded products that are often indispensable for the development of the merchandising competence of the retailer (see Chapter 11). Here, however, in most cases, only a few national or international providers (brand product manufacturers) or distributors with strong brands – often global brands – are available as suppliers. Furthermore, these are mostly categories with a high sourcing volume and a high turnover speed, e.g. food categories.

It must be assumed that sourcing situation 1 has a high potential for **supply chain management partnerships** because the basic patterns of the ECRapproach in the 1990s were based on this constellation. Accordingly, this sourcing situation should currently describe starting points for continuing ("advanced") collaborative forms of supply chain management – such as VMI, continuous replenishment (CRP) or collaborative planning, forecasting and replenishment (CPFR) – in order to obtain win–win situations (see Chapter 17). Traditional forms of electronic data exchange and newer web-based forms of cooperation are, in this case, an indispensable requirement.

Supply chain management partnerships and category management partnerships are not only relevant in the sector of fast-moving consumer goods (FMCG), but also in the non-food sector, such as the fashion industry. In the context of **controlled distribution concepts** (see Chapter 5), manufacturers take over replenishment and, at the same time, design sales areas, product ranges, promotions and so on. In the most extreme case, namely in **mono-brand stores**, the manufacturer in its role as franchisor takes over sourcing for franchisees.

15.4.3   Sourcing Situation 2: Commodities/Indirect Goods

Sourcing situation 2 is characterised by a large number of articles, usually with low sales importance ("C products"), for which there is a multitude of suppliers generally scattered worldwide, e.g. "everyday" watches, jeans, shirts, glassware and homewares. There is normally no transparency with regard to potential procurement sources. Furthermore, the importance of brands is either not given at all or is low (anonymous products or labels, no real brands) and sensitivity to quality is also low. This situation prevails for commodities, but generally also for **indirect goods**, i.e. goods that are not sold, but used in retail operations. Examples are photocopy paper or laptops for the internal use of food retailers (like maintenance, repair, operating (MRO) goods of manufacturers).

Because of the low relevance of differentiation, the question of the potential **outsourcing** of procurement arises in this situation, for example by bringing in **system suppliers**. In general, these suppliers are responsible for the operative sourcing of a complete category in the sense of a classic **rack jobber**. Manufacturers who complete their own product assortments with additional merchandise and wholesale companies can be considered **system suppliers**. In this context, the reduction of general procurement costs, namely the reduction of purchases (at cost) and process costs, is a dominant target.

In sourcing situations of type 2, **electronic marketplaces** can also be used to find new suppliers or to run reverse auctions.

15.4.4   Sourcing Situation 3: Store Brands

In sourcing situation 3, **customer-oriented differentiation** plays a significant role. Equally, companies aim to improve **gross margins** with store brands. As mentioned above, this sourcing situation is not characterised by a passive supply function, but by proper product development with proper designs. This does not preclude these tasks from being carried out collaboratively with **private label manufacturers**. With a view to producing store brands, one can distinguish between own production ("make") and contract manufacturing, usually under the quality management of the retailer.

This sourcing situation offers important potential for increasing **effectiveness** and **efficiency** by extensively combining value-added chains, for example, in the form of **collaborative supply chain management**. The potential offered by these characteristic forms should exceed the potentials of ECR partnerships in sourcing situation 1 because their levels of integration are higher.

15.4.5   Sourcing Situation 4: Fresh Food

Fresh food is increasingly important for market-oriented profiling in food retailing, and this sourcing situation is characterised by specific logistical challenges: shelf life/deterioration, ecological challenges such as organic cultivation methods, sustainability requirements such as avoidance of transport costs and consumer preferences such as those for local/regional products. From a mid- to long-term perspective, the abovementioned shortages represent further challenges.

The sourcing situation is accordingly diverse. It ranges from **local sourcing** to **global sourcing**, e.g. with exotic fruits and sea fruits, from local or worldwide production or cultivation, through contract manufacturing or contract farming, to passive sourcing at producers/plantations or wholesalers. Of outstanding importance in all cases is **product safety**. Not only buying activities but also logistical processes serve to secure it. Fresh products pose special requirements on the arrangement of the supply chain, e.g. the adherence to predefined temperatures in transport and storage areas.

15.5   Conclusion and Outlook

Starting from basic strategic trends in retail sourcing, new responsibilities are increasingly emerging for traditional buying. There are also shifts in the organisational relevance of various sectors. This results in changing requirements for future buyers.

In general, a consistent **customer orientation** is reflected in the company's organisation in such a way that marketing and sales (category management) gain influence, whereas the importance of buying seems to decline. By contrast, growing process orientation is reflected in the changing nature of **retailer–supplier negotiations**. Whereas price negotiations have so far been of prime importance within the frame of traditional buying, the importance of other terms – particularly conditions with regard to logistics and marketing, combined with a customer-oriented management of the supply chain according to the supply chain management philosophy – is rising.

Within the context of optimising the synergy potential of retail businesses by bundling the volume of purchase across countries and sales formats, **international purchasing organisations** are increasingly emerging, which coordinate sourcing across the group or company. In the course of international sourcing, the relevance of specialised knowledge in the field of quality assurance is also growing.

The introduction of **e-procurement** is also leading to an extensive change with regard to both organisational and personal aspects, and as far as corporate culture is concerned. In this regard, the learning aptitude of the company as a whole is also relevant. Thus, it is generally necessary to organise or reorganise purchasing and sourcing processes in the context of **electronic sourcing** and to ensure compatibility with previous systems with the help of standards.

One of the most important challenges from a mid- and long-term perspective is to guarantee supply security, especially in the food sector. The abovementioned measures, such as long-term contracts or the lease/acquisition of acreage in foreign countries, raise the ethical question of fair resource distribution. Non-profit organisations increasingly decry this phenomenon as "**land grabbing**".

| Further Reading

FERNIE, J.; SPARKS, L. (Eds.) (2009): Logistics & Retail Management, 3rd ed., London et al.

MOORE, C.M. (2005): The Anatomy of Retail Buying, in: BRUCE, M.; MOORE, C.M.; BIRTWISTLE, G. (Eds.): International Retail Management, Amsterdam et al., pp. 64-77.

15.6   Case Study: Coopernic[1]

15.6.1   Profile, History and Status Quo

Coopernic, the "Coopérative Européenne de Référencement et de Négoce des Indépendants Commerçants", was founded in November 2005 as Belgian cooperative society. In 2006, the legitimate transformation into a European cooperative society, or *Societas Cooperativa Europaea*, took place. The association acts as a **strategic alliance** of the founding members *Colruyt* (Belgium), *CONAD* (Italy), *Coop* (Switzerland), *E.Leclerc* (France) and *REWE Group* (Germany) (see **Figure 15.3**).

Each of the five independent retailers captures a strong position in its respective national market. For the fiscal year ending March 2010, *Colruyt* announced revenues of 5,212 million EUR for the retail business alone. In 2009, *CONAD* was ranked fourth in Italy with food sales of 6,707 million EUR. In 2009, *Coop* was ranked number 2 in the Swiss market with food sales of 8,345 million EUR and *E. Leclerc* was number 2 in France with food sales of 22,921 million EUR. In 2010, *REWE* Group was ranked second in Germany with food sales totalling 26,231 million EUR (LP international 2010).

The structure of *Coopernic* is efficient, given that it has one managing director who coordinates the cooperation in Brussels together with a few employees. This position is currently held by Gianluigi Ferrari. Mostly, projects are conducted by teams made up of representatives of the partner companies' management teams. Additionally, an administrative board of ten members, two representatives per member company, hold shares and votes in an egalitarian breakdown. A president chairs the group, appointed within one of the member companies. Michel-Eduard Leclerc, CEO of *E.Leclerc*, was the first president of *Coopernic* from 2006 to 2008. From 2008 to 2010, he was followed by Alain Caparros, CEO of the *REWE Group*, and from 2010 to 2012 by the current president Hansueli Loosli, CEO of *Coop*.

---

[1] Sources used in this case study include miscellaneous annual reports and press releases of the Coopernic founding members, the website http://www.lebensmittelzeitung.net as well as explicitly cited sources.

Figure 15.3   Geographical Scope of Coopernic Members

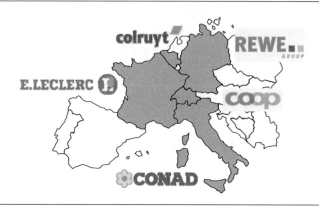

Financially, the European cooperative funds itself from membership fees and passes any savings or advantages obtained onto each grouping. The five partners of the alliance head-quartered in Brussels, represent a joint sales volume of 109.4 billion EUR and operate approx. 20,000 stores in 22 countries in 2009. **Table 15.3** illustrates the high growth rate within the group, which documents the success of the joint sourcing activities.

Table 15.3   Development of Coopernic

Year	Outlets in Europe	Countries	Cumulated Revenues
2006	17,208	17	96.0 billion EUR
2007	17,559	18	101.8 billion EUR
2009	20,000 (approx.)	22	109.4 billion EUR

What is special about the geographical scope of the members is that they operate their retail stores in **complementary markets** so there is – as far as possible – no direct competition between the companies (see **Table 15.4**).

Table 15.4   Geographical Complementarity of Store Locations

Company	FR	IT	DE	ES	PT	LUX	BE	CH	AT	HR	CZ	HU	SK	SI	PL	RO	UA	BG	RU
Colruyt	X					X	X												
CONAD		X																	
Coop								X											
REWE Group		X	X						X	X	X	X	X			X	X	X	X
E. Leclerc	X	X		X	X									X	X				

15.6.2   Drivers of Cooperative Sourcing

With *Coopernic,* the partners have established an alliance to face the growing challenges of competition in Europe and the internationalisation of retailing.

The growing challenge of competition arises in different fields. **Figure 15.4** illustrates the strategic importance of the top 10 grocery buying cooperatives or retail companies. With a grocery market volume of 1,382 billion EUR in Western and Central Europe in 2009 (EMD 2010), the top three **integrated purchasing groups** (*Coopernic, AMS* and *EMD*) account for almost 25 % of the market (figures include European countries only). The top 15 accounts for 65 % of the total market volume in Western and Central Europe (EMD 2010).

Figure 15.4   Top 10 Grocery Buyers 2009 in Europe

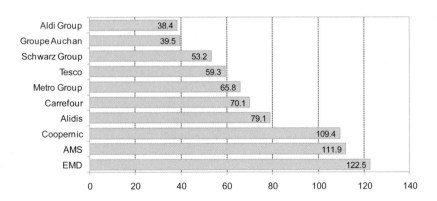

Aldi Group	38.4
Groupe Auchan	39.5
Schwarz Group	53.2
Tesco	59.3
Metro Group	65.8
Carrefour	70.1
Alidis	79.1
Coopernic	109.4
AMS	111.9
EMD	122.5

Source: IGD Research 2010.

One of the drivers of **cooperative buying** can be seen in this concentration process. The trend to bundle buying activities within global enterprises (*Walmart*, *Carrefour* and the *Metro Group*) increases critical mass in sourcing, thereby provoking the need for further concentration and building alliances (Liebmann/Zentes/Swoboda 2008, p. 731). As most *Coopernic* members concentrate on their national markets (see **Table 15.4**) and their sales volume is surmounted by the leading food retailers by far, it was a reasonable consequence to consolidate sourcing activities. As illustrated in **Figure 15.5**, only one of the five members of *Coopernic* ranks among the top 10 global retailers with regard to food sales in 2009. *E.Leclerc* is ranked 21st and *Coop* 48th, while *Colruyt* and *CONAD* are no longer in the top 50 (Lebensmittel Zeitung 2010).

Figure 15.5   Top 10 Global Retailers

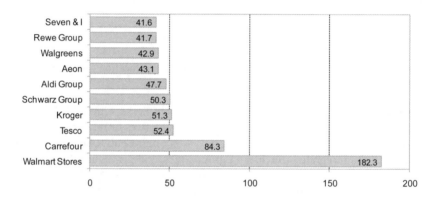

Source: Lebensmittel Zeitung 2010.

Furthermore, cooperative sourcing strengthens negotiation power against relevant manufacturers that are characterised by an increasing concentration as well. Coopernic (2006) described that situation as an oligopolistic trend, i.e. a small number of suppliers accounting for a high offer depending on the segment. Thus, the cooperative strengthens negotiation power relative to manufacturers.

The segmentation of markets through tariff and promotional strategies leads to disadvantages that can discriminate national retailers against their multinational counterparts. *Coop*, for example, which is headquartered in Switzerland and is limited to trading in that country, suffers from higher prices in comparison to the European average.

This form of cooperative sourcing allows for the consolidating of member performance, pooling know-how and optimising purchase activities. At the same time, it protects the autonomy of the companies, which allows them "to preserve their specific values, their organisation modes, entrepreneurial spirit, regional roots, and consumerism" (Coopernic 2006).

Sourcing is becoming more and more international and more cooperative (Liebmann/Zentes/Swoboda 2008, p. 730). This internationalisation of retail trade leads to an acceleration in movement and thus calls for greater flexibility in which markets to select in terms of market development and sourcing. *Coopernic* provides the necessary flexibility to profit from a European network.

15.6.3   Coopernic's Objectives

Coopernic (2006) aims at company- and group-level objectives, which are addressed to improve the individual situations of each partner company. It aims to:

■ make offers broader and more attractive,

■ achieve better prices,

■ reduce logistics costs,

■ mutualise negotiations with multinational manufacturers,

■ exchange know-how.

As the members of *Coopernic* mainly act in independent markets, they can exchange know-how openly, such as customer preferences or socio-cultural trends, and use **best practices** in commercial, logistics and ethics. This helps identify products that consumers desire and thus expands the offer. Additionally, more attractive product ranges can be arranged as each member's best product selections can be exchanged within the group. For example, *Coop's* company-owned production facility *Chocolats Halba* gained *CONAD* as a new customer in 2009 and now supplies finest Swiss chocolate to this Italian retailer. Another possibility to create a more attractive offer is to set up common specifications for **group-wide store brands**. In recent years, the members of *Coopernic* have integrated each other's store brands into their respective assortments in more than 60 cooperation projects. In this case, the branding remains specific to each retailer but the products are the same.

The main objective of the alliance is to pool sourcing volume to achieve cheaper prices and lower costs in the form of scale savings. "The simplest, and perhaps only, means of gauging the potential negotiating power of any buying group is to aggregate the grocery turnover of its members" (IGD Research 2010). **Figure 15.4** attests to the power of *Coopernic* in terms of sales volume. This improves *Coopernic's* position, especially in negotiations with branded goods manufacturers, to optimise the purchase conditions of branded products. To date, *Coopernic* has entered into **multinational purchasing agreements** with more than 100 suppliers. In accordance with that, suppliers profit from access to new markets and distribution channels resulting in a win-win-situation. Additionally, services can be delegated to the best provider – in terms of price performance – and this further reduces costs.

Another important objective is the significant reduction in logistics costs. The search for the best logistics sourcing conditions can be delegated or outsourced to the member with the best such knowledge in logistics on the respective market. This happened when *E.Leclerc* handled the supply of petrol to *CONAD* petrol stations in Northern Italy. Hence, the wider insight into transnational logistics services, from the eyes of the group, can help each partner identify more suitable logistics providers. Additionally, as the partners know each other's conditions, inter-company competition with logistics providers can be capitalised on.

The results of negotiations with multinational manufacturers can be shared among the group to improve each member's know-how in future negotiations. This can help optimise the purchasing of international brands. Furthermore, conditions – such as price spreads – can be made accessible to all members of the group.

In summary, the target of the alliance is to strengthen the positions of the members in their respective national markets through tight, transnational cooperation and to pass this resulting price advantage onto customers.

15.6.4   Current Challenges

One of the advantages of *Coopernic* is its financial strength. This enables members to invest quickly in fast-growing markets, while risks can be shared. The founding members of *Coopernic* acquired a majority stake of 80 % in *IKI Group*, a retailer operating in Lithuania and Latvia in supermarkets, discounters and convenience stores, but the purchasing price is unknown (see **Figure 15.6**). The remaining 20 % are still held by the Ortiz family (IKI Group 2007).

Figure 15.6   Ownership Structure of IKI Group

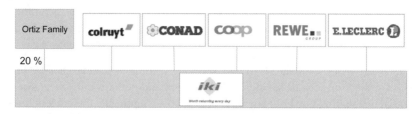

This strategic decision is supposed to make *Coopernic* more attractive to suppliers and it extends its area of influence to North-Eastern Europe, where the group members have not been present before (see **Table 15.4**). But this is a region where high growth and rising consumption and purchasing power is expected. "It is the first time in Europe that an alliance of independent retailers has jointly made an acquisition of this type" (IKI Group 2007). The acquisition should bring *IKI Group* considerable benefits in terms of resources, know-how and purchasing power. Aidas Mackevičius, CEO of *IKI Group*, expects Lithuanian and

Latvian consumers to profit from innovations, novelties in product range and better prices (IKI Group 2007).

At the end of 2010, *Coop* announced a complete takeover of a former joint venture with *REWE Group*, the *transGourmet Holding AG*. Taking over Europe's second largest cash & carry and foodservice company with sales of 5.8 billion EUR in 2009 contributes to its strategic focus on foodservice and wholesale for hotels, restaurants and businesses. As the acquisition does not influence the strategic partnership between *Coop* and *REWE Group*, the companies will continue to closely collaborate.

15.6.5   Summary and Outlook

What started as a sourcing partnership is now a strategic alliance of *Coopernic's* partners. Hence, the scope of the group has shifted from topics such as mere buying to **joint operations**, as illustrated with the example of the acquisition of *IKI Group*.

The cooperative provides further opportunities for joint activities concerning store brands, a field that is becoming more and more important in retailing. Currently, *REWE Group* is working on a store brand concept called *"Vivess"*. Omitting the manufacturer *REWE* from the brand name can be interpreted as intention to prepare for Europe-wide distribution. *"Vivess"* products could find a way into foreign markets using the partner's store network. Furthermore, multilateral exchange could exploit the opportunity to source from regional suppliers or small businesses and thus to profit from an increasing demand for regional products.

By demand pooling, buying groups have achieved such size that they are now among the largest grocery buyers in Europe, as illustrated in **Figure 15.4**. In practice, however, "such alliances bring a range of new strategic issues, such as maintaining the cohesion of the group and delivering on agreed activities, the latter of which is vital to securing concessions from suppliers" (IGD Research 2010). These issues have to be observed in the long run.

▌ Questions

1. List the possible advantages and disadvantages of horizontal cooperative purchasing and evaluate *Coopernic's* situation.

2. Describe the critical success factors that affect cooperative purchasing groups and assess to what extent *Coopernic* meets these factors.

3. Describe one of the two largest buying groups, *EMD* or *AMS*, and elaborate on the differences compared with *Coopernic*. How can the players be categorised concerning the dimensions "conceptual focus of purchasing" and "structural organisation of purchasing"?

▌ Hints

1. See e.g. Schotanus (2007, pp. 13-14) for a summary of the advantages and disadvantages of horizontal cooperative purchasing.

2. See Schotanus (2007, p. 109) on empirical evidence about critical success factors for managing purchasing groups.

3. Use press coverage and company websites for information about the buying groups. Use the framework of, for example, Essig (2000, p. 16) to categorise the players.

16 Logistics - Physical Distribution

This Chapter considers the strategic role of logistics in retail management. It is concerned with those issues that form the context for structuring logistical systems. There is also a discussion on distribution models for online purchases.

16.1 Logistics as a Core Competency

Traditionally, warehousing and distribution systems used by retail companies have been viewed as an operational instrument, delivering the goods at minimal costs. "Modern retailers, however, realise the advantages that can be derived from investment in such systems and view them as a trade-off between costs to the company and providing optimal service to the customer. As such, distribution and warehousing systems are an integral part of the companies' strategy and a major tool of competitive differentiation" (Bell/Davison 1997, p. 88).

Competitive advantage through warehousing and distribution systems means management control of the supply chain, i.e. **logistics leadership** (Liebmann/Zentes/Swoboda 2008, pp. 691-694). For example, as a top manager of Swiss retailer *Migros* states: "It is our belief that we should control the logistics, and that logistics and the supply chain is a core competency of *Migros* as a retailer" (cf. Cuthbertson 2004, p. 175).

The **logistics management responsibility** of retailers is concerned with managing the components of the "logistics mix" (Fernie/Sparks 2009). The following basic components can be identified:

- **Storage facilities**: these might be the stock rooms of the retail stores, warehouses or distribution centres.

- **Inventory**: the key question is the amount of stock to be held for each product.

- **Transportation**: products have to be transported – by ship, truck, rail or plane – from the factory to warehouses or distribution centres (**primary distribution**) and from these places to the retail outlets (**secondary distribution**).

- **Recycling/reuse**: over the last years, retailers have become much more involved in **reverse logistics operations**. This means an increased return of packaging material and handling products for recycling and/or reuse. This trend towards **circulation** has been reinforced by the EU packaging directive (Fernie/Sparks 2009, p. 11).

Information exchange can be regarded as a further basic component. "To get products to where retailers need them, it is necessary to have information, not only about demand and supply, but also about volumes, stock, prices and movements. Retailers have thus become increasingly concerned with being able to capture data at appropriate points in the system and to use that information to have a more efficient and effective logistics operation" (Fernie/Sparks 2009, p. 7). The enhanced role of communications can be demonstrated by reengineering the supply chain: from a **push supply chain** to a **pull supply chain** (Bell/Cuthbertson 2004). With regard to communications, but also with regard to the mentioned basic components, **enabling technologies**, such as identification/coding systems, standards for electronic data interchange (EDI), shared databases, etc. play a major role (see Chapter 17).

Managing retail logistics means balancing costs and service requirements (see **Figure 16.1**). In order to do this, retailers may outsource certain operational functions to specialist logistics service providers, while strategic functions are in most cases performed by the retailer: "Therefore, it is quite natural that we outsource very little of management control of the supply chain" (cf. Cuthbertson 2004, p. 175).

Figure 16.1   Management Tasks in Logistics

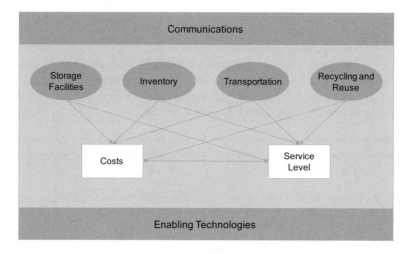

16.2   Structuring Logistical Systems

16.2.1   Basic Options of Supply Chain Structures

Supply chain structures differ according to the actor whose responsibility are the goods in the context of delivery (see **Figure 16.2**). As this responsibility lies with the manufacturer, the manufacturer controls the retailer's delivery as part of its own distribution. Options I and II represent two kinds of **direct store delivery** (DSL), option I without transhipment points and option II with a transhipment point, which operates as a **break-bulk point**, e.g. a platform of a logistics service provider from which the goods are delivered to the outlets.

Options IV and V characterise structures controlled totally by retailers ("**factory gate collecting**"). In option IV, the retailer controls the **primary distribution**, that is from the manufacturer to the central warehouse or regional warehouses, to distribution centres, cross-docking platforms or transhipment points, and the **secondary distribution** from these places to the outlets. Option V illustrates a structure without warehousing or intermediate points.

Combined structures are illustrated by option III. In this option, manufacturers manage the primary distribution to central or regional warehouses, distribution centres or cross-docking platforms of the retailers or to transhipment points. The secondary distribution is then coordinated by retailers.

Figure 16.2   Different Supply Chain Structures

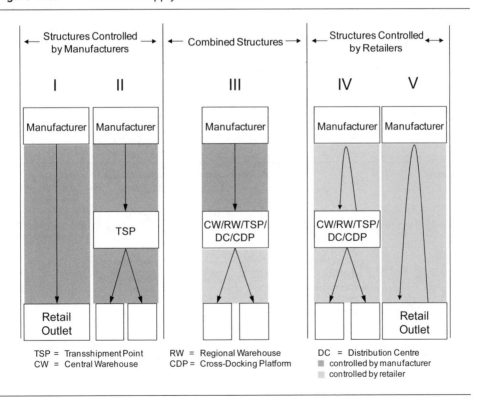

Source: adapted from Thorndike/Waltemath 1999, p. 21.

The main advantages and disadvantages of the basic alternatives of direct store delivery and central warehouses, neglecting the other forms of intermediate points, are summarised in **Table 16.1**.

Table 16.1   Advantages and Disadvantages of Direct Store Delivery and Central Warehouses

	Direct Store Delivery		Central Warehouse	
	Advantages	Disadvantages	Advantages	Disadvantages
Time	♦ just-in-time delivery ♦ quick response to consumer's demands and out-of-shelf situations		♦ centralised/ coordinated time schedule possible	♦ quick response difficult ♦ potential ordering delays
Costs		♦ high-cost-system ♦ high(er) transportation costs ♦ high(er) coordination costs	♦ efficiency in transportation costs ♦ efficiency in storage	♦ high cost for small retailers
Coordination	♦ high coordination efforts necessary		♦ coordination centralised ♦ coordinated merchandise	
Control		♦ higher control power of store managers	♦ higher control of retailers	♦ excessive centralised control possible
Quality of Goods	♦ advantageous for perishable goods or goods with a limited shelf life ♦ maximises the residual shelf life of a product ♦ freshness of products			♦ extra handling of perishables

Source: adapted from Berman/Evans 2010, p. 429; Fernie/Sparks 2009, pp. 146-151.

16.2.2   Increased Control over Primary and Secondary Distribution

Because of intensified competition, retailers, especially in the food and near-food sectors, have extended their control of the supply chain, both upstream and downstream. They have integrated primary and secondary distribution operations (Zentes 2006), and now manage all transport operations and run them as a single network system. This vertically integrated supply chain leads to a new pricing structure in the supplier-retailer relations: **factory gate pricing** (Ex Works, EXW).

Logistics not only constitutes a huge portion of the total costs, but also makes an essential contribution to the commercial value. If the handling of goods by the retailers is more efficient, then retailers are creating added value (Prümper/Pohl/Thoms 2006) (see **Figure 16.3**).

Figure 16.3   Value Added Through Logistics

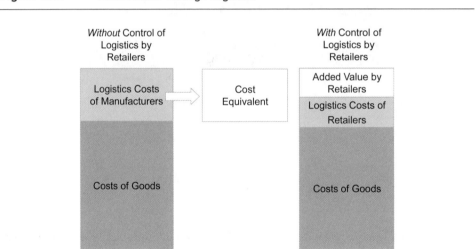

Source: adapted from Prümper/Pohl/Thoms 2006, p. 819.

The trend in food and near-food retailing (as well as in retailing with hard goods, e.g. electrical household appliances) is towards an increased control of the retailers over the supply chain, in sectors characterised by the **downstream verticalisation** of manufacturers (see Chapter 5). Thus, in the form of **secured distribution** or **controlled distribution**, manufacturers dominate the supply chain, which refers to logistical structures as well as to replenishment systems (see Chapter 17).

16.2.3 Rationalisation of Warehousing

In a traditional (central or regional) warehouse, goods are stocked, which is a very costly activity (see **Figure 16.4**). Inventory is expensive and can become obsolete. Furthermore, there are many operations associated with the physical flow of products: goods-in, let down, picking and goods-out (Bell/Davison 1997).

Figure 16.4   Structure of a Warehouse

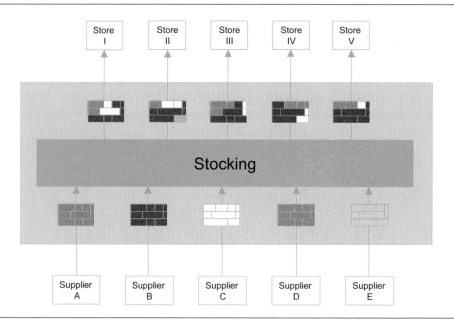

To reduce the inventory of goods and improve the speed of product flow, distribution centres and cross-docking systems have been developed and implemented. A **distribution centre** (DC) or **transit terminal** aims to run stockless in contrast to silos. The retailer can move from keeping stock to a **just-in-time** approach. The products needed in the retail stores are delivered to the "logistics platform" (by the manufacturers or collected/hauled by the retailer), bundled for the retail stores and transported to them. Ideally, no stock remains and the quantity delivered to the distribution centre is precisely that needed by the outlets. The job of the distribution centre is to partition (**break-bulk point**) the quantity delivered to the platform (usually on pallets) and to bundle (**consolidation point**) the different products for each store (usually on pallets or in roll cages.

In a pure **cross-docking system**, there is no partitioning. The products are delivered to the platform on separate pallets or in parcels for each retail store. The cross-docking process is reduced to the bundling of pallets or parcels for the various retail stores: "Cross-docking is a technique in which goods arriving at an RDC (regional distribution centre) are unloaded from the inbound vehicle and moved from the goods receiving area 'across the dock' for marshalling with the other goods for onward despatch without being put away into stock" (Whiteoak 2004, p. 143).

Both approaches, namely distribution centres and cross-docking platforms, have involved reducing order lead time and moving to a more frequent delivery of smaller volumes. This has greatly increased the rate of stock-turn or decreased the amount of goods being stored. The logistical facilities of warehouses and distribution centres/cross-docking platforms are quite different. Warehousing is related to silos, whereas distribution centres/cross-docking platforms are related to "**marshalling yards**".

16.2.4   Integrating Reverse Logistics

The increased return flow of packaging material and the handling of recycling and/or reuse of goods have become a major challenge in retail logistics (Cuthbertson 2004, p. 179). The integration of reverse logistics has extended the traditional linear flow of goods (see **Figure 16.5**). Recycling and reuse lead to a **circulation system** ("closed loop") in which retailers play an important role (Hertel/Zentes/Schramm-Klein 2011, pp. 2-5).

Figure 16.5   From Linear to Circular Logistics Systems

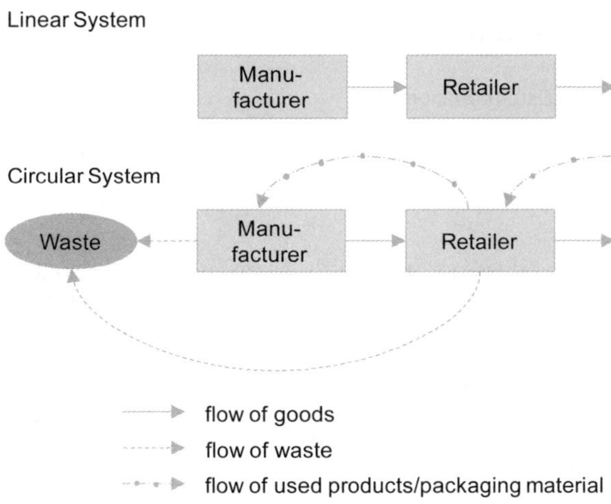

Linear System

Manu-facturer → Retailer → Consumer → Waste

Circular System

Waste ← Manu-facturer → Retailer → Consumer → Waste

→ flow of goods
⇢ flow of waste
⇠⇢ flow of used products/packaging material

16.3   Outsourcing and Joint Physical Distribution

With regard to **new institutional economics,** two polar options exist to realise activities: a value chain activity can be carried out internally (i.e. controlled or coordinated by **hierarchy/integration)** or externally (i.e. by other firms). Externalisation always means **buying** goods or services. In this case, the **market mechanism** takes up the task of coordination (see **Figure 16.6**). These two basic alternatives are also called in more practitioner-oriented terminology: **make or buy** (see Morschett/Schramm-Klein/Zentes 2010, pp. 261-262).

If an activity that is currently being realised internally is transferred to an external firm, this process is called **outsourcing**. By contrast, if an activity is integrated into the internal value chain (intra-firm transaction), this process is called **insourcing**. Between these two polar alternatives, a wide range of **cooperative arrangements** exists with fuzzy delimitations between externalisation and internalisation.

Figure 16.6   Transactional Modes

Managing physical distribution systems does not necessarily mean fulfilling the logistical operations. Retailers can outsource certain logistical functions such as transportation or warehousing to logistics operators, i.e. they can "**buy**" these services (**market transactions**). For example, by transport pooling logistics services providers derive benefit along and across many supply chains (see **Figure 16.7**).

Figure 16.7   Consolidation Opportunities along and across many Supply Chains

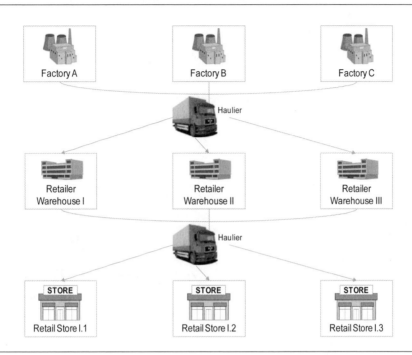

Source: adapted from Whiteoak 2004, p. 155.

These **consolidation opportunities** can also be achieved by joint physical distribution systems **(cooperative arrangements)**: "The broad principle here is that the greater the number of participants, the greater the synergy opportunities and the greater the chance of levering action within the logistics and network services provider community. […] A collaborative approach between manufacturers, their suppliers and customers is envisaged, aimed at optimising physical flows, executed via a community of service providers, working to common commercial principles" (Whiteoak 2004, p. 159).

Decision criteria to outsource logistical activities refer primarily to cost and service level (see **Figure 16.8**) (see Hertel/Zentes/Schramm-Klein 2011, pp 52-55).The decision to outsource logistics also depends on the importance of these activities for the company's success. This importance particularly depends on, and it is measured by, the extent of profiling and the differentiation of these services for the company. Despite possible saving potentials through outsourcing, differentiation effects may be more advantageous through the proper execution of the respective activities by the company.

Naturally, the decision to outsource further depends on the availability of competent partners within the supply chain. These partners need to be capable of taking over the respective activities. The availability of competent partners depends, for example, on the degree of the specificity of logistical activity (e.g. transport and stock resources) and the extent of service level the partners can realise.

Figure 16.8   Outsourcing Logistical Activities

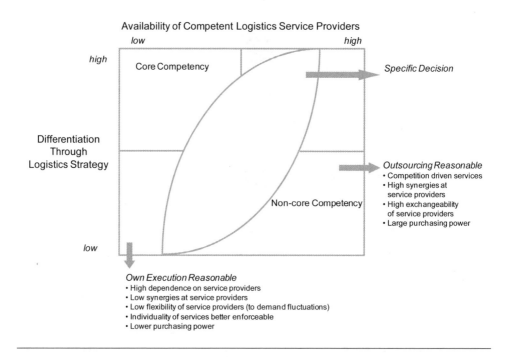

Source: adapted from Pirk/Türks/Mayer 1998, p. 259.

When comparing the two dimensions, the differentiation potential of the respective logisti-cal activity and availability of competent logistics service providers (see **Figure 16.8**), **out-sourcing potentials** can be derived (Pirk/Türks/Mayer 1998; Liebmann/Zentes/Swoboda 2008, pp. 715-718).

Processes and activities that are a company's **core competency** and thus contribute largely to the company's differentiation should be executed internally. **Possibilities for differen-tiation** in logistics exist, for example, in high flexibility, short lead times, high customer proximity and a high service level (with regard to timely, quantitative and qualitative as-pects). However, **non-core competencies** that only contribute to a slight extent to the com-pany's differentiation offer a high outsourcing potential.

According to the findings of study on „Trends and Strategies in Logistics" by Straube/Pfohl (2008), the procurement and distribution functions of retailers and wholesalers are gener-

ally outsourced. The degree of outsourcing transport planning, storage and return processing will most likely continue to increase until 2015 (see **Figure 16.9**).

Figure 16.9   Degree of Outsourcing of Logistical Activities in Retailing

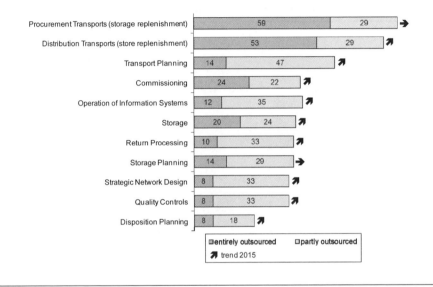

Source: Straube/Pfohl 2008, p. 5.

16.4   Distribution of Online Purchases

Online retailers providing a delivery service to the customer's home, especially grocery
retailers, are faced with the greatest logistical challenges: "Over the past decade many e-tail
businesses have failed primarily because of an inability to provide cost-effective order fulfilment. Several market research studies have identified delivery problems as a major constraint on the growth of home shopping" (Fernie/McKinnon 2009, p. 218). In store retailing
(**bricks-and-mortar stores**), these "fulfilment activities" (picking, transport to home) are
carried out by consumers.

Traditional catalogue mail order companies have long experience of delivering to homes.
They can extend this experience to online purchases. For new players (**pure players** and
multichannel retailers) in web-based retailing (e-commerce), online shopping imposes new
logistical requirements, such as new distribution centres and vehicle fleets. The greatest
challenge of e-commerce is to solve the "last mile problem" (Fernie/McKinnon 2009).

There are different logistics models for the distribution of online purchases. **Figure 16.10** describes a delivery model of online purchases that is characterised by the integration of an **e-fulfilment centre** (order picking centre), a possible solution for the last mile problem. Another option is **store-based picking** of online purchases.

Figure 16.10   Logistics Model for an E-Fulfilment Centre

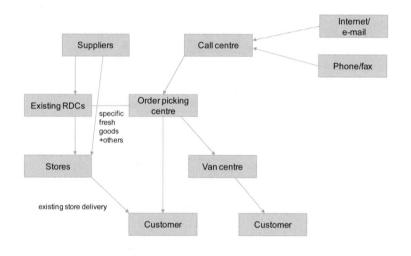

Source: adapted from Foresight Retail Logistics Task Force 2000, p. 15 (cf. Fernie/Sparks 2009, p. 29).

New solutions in the field of e-commerce are **drive-in concepts** or **click & collect concepts**. The consumer can order by phone or via the Internet and pick up the goods, which are commissioned by the retailer in an order picking centre. These solutions are used by *Auchan* in France and *Real* in Germany.

16.5   Instore Logistics

16.5.1   Roll Cage Sequencing

With a view to store retailing, instore logistics can be highlighted. The instore movement of goods presents an important part of the logistical process chain. The instore optimisation of shelf maintenance and the reduction of handling operations are major objectives in supply chain optimisation. This is because existing floor space is generally the most expensive within the entire chain and the sales staff should primarily handle other tasks.

At the same time, instore logistical processes feature close relations with other upstream logistical processes, such as commissioning processes. Stocking roll containers, which are the basis of retail outlet deliveries, may lead to inefficiencies in retail outlets when stocked by storage layout. The reason for this is that the ordered goods are commissioned in the sequence of the storage layout and not in the sequence of the retail outlet layout. Consequently, retail outlet staff are required to move the roll container through the entire store from one item location to another. When controlling the completeness of delivery, another problem arises: all roll containers must be searched for all items of one sales unit. These problems can be reduced through **roll cage sequencing**.

Roll cage sequencing primarily concerns central warehouses. The roll containers are loaded in the reverse sequence in which they are unloaded in the store. Ideally, the store layout determines the central warehouse layout. This means that articles of the same assortment segment are placed on the same roll container. Additionally, articles are sorted by store layout within the roll container, meaning that the articles that are unloaded instore first are placed on top. The results are cost disadvantages in the central warehouse. The higher amount of buffer space needed leads to higher space costs. In addition, the installation of the needed software leads to a one-off investment. Measureable disadvantages result from commissioning because of meticulous picking and longer in-storage distances owing to buffer zones. The most significant disadvantage results from roll containers that are not fully loaded, which in turn leads to unused loading capacities on trucks.

However, significant cost savings can be realised in the central warehouse. For example, the inspection of outgoing goods is more efficient because of the use of clearly arranged roll containers. Consequently, time savings can be realised when placing items on shelves because staff do not have to move the roll container from one assortment sector to another.

16.5.2 RFID Systems at Store Level

Radio frequency identification (RFID) is an emerging technology that "has been over-hyped and raised many concerns, but there seems little doubt that it holds some promise for improving key aspects of logistics and supply chain performance" (Sparks 2009, p. 234). However, there are still a number of problems in RFID implementation, such as technology (e.g. scanning accuracy, size and data storage), costs (infrastructure costs), standardisation and consumer privacy (Sparks 2009, p. 243).

Radio frequency identification is a technology that uses communication via radiowaves to exchange data between a reader and an electronic tag attached to an object for the purpose of identification and tracking. Some tags can even be read from several metres away beyond the line of sight of the reader. The application of bulk reading enables an almost parallel reading of tags. Radio frequency identification involves **interrogators** (also known as **readers**) and tags (also known as **labels**). Most RFID tags contain at least two parts. One is an integrated circuit for storing and processing information, modulating and demodulating a radio frequency signal and other specialised functions. The other is an antenna for receiving and transmitting the signal.

Fields for the application for RFID in retail are primarily transport and storage (e.g. the attachment of RFID tags on pallets, outer packaging or individual products). Additionally, RFID can be used in back store areas or in instore sales areas, for example in connection with "**intelligent shelves**". Intelligent shelves transmit information on shelf inventories based on RFID systems. Furthermore, RFID can be used in **payment procedures**. In this case, there is an automated registration of the customer's purchases based on RFID tags on each article respectively consumption unit. Beyond that, the usage of RFID is discussed in the context of "**traceability**".

Figure 16.11   RFID-Systems in Retail Outlets

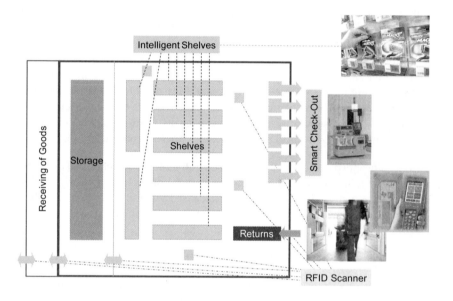

16.6   Conclusion and Outlook

Physical distribution systems in retailing or the consumer goods industry are not only influenced by technological innovations such as RFID. Environmental and societal issues play an important role, too. **Sustainability** has become the hot topic in business strategy, including logistics. By looking at logistics or physical distribution systems from this point of view, questions of **climate protection** and the reduction of CO_2 emissions surface. With regard to supply chains or logistical systems, transport activities and warehousing are primary concerns. Responsible solutions include the alternative consolidation opportunities, e.g. by cooperative arrangements, a new balance between the different modes of transportation (rail, truck, shipping), a new balance between stock and delivery frequency and a new balance between national/global production and transport (see Hertel/Zentes/Schramm-Klein 2011, p. 64-66).

Further Reading

AYERS, J.B.; ODEGAARD, M.A. (2008): Retail Supply Chain Management, New York et al.

FERNIE, J. (2005): Retail Logistics, in: BRUCE, M.; MOORE, C.M.; BIRTWISTLE, G. (Eds.): International Retail Management, Amsterdam et al., pp. 39-63.

FERNIE, J.; SPARKS, L. (2009a): Logistics & Retail Management, 3rd ed., London et al.

HINES, T. (2005): The Emergence of Supply Chain Management as a Critical Success Factor for Retail Organisations, in: BRUCE, M.; MOORE, C.M.; BIRTWISTLE, G. (Eds.): International Retail Management, Amsterdam et al., pp. 108-122.

LEEMAN, J.J. (2010): Supply Chain Management, Duesseldorf.

16.7   Case Study: Sainsbury's[1]

16.7.1   Profile, History and Status Quo

The roots of *Sainsbury's Supermarkets* go back to 1869 when John James and Mary Ann Sainsbury opened their first small dairy shop in London. Today, it is the United Kingdom's longest standing major food retailing chain. The company is a leading UK food retailer with interests in financial services. The parent company *J Sainsbury plc* consists of *Sainsbury's Supermarkets, Sainsbury's Local, Bells Stores, Jacksons Stores* and *JB Beaumont, Sainsbury's Online* and *Sainsbury's Bank*, thus encompassing the business segments of supermarkets and convenience stores, banking services (established in 1997) and online shopping (since 1999). *J Sainsbury plc* is listed on the London Stock Exchange.

Since the disposal of its US engagement in March 2004, when its 37 % share in *Shaw's Supermarkets* was sold to *Albertson's Inc.*, the company has focused on its core UK business in order to increase growth and strengthen its market position. *Sainsbury's* 150,000 employees serve over 19 million customers each week in 872 stores, of which 537 are main *Sainsbury's* supermarket outlets and 335 are convenience stores. For the financial year 2009/10, group

---

[1] Sources used for this case study include various annual reports, financial results 2009/10, press releases, the websites http://www.jsainsburys.co.uk/, http://www.sainsburys.co.uk/sol/index.jsp as well as explicitly cited sources.

sales totalled 21.4 billion GBP, which represented an increase of 5.1 % compared with the previous year.

Sainsbury's is currently the no. three UK supermarket behind its competitors *Tesco* and *ASDA* (owned by *Walmart*). Whereas *Tesco* is the clear leader with about 30 % of the market, the followers are close to each other: *ASDA* with a market share of about 17 % and *Sainsbury's with* a market share of 16 %.

16.7.2 Sainsbury's Outdated Distribution System and the "7-in-3" Supply Chain Management Programme

Since *Tesco* first overtook *Sainsbury's* as the country's largest supermarket in 1995, the former market leader has constantly lost market share. The reasons generally given include the increasingly competitive environment, *Sainsbury's* own complacent attitude and relying on its reputation as a market leader instead of ensuring continuous improvement. Accordingly, the company was still operating with the same supply chain as it had 40 years ago. Not surprisingly, a benchmarking study conducted in 2000 revealed outdated systems and warehousing infrastructure as well as a supply chain-related cost gap of 60 million GBP between *Sainsbury's* and its best-practice competitors (Corsten 2005, p. 70). During the 1960s, *Sainsbury's* had been one of the first retailers to centralise its distribution and to implement **regional distribution centres (RDC)**; about 1-2 % of the company's net profit margin could then be attributed to the resulting efficiency in retail distribution. However, as the distribution network had not been changed for 40 years, it was aging badly. As a result, a single store was sometimes receiving goods from as many as eleven different depots within a single day (Campbell 2003, p. 20). With the introduction of home shopping, the increasing variety of commodities sold, changing consumer tastes and less predictable shopping behaviour, the need to manage this complexity efficiently grew considerably. This outdated supply chain infrastructure was just no longer capable of efficiently organising the supply chain process (Campbell 2003, p. 20). This is why, in 2001, under the leadership of CEO Peter Davis, *Sainsbury's* started one of the "most talked about re-engineering projects ever undertaken by a supermarket retailer" (Campbell 2003, p. 20). Rivals "watched in utter disbelief" as the company embarked on its radical supply chain overhaul (cf. Watson 2005, p. 29). *Sainsbury's* wanted to develop a new **"all-or-nothing" supply chain strategy** in which four key areas were supposed to be tackled:

- Network renewal

- Systems and technology

- Processes and partnerships

- People and culture (Sainsbury's Supermarkets 2001, p. 1).

When the proposals for the overhaul were first presented, the company's former supply chain manager estimated it would take seven years to complete. However, *Sainsbury's* management board pointed out that there was no time to experiment and requested completion within three years. Hence, the stretch target was "7-in-3", which gave the programme its name (Mitchell 2004, p. 32). Given the urgency, this radical "all-or-nothing" approach to rejuvenate the supply chain was chosen (Corsten 2005, p. 70). A reduction in the overall cost base by 700 million GBP within three years was targeted. Key measures for achieving this goal included:

- Replacing the current depots with automated fulfilment factories (FFs) and primary consolidation centres (PCCs)

- An integrated management of transportation from the factory gate to the store back door

- Replacing core supply chain systems, which were old and inflexible

- Ensuring clear performance measurement by reorganising the supply chain structure and processes.

Furthermore, the following key principles were considered as the basis of the future distribution system: paperless, stockless, accurate, simple and automated where appropriate. Traditionally, so-called logistics teams had been responsible for managing the flow of information along the supply chain, whereas distribution teams had cared for the physical storage and delivery of goods. As part of the reform, these two areas were supposed to work as a single organisational division to achieve shared objectives and make the supply chain a seamless flow of products and information.

The "7-in-3" programme aimed at establishing a simplified and efficient supply chain/distribution network, providing for the substitution and supplementation of the RDCs with four types of distribution facilities, designed to increase the product flow (see **Table 16.2**).

Additionally, 60 % of the prior existing facilities were closed (Tulip 2003, p. 52). The transformation of the entire supply chain was largely based around the fulfilment factories which were supposed to both receive goods and despatch them to stores. *Sainsbury's* change from predominantly stockholding RDCs to flow-through FFs was supposed to move "from an infrastructure chiefly comprising conventional wide aisle racking to one combining automated storage and retrieval systems (AS/RS), pick conveyors and sophisticated sortation systems" (Baker 2004, p. 119).

Figure 16.12 gives an overview of the intended flows of goods through the supply chain, which is characterised as a supplier-facing network linked to store-facing facilities.

The rationale behind the automated facility was that economies of scale should be increased because fewer suppliers were able to deliver more volume and because automated sortation and case picking entailed greater accuracy and reduced costs.

Table 16.2   Planned Distribution Facilities in Line with the "7-in-3" Programme

Distribution Facility	Planned functions
Primary Consolidation Centres (PCCs)	◆ handling shipments from local suppliers ◆ holding stock and replenishing fulfilment factories ◆ link between local suppliers and RDCs
Fulfilment Factories (FFs)	◆ handling around 10,000 lines of high-volume commodities ◆ handling waived deliveries to store on a round-the-clock basis
K Line Depots	◆ specialist distribution centres ◆ using highly-automated sorting systems enabling them to efficiently pick low volumes of a wide range of up to 16,000 slow moving and bulky products
Frozen Food Depots	◆ delivering products directly to stores

Source: adapted from Sainsbury's Supermarket Ltd 2001, p. 3.

Figure 16.12   Possible Flows through the Supply Chain

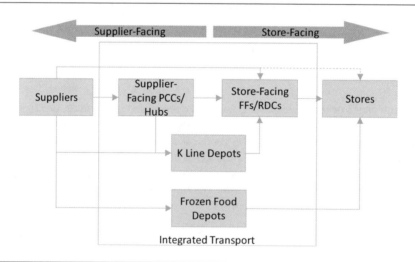

The new structure of the supply chain was supposed to be supported by factory gate pricing (FGP), which has been one of the major developments in UK retailing in recent years, driven primarily by *Tesco*, but also *Sainsbury's*. Suppliers are asked to state the prices of their products with and without delivery costs to the retailer's distribution facility. Hence, FGP "involves a retailer separating the transport costs that the supplier has imposed on products and looking for a cheaper way to transport the goods. This may mean the retailer using its own vehicles, or using a third party logistics provider to pick the goods up directly from the supplier — at the factory gate" (Davies 2004, p. 15). By taking responsibility for primary distribution, i.e. collecting the supplies from the manufacturer (see section "Logistics as a Core Competency"), the retailer can optimise the use of its existing fleet, thereby realising a competitive advantage as well as environmental benefits through the reduction of fuel usage.

Additionally, *Sainsbury's* established a **national transport service centre** (NTSC) to optimise the effectiveness of its transport operations. This was supposed to lead to greater efficiency and effectiveness, enabling *Sainsbury's* to save costs and reduce vehicle usage and kilometres travelled. The NTSC presents opportunities for reducing total truck distance through the better planning of vehicle movements, while optimising truck fill. All trucks are equipped with a global positioning system (GPS) that helps achieve this. In this respect, when it is beneficial to do so, collections of products from suppliers using *Sainsbury's* own fleet are organised, thus reducing the number of vehicles on the roads.

16.7.3   The Outcomes of the "7-in-3" Programme and "Making Sainsbury's Great Again"

In October 2004, Justin King replaced Peter Davis as CEO and introduced a three-year recovery plan worth 550 million GBP called "Making Sainsbury's Great Again". This was based on the outcomes of the "7-in-3" programme. Despite the enormous 700 million GBP investment in the programme and it being honoured with the Global Retail Achievement Award in the category "Best in International Logistics and Distribution" in 2004, and despite consensus that a reform of the distribution system was necessary, the actual performance of the supply chain was not as good as projected (Rode 2008).

In particular, the automated FFs did not utilise their performance potential. At their lowest point, Hams Hall, Waltham Point and Rye Park were turning away 50 % of supplier deliveries. In October 2004, the fulfilment factories were each operating at a capacity of only 800,000 cases a week being picked and delivered and systems were breaking down regularly. One of the biggest problems was massive difficulties in product availability because data on delivered goods were not accurate enough (Rode 2008). Since automated warehouses need near-perfect conditions to work properly and since the strict catalogue of rules led to confusion and annoyance on the part of many manufacturers, the FFs did not work as efficiently as expected and this led to out-of-stocks and availability problems in the stores (Watson 2005, p. 29). Whereas the automation was expected to raise labour productivity and deliver store-friendly product sequencing to reduce replenishment labour at the store, the sensitivity of the FFs sometimes led to the opposite effect and manual assistance and intervention was required (Rode 2008).

As one consequence of the results of the "7-in-3" programme, *Sainsbury's* changed its IT focus and decided to rebuild its expertise back in-house in order to gain more control over its IT system. Therefore, its IT services, which were formerly outsourced to *Accenture*, were migrated back to *Sainsbury's* together with a number of *Accenture* employees and the outsourcing contract with *Accenture* was terminated. The transfer of 470 employees cost approximately 63 million GBP. However, the company expected that future cost savings through the regained control of IT processes and systems would amortise the investment made (J Sainsbury plc 2006).

16.7.4   Sainsbury's Logistics Structure today

Today, *Sainsbury's* is further developing its distribution network, indicating the responsibility being taken for the optimisation of the existing structure. The company has learned from the mistakes made and it tries to constantly improve the network to never again operate with an outdated supply chain. Consequently, the remaining problems in the supply chain process led to the decision not to build any more of the planned fulfilment factories. Even in the existing FFs, automation was partly removed, which led to increased capacity. In line with the new trend to dismantle the automation, even some of *Sainsbury's* depots were partly changed back to **manual labour** (Rode 2008).

Today, ten Primary Consolidation Centres exist (Sainsbury's 2011a). Two different kinds of PCC networks are operated: one for suppliers of non-perishable and frozen goods and one for suppliers of perishable goods. More than 350 suppliers utilise *Sainsbury's* PCCs, which provide the link between suppliers and Regional Distribution Centres. Ambient and frozen food suppliers can benefit from the PCCs as they enable them to meet seven-day order placement and 24-hour lead times and, therefore, allow customer availability to increase. Suppliers of perishable goods benefit from a faster delivery of fresh products to stores. The suppliers receive an order on day one, by day two the perishables have reached a RDC and on day three customers can buy the product (Sainsbury's 2011b).

Originally, nine FFs were planned, six automated and three manual (Sainsbury's 2011c). Today however, *Sainsbury's* only operates three FFs by itself: Hams Hall, Haydock and Waltham Point. One e-fulfilment centre at Corby is operated by iForce, a third-party operator, and one manual fulfilment centre at Emerald Park is operated by the third-party operator *Exel*. Furthermore, about 15 depots for ambient, chilled and frozen food are operated throughout the country (Sainsbury's 2011a).

Today, a holistic supply chain system does not only comprise meeting efficiency goals but also includes dealing with sustainability issues. Therefore, sustainability aspects play a major role in *Sainsbury's* business strategy. With sales of over 218 million GBP, *Sainsbury's* is the world's largest retailer of fair trade products and the company received an "A rating" in the "Green to the Core?" survey by Consumer Focus. Therefore, it seems plausible for it to invest in ecologically friendly transport technologies in order to lessen negative influences on the environment during the logistics process. *Sainsbury's* increasingly uses transport by train and emphasises the use of biogas. After a successful test phase, *Sainsbury's* decided to equip more vehicles with this "dual-fuel system", which mainly uses biogas but also has a diesel engine. This technique reduces CO_2 emissions by 60 %. *Sainsbury's* plans to reduce CO_2 emissions by 15 % per trading unit by 2012. To do so, they have introduced a **transport**

management system, which coordinates the planning of the depots and so reduces unnecessary routes of transport and enables fuel economy (Kapell 2009).

16.7.5   Summary and Outlook

Even after the introduction of the "Making Sainsbury's Great Again" programme, the company's automated warehouses are not totally working as intended and a continued improvement of the structure seems to be necessary. However, measures taken such as the transport management system, which functions as the "central brain" for the entire transport fleet and for suppliers, have been successful. Nevertheless, plans to alter the current warehouse management systems are still being mooted. Today, FFs partly work with manual labour again to ensure product availability, and the original plans for FFs have not been realised (Sainsbury's 2011a; Sainsbury's 2011c). Furthermore, *Sainsbury's* has realised that suppliers found the rules, guides and processes that were necessary for a smooth working system complex and confusing and, therefore, has tried to improve the communication with suppliers. This is, by way of an example, carried out via the portal "Sainsbury's Information Direct" where useful information for suppliers can be found. Nevertheless, a 5.1 % increase in turnover for the commercial year 2009/10 proves the success of the measures hitherto taken. *Sainsbury's* won the "supermarket of the year" retail industry award in 2009, is the world's largest retailer of fair trade products and opened 38 new supermarkets in the same year. These facts show the strong progress made over recent years and prove that the restructuring efforts have been successful.

| Questions

1. *Sainsbury's* supply chain comprises different types of distribution facilities. Why is this distinction normally used?

2. Factory gate pricing (FGP) is becoming increasingly popular. What are the reasons and motivations for this development? Which possible limitations and risks can be identified?

3. What advantages and disadvantages are associated with the outsourcing of physical distribution processes by *Sainsbury's*?

| Hints

1. See Bell/Cuthbertson 2004 and Smith/Sparks 2009 for a description of the different supply chains that operate in terms of type of product.

2. See e.g. Fernie 2009b.

3. See e.g. Levy/Weitz 2009 for a discussion on logistics outsourcing.

17 Logistics – Supply Chain Management and Information Management

In this Chapter, supply chain management is presented as a strategic approach for retail companies. With a focus on logistics activities, efficient consumer response is discussed as a collaborative approach to supply chain management. Information technology is a major enabler of supply chain activities. Therefore, the general principles of information management in retail companies, in a logistics context, are outlined.

17.1 The Supply Chain in the Consumer Goods Industry

Traditionally, manufacturers were the dominant forces in the supply chain in the consumer goods industry. With the trend towards **retail consolidation** and the emergence of large retailers, power in the supply chain has been shifting towards the retail level (Fernie/Fernie/Moore 2004, p. 198). Whereas manufacturers previously designed, produced, promoted and distributed their products or brands and retailers depended on their leadership, retailers have been able to exert pressure back into the supply chain. They have forced manufacturers to change their supply chain strategies, for example, by including tailored pallet packs, scheduled deliveries, continuous replenishment systems and so on (Coyle/Bardi/Langley 2003, p. 6).

The **supply chain** in the consumer goods industry includes all parties directly or indirectly involved in receiving and fulfilling customer requests, namely manufacturers, suppliers, wholesalers, retailers, third-party service providers (transporters, warehouses) and customers (Chopra/Meindl 2010, p. 20). Supply chains are dynamic and they involve the constant flow of products, information and finance between the different stages (see **Figure 17.1**).

The first flow, the flow of **products and related services** from the manufacturer (and its suppliers) to the retailer and eventually the customer, is the core element in supply chain management. Traditionally, it has been the major topic in logistics because customers expect their orders to be delivered on time, reliably and damage-free. **Information flows** comprise, for example, orders, inventory, demand or sales data. These flows are important for replenishment and (demand) forecasting at all stages of the supply chain. **Financial flows** include the transfer of funds or cash between the supply chain partners (Coyle/Bardi/Langley 2003, pp. 18-19).

Figure 17.1   Flows in the Supply Chain of the Consumer Goods Industry

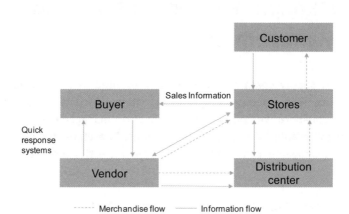

Source: adapted from Levy/Weitz 2009, p. 282.

17.2   Supply Chain Management

17.2.1   Overview

Supply chain management is defined as the planning and management of all business activities involved in fulfilling customer requests, such as sourcing, procurement, operations, marketing and logistics management. It not only focuses on processes or functions within one particular company, but also includes **coordination and collaboration** with other parties in the supply chain (Stank/Davis/Fugate 2005).

The main goal of supply chain management is to facilitate the **integration** of supply and demand management for the purposes of improving the performance of individual companies and the supply chain as a whole. The objective of supply chain management is thus to maximise overall value generated and thus it focuses strongly on **supply chain profitability** (Mentzer et al. 2001).

17.2.2   The Bullwhip Effect

The fundamental idea of supply chain management is that all parties involved should coordinate their activities and collaborate, thus improving the profitability of all supply chain partners. If each value-added partner optimises its own part of the supply chain in isolation, **inefficiencies** in the supply chain are likely to occur. These result mainly from the isolated planning and forecasting of materials or order quantities along the value chain, a scenario that is described as the **bullwhip effect**. This occurs when sales or order quantity fluctuations swing upwards through the various value-added stages, with the amplitudes increasing at each stage. The bullwhip effect results from the fact that customer demand is often unstable. Thus, each company in the supply chain must forecast demand. Because of incomplete information and uncertainties, forecasting errors are common and companies therefore usually carry safety stock in their inventories.

Moving up the supply chain from the consumer to suppliers, each participant observes higher fluctuations in demand and, therefore, has a greater need for safety buffers in its inventory. If demand rises, supply chain participants tend to increase stock and orders. However, if demand declines, companies tend to reduce inventory stocks. The bullwhip effect is characterised by variations amplifying the further one moves up the supply chain from the consumer to suppliers (Lee/Padmanabhan/Whang 1997b; see **Figure 17.2**).

Figure 17.2   The Bullwhip Effect

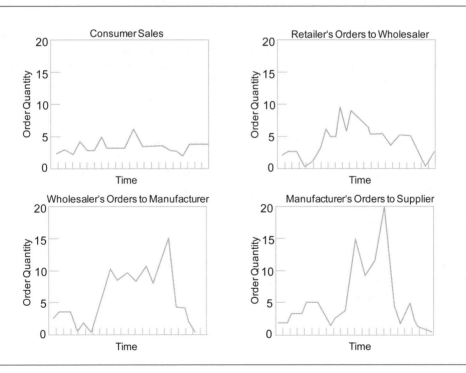

Source: Lee/Padmanabhan/Whang 1997b, p. 94.

The effect demonstrates how pervasive **inefficiencies** can arise from delays caused by **uncoordinated planning cycles** (e.g. because of order batching, price fluctuations or the rationing of quantities by manufacturers) as well as inconsistent and possibly out-of-date customer information or sales data (Lee/Padmanabhan/Whang 1997a, 1997b; Disney/Towill 2003). This then impacts planning and reduces the transparency of supply and material quantities beyond the specific value-added stage (Lee/Padmanabhan/Whang 1997b).

The main approach to solving these difficulties is the implementation of comprehensive **interorganisational information and planning systems**, developing an information flow in the supply chain that reduces inefficiency (Schramm-Klein/Morschett 2006).

Apart from information sharing, other sales and marketing practices in the supply chain, such as the price schedule offered by manufacturers, frequency and depth of price promotion, demand forecasting methods and allocation rules in case of shortages, are important (Lee/Padmanabhan/Whang 2004).

17.3   Efficient Consumer Response

The consequence of the problems encountered with isolated planning is that cooperation and collaboration among supply chain participants are at the core of industry efforts to attenuate the bullwhip phenomenon. The concept of **efficient consumer response** (ECR) is significant in this context. ECR comprises a number of collaborative strategies and operating practices between retailers and suppliers that focus on fulfilling consumer needs better, faster and at less cost (ECR Europe 1998).

The ECR concept implies a shift from the traditional **push-oriented** view of the supply chain that relied on "pushing" merchandise through the supply chain, initiated and performed in anticipation of customer orders, to a **pull-oriented supply chain**. Pull processes, from this view, are triggered by consumer demand and are executed in response to consumer needs. ECR is thus a demand-driven system that has an affinity to the concept **of just-in-time** (Kracklauer et al. 2004, p. 59).

Efficient consumer response is central to the development of concepts for exploiting interorganisational potential through the structuring and control of value chains and it offers a range of supply management- and demand management-oriented concepts based on **retailer-supplier collaboration** (see **Figure 17.3**).

Figure 17.3   Elements of Efficient Consumer Response

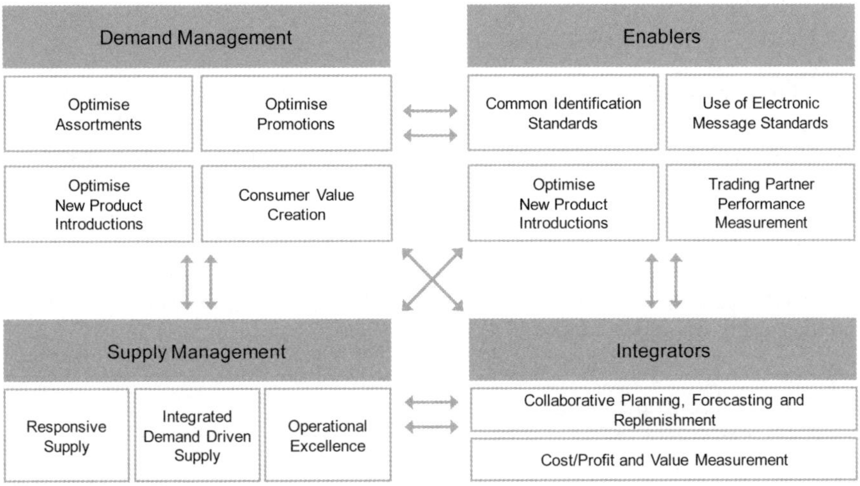

Demand Management		Enablers	
Optimise Assortments	Optimise Promotions	Common Identification Standards	Use of Electronic Message Standards
Optimise New Product Introductions	Consumer Value Creation	Optimise New Product Introductions	Trading Partner Performance Measurement

Supply Management			Integrators	
Responsive Supply	Integrated Demand Driven Supply	Operational Excellence	Collaborative Planning, Forecasting and Replenishment	
			Cost/Profit and Value Measurement	

Source: Global Scorecard 2011.

17.4   Supply Management Concepts in ECR

17.4.1   Overview

Whereas demand management-oriented concepts focus on cooperation in marketing, supply side-oriented concepts strongly emphasise **logistical issues**. Following the pull-oriented view, they relate mainly to the satisfaction of demand in terms of delivering the right products to the right destinations at the right time and in the right quantities ("4rs") (Mollenkopf/Gibson/Ozanne 2000) throughout the supply chain at the lowest possible costs. The emphasis is on **minimising logistics costs**, such as transport costs, in particular inventory costs and costs related to asset commitment.

The main areas of collaboration in supply management are (www.globalscorecard.net):

- **Responsive supply**: the main goal of responsive supply concepts is to synchronise manufacturer and supplier operations with retail sales in terms of a just-in-time pull-oriented supply chain driven by retail sales. Responsive supply, therefore, focuses on distribution methods that integrate product flow from the manufacturers' production lines to consumer demand using actual consumer demand to drive replenishment. The aim is to generate very high service levels, which need to be balanced against cost and inventory levels.

■ **Integrated demand-driven supply**: within integrated demand-driven supply, the focus is on synchronising both production and purchased goods supply to demand. It thus comprises planning and control methods that align supply frequency and volumes with actual demand. Key objectives are minimum inventory levels and response flexibility and speed, which must be balanced against well-managed costs.

■ **Operational excellence**: the objective of these concepts is to enhance efficiency by establishing industry-wide standards and management methods to increase the reliability of operations with regard to problems such as out-of-stocks, late deliveries or administrative errors. Very important in this context are efficient administrative processes between the supply chain parties and **electronic data interchange** (EDI) and other technologies that enable, for example, process automation.

In this context, various concepts have been established to increase efficiency and effectiveness in the supply chain (see **Figure 17.4**).

Figure 17.4   Concepts in Supply Management

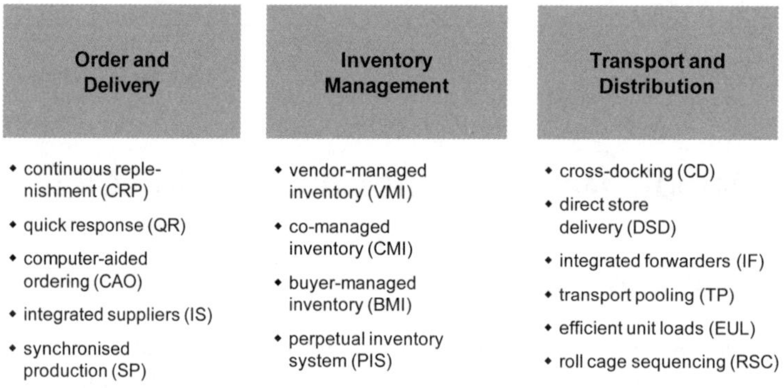

Order and Delivery	Inventory Management	Transport and Distribution
◆ continuous replenishment (CRP)	◆ vendor-managed inventory (VMI)	◆ cross-docking (CD)
◆ quick response (QR)	◆ co-managed inventory (CMI)	◆ direct store delivery (DSD)
◆ computer-aided ordering (CAO)	◆ buyer-managed inventory (BMI)	◆ integrated forwarders (IF)
◆ integrated suppliers (IS)	◆ perpetual inventory system (PIS)	◆ transport pooling (TP)
◆ synchronised production (SP)		◆ efficient unit loads (EUL)
		◆ roll cage sequencing (RSC)

Source: adapted from Gleißner 2000, p. 169.

17.4.2   Order and Delivery

The superordinate concept in inventory management for ECR is **continuous replenishment (CRP)** which implies the continuous flow of merchandise based on consumer demand (i.e. retail sales). The fundamental idea is to transfer the just-in-time concept to retail outlets and thus reduce overall inventory at all stages of the supply chain (see **Figure 17.5**). Continuous replenishment systems require integrated information systems (e.g. EDI) that enable close to the **real-time transfer** of sales and inventory data between retailer and supplier. This information transfer enables suppliers and retailers to **reduce lead times** in production and delivery.

Quick response (QR) is a specific type of CRP, and a concept that has been developed to accelerate product flows in the supply chain. The concept was developed in the textiles industry to reduce replenishment lead times and it is especially well suited to markets with high volatility in demand and rapidly changing assortments. The main objective is to decrease the number of **overstocks** and **out-of-stocks** in the fashion industry, which is characterised by a high number of product variants and short fashion cycles with low demand predictability and a high share of impulse purchases (Christopfer/Lowson/Peck 2004, p. 82; see Chapter 6). By allowing **for multiple orders** to be placed in the selling season, quick response enables a better match between demand and supply.

Figure 17.5   Continuous Replenishment

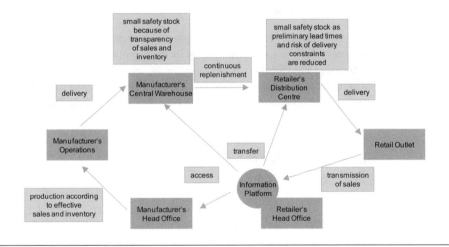

Source: adapted from Swoboda/Janz 2002, p. 207.

A manufacturers' **postponement strategy** is closely linked to this concept and it refers to the delay of product differentiation until temporarily closer to the sale of the product (Birtwistle/Moore/Fiorito 2006).

17.4.3   Inventory Management Concepts

Inventory management strategies in efficient replenishment can be classified according to the party responsible for maintaining inventory levels in vendor-managed inventory (VMI), buyer-managed inventory (BMI) or co-managed or jointly managed inventory (CMI).

The focus of attention is on **VMI**, which is characterised by the vendor being responsible for maintaining the retailer's inventory in the retailer's distribution centre or in each of the outlets (Lee/Padmanabhan/Whang 1997b). The main objective is to reduce out-of-stocks in stores and inventory in the supply chain by centralising forecasting at the supplier and shortening the supply chain. For retailers, VMI is sometimes associated with a loss of control in the supply chain. VMI requires a **continuous information transfer** between both parties in terms of sales and inventory data, and the vendor generates the orders (i.e. reverse purchase orders). Under ideal conditions, inventories are replenished in quantities that meet the retailer's immediate demand, reducing out-of-stocks with minimal inventory levels (Levy/Weitz 2009, p. 298).

Buyer-managed inventories imply retailers maintain suppliers' inventories. They are thus inversely related to VMI. **Jointly managed inventories** entail cooperation between vendor and retailer in inventory management.

17.4.4   Transport and Distribution

Several transport and distribution strategies are applied in efficient replenishment. They serve mainly to guarantee continuous product flows in the supply chain (see Chapter 16). For example, **cross-docking** allows for stockless distribution processes and transport optimisation. **Direct store delivery** (DSD) means that merchandise is shipped directly to the outlets and **transport pooling** helps use transport capacities fully (Coyle/Bardi/Langley 2003, p. 109).

17.4.5   Collaborative Planning, Forecasting, and Replenishment (CPFR)

Collaborative planning, forecasting, and replenishment is a concept that integrates the idea of supply side and demand side concepts in ECR. The concept focuses mainly on **promotion processes** and thus relates primarily to HiLo pricing strategies that, in contrast to EDLP pricing strategies, are usually characterised by a high risk of running out of stock because of high demand uncertainty (see Chapter 12).

The main goal of CPFR is to increase **sales forecast** accuracy by joint sales planning by manufacturer and retailer, using all available data from both parties. Based on this forecast, production, delivery, warehousing and advertising are coordinated to achieve higher product availability and reduce inventory costs. Additionally, as information on customer behaviour is available simultaneously to all participants, reaction to sudden, unanticipated changes in demand is possible (Kracklauer et al. 2004, p. 59). The CPFR process is depicted in **Figure 17.6**.

Figure 17.6   CPFR-Process

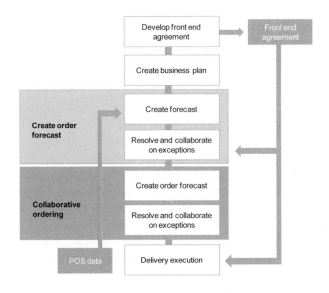

Source: Global Scorecard 2011.

17.4.6   Enabling Technologies

Supply chain management requires efficient information-sharing processes between the parties at each stage of the value chain. Many available technologies enable such information flows (Sanders/Premus 2005).

In order to facilitate interorganisational data exchange, **EDI** and communication networks that enable instantaneous, real-time information transfers such as the Internet, Intranet or Extranet are necessary (Chopra/Meindl 2010, p. 71). Standardisation and automation are important to increase the efficiency of such information processes. Other particularly important enablers of interorganisational information exchange are (Hertel/Zentes/Schramm-Klein 2011, pp. 67-85):

- **Automated identification systems**: important auto-id systems are barcodes, optical character recognition or RFID (see Chapter 16). These are based on coding systems such as global trade item numbers (GTIN) that identify each SKU (item) in the supply chain, global location numbers (GLN) for identifying each participant in the supply chain or the serial shipping container code (SSCC) for identifying shipping units.

- **Communication standards**: standardised message formats that can be processed by the IT systems of all involved parties are important for interorganisational data transfer.

Examples are UN/EDIFACT (United Nations Electronic Data Interchange for Administration, Commerce and Transport), EANCOM (a subset of UN/EDIFACT in the consumer goods industry) or GS1-XML, which is a more flexible message format.

■ **Master data**: master data are the basic data in information processing. They characterise each object in the supply chain, for example, each customer or supplier. Customer and supplier master data are usually company-specific, whereas article master data are usually exchanged between parties. Thus, standardisation in this field is important.

17.5   Information Management

As the bullwhip effect demonstrates, information availability is extremely important in all stages of the supply chain. For example, suppliers need information from the retailer on sales, inventory turnover and feedback on competitors or on the level of customer returns. Information is also needed from consumers on attitudes towards the products, brand loyalty and willingness to pay. Retailers need, for example, sales forecasts, information on product specifications, advance notice of new models, training materials for complex products and information from consumers on their shopping needs, where else they shop and their satisfaction levels with the retailer and the merchandise (Berman/Evans 2010, p. 227). Retailers play a crucial role in collecting information on consumers because they have direct contact with customers at the **point-of-sale** and can collect information that goes beyond sales or scanning data. They thus can act as **gatekeepers** in the supply chain and are able to control information flows.

The above examples demonstrate the need for **information flows** between the different departments of the retailer (e.g. marketing and logistics) as well as at an interorganisational level (Schramm-Klein/Morschett 2006). The main information flows that are important in logistics are shown in **Figure 17.7**. In order to guarantee efficient and timely information flows and to reduce errors in information transmission, **information technology (IT)** plays a vital role.

In a pull-oriented supply chain, the starting point for information flows is the retail outlet. Thus, *store-based IT*, especially point-of-sale systems that enable the scanning of barcodes, is of particular importance. Such point-of-sale systems do not only increase efficiency and productivity in the stores (e.g. faster checkouts), but, in terms of logistical benefits, enable the immediate recording of sales and rapid flow of sales and inventory information. In addition, orders can be automatically recommended or triggered (**sales-based ordering (SBO)**) (McGoldrick 2002, p. 15).

Figure 17.7   Information Flows in the Supply Chain

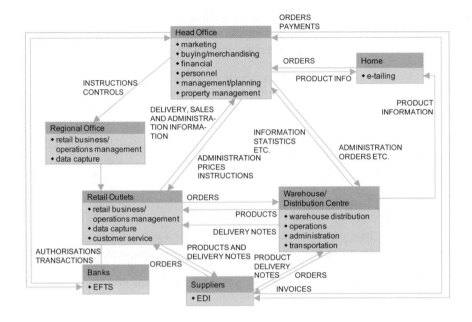

Source: adapted from Dawson 1995.

Also important are enterprise software systems such **as enterprise resource planning systems** (ERP) or **merchandise information systems** (MIS). ERP systems integrate all data and processes of the retail company into a single unified system. They usually consist of various components such as human resources, finance logistics. In retail companies, MIS, as an integral part of ERP systems, play a particularly central role. MIS such as *SAP for Retail* or *Oracle Retail* support all information processes related to product flows in the retail channel, for example, merchandise planning, ordering and inventory processes.

As illustrated, in all stages of the supply chain, data are important for **decision support**. The information (e.g. merchandise information, sales, customer data or supplier information) is "stored" in huge databases that are referred to as **data warehouses**. This information can be accessed by different departments within a retail company (e.g. marketing, buying or logistics) and it serves as an input for the various software systems such as ERP, MIS or **data mining** systems.

17.6   Conclusion and Outlook

In the past, suppliers and retailers were intent on minimising their own logistics costs. This optimisation in one stage of the supply chain often leads to additional costs at other stages, either for retailers or for suppliers. Recently, more integrative views on the supply chain have evolved, which has led to supply chain management and the various concepts of ECR.

Apart from this change to a more strategic view of the supply chain in terms of focussing on total system efficiency, **efficient information processing** is of central importance in collaborative supply chain management. In this context, new technological developments such as data warehousing, webEDI, RFID or Internet apps have added new dimensions to collaboration in the value chain and have enabled the various new concepts in supply chain management.

❘ Further Reading

BELL, R.; CUTHBERTSON, R. (2004): Collaboration in the Retail Supply Chain, in: REYNOLDS, J.; CUTHBERTSON, C. (Eds.): Retail Strategy, Amsterdam et al., pp. 52-77.

SEIFERT, D. (2004): Collaborative Planning, Forecasting and Replenishment - How to Create a Supply Chain Advantage, Bonn.

17.7   Case Study: Procter & Gamble and Walmart[1]

17.7.1   Overview

This case study describes the supply chain cooperation between a manufacturer, *Procter & Gamble (P&G)*, and a retailer, *Walmart*. Both corporations have applied the ECR methods described in the previous Chapter in a variety of ways and thus have coordinated channel activities better than prior to their cooperation. Specifically, the result has been a more efficient supply chain with reduced needs for inventories and more sales, with product lines that were harmonised with regional customer needs.

---

[1] Sources used for this case study include various annual reports, press releases, the websites www.walmart.com and www.pg.com as well as explicitly cited sources.

17.7.2   Profiles of the Channel Partners

17.7.2.1   Walmart

Walmart was founded in 1962 by Sam Walton. Walton opened his first store in Arkansas, USA. Early on, he focused on offering significant discounts on product prices to expand volumes and increase overall profits. This strategy proved to be successful, so that Walton opened a second store within three years. Since then, *Walmart* has focused on growth. Since 1984, over 3,600 *Walmart* stores (including more than 700 *Walmart Discount Stores* and approx. 2,900 *Walmart Supercenters*) have opened in the US. Most of these stores are located in small towns. Walton described the underlying business model: "When we arrived in these small towns offering low prices every day, guaranteed customer satisfaction, and hours that were realistic for the way people wanted to shop, we passed right by that old variety store competition, with its 45 % mark-ups, limited selection and limited hours" (quoted in Chandran 2003). In the 1990s, *Walmart* continued its expansion strategy with the opening of stores outside the US, e.g. Mexico (1992) and Canada (1994).

Walmart is one of the largest business groups in the world in terms of turnover and profits. The corporation generates a turnover of 405 billion USD and a profit of 14.3 billion USD (Fortune 2011). In the US alone, *Walmart* operates more than 4,300 facilities including *Walmart Supercenters*, discount stores, neighbourhood markets and Sam's Club warehouses (Walmart 2011a).

Walmart's strategic orientation has hardly changed since its beginnings. The range is focused on the needs of the customer, offering significant discounts on product prices to expand volumes and increase overall profits (Walmart 2011b). Cost reductions as well as fast reactions to customer wishes with regard to product ranges are essential for this. Efficient supply chain management is thus particularly important for *Walmart* (Seifert 2001, Walmart 2011c).

17.7.2.2   Procter & Gamble

Procter & Gamble's history goes back to 1837, when William Procter and James Gamble founded a small family-operated soap and candle company in the USA. It was the stated aim of the founders to manufacture products that make people's everyday lives a little better (Procter & Gamble 2011a). In the early decades, these products were primarily soap and candles. Other product ranges were only added at the beginning of the 1910s.

Today, *Procter & Gamble* manufactures a wide range of consumer goods. The company offers its products as a multitude of brands, so that the corporate brand *Procter & Gamble* often fades into the background. In this way, the corporation owns 50 brands described as **leadership brands** that account for 90 % of *P&G* sales and profits; 23 of *P&G*'s brands have more than a billion USD in net annual sales (Procter & Gamble 2011b). Net sales of 78.9 billion USD (in 2010) make *P&G* one of the world's leading consumer products companies. In total, 48 % of the net sales were made in the household care segment, 34 % in the beauty and grooming segment and 18 % in the health and well-being segment (Procter & Gamble 2011b).

Procter & Gamble is associated with a high market research and category management competence (Seifert 2001). In particular, the term **"first moment of truth"** (Nelson/Ellison 2005) has gained some importance in the past couple of years (cf. Inman et al. 2009). This designates the seconds after a shopper first encounters a product on a store shelf. According to *Procter & Gamble*, shoppers make up their minds about the product in these first few seconds; this becomes behaviour-relevant. The inherent significance of the point-of-sale in this idea is reflected in the emphasis on category management and ECR.

17.7.3   Initial Position and Aims of the Cooperation

Before *Walmart* and *Procter & Gamble* began their supply chain cooperation in 1988, the business relationship between the two companies was poor. *Procter & Gamble* was divided into 12 different product divisions at the time. Each division was independently organised and fully responsible for its area, independent of the other divisions. As a direct result, the sales managers of the individual divisions of *Procter & Gamble* contacted *Walmart* separately and independently. An opportunity for the sales managers of the individual divisions to come together and arrange for a uniform strategy of *Procter & Gamble* towards *Walmart* was not intended.

Grean/Shaw (2003 p. 158) described the cooperation of the two companies before establishing the channel partnership as "anything but collaborative". The business relationship was adversarial, as the structures of the two companies did not fit each other: *Procter & Gamble* was too inflexible and complicated from *Walmart*'s viewpoint. The relationship of the two companies was cluttered with day-to-day transactions rather than long-term planning and customer relationship management. Furthermore, information systems in the relationship were non-existent.

One incident characterised the two companies' relationship at the time. According to Grean/Shaw (2003), in 1985 Sam Walton tried to inform *Procter and Gamble's* CEO about *Walmart*'s intention to award *P&G* its "Vendor of the Year" award. Instead of getting through to *Procter & Gamble*'s CEO, he reached the sales organisation who redirected Walton to the corporate office. After being transferred from one *P&G* office without ever reaching *P&G*'s CEO, *Walmart* decided to award it to another vendor (Grean/Shaw, 2003, p. 159).

Both companies started to rethink their **business relationship** in the mid-1980s. They hoped for:

- reductions in the costs arising from inefficiencies between the organisations,
- a better coordination of order amounts and produced goods for effective demand,
- reductions in storage costs resulting in out-of-stocks and a
- better production planning.

In 1988, *Procter & Gamble* and *Walmart* established **business teams** that developed the use of joint scorecards, annual plans and technology as a method to eliminate costs and openly share data. *Procter & Gamble* and *Walmart* developed a mission statement that clarified the nature of the cooperation:

"The mission of the *Walmart/P&G* business team is to achieve the long-term business objectives of both companies by building a total system partnership that leads our respective companies and industries to better serve our mutual customer - the consumer" (quoted in Ehring 2006).

The changes in the cooperation of the two companies were characterised by a change in contact points. While prior to the establishment of the channel partnership, there were very few contact points between the companies and they did not exchange much information, the interface between the two companies broadened with wider methods afterwards.

While establishing and evolving their business relationship, both companies developed a new approach to collaboration between manufacturers, retailers and, later on, other intermediaries in the supply chain. Through its outstanding success, the channel partnership between *Procter & Gamble* and *Walmart* has been a prototype of an **ECR strategy** since then.

17.7.4   Cooperation in Supply Chain Management

17.7.4.1   Inventory Management Concepts

Procter & Gamble established a **vendor managed inventory programme** for the implementation of efficient replenishment. Within the VMI programme and within contractually agreed boundaries, it is responsible for all decisions regarding its product stock at *Walmart*. *Procter & Gamble* thus has control over the frequency, quantity and timing of shipments – an explicit order by *Walmart* is no longer necessary.

A prerequisite for this to occur was *Procter & Gamble's* access to *Walmart's* inventory data. *Procter & Gamble* replenished *Walmart's* inventory-based system with inventory data received from *Walmart's* distribution centre (DC). *Procter & Gamble* used its data access to fundamentally change the replenishment process by linking *Walmart's* inventory data at its distribution centres and *Procter & Gamble's* replenished inventory, based on the movement of products through the distribution centres. The project team referred to three types of information for efficient replenishment: actual warehouse on-hand quantity, actual warehouse on-order quantity and projected sales demand from the stores.

The Procter & Gamble and Walmart channel partnership has dramatically improved Procter & *Gamble's* on-time deliveries to *Walmart*, while increasing inventory turnover (Simchi-Levi et al., 2000; Handfield/Nichols 1999): *Procter & Gamble* has reduced the order cycle time by 3-4 days (Grean/Shaw 2003). At the same time, it has saved *Walmart's* resources and demonstrated how information sharing leads to mutual advantages for both parties in such partnerships (Solis 2001).

17.7.4.2 Collaborative Planning, Forecasting, and Replenishment

Walmart and *P&G* have been the initiators of a whole series of pilot projects within CPFR (LebensmittelZeitung 1999), a cooperative planning system within which out-of-stocks and stock costs along the supply chain are supposed to be reduced. The pilot projects have generally achieved 30 - 40 % improvements in forecast accuracy. Besides this, significant increases of between 15 % and 60 % in customer service and sales have been reported as well as distinctive reductions in days of supply (Sheffi 2002; Ireland/Bruce 2000).

The Collaborative Planning, Forecasting and Replenishment Committee aims to "improve the existing guidelines, tools and critical first steps that enable the implementation of CPFR" (http://www.vics.org/committees/cpfr/). The committee furthermore strives to promote the integration of category management with CPFR.

Procter & Gamble has been engaged in CPFR for at least 15 years and it also carries out collaborative planning with hundreds of partners (D'Souza et al. 2008; Sliwa 2002). The company has implemented CPFR with its retail customers and suppliers, and even inside the company between functions and divisions (Sheffi 2002).

Walmart laid an important foundation for the further spreading of CPFR with its decision to largely insist on the use of RFID with its suppliers (D'Souza et al. 2008). In order to secure this, *Walmart* ensured its suppliers that the data saved in the RFID tags, which contain significantly more information than do barcodes, will be exchanged within 30 minutes of their cargos arriving at *Walmart* (Schwartz 2005). In this way, the supplier has an unprecedented level of data for planning its replenishment operation. In 2003, *Walmart* reduced its operating expenses by establishing over 600 trading partners through CPFR (Andraski/Haedicke 2003; Kim/Mahoney 2006).

In its CPFR partnership, *Walmart*'s market information is integrated with *P&G*'s **data management systems**. In this way, effective vertical coordination across their firm-level boundaries can be achieved (Kim/Mahoney 2006). Thus, *P&G* and *Walmart* come to better consumer-based decisions. For example, *P&G* receives actual demand information on what is selling and the selling price by analysing *Walmart*'s POS data. Thus, the development, production and delivery of *Procter & Gamble*'s products can be arranged in a way to meet customer needs in a timely manner.

17.7.5 Information Management

One of the most important challenges within supply chain management is the design of the information exchange between the partners along the supply chain. As with almost all business collaborations that involve the exchange of information, *Walmart* and *Procter &*

Gamble were faced with the challenge of creating an infrastructure that could combine two different and independently operating data management systems.

In all of its stores, *Walmart* recorded data with scanners to track, measure and analyse business. For this, the company built a new data warehouse before the establishment of the channel partnership with *Procter & Gamble* that allowed it to track the sales of all products in each of its stores (Grean/Shaw 2003). When analysing the data, *Walmart* wanted to answer the following questions:

- How much of the product was sold at stores during a certain time period?

- How many customers bought *P&G* products?

- What was the profitability of these products for both *P&G* and *Walmart*?

Procter & Gamble also collected data primarily related to the (potential) buyers of its products. As a result of *P&G*'s market research, *P&G* answered these questions: who is the buyer of a certain product? For which occasions are relevant products bought in what channels? Beyond this, *Procter & Gamble* researched consumer needs and shopper behavior independent of whether the customers were actually buyers of its products or not. In this way, the manufacturer generates insights that the retailer generally does not have. A third data source is third-party data. These data come from scientific research or research by a market research company, and was not specifically generated for one of the partner companies, but was gathered and saved by them.

It was the task of information management within the cooperation between *Walmart* and *Procter & Gamble* to create the infrastructure so that both companies could combine their gathered data and relate it. The combined, or matched, data were the basis for a multitude of analyses. The market and acting market participants could then be described better and much more completely.

This request was achieved with a **"Data Delivery Highway"** (see **Figure 17.8**). This architecture allows for interface integration for individual applications. Furthermore, joint business cards and different analysis tools were developed to use these interfaces and thus offered *Walmart* and *Procter & Gamble* employees access to the prepared and combined data of both companies.

Figure 17.8   The Data Highway for the Manufacturing/Retail Integration

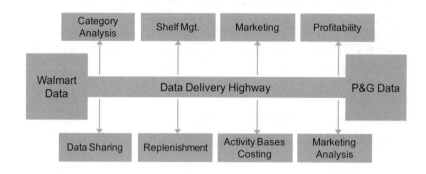

Source: Grean/Shaw 2003, p. 161.

In this cooperation, the partners in the supply chain were meant to be connected by using the industry-standard EDI, so that key business documents could be easily exchanged using one standard. Examples of such documents were purchase orders, invoices, advanced shipment notifications and financial payments. Thus, it was important that EDI would not be used to automate poor business practices. Accordingly, the introduction of EDI was started only after the reorganisation of the companies' communication was advanced, otherwise the exchange via EDI would have resulted in the quicker exchange of bad data.

This can be illustrated by the following example: *Procter & Gamble* and *Walmart* automated all purchase orders and invoices through EDI. The system automatically balanced all *Procter & Gamble* invoices that matched *Walmart*'s purchase orders. If they did not match, they were treated manually, which took extra time and incurred higher costs. After establishing this system, the high count (85 %) of invoices not matching purchase orders became evident. Detailed enquiries revealed that the same product was often saved with differing prices in the respective *Procter & Gamble* and *Walmart* databases. The automatic exchange via EDI had thus only exchanged bad data faster, but it did not lead to better communication. To respond to this problem, a tool ("Customer Table Checking") was created that automatically harmonised the prices in both companies' databases at the beginning of each week (Grean/Shaw 2003).

Table 17.1   Walmart and Procter & Gamble Scorecard

	Walmart FYs		
	Last Year	This Year	Index
Retail Sales (W-M POS Data Walmart Stores			
Gross Margin % (W-M POS Data) Walmart, Inc.			

Inventory Management (Walmart Stores)
    Store Inventory DOH
    Total DOH
    Serivce Levels (% Fill)
    In Stock Level
    On-Time Delivery to Whse			

Financial
    PO/Invoice Match Rate
    Deduction Rolling Balance
    Past Due Invoice Payment Rolling Balance
    Customer Pick-Up Revenue			

(Abbr.: W-M - Walmart; POS - Point-of-Sale; DOH - Days on Hand; FY - Fiscal Year)

Source: Grean/Shaw 2003, p. 162.

An important interface that links *Walmart*'s data with its key vendor partners and carriers is called "Retail Link". This application can be accessed through the Internet and is thus usable independent of location. "Retail Link" provides information and several tools that allow suppliers to analyse information about many areas of their relationships with *Walmart*. "Retail Link" enables participating suppliers to plan, execute and analyse production amounts and delivery dates.

One example of the use of the combined information of both companies in the channel partnership was the **joint common scorecard** (see **Table 17.1**), which allowed the partners to measure joint progress in order to design starting points for the modification of the cooperation. The scorecard contained the sales of *Procter & Gamble* products at *Walmart* as well as margins, profit results, inventory turns and other financial and logistics measurements (Grean/Shaw 2003).

17.7.6   Summary and Outlook

From a difficult starting point, *Procter & Gamble* and *Walmart* designed a prototype of an **ECR strategy** in the US in the late 1980s. By doing so, both companies attached particular importance to an efficient design of the administrative processes in the cooperation of the channel partners. Industry standards used automated and accelerated repeating processes such as orders and invoicing. Special attention was given to the development of a **VMI programme**, in which *Procter & Gamble* gained access to *Walmart*'s inventory data and was thus able to independently control the stock of its products in *Walmart* stores. The basis for this process was a far-reaching information management system that allows respective access for both involved channel partners to the other's data. At the same time, applications allow analyses and further earmarked use of the data.

The cooperation of the two companies has resulted in some remarkable successes. Not least, both *Walmart* and *Procter & Gamble* have achieved top scores in independent analyses on meeting consumer and shopper needs (Promo 2006; Kantar Retail 2010). The reported benefits attracted the attention of the *Metro Group* in Germany and were the beginning of another close collaboration (ECR Europe 2005).

▌ Questions

1. Why did *P&G* and *Walmart* establish their first channel partnership at the end of the 1980s?

2. Why is the design of the information exchange between partners along the supply chain one of the most important challenges within supply chain management?

3. Which criteria would you use to measure the success of the channel partnership?

▌ Hints

1. Bear in mind both the starting position and the converging goals of both companies.

2. Consider the prerequisites for file formats and database structure.

3. Consider what effect the channel partnership has on both partners.

18   Monitoring Operational and Financial Performance

The aims of this Chapter are to consider the relationships between retail strategy and performance, to review the ratios and tools of productivity and effectiveness, inventory/supply chain evaluation, profit/turnover evaluation and financial performance evaluation and to consider new conceptual frameworks.

18.1   Retail Strategy and Performance

Retailers develop their strategies for sustaining a competitive advantage (see Part II of this book) in a market situation characterised by intensified competition. In such a situation, there is growing pressure on retailers to perform, so they must measure or evaluate their performances. Different kinds of performance measures can be identified:

- Productivity/effectiveness evaluation
- Inventory/supply chain evaluation
- Profit/turnover evaluation
- Financial performance evaluation.

The study of productivity in retailing has a long history (McGoldrick 2002, p. 211). Many different measures have been developed as useful and practical indicators of retail performance. In discussing operational performance, not only retail performance, the terms **productivity**, **efficiency** and **effectiveness** have to be defined and distinguished. According to Goodman (1985), the following distinct definitions can be used (McGoldrick 2002, p. 211):

- Productivity relates a single input factor to an output measure, other inputs assumed constant.
- Efficiency measures the effects of all inputs in combination and thus recognises that all inputs and the proportions in which they are employed may vary.
- Effectiveness takes into account goal achievement as well.

These measures are distinct, but a hierarchical relationship exists between them (Goodman 1985): "High productivity is a necessary but not sufficient condition for high efficiency, as individual productive factors may not be combined in an optimal manner. Similarly, high efficiency is a necessary but not sufficient condition for high effectiveness, as the efficient combination may be directed to less than optimal goals".

The inventories of retail companies has an important influence on profits and financial performance. A large variety of ratios and performance indicators has been developed to evaluate how efficiently and effectively retailers utilise their investments, for example, stock turnover or inventory turnover. To balance inventory levels and out-of-stocks with regard to **customer satisfaction** and **customer loyalty**, new tools have been created such as the **performance measurement** of the supply chain (Zentes 2004).

Profit and turnover evaluation are more specific in retailing compared with other industries because of the huge number of **stock-keeping units** (**SKU**s) and large number of organisational units, such as outlets in a retail chain. This complexity leads to specific turnover and profit paths in analysing retail performance.

The financial performances of retailers can be examined based on the balance sheet, profit and loss account (P&L statement), and cash flow statement. There is no difference in principle, in measuring the financial performance of the retail industry compared with other industries using, for example, liquidity ratios, return ratios, earnings coverage ratios and value metrics.

In addition to these tools, various other instruments have been developed for the monitoring of operational and financial performance, such as activity-based costing, benchmarking and balanced scorecards (Liebmann/Zentes/Swoboda 2008; Morschett 2004).

18.2   Productivity/Effectiveness Evaluation

Many retailers give great priority on improving productivity. Various ratios can be calculated to measure **retail productivity** or different aspects of retail productivity. The most common ratios are:

- Sales per square metre (or square foot)

- Sales per employee (i.e. per full-time equivalent).

Actual examples of these two ratios are given in **Table 18.1**.

Table 18.1 illustrates considerable differences within and between the sectors. It is important to notice that the lower value of these measures does not necessarily mean lower effectiveness. "A relatively high number and/or quality of stuff **may** be a natural outcome of higher service positioning. Likewise, more space per unit of sales **could** reflect a more comfortable selling environment"(McGoldrick 2002, p. 211).

Table 18.1   Retail Productivity Measures of Selected Companies

Company	Sales per m² (EUR)	Sales per employee (EUR)
Carrefour	6,065	219,325
JC Penny	1,213	83,924
Kohl's	1,691	92,613
Kroger	3,742	167,491
Macy's	1,173	104,613
Marks & Spencer	6,168	133,928
Sears	1,181	98,078
Tesco	7,675	122,551
Walmart	3,317	134,199

Source: Annual Reports 2009.

Nevertheless, these ratios provide **benchmarks** within sectors or **strategic clusters** of retail companies. Retail managers can detect and analyse deviations from the benchmarks or just from the averages. Productivity measures, such as sales per square metre or sales per employee, can support monitoring the store management performance within retail chains. **Table 18.2** illustrates the different ratios used in German grocery retailing in 2008.

Table 18.2   Retail Productivity Measures of German Grocery Formats

Grocery Format	Sales per m² (EUR)	Sales per employee (EUR)
Discounters	4,580	422,857
Hypermarkets	4,291	325,285
Superstores	4,047	272,831
Small Grocery Retailers	3,743	150,028
Conventional Supermarkets	3,623	204,411

Source: EHI Retail Institute 2009.

18.3   Inventory/Supply Chain Evaluation

With regard to **financial inventory control**, two main metrics are applied in retail companies:

- Stock turnover

- Gross margin return on investment.

"**Stock turnover** represents the number of times during a specific period, usually one year, that the average inventory on hand is sold" (Berman/Evans 2010, p. 457). This ratio can be calculated in units or currency (e.g. EUR, USD or GBP). In computing stock turnover in currency, two dimensions can be distinguished: retail prices ("at retail") or purchasing prices ("at cost").

Different formulas can be applied (Berman/Evans 2010, p. 456):

$$(1)\ \text{annual rate of stock turnover (in units)} = \frac{\text{number of units sold during year}}{\text{average inventory on hand (in units)}}$$

$$(2)\ \text{annual rate of stock turnover (at retail)} = \frac{\text{net yearly sales}}{\text{average inventory on hand (at retail)}}$$

$$(3)\ \text{annual rate of stock turnover (at cost)} = \frac{\text{cost of goods sold during the year}}{\text{average inventory on hand (at cost)}}$$

In order to increase stock turnover, retailers can reduce the stocks of slow-selling items ("stock reduced", see Chapter 15), buy in a timely manner ("stockless"), apply collaborative planning tools and supply chain techniques such as CRP or VMI (see Chapter 17) or use reliable suppliers.

High stock turnover may result in the loss of volume discounts and in higher transportation charges. One way of monitoring inventory investment and profit per unit is to compute **gross margin return on investment** (GMROI). This metric represents the relationship between gross margin and average inventory at cost, by combining profitability and sales-to-stock measures (Berman/Evans 2010, p. 457):

$$(4)\ \text{GMROI} = \frac{\text{gross margin}}{\text{net sales}} \times \frac{\text{net sales}}{\text{average inventory at cost}} = \frac{\text{gross margin}}{\text{average inventory at cost}}$$

18.4   Profit/Turnover Evaluation

18.4.1   Profitability Ratios

Metrics from this group are designed to measure the ability of a retail company to achieve, sustain and increase profits (Dragun 2004a). Profitability can be measured by different indicators. One important relationship is between profits and sales (**margin ratios**); another dimension of profitability relates profits to capital. These so-called **return ratios** are discussed below within the context of financial performance evaluation.

"Top-level" indicators of profitability are (Dragun 2004a):

■ Gross margin in %

■ Net profit margin in %.

Gross margin, also called gross profit, is defined as:

(5) gross margin = net sales − costs of goods sold

"It is an important measure in retailing because it indicates how much profit the retailer is making on merchandise sales without considering the expenses associated with operating the store and corporate overhead expenses" (Levy/Weitz 2009, p. 174). Like other performance measures, this indicator can be expressed as a percentage of net sales (**gross margin in %**):

(6) gross margin in % $= \frac{\text{gross margin}}{\text{net sales}} \times 100$

The term **net sales** expresses the total volume of money (e.g. EUR, USD or GBP) after all refunds have been paid and payments have been collected from vendors for promotions (Levy/Weitz 2009, p. 173) (and after sales tax):

(7) net sales = gross amount of sales + promotional allowances − customer returns

The net profit margin in % relates net profits (see **Figure 18.1**) to sales:

(8) net profit margin in % $= \frac{\text{net profit}}{\text{net sales}} \times 100$

This **"bottom-line" profitability** is useful for comparisons across companies.

18.4.2   Profit Path

Different profit margin models or formulas can be illustrated by a firm's profit path (see **Figure 18.1**).

Expenses are the costs incurred by a retail company in the normal course of business. There are three types of **retail operating expenses** (Levy/Weitz 2009, pp. 174-175):

- Selling expenses

- General expenses

- Administrative expenses.

Selling expenses comprise sales staff salaries, commission and benefits. **General expenses** include rent and utilities. **Administrative expenses** include salaries of all employees other than sales personnel, operational costs incurred by buying offices and other administrative expenses.

Figure 18.1   Profit Path - Example Kohl's (in billion USD)

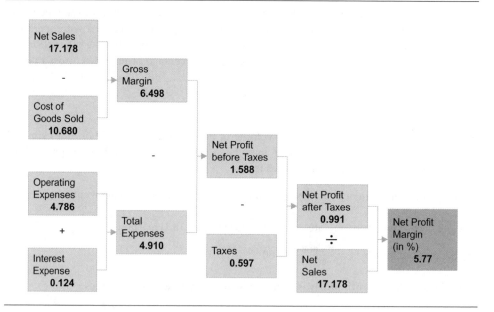

Source: Kohl's 2010, p. 20.

18.4.3 Operating Profit Analysis in Retail Chains

As a simplified example of an **operating profit analysis** in retail chains, **Table 18.3** provides a calculation of gross margin and operating profit for a fictitious retail store and the aggregation from store level to company level.

Table 18.3 Operating Profit: Department, Store and Company Level (in 1,000 EUR) (fictitious example)

Step	Position	Store A			Store B			Com-pany
		Dep. 1	Dep. 2	Total	Dep. 1	Dep. 2	Total	
0	net sales	278.0	424.0	702.0	723.5	381.5	1,105.0	
	./. costs of goods sold	159.4	242.2	401.6	435.9	234.6	670.5	
1	gross margin	118.6	181.8	300.4	261.3	174.2	435.5	
	./. salaries	57.5	96.3	153.8	150.5	93.5	244.0	
	./. rent	24.0	16.0	40.0	33.0	22.0	55.0	
2	operating profit (department level)	37.1	69.5	106.6	77.8	58.7	136.5	
	./. other store level expense			55.0			68.8	
3	operating profit (store level)			51.6			67.7	119.3
	./. expenses of headquarters							33.2
4	operating profit (company level)							86.1

18.5 Financial Performance Evaluation

18.5.1 Financial Ratios

To evaluate the financial performances of retailers, **financial ratios** can be applied. In retail companies, four groups of financial ratios are utilised (Dragun 2004a):

- Internal liquidity ratios
- Return ratios

- Financial leverage ratios

- Earnings coverage ratios.

In this Chapter, internal liquidity ratios and return ratios are discussed.

The limitations of ratio analysis have led to the development of a new class of measures called **value metrics**. "The idea behind a value metric is simple and powerful: value is only created if the company generates return on capital exceeding the cost of that capital" (Dragun 2004a, p. 161). This approach will be discussed briefly and illustrated in the following case study.

18.5.2   Liquidity Ratios

Metrics from this group "measure the ability of the firm to sustain current and meet future obligations. Internal liquidity ratios usually compare the short-term assets such as cash and marketable securities with the near-term financial obligations such as accounts payable" (Dragun 2004a, p. 149).

The current ratio is one of the best-known liquidity metrics:

(9) $\text{current ratio} = \frac{\text{current assets}}{\text{current liabilities}}$

Other metrics from this group are (Dragun 2004a):

(10) $\text{quick ratio} = \frac{\text{cash and equivalents+accounts receivables}}{\text{current liabilities}}$

(11) $\text{cash ratio} = \frac{\text{cash equivalents}}{\text{current liabilities}}$

(12) $\text{cash flow from operations ratio} = \frac{\text{cash flow from operations}}{\text{current liabilities}}$

The quick ratio and cash ratio are more conservative ratios, because inventories and other assets included in current assets may not be liquid enough (Dragun 2004a). Formula 12 integrates a cash flow perspective.

18.5.3   Return Ratios and Return Path

These metrics relate profits to capital in contrast to profitability ratios, which relate profits to sales. A "top-level" indicator measures the efficiency of a company in utilising assets for profit generation: **return on assets** (ROA). This indicator is usually calculated on an **EBIT** basis (earnings before (b) interest and taxes):

(13) $\text{ROA}^{(b)} = \dfrac{\text{EBIT}}{\text{average total assets}}$

On an after-tax and after-interest basis (a), a second metric return on assets can be computed:

(14) $\text{ROA}^{(a)} = \dfrac{\text{net profit after tax}}{\text{average total assets}}$

Other return metrics are **return on invested capital** (ROIC) and **return on equity** (ROE) (see Dragun 2004a; 2004b). **Table 18.4** shows returns on assets (ROA) of selected retail companies operating worldwide.

Table 18.4   Return Ratios of Selected Retailers

Company	Return on Assets (%)
Carrefour	5.4 (b)
JC Penny	3.5 (a)
Kohl's	8.1 (a)
Macy's	1.6 (a)
Marks & Spencer	7.2 (a)
Sears	1.2 (a)
Tesco	5.7 (a)
Walmart	8.9 (a)

a = after-tax basis
b = before-tax basis

Source: adapted from Annual Reports 2009.

The net profit margin model (**Figure 18.1**) can be combined with the **asset turnover model**, which yields asset turnover by dividing net sales by total assets. As a result, the **ROA path** can be derived (see **Figure 18.2**).

Figure 18.2   ROA Path

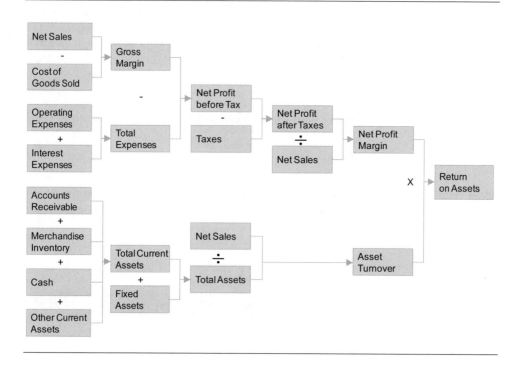

18.5.4   Value Metrics

18.5.4.1   Economic Value Added

These metrics measure the financial performances of firms by their ability to generate or add **economic value**. Measures of economic value include **market value added** (MVA), which is a purely stock market-based measure, and **economic value added (EVA)**. Economic value added is computed according to formula (15) (see Dragun 2004a, p. 162):

(15)   EVA = net operating profit (after taxes) − WACC × capital

The **weighted average cost of capital** (WACC) is calculated as a weighted average of the costs of debt and the costs of equity capital. The costs of debt are the interest expenses required to serve the debt. "For equity, the cost is the rate of return on common stock expected by the shareholders" (Dragun 2004a, p. 161). These costs are more difficult to calculate because they depend "on the uncertain factors such as overall stock market risk, return expectations and the risk-free rate of return available to investors" (Dragun 2004a, p. 161).

Table 18.5 shows a calculation scheme for EVA.

Table 18.5   Calculation of EVA

	Component	Calculation
1.	Operating profit before taxes	
2.	Income tax expense	
3.	NOPAT (Net operating profit after tax)	Item1 ./. Item 2
4.	Capital	a = interest-bearing debt b = equity capital C = a + b
5.	Debt-to-equity-ratio	$= \frac{a}{b}$
6.	Cost of debt	α (%)
7.	Cost of equity	β (%)
8.	WACC	$= \frac{a}{c} \times \alpha\ (\%) + \frac{b}{c} \times \beta(\%)$
9.	Capital charge	Item 4 x Item 8
10.	EVA	Item 3 ./. Item 9

Source: adapted from Dragun 2004a, p. 163.

18.5.4.2   EVA and Supply Chain Performance

Supply chain performance evaluation can be combined with financial performance evaluation. **Figure 18.3** illustrates the means by which supply chain management can improve value metrics such as EVA (Morschett 2004).

Figure 18.3   EVA and Order Fulfilment

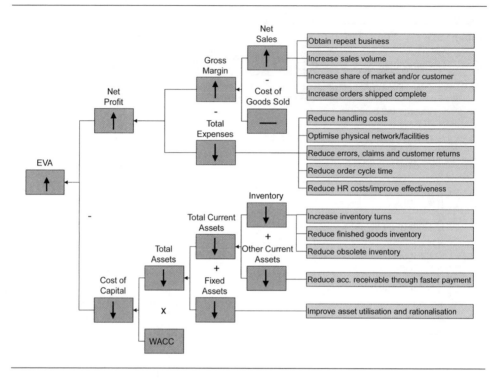

Source: adapted from Lambert/Pohlen 2001, p. 13; Neher 2003, p. 38.

18.6   Conclusion and Outlook

Apart from the concepts of monitoring operational and financial performance discussed here, new approaches have been developed in which the measurement of **consumer satisfaction** comes to the fore (for details, see Zentes 2005). These approaches enlarge the scope of traditional performance measurement.

A new challenge for performance measurement is emerging from the increasing importance of **corporate social responsibility** (CSR) and **sustainability** (Zentes et al. 2009a; 2009b). The extension of the corporate goal system into ecological and social dimensions also requires advanced concepts of monitoring social performance (**corporate social performance**).

| Further Reading

AYERS, J.B.; ODEGAARD, M.A. (2008): Retail Supply Chain Management, New York et al.

BREALEY, R.A.; MYERS, S.C.; ALLEN, F. (2010): Principles of Corporate Finance, 10th ed., Boston et al.

MEYER, M.W. (2009): Rethinking Performance Measurement: Beyond the Balanced Scorecard, New York.

18.7   Case Study: Metro[1]

18.7.1   Profile, History and Status Quo

With net sales amounting to 67.3 billion EUR in 2010, the *Metro Group* is currently third in the worldwide ranking list of retail companies, directly behind *Walmart* and *Carrefour* (Metro AG 2010a, p. 11). The *Metro Group* was created in 1964 when the first German *Metro* cash & carry market for commercial customers opened. The *Metro Group* emerged in its current form in 1996 after mergers with other companies and several portfolio adjustments. After a broad programme focussing on value and efficiency enhancement called "Shape 2012", the publicly listed DAX company introduced a new group structure in 2009. The guiding theme of this change was as decentral as possible, as central as necessary. The *Metro Group* concentrates on four key business segments: **wholesale**, **food retail** (hypermarkets/superstores), **non-food specialist markets** and **department stores**. These are organised in four sales divisions: *Metro Cash & Carry, Real, Media Markt* and *Saturn* as well as *Galeria Kaufhof* (see **Figure 18.4**).

Figure 18.4   Metro Group's Structure

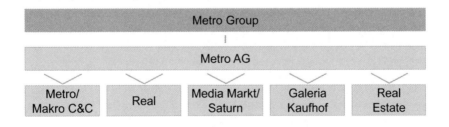

Source: adapted from Metro AG 2011, p. 72.

---

[1] Sources used for this case study include the website http://www.metrogroup.de, the annual report 2010 as well as explicitly cited sources.

Metro AG leads the group as a strategic management holding that is responsible, for instance, for the group-wide finance, controlling and compliance functions. The *Metro Group's* real estate portfolio is managed by *Metro Group Asset Management*, which acts as an independent profit centre. The sales divisions are independently responsible for their respective operative businesses and, in some cases, operate in the market with several **retail brands**. They are supported by so-called **cross-divisional service companies** that provide them with procurement and logistics services.

The company currently employs about 283,000 employees in 33 countries. Sales per employee have been volatile but they have remained at a comparatively high level over recent years (see **Figure 18.5**).

Figure 18.5   Retail Productivity Measures: Sales per Employee (EUR) at Metro Group

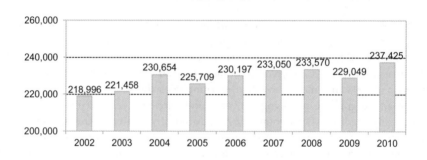

Source: adapted from Metro AG 2010a, p. 11; Metro AG 2011.

With regard to sales per square metre, the *Metro Group* has also shown relatively high values over recent years, with an increase in 2010 (see **Figure 18.6**).

Altogether, 61.1 % of the turnover in 2010 was earned abroad. The internationalisation of the cash & carry concept contributed considerably to this success by generating more than 82 % of its turnover outside the domestic market.

Figure 18.6   Retail Productivity Measures: Sales per Square Metre (EUR) at Metro Group

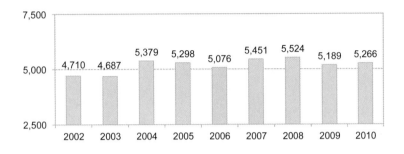

Source: adapted from Metro AG 2010a, p. 11; Metro AG 2011.

18.7.2   Shareholder Value Concept

Within the framework of the internationalisation and liberalisation of capital markets, shareholder value for publicly listed corporations is becoming more and more important. Rational investors select an investment with the same risk level from which they expect the highest returns on their investments (Stern/Shiely/Ross 2001, p. 3). Generally, there is a differentiation between investments in a company and capital market investments. As owners of a stock corporation, shareholders expect returns on their invested capital in the form of dividends or rising stock prices. Furthermore, especially since the 1990s, the problem of measuring company value adequately has become apparent through the high number of mergers & acquisitions. The basic principle behind the shareholder value approach is that the company's strategy is aligned with its owner's interests and that decisions are made in the context of their effects on the company's value. This approach is, among other factors, designed to counteract **opportunistic actions** on the part of managers.

Generally, the shareholder value concept results in the implementation of **value-based management** in the company. Value metrics aim to counteract the deficiencies in conventional performance benchmarks such as return on investment (Freeman 2004, p. 60) and to measure the actual value or value creation of a company according to the thesis "you can't manage and improve what you can't measure". **Figure 18.7** shows a survey of shareholder value key data that were most commonly used by the German DAX-23 in 2007. Companies most frequently revert to **economic value added** (EVA) or **return on capital employed** (ROCE).

Figure 18.7   Shareholder Value Metrics in German DAX-23 Corporations (without
                      Banking, Finance and Insurance) (1st quarter of 2007)

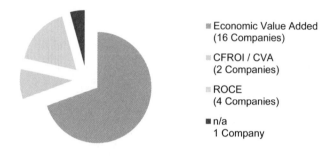

■ Economic Value Added
  (16 Companies)

■ CFROI / CVA
  (2 Companies)

■ ROCE
  (4 Companies)

■ n/a
  1 Company

Source: Bausch/Hunoldt/Matysiak 2009, p. 20.

18.7.3   Value-oriented Performance Metrics at Metro Group: EBIT after Cost of Capital (EBITaC)

To ensure sustained value creation, the *Metro Group* has been using value-oriented performance metrics since 2000. At that time, EVA (economic value added) was implemented
across the entire group as the standardised management instrument and this was actively
and externally communicated, especially to capital markets and shareholders.

However, in 2009 the *Metro Group* decided to use EBIT after the cost of capital (EBITaC)
instead, a different concept in terms of value-based management. Because a positive value
contribution is achieved when EBIT rises above the costs of capital needed to finance the
average capital employed, a more focused orientation towards the *Metro Group's* value
drivers ought to be ensured.

The following formula is used for calculating the key performance indicator EBITaC with
the purpose of ensuring value contribution (see **Figure 18.8**).

Figure 18.8   EBITaC Formula used in 2010 by the Metro Group

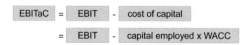

Source: Metro AG 2011, p. 86.

The determination of value creation using EBITaC concentrates on key drivers of the operative business that can be influenced actively by management. These drivers comprise increases in operational efficiency, value-creating growth and the optimisation of capital employed. The group-wide programme Shape 2012 that aims to increase operational efficiency and optimise capital employed is a contribution to value enhancement in the *Metro Group*.

The weighted average cost of capital (WACC) is calculated based on the average cost of equity and borrowed capital, weighted by the company's capital structure. It reflects the risk inherent in an investment. Multiplying the capital employed by WACC provides the cost of capital, reflecting the expected remuneration to investors for the capital provided by them as well as for their investment risks before taxes. Previously, the cost of capital was calculated based on a uniform risk for all sales divisions, but as this did not distinguish between the trade and real estate business, and the WACC-calculation for the segments did not reflect a weighting of country risks, the *Metro Group* adjusted the capital cost calculation in 2010. By using risk adequate capital costs that are differentiated by countries and segments the company can optimise the allocation of available investment funds. The beta factor reflects the assessment of the segment's business risk. This assessment was implemented by means of an analysis of peer companies for the respective sales divisions and the real estate segment. Furthermore, the new way of calculating WACC considers sector-specific financing structures and accounts for individual country risks to calculate segment WACCs.

In the case of a positive spread between operative profit and financing costs, a company generates value.

Equity cost of capital is determined based on the **capital asset pricing model** (CAPM), which states that investors only invest in a company if they receive at least the return of a risk-free alternative plus a premium for their market risk, which is weighted by a company-specific risk factor (Bühner/Tuschke 1999, p. 17). In the case of *Metro*, this beta factor equals one.

The *Metro Group's* cost of capital before taxes was 9.8 % in 2010, corresponding to the minimum return on capital demanded by capital providers. This reflects a return that investors would generate from an alternative investment in a portfolio of shares and bonds with a comparable level of risk. The **cost of capital** should be interpreted as the sum of both equity and debt capital costs and, therefore, it reflects the entire cost of employed capital.

Capital employed represents interest-carrying assets, comprising the following components: segment assets plus net working capital less trade payables as well as deferred liabilities. In contrast to the previously used EVA, one-off effects are not capitalised within capital employed, for example in the course of restructuring expenses. The usage of balance sheet items to determine EBITaC enhances traceability in comparison to system-related adjustments in the calculation of EVA.

Figure18.9   Calculation of Weighted Average Cost of Capital (WACC) for Metro
                   Group in 2010

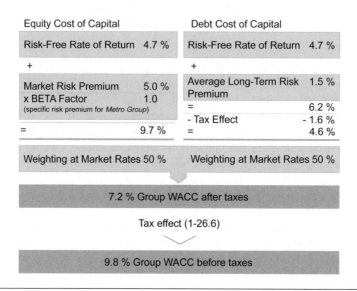

Source: Metro AG 2011, p. 87.

Within the *Metro Group*, EBITaC is not only used as a group management system but also in terms of remuneration for its employees. In this context, the **performance-based remuneration** of members of the sales divisions' management is based on the achievement of decided EBITaC targets for individual countries and sales divisions (Metro AG 2010b, p. 79). Thus, employees participate directly in the company's business success, which increases their identification with the *Metro Group* and enhances their awareness of the opportunities and risks associated with all entrepreneurial decisions. Accordingly, employees ideally become "co-entrepreneurs" and "act as portfolio managers" (Bell 2004, p. 223). The remuneration of *Metro* AG's management board is also performance-dependant, but based on two other financial metrics. The first is **return on capital employed,** (ROCE) which is directly related to the performance metric EBITaC and calculated by dividing the reported EBIT by the average capital employed. **Net profit** for the period (net earnings) of *Metro Group* is the second pillar for the calculation of the performance-based remuneration of the management board.

Concerning the calculation of EBITaC, special items resulting from Shape 2012 are generally distributed over four years on a straight-line basis and are considered in earnings before interests and taxes (EBIT). This periodisation with regard to EBITaC is conducted for economic reasons, because special items from Shape 2012 that were recorded in 2010 are largely the result of an optimisation of the location portfolio, selling spaces or organisational structures and thus positive effects on EBIT largely arise with a time lag. A distribution of the special items over several years, therefore, provides for an accurate presentation of operating performance and, consequently, short-term special effects do not fully influence earnings in the period in which they occur. This way of thinking is also transferred to performance-based incentives for members of the management that are also based on the EBITaC system. Thus, it is assured that measures creating value from a long-term perspective are not abandoned because of negative short-term earnings.

The results of the EBITaC analysis are used – for instance – for the management of the *Metro Group's* portfolio or the allocation of investment funds. In 2010, a positive EBITaC of 668 million EUR was achieved (see **Table 18.6**).

Table 18.6   Key Financial Ratios of Metro Group in the Financial Years 2009 and 2010 (in million EUR)

	2010	2009[1]	Delta
EBIT before special items	2,415	2,024	391
EBIT after periodisation of special items from Shape 2012[2]	2,219	1,879	340
Ø Business assets	15,895	15,798	97
WACC before taxes	9,8 %	9,8 %	-
Cost of capital	-1,551	-1,542	-9
EBITaC	668	337	331

[1]Previous year's figure adjusted for comparability reasons

[2]The effects of the special items from Shape 2012 are distributed over four years

Source: adapted from Metro AG 2011, p. 88.

The periodisation of special items from Shape 2012, totalling 204 million EUR, and the consideration of periodised expenses from 2008 (237 million EUR for streamlining of the *Real* store network) and 2009 (343 million EUR one-off expenses from Shape 2012) led to an EBIT of 2,219 million EUR in 2009. The cost of capital amounted to 1,551 million EUR, with average business assets of 15,895 million EUR in 2010. The main reason for the growth of capital employed was increased international expansion. The sales divisions *Media Markt, Saturn* and *Metro Cash & Carry* achieved positive value added in 2010, with the latter even exceeding the previous year's level. *Galeria Kaufhof* also earned its cost of capital, and *Real* even posted a significant increase in EBITaC compared with 2009.

18.7.4   Conclusion and Outlook

As the global economy developed positively in 2010, leading to a recovery from the impact of the economic and financial crisis, nearly all countries in which the *Metro Group* enhances its activities returned to growth. For the company, 2010 was a successful financial year, and all sales divisions increased their sales compared with the year before. In early 2009, *Metro* launched its efficiency and value-enhancing programme Shape 2012. This programme aimed at ensuring the sustainable and profitable long-term growth of the *Metro Group* with an overall profit potential of 1.5 billion EUR from 2012 resulting from cost savings and productivity gains (Metro AG 2010b, p. 33).

▌ Questions

1. Although the *Metro Group* changed its management system from EVA to EBITaC, several companies such as *Henkel* and *ArcelorMittal* still use the more common EVA. Discuss the possible limits and risks of EVA as a group management system.

2. Compare the EVA concept with EBITaC and discounted cash flow approaches, and make a comparative analysis.

3. Financial metrics facilitate the management of a company as they interpret the quantitative image of its performance capability. However, the main strength of a company is in its resources, capabilities and competences, which are qualitative aspects at the heart of financial performance. Which value potentials are strategic to the *Metro Group* in this context?

▌ Hints

1. See Metro AG 2011 for details of the computation of EBITaC.

2. See Stewart 1990 for a detailed analysis of the relationship between EVA and MVA.

3. See www.metrogroup.de and press coverage for details on the strategic value drivers of the *Metro Group*.

References

7-ELEVEN (2011a): About us, http://corp.7-eleven.com/AboutUs/tabid/73/Default.aspx, accessed on February 22, 2011.

7-ELEVEN (2011b): Real Estate, http://corp.7-eleven.com/RealEstate/tabid/180/Default.aspx, accessed on February 22, 2011.

7-ELEVEN (2011c): Real Estate Requirements, http://corp.7-eleven.com/RealEstate/Real Estate Requirements/tabid/181/ Default.aspx, accessed on February 22, 2011.

7-ELEVEN (2011d): Corporate Website, http://careers.7-eleven.com/job_detail.html? id=411&title=Internship%20-%20Urban%20Walk-Up%20Store%20Site%20Selection, accessed on February 22, 2011.

7-ELEVEN (2011e): In the Spotlight, http://bcp.7-eleven.com/index.php/in-the-spotlight/ before-and-after-gallery, accessed on February 22, 2011.

AAKER, D. (1996): Building Strong Brands, New York et al.

ABSATZWIRTSCHAFT (Ed.) (1976): Aldi am Ende?, in: Absatzwirtschaft, Vol. 18, No. 11, pp. 23-26.

ADIDAS GROUP (Ed.) (2010): Die adidas Gruppe präsentiert den strategischen Business Plan 2015, http://www.adidas-group.com/de/pressroom/archive/2010/08Nov2010.aspx, accessed on February 24, 2011.

AHOLD (2010): Annual Report 2009, http://www.annualreport 2009.ahold.com/documents/ reports/Ahold_AR_2009.pdf, accessed on February 22, 2011.

AHOLD (2011a): Ahold's History, http://www.ahold.com/en/about/history, accessed on February 22, 2011.

AHOLD (2011b): Ahold Press Pack, February 2011, http://www.ahold.com/_files/ ahold_press_pack_february_2011.pdf, accessed on February 22, 2011.

AILAWADI, K.; KELLER, K. (2004): Understanding Retail Branding: Conceptual Insights and Research Priorities, in: Journal of Retailing, Vol. 80, pp. 331-342.

AKEHURST, G.; ALEXANDER, N. (1997): The Internationalisation of Retailing, London.

ALBA, J.; LYNCH, J.; WEITZ, B.; JANISZEWSKI, R.L.; SAWYER, A.; WOODS, S. (1997): Interactive Home Shopping: Consumer, Retailer, and Manufacturer Incentives to Participate in Electronic Marketplaces, in: Journal of Marketing, Vol. 61, No. 3, pp. 38-53.

ALDERSON, W. (1954): Factors governing the development of marketing channels, in: Clewitt, R.M. (Ed.): Marketing Channels for Manufactured Products, Homewood/Ill., pp. 5-34.

ALEXANDER, N.; DOHERTY, A.M. (2009): International Retailing, Oxford et al.

ALEXANDER, N.; QUINN, B.; CAIRNS, P. (2005): International Retail Diversity Activity, in: International Journal of Retail and Distribution Management, Vol. 33, No. 1, pp. 5-22.

ANDRASKI, J.C.; HAEDICKE, J. (2003): CPFR: Time for the breakthrough?, in: Supply Chain Management Review, Vol. 7, No. 3, pp. 54-61.

ANSOFF, H. (1988): Corporate Strategy, 4th ed., New York.

APPLEBAUM, W. (1966): Methods for Determining Store Trade Areas, Market Penetration, and Potential Sales, in: Journal of Marketing Research, Vol. 3, No. 2, pp. 127-141.

ARNOLD, S.J.; FERNIE, J. (2000): Wal-Mart in Europe: Prospects for the UK, in: International Marketing Review, Vol. 17, No. 4/5, pp. 416-432.

ARNOLD, U. (1998): Global Sourcing – Strategische Neuorientierung des Einkaufs, in: ZENTES, J.; SWOBODA, B. (Eds.): Globales Handelsmanagement, Frankfurt, pp. 235-256.

ARNOTT, D. (1993): Positioning: Redefining the Concept, Warwick Business School Research Papers, No. 8.

A.S. WATSON (Ed.) (2002): WatsOn, No. 55, October 2002.

A.S. WATSON (Ed.) (2003): WatsOn, No. 56, January 2003.

A.T. KEARNEY (Ed.) (2010): 2010 Global Retail Development Index, www.atkearney.com, accessed on October 24, 2011.

AVERY, J.; CARAVELLA, M.; DEIGHTON, J.; STEENBURGH, T.J. (2007): Adding Bricks to Clicks: The Effects of Store Openings on Sales through Direct Channels, Working paper, Havard Business School Boston, pp. 07-43.

AYAL, I.; ZIF, J. (1979): Market Expansion Strategies in Multinational Marketing, in: Journal of Marketing, Vol. 43, pp. 84-94.

AYERS, J.B.; ODEGAARD, M.A. (2008): Retail Supply Chain Management, New York et al.

BAKER, P. (2004): Aligning Distribution Center Operations to Supply Chain Strategy, in: International Journal of Logistics Management, Vol. 15, No. 1, pp. 111-123.

BABIN, B; DARDEN, W; GRIFFIN, M (1994): Work and/or Fun: Measuring Hedonic and Utilitarian Shopping Value, Journal of Consumer Research, Vol. 20, No. 4, pp. 644-656.

BALIGH, H.; RICHARTZ, L. (1964): An Analysis of Vertical Market Structure, in: Management Science, Vol. 10, No. 4, pp. 667-689.

BARTLETT, C.; GHOSHAL, S. (1989): Managing Across Borders: The Transnational Solution, Boston, MA.

BARTSCH, A. (2004): Transaktionales vs. relationales Lieferantenmanage-ment – Eine vergleichende Analyse, in: ZENTES, J.; BIESIADA, H.; SCHRAMM-KLEIN, H. (Eds.): Performance-Leadership im Handel, Frankfurt, pp. 159-190.

BÄURLE, I. (1996): Internationalisierung als Prozessphänomen: Konzepte – Besonderheiten – Handhabung, Wiesbaden.

BAUM, S. (2006): French Dressing, in: Cabinet Maker, Vol. 10, No. 5472, pp. 65-68.

BAUSCH, A.; HUNOLDT, M.; MATYSIAK, L. (2009): Superior Performance Through Value-based Management, in: BAUSCH, A.; SCHWENKER, B. (Eds.): Handbook Utility Management, Berlin et al., pp. 15-36.

BECHWATI, N.; ESHGHI, A. (2005): Customer Lifetime Value Analysis: Challenges and Words of Caution, in: The Marketing Management Journal, Vol. 15, No. 2, pp. 87-97.

BECKETT, A.; NAYAK, A. (2005): Governing the Consumer: Every Little Helps, Paper for the 4th International Critical Management Studies Conference, University of Cambridge, Cambridge.

BELL, D. (1999): Creating A Global Retail Brand: Interview with Sir Geof-frey Mulcahy, Group Chief Executive, Kingfisher plc., in: European Retail Digest, Vol. 7, No. 21, pp. 14-18.

BELL, D.; WANG, Y.; PADMANABHAN, V. (2003): The Effect of Partial Forward Integration on Retailer Behavior: An Explanation for Co-Located Stores, http://marketing.wharton.upenn.edu/ideas/pdf/Bell/partial_forward_ integration_2003.pdf.

BELL, R. (2004a): Creating a Global Retail Brand, in: REYNOLDS, J.; CUTHBERTSON, C. (Eds.): Retail Strategy: The View from the Bridge, Amsterdam et al., pp. 275-283.

BELL, R. (2004b): Metro in China or a Chinese Metro?, in: REYNOLDS, J.; CUTHBERTSON, C: (Eds.): Retail Strategy: The View from the Bridge, Amsterdam et al., pp. 218-224.

BELL, R.; CUTHBERTSON, R. (2004): Collaboration in the Retail Supply Chain, in: REYNOLDS, J.; CUTHBERTSON, C. (Eds.): Retail Strategy: the View from the Bridge, Amsterdam et al., pp. 52-77.

BELL, J.; DAVISON, J. (1997): Warehouse Management Systems at Tesco, in: HART, C. et al. (Eds.): Cases in Retailing, Oxford, pp. 88-96.

BENDER, H. (2006): Invasion der Center, in: Der Handel, Vol. 35, No. 7-8, pp. 18-24.

BENDER, H. (2011): Butlers und Depot auf Expansionskurs, in: Der Handel, http://www.derhandel.de/news/unternehmen/pages/Butlers-und-Depot-auf-Expansionskurs_6998.html, accessed on February 21, 2011.

BENETTON (Eds.) (2006a): Benetton Group - Annual Report 2005, Treviso/Italy.

BENETTON (Eds.) (2006b): Benetton Group 2004-2007 Guidelines – Key Highlights, Treviso/Italy.

BENNET, S. (1999): The Quest for Value, New York.

BERGER, S. (1977): Ladenverschleiß, Göttingen.

BERGMANN, J. (2004): Mode für die neue Mitte, in: brand eins, Vol. 6, No. 4, pp. 22-29.

BERMAN, B.; EVANS, J. (2010): Retail Management, 11th ed., Upper Saddle River/NJ.

BERMAN, B.; THELEN, S. (2004): A guide to developing and managing a well-integrated mulit-channel retail strategy, in: International Journal of Retail & Distribution Management, Vol. 32, No. 2/3, pp. 147-156.

BERRY, L.; SEIDERS, K.; GREWAL, D. (2002): Understanding Service Convenience, in: Journal of Marketing, Vol. 66, No. 3, pp. 1-17.

BEST BUY (2010): Oppenheimer 10th Annual Consumer, Gaming, Lodging & Leisure Conference, http://phx.corporate-ir.net/External.File?item=UGFyZW50SUQ9NTIyNjB8Q2hpbG RJRD0tMXxUeXBlPTM=&t=1, accessed on February 10, 2011.

BEST BUY (2011): Store Stats, http://phx.corporate-ir.net/External.File?item=UGFy ZW50SUQ9NTA1NzR8Q2hpbG RJRD0tMXxUeXBlPTM=&t=1, accessed on February 10, 2011.

BIEL, A. (1992): How Brand Image Drives Brand Equity, in: Journal of Advertising Research, Vol. 32, No. 6, pp. RC6-RC12.

BIESIADA, H.; NEIDHART, M. (2004): Retail-Performance-Management – Konzeption eines modernen Business-Intelligence-Systems für die Planung, Steuerung und Kontrolle von Handelsprozessen, in: ZENTES, J.; BIESIADA, H.; SCHRAMM-KLEIN, H. (Eds.): Performance-Leadership im Handel, Frankfurt, pp. 93-115.

BIRTWISTLE, G.; MOORE, C.M.; FIORITO, S.S. (2006): Apparel Quick Response Systems: The Manufacturer Perspective, in: International Journal of Logistics: Research & Applications, Vol. 9, No. 2, pp. 157-168.

BLOIS, K.J. (1972): Vertical Quasi-Integration, in: The Journal of Industrial Economics, Vol. 20, No. 3, pp. 253-272.

BLOOMBERG (2010): Asia, Latin America Propel UPS, Nike Profits as US Economic Growth Slows, http://www.bloomberg.com/news/2010-07-24/asia-latin-america-propel-ups-nike-profits-as-u-s-economic-growth-slows.html, accessed on February 02, 2011.

BLOOMBERG BUSINESSWEEK (2007): Can Nike Do It?, http://www.businessweek.com/b wdaily/dnflash/content/feb2007/db20070206_233170.htm, accessed on February 14, 2011.

BOATWRIGHT, P.; NUNES, J. (2001): Reducing Assortment: An Attribute-Based Approach, in: Journal of Marketing, Vol. 65, No. 3, pp. 50-63.

BOLTON, R.; SHANKAR, V.; MONTOYA, D. (2008): Recent Trends and Emerging Practices in Retailer Pricing, in: KRAFFT, M.; MANTRALA, M. (Eds.): Retailing in the 21st Century, 2nd ed., Berlin et al., pp. 301-318.

BOOTH, H. (2005): Clean Sweep, in: Design Week, Vol. 20, No. 19, p. 22.

BOSE, S. (2005): Carrefour in 2004 – Managing Globalisation, Case Study, http://www.ecch.com.

BOYLE, M. (2006): Best Buy's giant gamble, in: Fortune, March 29, 2006, http://money.cnn.com/magazines/fortune/fortune_archive/2006/04/03/8373034.

BRADLEY, F. (2005): International Marketing Strategy, 5th ed., London et al.

BRADLEY, S.P.; GHEMAWAT, P.; FOLEY, S. (1994): Wal-Mart Stores, Inc., Harvard Business School Case, Boston, MA.

BRAND, M. (2005): KINGFISHER, in: Brand Strategy, Vol. 5, No. 196, pp. 10-11.

BREALEY, R.A.; MYERS, S.C.; ALLEN, F. (2010): Principles of Corporate Finance, 10th ed., Boston et al.

BRODERSEN, T. (2006): Franchising als Wachstumsstrategie – Modernes Partnership-for-Profit, in: ZENTES, J. (Ed.): Handbuch Handel, Wiesbaden, pp. 299-320.

BRONSON, J.W.; FAIRCLOTH, J.B.; CHAKO, J.M. (1999): Toward a Strategic Model of the Franchise Form of Business Organization, http://www.usa-sbe.org/knowledge/proceedings/1999/bronson.pdf.

BROWN, S. (1988): The Wheel of the Whell of Retailing, in: International Journal of Retailing, Vol. 3, No. 1, pp. 16-37.

BROWN, S. (1992): Retail Location: A Micro-Scale Perspective, Aldershot et al.

BROWN, S.; GULYCZ, M. (2002): Performance Driven CRM, Etobicoke/ON.

BRUCE, M.; CHRISTOPHER, M.M.; BIRTWISTLE, G. (2005): International Retail Marketing – A Case Study Approach, Burlington.

BRUCE, M.; MOORE, C.M.; BIRTWISTLE, G. (2005): International Retail Marketing, Amsterdam et al.

BRUHN, M. (2001): Relationship Marketing, Munich.

BÜHNER, R.; TUSCHKE, A. (1999): Wertmanagement – Rechnen wie ein Unternehmer, in: BÜHNER, R.; SULZBACH, K. (Eds.): Wertorientierte Steuerungs- und Führungsinstrumente, Stuttgart, pp. 3-41.

BUCKLIN, L.P. (1966): A theory of distribution channel structure, Berkeley/CA.

BUCKLIN, C.B.; THOMAS-GRAHAM, P.A.; WEBSTER, E.A. (2004): Channel conflict: When is it dangerous?, McKinsey Quarterly 1997, No. 3, p. 36-43.

BURT, S.; DAVIS, S. (1999): Follow my leader? Lookalike Retailer Brands in Non-Manufacturer Dominated Product Markets in the UK, in: The International Review of Retail, Distribution and Consumer Research, Vol. 9, No. 2. pp. 163-185.

BURT, S.; LIMMACK, R. (2001): Takeovers and Shareholder Returns in the Retail Industry, in: The International Review of Retail, Distribution and Con-sumer Research, Vol. 11, No. 1, pp. 1-21.

BURT, S.; DAWSON, J.; SPARKS, L. (2008): International Retail Divestment: Reviews, Case Studies and (E)merging Agenda, in: SWOBODA, B. et al. (Eds.): European Retail Research, Vol. 22, pp. 29-49.

BUTLER, R.S. (1917): Marketing Methods, New York.

BUZZ, D.D. (1997): Entertailing, Nation's Business, December 1997.

C&A (2010): C&A-Report 2010, Duesseldorf – Brussels.

CAMPBELL, A. (2003): Sainsbury Takes Bold Supply Chain Steps to Claw Back Market Share, in: Frontline Solutions Europe, Vol. 12, No. 8, pp. 20-23.

CAMUFFO, A.; ROMANO, P.; VINELLI, A. (2001): Back to the Future: Benetton Transforms its Global Network, in: MIT Sloan Management Review, Vol. 43, No. 1, pp. 46-52.

CAPELL, K. (2005): IKEA: How the Swedish Retailer Became a Global Cult Brand, in: BusinessWeek, 14.11.2005, pp. 46-54.

CARREFOUR (2009): Improve price Image, company presentation, http://www.carrefour.com/docroot/groupe/C4com/Pieces_jointes/Presentation_aux_analystes/2009/03.pdf, accessed on March 02, 2011.

CARTER, J.R.; PEARSON, J.N.; PENG, L. (1997): Logistics Barriers to International Operations: The Case of the People's Republic of China, in: Journal of Business Logistics, Vol. 18, No. 2, pp. 129-145.

CATALOGUE-CONNECTION (2011): 21 years of Next Directory catalogue, http://www.catalogue-connection.co.uk/content/21_years_of_Next_Directory.htm, accessed on February 25, 2011.

CAZENOVE (Eds.) (2005): Benetton Group, London et al.

CCN MARKETING (Ed.) (1993): Strategies for Retail Network Planning, Nottingham.

CHAIN STORE AGE (Ed.) (2004): Esprit Returns to American Retail, in: Chain Store Age, Vol. 80, October 2004 supplement, p. 7.

CHAIN STORE AGE (Ed.) (2005): Retail Stores of the Year, in: Chain Store Age, Vol. 81, No. 2, pp. 69-117.

CHANDRAN, P.M. (2003): Walmart's supply chain management practices, in: ICMR Case Collection, Hyderabad: ICFAI Center for Management Research.

CHOPRA, S.; MEINDL, P. (2010): Supply Chain Management, 4th ed., Upper Saddle River.

CHRISTOPHER, M.; LOWSON, B., PECK, H. (2004): Fashion Logistics and Quick Response, in: FERNIE, J.; SPARKS, L. (Eds.): Logistics and Retail Management, 2nd ed., London et al., pp. 82-100.

CLIQUET, G. (2000): Plural Forms in Store Networks: A Model for Store Net-work Management, in: The International Review of Retail, Distribu-tion and Consumer Research, Vol. 10, No. 4, pp. 369-387.

CLIQUET, G. (2006): Retailing in Western Europe – Structures and Development Trends, in: ZENTES, J. (Ed.): Handbuch Handel, Wiesbaden, pp. 111-138.

COFRA HOLDING AG (2011): COFRA Holding AG, http://www.cofraholding.com/en/hol.asp, accessed on February 17, 2011.

COMMITTEE FOR DEFINITIONS OF TERMS IN TRADE AND DISTRIBUTION (2009): Katalog E – Definition of Terms in Trade and Distribution, Cologne.

CONSUMER CONFIDENCE SURVEY-Q1 (Eds.) (2008): Field dates March 8, 2010 – March 28, 2010.

CONVENIENCESTORENEWS (2009): 7-Eleven, Inc. Expands in Indonesia, http://www.csnews.com/top-story-international_news__7_eleven__inc._expands _in_indonesia-44402.html, accessed on March 23, 2011.

COOK, B. (2003): IKEA – put together, http://www.brandchannel.com.

COONEY, J. (2002): One Brand. One Esprit., in: License!, Vol. 5, No. 5, pp. 128-129.

COOPER, J.; BROWNE, M.; PETERS, M. (1992): European Logistics, Oxford.

COOPERNIC (2006): Coopernic, Alliance of independent European distribution retailers, http://www.rewe-group.com/fileadmin/content/image/Unternehmen/PDFs/Presse_PDFs_EN/Charts_Coopernic_06b.pdf, accessed on October 10, 2010.

CORIOLIS RESEARCH (Ed.) (2004): Tesco: A Case Study in Supermarket Excellence, Auckland.

CORSTEN, D. (2005): History in the Making?, in: ECR Journal, Vol. 5, No. 1, pp. 70-78.

CORSTJENS, M.; LAL, R. (2000): Building Store Loyalty Through Store Brands, in: Journal of Marketing Research, Vol. 37, August, pp. 281-291.

COSTELLO, B. (2005): Galeries Lafayette Revamping Flagship Beauty Department, in: WWD: Women's Wear Daily, Vol. 190, No. 11, p. 21.

COUGHLAN, A.; ANDERSON, E.; STERN, L.; EL-ANSARY, A. (2008): Marketing Channels, 7th ed., Upper Saddle River/NJ.

COYLE, J.J.; BARDI, E.J.; LANGLEY, C.J. (2003): The Management of Busi-ness Logistics: A Supply Chain Perspective, 7th ed., Mason, OH.

CRAIG, C.S.; GHOSH, A.; MCLAFFERTY, S. (1944): Models of the Retail Location Process: A Review, in: Journal of Retailing, Vol. 60, No. 1, pp. 5-35.

CSDECISIONS (2011): 7-Eleven Expands in Manhatten, www.csdecisions.com/7-eleven-expands-manhattan/, accessed on February 25, 2011.

CUTHBERTSON, R. (2004): Supply Chain: A Core Competency for Retailers – Interview with Armin Meier, IT and Logistics Director of Migros, in: REYNOLDS, J.; CUTHBERSON, C. (Eds.): Retail Strategy, Amsterdam et al., pp. 173-180.

CUTHBERTSON, R.; LAINE, A. (2004): The Role of CRM within Retail Loyalty Marketing, in: Journal of Targeting, Measurement and Analysis for Marketing, Vol. 12, No. 3, pp. 290-304.

DAHLSRUD, A. (2008): How corporate social responsibility is defined: An analysis of 37 definitions, Corporate Social Responsibility and Environmental Management, Vol. 15, No. 1, pp. 1-13.

DANAHER, T. (2009): A.S. Watson: Gunning for the Chinese lion's share, in: Retail Week, December 04, 2009.

DATAMONITOR PLC (Ed.) (2005a): Benetton Group SpA - Company Profile, New York et al.

DATAMONITOR PLC (Ed.) (2005b): Carrefour S.A. – Company Profile, New York et al.

DATAMONITOR PLC (Ed.) (2005c): Food Retail in the United Kingdom: Industry Profile, New York et al.

DATAMONITOR PLC (2005d): Global Food Retailing – Industry Profile, New York et al.

DATAMONITOR PLC (2010): 7-Eleven, Inv., www.datamonitor.com, accessed on February 22, 2011.

DAVIES, C. (2004): Cutting-edge Logistics: Factory Gate Pricing, in: Supply Chain Europe, Vol. 13, No. 6, pp. 15-18.

DAVIES, M.; CLARKE, I. (1994): A Framework for Network Planning, in: International Journal of Retail and Distribution Management, Vol. 22, No. 6, pp. 6-10.

DAVIES, R. (Ed.) (1995): Retail Planning Policies in Western Europe, London and New York.

DAVIS, J.; DEVINNEY, T. (1997): The Essence of Corporate Strategy, Crows Nest/Australia.

DAVIS, S.; GREEN, J. (2000): One Day and a Lifetime of Brand Lessons, in: Brandweek, Vol. 41, No. 34, pp. 30-31.

DAWSON, J. (1993): The Internationalisation of Retailing, in: Bromley, R.D.; Thomas, C.J. (Eds.): Retail Change: Contemporary Issues, London.

DAWSON, J. (1994): Internationalisation of Retail Operations, in: Journal of Marketing Management, Vol. 10, pp. 267-282.

DAWSON, J. (1995): Retail Change in the European Community, in: DAVIES, R. (Ed.): Retail Planning Policies in Western Europe, London and New York, pp. 1-30.

DAWSON, J. (2010): Retail Trends in Europe, in: KRAFFT, M.; MANTRALA, M. (Eds.): Retailing in the 21st Century – Current and Future Trends, 2nd ed., Berlin et al., pp. 63-81.

DAWSON, J.; USUI, K. (2011): Renewal and Transformation of Value in an International Retailer: Dixons Retail plc, in: ZENTES, J.; SWOBODA, B.; MORSCHETT, D. (Eds.): Fallstudien zum Internationalen Management: Grundlagen – Praxiserfahrungen – Perspektiven, 4th ed., Wiesbaden, pp. 589-610.

DAWSON, M. (2011): Neues Kommando, in: Lebensmittel Zeitung, No. 8, February 25, 2011, pp. 32-33.

DECARLO, L. (2005): Esprit Dealing With Uncertainty, in: WWD: Women's Wear Daily, Vol. 190, No. 71, p. 5.

DELOITTE (2009): Emerging from the downturn: Global Powers of Retailing 2010, London.

DHAR, S.; HOCH, S. (1997): Why Store Brand Penetration Varies by Retailer, in: Marketing Science, Vol. 16, No. 3, pp. 208-227.

DICK, A.; BASU, K. (1994): Customer Loyalty, Toward an Integrated Conceptual Framework, in: Journal of the Academy of Marketing Science, Vol. 22, pp. 99-113.

DIEHL, S. (2003): Erlebnisorientiertes Internetmarketing – Analyse, Konzeption und Umsetzung von Internetshops aus verhaltenswissenschaft-licher Perspektive, Wiesbaden.

DILLER, H.; ANSELSTETTER, S. (2006): Preis- und Sonderangebotspolitik, in: ZENTES, J. (Ed.): Handbuch Handel, Wiesbaden, pp. 597-630.

DIRECT SELLING NEWS (2010): DSN Global 100, www.directsellingnews.com, accessed on November 17, 2010.

DISCOUNT STORE NEWS (Ed.) (1999): Complex System Grounded in EDLP, in: Discount Store News, October 1999 Special Commemorative Issue, Vol. 38, No. 18, pp. 107-108, 187.

DISNEY, S.M.; TOWILL, D.R. (2003): The Effect of Vendor Managed Inventory (VMI) Dynamics on the Bullwhip Effect in Supply Chains, in: International Journal of Production Economics, Vol. 85, No. 2, pp. 199-216.

DISPLAY AND DESIGN IDEAS (Ed.) (2004): Lafayette Maison is Galeries Lafayette's new, http://www.ddimagazine.com.

DONOVAN, R.; ROSSITER, J. (1982): Store atmosphere: An Environmental Psychology Approach, in: Journal of Retailing, Vol. 28, No. 1, pp. 34-57.

DRAGUN, D. (2004a): The Financial Implications of Retail Strategy, in: REYNOLDS, J.; CUTHBERTSON, C. (Eds.): Retail Strategy, Amsterdam et al., pp. 137-169.

DRAGUN, D. (2004b): Financial Management at Sainsbury's, in: REYNOLDS, J.; CUTHBERTSON, C. (Eds.): Retail Strategy, Amsterdam et al., pp. 298-308.

DUELFER, E.; JOESTINGMEIER, B. (2011): International Management in Diverse Cultural Areas, 2nd ed., Munich.

ECC (Ed.) (2010): ECC-Monitor Markenhersteller Sportartikel, http://www.ecc-handel.de/sportartikelhersteller_im_internet_zwischen_12851 501.php, accessed on January 22, 2011.

ECE PROJEKTMANAGEMENT GMBH & CO. KG (Ed.) (2003): Vibrant Marketplaces, Hamburg.

E-COMMERCE-CENTER HANDEL (Ed.) (2005): Relaunch des Online-Shops – Reaktion auf Billig-Angebote der Konkurrenz – Branchenkenner reagieren skeptisch, www.ecc-handel.de/best_practise.

ECR EUROPE (Ed.) (1997): Category Management Best Practice Report, Brussels.

ECR EUROPE (Ed.) (1998): Assessing the Profit Impact of ECR, www.ecrnet.org.

ECR EUROPE (Ed.) (2005): The Case for ECR: A review and outlook of continuous ECR adoption in Western Europe, Brussels.

EHI RETAIL INSTITUTE (Ed.) (2009): Flächenproduktivität der Lebensmittelfilialbetriebe in Deutschland nach Betriebsformen im Jahr 2009 in Euro pro Quadratmeter und Mitarbeiter, www.ehi.org, accessed on November 22, 2010.

EHRING, D. (2006): THE WAL*MART MODEL, IN: Mortgage Banking, October 1st, www.dorado.com/pdf/WALMART_10.06.pdf.

EMAP BUSINESS PUBLICATIONS (2010): Multiples – TK Maxx ramps up ad spend for Christmas TV campaign, http://news.reportlinker.com/n03864919/Multiples-TK-Maxx-ramps-up-ad-spend-for-Christmas-TV-campaign.html, accessed on March 14, 2011.

EMD (Ed.) (2010): European Marketing Distribution – auf einen Blick, http://emd-eg.com/d/untern001.shtm, accessed on October 21, 2010.

ERLINGER, M. (2010): Die Post wird richtig abgehen, http://www.textilwirtschaft.de/servi ce/archiv/pages/show.php?id=766039&a=1, accessed on February 17, 2011.

ESPRIT HOLDINGS LIMITED (Ed.) (2005): Annual Report 04/05, Hong Kong.

ESPRIT HOLDINGS LIMITED (Ed.) (2006): fy05/06 interim results, Hong Kong.

ESSIG, M. (2000): Purchasing consortia as symbiotic relationships: Developing the concept of "consortium sourcing", in: European Journal of Purchasing & Supply Management, Vol. 6, No. 1, pp. 13-22.

FAITHFULL, M. (2005): All the Store's a Stage, in: Display & Design Ideas, http://www.ddimagazine.com/displayanddesignideas/search/article_display.jsp?vnu_conte nt_id=1000928726.

FERDOWS, K.; LEWIS, M.A.; MACHUCA, J.A. (2004): Rapid-Fire Fulfillment, in: Harvard Business Review, Vol. 82, No. 11, pp. 104-110.

FERDOWS, K.; LEWIS, M.A.; MACHUCA, J.A.D. (2005): Über Nacht zum Kunden: in: Harvard Business Manager, Vol. 10, No. 2, pp. 80-89.

FERNIE, J. (2004a): The Internationalization of the Retail Supply Chain, in: FERNIE, J.; SPARKS, L. (Eds.): Logistics and Retail Management, 2nd ed., London et al., pp. 48-61.

FERNIE, J. (2004b): Relationships in the Supply Chain, in: FERNIE, J.: SPARKS, L. (Eds.): Logistics and Retail Management, 2nd ed., London et al., pp. 26-47.

FERNIE, J. (2005): Retail Logistics, in: BRUCE, M.; MOORE, C.M.; BIRTWISTLE, G. (Eds.): International Retail Marketing, Amsterdam et al., pp. 39-63.

FERNIE, J. (2009a): Relationships in the supply chain, in: FERNIE, J.; SPARKS, L. (Eds.): Logistics & Retail Management, 3rd ed., London et al., pp. 38-62.

FERNIE, J. (2009b): The internationalization of the retail supply chain, in: FERNIE, J.; SPARKS, L. (Eds.): Logistics & Retail Management, 3rd ed., London et al., pp. 63-79.

FERNIE, J.; McKINNON, A. (2009): The Development of E-tail Logistics, in: FERNIE, J.; SPARKS, L. (Eds.): Logistics & Retail Management, 3rd ed., London et al., pp. 207-232.

FERNIE, J.; PERRY, P. (2011): The International Fashion Retail Supply Chain, in: ZENTES, J.; SWOBODA. B.; MORSCHETT, D. (Eds): Fallstudien zum Internationalen Management: Grundlagen – Praxiserfahrungen – Perspektiven, 4th ed., Wiesbaden, pp. 271-290.

FERNIE, J., SPARKS, L. (2004): Retail Logistics: Changes and Challenges, in: FERNIE, J.; SPARKS, L. (Eds.): Logistics and Retail Management, 2nd ed., London et al., pp. 1-25.

FERNIE, J.; SPARKS, L. (2009): Logistics & Retail Management, 3rd ed., London et al.

FERNIE, J.; FERNIE, S.; MOORE, C. (2004): Principles of Retailing, Amsterdam et al.

FISHMAN, C. (2003): The Wal-Mart You Don't Know, in: FastCompany, No. 77, New York, pp. 68-84.

FOREMAN, K. (2006): Los Angeles Fashion Invades Paris, in: WWD: Women's Wear Daily, Vol. 191, No. 78, p. 10.

FORTUNE (Ed.) (2010): Fortune 500 – Nike http://money.cnn.com/magazines/fortune/fortune500/2010/snapshots/2184.html, accessed on January 20, 2011.

FORTUNE MAGAZINE (Ed.) (2011): Global 500, http://money.cnn.com/magazines/fortune/global500/2010/full_list/, accessed on February 21, 2011.

FOX, E.J.; SETHURAMAN, R. (2010): Retail Competition, in: KRAFFT, M.; MANTRALA, M. (Eds.): Retailing in the 21st Century – Current and Future Trends, Berlin et al., pp. 239-254.

FOXALL, G.; HACKETT, P. (1992): Consumers' perceptions of micro-retail location: Wayfinding and cognitive mapping in planned and organic shopping environments, in: International Review of Retail, Distribution & Consumer Research, Vol. 2, No. 3, pp. 309-327.

FREEMAN, L.N. (2004): Economic Value Added Reflects Long-Term Benefits of Investments, Projects, in: Ophthalmology Times, Vol. 29, No. 14, p. 60.

FREITAG, M.; HIRN, W.; RICKENS, C. (2006): Die Inventur, in: Manager Magazin, Vol. 19, No. 2, pp. 29-39.

FÜSSLER, A. (2004): Auswirkungen der RFID-Technologie auf die Gestaltung der Versorgungskette, in: ZENTES, J.; BIESIADA, H.; SCHRAMM-KLEIN, H. (Eds.): Performance-Leadership im Handel, Frankfurt, pp. 137-155.

FUNDINGUNIVERSE (Ed.) (2011): 7-Eleven, Inc. – Company History, www.fundinguniverse.com/company-histories/7Eleven-Inc-History.html, accessed on February 22, 2011.

FUNG, V.K.; FUNG, W.K.; WIND, Y. (2008): Competing in a Flat World, New Jersey.

GALLAGHER, L. (2003): Esprit du Monde, in: Forbes Global, Vol. 6, No. 11, p. 24.

GEBAUER, E. (2003): Die Legende lebt, in: Stores & Shops, Vol. 6, No. 3, pp. 42-45.

GEDENK, K.; NESLIN, S.; AILAWADI, K. (2008): Sales Promotion, in: KRAFFT, M.; MAN-TRALA, M. (Eds.): Retailing in the 21st century, 2nd ed., Berlin et al., pp. 393-408.

GFK (Ed.) (2010): Detailhandel Schweiz, Hergiswil.

GILBERT, D. (2003): Retail Marketing Management, 2nd ed., Harlow et al.

GLEIßNER, H. (2000): Logistikkooperationen zwischen Industrie und Handel, Göttingen.

GLOBAL INSIGHT (Ed.) (2005): The Economic Impact of Walmart, Waltham, MA.

GLOBAL SCORECARD (Ed.) (2011): Global Scorecard, http://www.globalscorecard.net/, accessed on January 28, 2011.

GLOBAL SOURCES (2011): Buyer profile A.S. Watson group, http://www.globalsources.com/PEC/PROFILES/WATSON.HTM, accessed on January 07, 2011.

GOOD INDONESIA (Ed.) (2010): Will Convenience Store Giant 7-Eleven Be Coming to a Jakarta Street Near You?, http://news.goodindonesia.info/will-convenience-store-giant-7-eleven-be-coming-to-a-jakarta-street-near-you, accessed on February 22, 2011.

GOODMAN, C.S. (1985): Comment: On Output Measures of Retail Performance, in: Journal of Retailing, Vol. 61, No. 3, pp. 77-82.

GOTTERBARM, C. (2004): US-amerikanische Einzelhandelsunternehmen in Deutschland – Fakten, Trends und Theorien, Diss., Passau.

GREAN, M.; SHAW, M.J. (2003): Supply Chain Integration through Information Sharing: Channel Partnership between Walmart and Procter & Gamble, in: Shaw, M.J. (ed.): E-Business Management, Norwell, MA, pp. 155-171.

GREENBERG, J. (2004): The Hip List, in: WWD: Women's Wear Daily, Vol. 188, WWD100, pp. 58-59.

GRÖPPEL-KLEIN, A. (2006): Point-of-Sale-Marketing, in: ZENTES, J. (Ed.): Handbuch Handel, Wiesbaden, pp. 671-692.

GRÖPPEL-KLEIN, A.; BAUN, D. (2001): The Role of Customers' Arousal for Retail Stores – Results from an Experimental Pilot Study Using Electroder-mal Activity as Indicator, in: GILLY, M.; MEYERS-LEVY, J. (Eds.): Advances in Consumer Research, Vol. 28, Valdosta, GA, pp. 412-419.

GROUPE GALERIES LAFAYETTE (Ed.) (2006): Galeries Lafayette Paris Launches its New "Souvenirs Boutique", Press Release April 2006, Paris.

H&M (2009): Style & Substance Sustainability Report 2009, www.hm.com, accessed on December 09, 2010.

H&M (Ed.) (2011): H&M, http://www.hm.com, accessed on January 27, 2011.

HAAS, A. (2000): Discounting – Konzeption und Anwendbarkeit des Discount als Marketingstrategie, Nürnberg.

HAMBURGER ABENDBLATT (Ed.) (2011): IKEA, http://www.abendblatt.de, accessed on March 07, 2011.

HANDFIELD, R.B.; NICHOLS, E.L. (1999): Introduction to Supply Chain Management, Upper Saddle River, N.J.

HANKE, G. (2004): Media Markt in der Klemme, in: Lebensmittel Zeitung, No. 14, April 2, 2004, p. 5.

HANSIOTA, B.; RUKSTALES, B. (2002): Direct Marketing for Multichannel Retailers: Issues, Challenges and Solutions, in: Journal of Database Market-ing, Vol. 9, No. 3, pp. 259-266.

HART, C. (1997): A Tale of Two Store Managers: Performance Measurement at Sainsbury's, in: HART, C. et al. (Eds.): Cases in Retailing, Oxford, pp. 216-225.

HARTLEY, R.F. (2009): Marketing Mistakes & Successes, 11th ed., Westford.

HAUPTKORN, B.; MANGET, J.; RASCH, S. (2005): Taking Care of Brands Through Vertical Integration, The Boston Consulting Group, Munich.

HAYWARD, M. (2009): Any colour you like as long it's any colour you like, London.

HEDEWIG-MOHR, S. (2000): Media Markt testet Web-Verkauf: Metro-Tochter bietet in Italien 500 Artikel online, www.lz-net.de, accessed on February 24, 2000.

HELFFERICH, E.; HINFELAAR, M.; KASPER, H. (1997): Towards a Clear Terminology on International Retailing, in: International Review of Retail, Distribution and Consumer Research, Vol. 7, pp. 287-307.

HERNANDÉZ, T.; BENNISON, D. (2000): The Art and Science of Retail Location Decisions, in: International Journal of Retail & Distribution Management, Vol. 28, No. 8, pp. 357-367.

HERTEL, J.; ZENTES, J.; SCHRAMM-KLEIN, H. (2011): Supply-Chain-Management und Warenwirtschaftssysteme im Handel, 2nd ed., Berlin et al.

HILT, C.; SCHEER, L. (2006): Handel in Nordamerika, in: ZENTES, J. (Ed.): Handbuch Handel, Wiesbaden, pp. 161-182.

HINES, T. (2005): The Emergence of Supply Chain Management as a Critical Success Factor for Retail Organisations, in: BRUCE, M.; MOORE, C.M.; BIRTWISTLE, G. (Eds.): International Retail Marketing, Amsterdam et al., pp. 108-122.

HIRSCHKORN, J. (2004): Retail Therapy, in: Accountancy, Vol. 134, No. 1336, pp. 45-46.

HO, F. (2003): Esprit – An Unfading Legend, Cash Research, Hong Kong.

HOCH, S.; BRADLOW, E.; WANSINK, B. (1999): The Variety of an Assortment, in: Marketing Science, Vol. 18, No. 4, pp. 527-546.

HOCH, S.; DRÉZE, X.; PURK, M. (1994): EDLP, Hi-Lo, and Margin Arithmetic, in: Journal of Marketing, Vol. 58, No. 4, pp. 16-27.

HOFER, J. (2010): Markenhersteller wandern zielstrebig aus der Krise, http://www.handels blatt.com/unternehmen/mittelstand/nachrichten-trends/markenhersteller-wandern-zielstrebig-aus-der-krise/3365440.html, accessed on January 22, 2011.

HOFFMAN, R.; PREBLE, J. (2003): Convert to Compete: Competitive Advantage through Conversion Franchising, in: Journal of Small Business Management, Vol. 41, No. 2, pp. 187-204.

HOFFMANN, W. (2006): Straight from the Source, in: Journal of Commerce, Vol. 7, No. 2, p. 23.

HOMBURG, C.; WERNER, H. (1998): Kundenorientierung mit System, Frankfurt a.M.

HOMBURG, C.; TOKSAL, A.; GÖDDE, D. (Eds.) (2004): Corporate Governance und Value Based Management – eine empirische Untersuchung der DAX-, MDAX- und TecDAX-Unternehmen, Cologne.

HORNBLOWER, S. (2004a): Always Low Prices, in: Public Broadcasting Service (2006): Is Wal-Mart Good for America?, http://www.pbs.org/wgbh/pages/frontline/shows/walmart/secrets/pricing.html.

HORNBLOWER, S. (2004b): Wal-Mart & China: A Joint Venture, in: Public Broadcasting Service (2006): Is Wal-Mart Good for America?, http:// www.pbs.org/wgbh/pages/frontline/shows/walmart/secrets/wmchina.html.

HOUZÉ, P. (2006): Les Galeries Lafayette Veulent s'Exporter, in: Le Figaro, 06 April 2006.

HOWARD, E. (2004a): Retail Internationalization: How to Grow, in: REYNOLDS, J.; CUTHBERTSON, C. (Eds.): Retail Strategy, Amsterdam et al., pp. 96-118.

HOWARD, E. (2004b): Straightforward British Approach Works in China, in: REYNOLDS, J.; CUTHBERTSON, C. (Eds.): Retail Strategy, Amsterdam et al., pp. 208-217.

HUBER, M (2009): Expansion durch Anpassung, http://www.sport-fachhandel.com/ Firmenportrait/Interview/expansion-durch-anpassung-sportlicher-aldi-soll-kommen.html, accessed on March, 8, 2011.

HUDETZ, K. (2005): E-Commerce im Einzelhandel mit Consumer Electronics, in: Handel im Fokus – Mitteilungen des Instituts für Handel an der Universität zu Köln, No. 2, pp. 112-124.

HUFF, D.L. (1964): Defining and Estimating a Trading Area, in: Journal of Marketing, Vol. 28, No. 3, pp. 34-38.

HUMBY, C.; HUNT, T.; PHILLIPS, T. (2007): Scoring Points: How Tesco is Winning Customer Loyalty, London et al.

HURTH, J. (2006): Angewandte Handelspsychologie, Stuttgart.

HUTCHISON WHAMPOA (2011a): Group structure, http://www.hutchison-whampoa.com/eng/about/structure/structure.htm, accessed on January 10, 2011.

HUTCHISON WHAMPOA (2011b): Audited Results for the Year ended 31 December 2010, http://www.aswatson.com/LTN20110329307.pdf, April 06, 2011.

IGD (Ed.) (2005): The Challenges & Opportunities Facing the Swiss Grocery Industry as Discounters Enter the Market, London.

IGD RESEARCH (2010): Grocery Buying Groups, http://www.igd.com/index.asp?id=1&fid= 1&sid=7&tid=26&cid=130, accessed on February 27, 2011.

IHA-GFK AG (Ed.) (2003): Detailhandel Schweiz 2003, Hergiswil.

IHA-GFK AG (Ed.) (2005): Detailhandel Schweiz 2005, Hergiswil.

IKI GROUP (2007): Coopernic Partners invest into the IKI Group retail network, http://www.iki.lt/en.php/press/?id=242&y=2007&page=1, accessed on February 27, 2011.

INFORMATION RESOURCES GMBH (Ed.) (2005): Grundgesamtheiten Deutschland 2005, Nürnberg.

INMA, C. (2005): Purposeful Franchising: Re-thinking of the Franchising Rationale, in: Singapore Management Review, Vol. 27, No. 1, pp. 27-48.

INMAN, J.; WINER, R.S.; FERRARO, R. (2009): The Interplay Among Category Characteristics, Customer Characteristics, and Customer Activities on In-Store Decision Making, in: Journal of Marketing, Vol. 73, pp. 19-29.

INTERBRAND (2010): Best Global Brands – 2010 Rankings, http://www.interbrand.com/en/ knowledge/best-global-brands/best-global-brands-2008/best-global-brands-2010.aspx, accessed on February 14, 2011.

INTERMEC TECHNOLOGIES CORPORATION (Ed.) (2004): Supply Chain RFID: How it Works and Why it Pays, White Paper, Everett.

IRELAND, R; BRUCE, R. (2000): CPFR: Only the Beginning of Collaboration, in: Supply Chain Management Review, September-October, http://www.surgency.com/news/news/publications.htm, accessed on February 22, 2011.

JAPAN NEWS REVIEW (Ed.) (2007): 7-Eleven world's largest chain store, http://www.japannewsreview.com/business/business/20070712page_id=598, accessed on February 22, 2011.

JANZ, M.; SWOBODA, B. (2007): Vertikales Retail-Management in der Fashion-Branche, Frankfurt a.M.

JENNINGS, D. (2001): Thorntons: The vertically integrated retailer, questioning the strategy, in: International Journal of Retail & Distribution Management, Vol. 29, No. 4, pp. 176-187.

KAHN, B.E. (1999): Introduction to the Special Issue: Assortment Planning, in: Journal of Retailing, Vol. 75, No. 3, pp. 289-293.

KALISH, I. (1999): Insights on Wal-Mart in Europe, http://www.retailforward.com/retailintel/specialreports/walmart.pdf.

KALTCHEVA, V.; WEITZ, B. (2006): When Should a Retailer Create an Exciting Store Environment?, in: Journal of Marketing, Vol. 70, No. 1, pp. 107-118.

KALYANAM, K.; LAL, R.; WOLFRAM, G. (2006): Future Store Technologies and their Impact on Grocery Retailing, in: KRAFFT, M.; MANTRALA, M. (Eds.): Retailing in the 21st Century, Berlin et al., pp. 95-112.

KANTAR RETAIL (2010): Kantar Retail Releases 2010 Powerranking® Study: Procter & Gamble tops manufacturers list; Walmart retains #1 rank among retailers; Press release, http://www.retailforward.com/pressroom/pressreleases/110810.htm, accessed on February 22, 2011.

KAPELL, E. (2002): Media Markt testet digitalen Musikvertrieb, www.lz-net.de, accessed on April 04, 2002.

KAPELL, E. (2005a): Größeres Angebot: Media Markt frischt Internet-Shop optisch und technisch auf, www.lz-net.de, accessed on July 28, 2005.

KAPELL, E. (2005b): Zweistelliges Plus bei Media Online: Kräftiges Wachstum – Relaunch geplant, www.lz-net.de, accessed on June 13, 2005.

KAPELL, E. (2009): Sainsbury's lässt rollen, http://www.lebensmittelzeitung.net/news/top/protected/meldung_77050.html, accessed on March 1st, 2011.

KAPLAN, R.S.; NORTON, D.P. (1993): Putting the Balanced Scorecard to Work, in: Harvard Business Review, Vol. 71, No. 5, pp. 134-157.

KEAVENEY, S.; HUNT, K. (1992): Conceptualization and Operationalization of Retail Store Image, in: Journal of the Academy of Marketing Science, Vol. 20, No. 2, pp. 165-75.

KELLER, K. (1993): Conceptualizing, Measuring, and Managing Customer-Based Brand Equity, in: Journal of Marketing, Vol. 57, No. 1, pp. 1-22.

KELLER, K. (2003): Strategic Brand Management, 2nd international ed., Upper Saddle River/NJ.

KIM, S.M.; MAHONEY, J.T. (2006): Collaborative Planning, Forecasting, and Replenishment (CPFR) as a Relational Contract: An Incomplete Contracting Perspective, http://www.business.uiuc.edu/Working_Papers/papers/06–0102.pdf, accessed on February 22, 2011.

KINGFISHER PLC (Ed.) (2004a): Group Direct Sourcing, London.

KINGFISHER PLC (Ed.) (2004b): Presentation for Goldman Sachs, London.

KINGFISHER PLC (Ed.) (2005a): Annual Review 2004, London.

KINGFISHER PLC (Ed.) (2005b): Steps to Responsible Growth: Social Responsibility Report 2005 Summary, London.

KINGFISHER PLC (Ed.) (2006): Preliminary Results for the 52 Weeks Ended 28 January 2006, London.

KLING, K.; GOTEMAN, I. (2003): IKEA CEO Anders Dahlvig on International Growth and IKEA's Unique Corporate Culture and Brand Equity, in: Academy of Management Executive, Vol. 17, No. 1, pp. 31-37.

KNIGHT, M. (2005): Heading to Germany, in: International Council of Shopping Centers, http://www.icsc.org/srch/sct/sct1205/Investing_in_Germany.php.

KNUTT, E. (2003): Master Kraftsmen, in: Estates Gazette, Vol. 145, Supplement Issue No. 324, pp. 19-20.

KOHL'S (2010): Annual Report on Form 10-k, Wisconsin.

KOTLER, P.; BLIEMEL, F. (2001): Principles of Marketing, 9th international ed., New York.

KOTLER, P.; ARMSTRONG, G.; SAUNDERS, J.; WONG, V. (2002): Principles of Marketing, 3rd European ed., Harlow.

KOZINETS, R.V.; SHERRY, J.F.; DEBERRY-SPENCE, B.; DUHACHEK, A.; NUTTAVUTHISIT, K.; STORM, D. (2002): Theme Flagship Brand Stores in the New Millennium: Theory, Practice, Prospects, Journal of Retailing, Vol. 78, No. 1, pp. 17-29.

KPMG (Ed.) (2001): Verticalization in the Trade: Effects in the Future Sales Channel Structure, Cologne.

KPMG (Ed.) (2004): Internationalisierung im Lebensmitteleinzelhandel: Status Quo und Perspektiven, Cologne.

KRACKLAUER, A.H.; MILLS, D.Q.; SEIFERT, D.; BARZ, M. (2004): The Integration of Supply Chain Management and Customer Relationship Management, in: KRACKLAUER, A.H.; MILLS, D.Q.; SEIFERT, D. (Eds.): Collaborative Customer Relationship Management, Berlin et al., pp. 57-69.

KRAFFT, M.; MANTRALA, M. (2010): Retailing in the 21st Century – Current and Future Trend, 2nd ed., Berlin et al.

KRISHNAN, H. (1996): Characteristics of Memory Associations: A Consumer-Based Brand Equity Perspective, in: International Journal of Research in Marketing, Vol. 13, pp. 389-405.

KUCHMENT, A.; THEIL, S. (2004): Esprit Redux, in: Newsweek, Vol. 143, No. 20, p. E24.

KUTSCHKER, M.; SCHMID, S. (2011): Internationales Management, 7th ed., Munich.

LAMBERT, D.; POHLEN, T. (2001): Supply Chain Metrics, in: International Journal of Logistics Management, Vol. 12, No. 1, pp. 1-19.

LAMEY, I. (1997): Retail Internationalisation: Cross Border Strategies, London.

LANE, C.; PROBERT, J. (2009): National Capitalisms, Global Production Networks, Oxford et al.

LASSAR, W.; MITTAL, B.; SHARMA, A. (1995): Measuring Customer-Based Brand Equity, in: Journal of Consumer Marketing, Vol. 12, No. 4, pp. 11-19.

LAU, P.; KUNERT, A.H. (2005): Die sind doch nicht blöd – und andere Gründe für den unglaublichen Erfolg von Media Markt, in: brand eins, No. 4, pp. 22-28.

LEBENSMITTEL ZEITUNG (2010): Top 50 LEH Welt 2010, http://www.lebensmittelzeitung .net/business/handel/rankings/pages/Top-50-LEH-Welt-2010_110.html#rankingTable,   accessed on February 28, 2011.

LECOQ, F. (2008): La R et D à la manière de Décathlon, LSA, pp. 50-51.

LEE, H.L.; PADMANABHAN, V.; WANG, S. (1997a): The Bullwhip Effect in Supply Chains, in: Sloan Management Review, Vol. 38, No. 3, pp. 93-102.

LEE, H.L.; PADMANABHAN, V.; WANG, S. (1997b): Information Distortion in a Supply Chain: The Bullwhip Effect, in: Management Science, Vol. 43, No. 4, pp. 546-558.

LEE, H.L.; PADMANABHAN, V.; WANG, S. (2004): Comments on "Information Distortion in a Supply Chain: The Bullwhip Effect": The Bullwhip Effect: Reflections, in: Management Science, Vol. 50, No. 12 Supplement, pp. 1887-1893.

LeHONG, H. (2004): Both EDLP and Hi-Lo Retail Pricing Can Work if Executed Properly, Gartner G2 Report June 2004.

LEISCHNIG, A.; SCHWERTFEGER, M.; GEIGENMÜLLER, A. (2010): Shopping events, shopping enjoyment, and consumer's attitude toward retail brands – An empirical examination, in: Journal of Retailing and Consumer Services, Vol. 18, No. 3, pp. 218-223.

LEEMAN, J.J. (2010): Supply Chain Management, Duesseldorf.

LEVEQUE, E. (2004): Galeries Lafayette: Opération Séducation auprès des Jeunes, http://www.journaldunet.com/ 0409/040922lafayettevo.shtml.

LEVY, M.; WEITZ, B. (2009): Retailing Management, 7th ed., Boston et al.

LEWALLEN, B. (2004): Wal-Mart & the Bar Code, in: Public Broadcasting Service (2006): Is Wal-Mart Good for America?, http://www.pbs.org/ wgbh/pages/frontline/shows/walmart/ secrets/barcode.html.

LEWIS, E. (2005): Is IKEA for Everyone?, http://www.brandchannel.com.

LHERMIE, C. (2001): Carrefour ou l'Invention de l'Hypermarché, Quercy.

LIEBMANN, H.-P.; ZENTES, J. (2001): Handelsmanagement, Munich.

LIEBMANN, H.-P.; ZENTES, J.; SWOBODA, B. (2008): Handelsmanagement, 2nd ed., Munich.

LINDSTROM, M. (2001): Clicks, Bricks & Brands, London.

LIU, H.; McGOLDRICK, P.J. (1995): International Sourcing: Patterns and Trends, in: MCGOLDRICK, P.J.; DAVIES, G. (Eds.): International Retailing, London, pp. 99-116.

LP INTERNATIONAL (Ed.) (2010): Top 30 des Deutschen Lebensmittelhandels 2009, in: LP international, No. 7, p. 2.

LZNET (Ed.) (2004): 7-Eleven: große Pläne mit kleinen Läden, http://www.lebensmittelzeitung.net/news/markt/protected/7-Eleven-Grosse-Plaene-mit-kleinen-Laeden_40923.html?a=1, accessed on February 22, 2011.

LZNet (Ed.) (2006): Neuer Shoppingcenter-Boom in Sicht, http://www.lz-net.de/news/ topnews/pages/protected/show53974.html, accessed on February 25, 2011.

LZNet (Ed.) (2010): Neue Umlaufbahn, http://www.lebensmittelzeitung.net/ business/ handel/ internationale-maerkte/protected/Handel-in-Europa_5408_7932.html, accessed on February 23, 2011.

MAGAUD, C. (2009): Décathlon assure son titre de champion, in: Points de Vente, Avril 2009, www.pointsdevente.fr, accessed on March 14, 2011.

MAGEE, S.K. (2009): 7-Eleven to expand in North America, in: The Japan Times, http://search.japantimes.co.jp/cgi-bin/nb20090214a3.html, accessed on February 22, 2011.

MARKETING WEEK (UK) (Ed.) (1998): Silver Award Winner, in: Marketing Week (UK), Vol. 21, No. 12, p. 77.

MARKETING WEEK (UK) (Ed.) (2005): Tesco Clubcard Relaunch, in: Marketing Week (UK), Vol. 36, No. 41, p. 89.

MARSH, E. (2004): 4 Corners of the World, in: WWD: Women's Wear Daily, Vol. 188, No. 86, pp. 28-30.

MARTENSON, R. (1987): Is Standardisation of Marketing Feasible in Culture-Bound Industries?, in: International Marketing Review, Vol. 4, No. 3, pp. 7-17.

MARTENSON, R. (2001): IKEA: Visionary Brand Building Through Employees, in: European Retail Digest, Vol. 9, No. 31, pp. 32-33.

MATTMÜLLER, R.; TUNDER, R. (2004): Strategisches Handelsmarketing, Munich.

McGOLDRICK, P. (2002): Retail Marketing, 2nd ed., London et al.

McGOLDRICK, P.J. (1995): Introduction to International Retailing, in: McGOLDRICK, P.J.; DAVIES, G. (Eds.): International Retailing, London, pp. 1-14.

McGOLDRICK, P.J; BLAIR, D. (1995): International Market Appraisal and Positioning, in: McGOLDRICK, P.J.; DAVIES, G. (Eds.): International Retailing, London, pp. 168-190.

McKELVEY, C. (2005): Can Data Ease Boots Headache?, in: Precision Marketing, Vol. 17, No. 15, p. 13.

McKINSEY & COMPANY (Ed.) (2004): Strategien für den traditionellen Handel im Wettbewerb mit den Discountern, Frankfurt.

McNAIR, M.P. (1931): Trends in Large Scale Retailing, in: Harvard Business Review, Vol. 10, No. 1, pp. 30-39.

McNAIR, M.P.; MAY, G.E. (1978): The Next Revolution of the Retailing Wheel, in: Harvard Business Review, Vol. 56, No. 5, pp. 81-91.

MEDIA MARKT (Ed.) (2006a): About Media Markt, www.mediamarkt.com, accessed on March 09, 2006.

MEDIA MARKT (Ed.) (2006b): Wer wir sind, www.mediamarkt.de, accessed on March 02, 2006.

MEDIAONLINE (Ed.) (2006): Wer sind wir, www.mediaonline.de, accessed on March 09, 2006.

MEHRABIAN, A.; RUSSEL, J. (1974): An Approach to Environmental Psychology, Cambridge/MA.

MENGELE, A. (1999): Shareholder-Return und Shareholder-Risk als unternehmensinterne Steuerungsgrößen, Stuttgart.

MENTZER, J.T.; DE WITT, W.; KEEBLER, J.S.; MIN, S.; NIX, N.W.; SMITH, C.D.; ZACHARIA, Z.G. (2001): Defining Supply Chain Management, in: Journal of Business Logistics, Vol. 22, No. 2, pp. 1-25.

MERKEL, H.; BREUER, P.; ELTZE, C.; KERNER, J. (2008): Global Sourcing im Handel, Berlin – Heidelberg.

METRO AG (Ed.) (2004): EVA Economic Value Added: Information Handbook for Employees, 2nd ed., Düsseldorf.

METRO AG (Ed.) (2005a): Annual Report 2004: Consolidated Financial Statements of the Metro Group, Düsseldorf.

METRO AG (Ed.) (2005b): Metro-Handelslexikon 2005/2006: Daten, Fakten und Adressen zum Handel in Deutschland, Europa und weltweit, Düsseldorf.

METRO AG (Ed.) (2006): Annual Report 2005: Consolidated Financial Statements of the Metro Group, Düsseldorf.

METRO AG (2010a): Investor Factbook: Version December 2010, Duesseldorf.

METRO AG (2010b): Annual Report 2009: Consolidated Financial Statements of Metro AG, Duesseldorf.

METRO AG (2011): Annual Report 2010: Consolidated Financial Statements of Metro AG, Duesseldorf.

METRO GROUP (Ed.) (2010): METRO Group, http://www.metrogroup.de/, accessed on February 26, 2011.

MEYER, K. (2001): Institutions, Transaction Costs and Entry Mode Choice in Eastern Europe, in: Journal of International Business Studies, Vol. 32, No. 2, pp. 357-367.

MEYER, M.W. (2009): Rethinking Performance Measurement: Beyond the Balanced Scorecard, New York.

MILLER, P. (2004): IKEA with Chinese Characteristics, in: The China Business Review, Vol. 31, No. 4, pp. 36-38.

MINTZBERG, H.; QUINN, J. (1996): The Strategy Process, 3rd ed., Upper Saddle River/NJ.

MITCHELL, A. (2004): The Back-to-Basics Way to Stand out from the Crowd, in: Marketing Week, Vol. 27, No. 40, pp. 32-33.

MOIN, D. (2004): Esprit Tweaks US Return With Juniors, in: WWD: Women's Wear Daily, Vol. 188, No. 136, p. 3.

MOLLENKOPF, D.; GIBSON, A.; OZANNE, L. (2000): The Integration of Marketing and Logistics Functions: An Empirical Examination of New Zealand Firms, in: Journal of Business Logistics, Vol. 21, No. 2, pp. 89-112.

MOON, Y. (2005): Break Free from the Product Life Cycle, in: Harvard Business Review, Vol. 83, No. 5, pp. 86-94.

MOORE, C.M. (2005): The Anatomy of Retail Buying, in: BRUCE, M.; MOORE, C.M.; BIRTWISTLE, G. (Eds.): International Retail Marketing, Amsterdam et al., pp. 64-77.

MOORE, C.M.; DOHERTY, A.M. (2007): The International Flagship Stores of Luxury Fashion Retailers, in: HINES, T.; BRUCE, M. (Eds.): Fashion Marketing: Contemporary Issues, 2nd ed., Oxford, pp. 277-295.

MOORE, C.M.; FERNIE, J. (2005): Retailing within an International Context, in: BRUCE, M.; MOORE, C.M.; BIRTWISTLE, G. (Eds.): International Retail Marketing, Amsterdam et al., pp. 3-38.

MORGAN, R.; HUNT, S. (1994): The Commitment-Trust Theory of Relationship Marketing, in: Journal of Marketing, Vol. 58, No. 3, pp. 20-38.

MORSCHETT, D. (2002): Retail Branding und Integriertes Handelsmarketing, Wiesbaden.

MORSCHETT, D. (2004): Retail-Performance-Measurement – Konzepte und Perspektiven des Prozess-Controllings im Handel, in: ZENTES, J., BIESIADA, H.; SCHRAMM-KLEIN, H. (Eds.): Performance-Leadership im Handel, Frankfurt, pp. 63-92.

MORSCHETT, D. (2006): Retail-Branding – Strategischer Rahmen für das Handelsmarketing, in: ZENTES, J. (Ed.): Handbuch Handel, Wiesbaden, pp. 525-546.

MORSCHETT, D.; NEIDHART, M. (2006): Internationalisierung im Handel – Das Beispiel der Fressnapf-Gruppe, in: Wirtschaftswissenschaftliches Studium, Vol. 35, No. 3, pp. 174-180.

MORSCHETT, D.; SCHRAMM-KLEIN, H.; ZENTES, J. (2010): Strategic International Management – Text and Cases, 2nd ed., Wiesbaden.

MORSCHETT, D.; SWOBODA, B.; SCHRAMM-KLEIN, H. (2006): Competitive Strategies in Retailing - An Investigation of the Applicability of Porter's Framework for Food Retailers, in: Journal of Retailing and Consumer Services, Vol. 13, No. 4, pp. 275-287.

MOTTEZ, D. (2005): Ça y est: Les 0 – 12 Ans ont leur Espace aux Galeries Lafayette, in: Le Journal des Femmes, http//www.internaute.com/femmes/actu/05/0210galeries-enfant.shtml.

MOUTINHO, L.; CURRY, B.; DAVIES, F. (1993): Comparative Computer Approaches to Multi-outlet Retail Site Location Decisions, in: Service Industries Journal, Vol. 13, No. 4, pp. 201-220.

MULHERN, F. (1997): Retail Marketing: From Distribution to Integration, in: International Journal of Research in Marketing, Vol. 14, pp. 103-124.

MURPHY, G. (2006): "Je suis fier de Casto et de Brico Dépôt", in: Rayons JB, No. 51, pp. 16-19.

NCR STORE PERFORMANCE CONSULTING (Ed.) (2003): 50 Ideas for Revolutionizing the Store through RFID, Dayton.

NEHER, A. (2003): Wertorientierung im Supply Chain Controlling, in: STÖLZLE, W.; OTTO, A. (Eds.): Supply Chain Controlling in Theorie und Praxis, Wiesbaden, pp. 27-48.

NELSON, R.L. (1958): The Selection of Retail Locations, New York.

NELSON, E.; ELLISON, S. (2005): Shelf Promotion: In a Shift, Marketers Beef Up Ad Spending Inside Stores, The Wall Street Journal, September 21, p. A1

NESLIN, S.A.; VENKATESH, S. (2009), Key Issues in Multichannel Customer Management: Current Knowledge and Future Directions, Journal of Interactive Marketing, Vol 23, No. 1, pp. 70-81.

NETIMPERATIVE (Ed.) (2010): UK online retail 'to sustain double-digit growth over the next 5 years', http://www.netimperative.com/news/2010/march/uk-online-retail-to-sustain-double-digit-growth, accessed on February 24, 2011.

NEW MEDIA AGE (2007): TK Maxx uses online to push itself as a key destination, 20.09.2007, p. 2, accessed on February 25, 2011.

NEXT (Ed.) (2011): NEXT, www.next.co.uk, accessed on March 03, 2011.

NEXT PLC (2010): January 2010 Annual Report & Accounts, http://ir2.flife.de/data/next/igb_html/pdf/1000003_e.pdf, accessed on February 25, 2011.

NEXT PLC (2011a): About Next – Our History, http://www.nextplc.co.uk/nextplc/aboutnext/ourhistory/, accessed on February 25, 2011.

NEXT PLC (2011b): Trading Statement – 5 January 2011, http://www.nextplc.co.uk/nextplc/financialinfo/reportsresults/2010/2011-01-05/2011-01-05a.pdf, accessed on February 26, 2011.

OGDEN, J.R.; OGDEN, D.T. (2005): Retailing – Integrated Retail Management, Boston et al.

OHMAE, K. (1985): The Triad World View, in: Journal of Business Strategy, Vol. 7, No. 4, pp. 8-19.

OLIVAREZ-GILES, N. (2010): Nike's retail expansion: 15th California store open and 250 to 300 new stores planned globally, http://latimesblogs.latimes.com/money_co/2010/11/ nike-to-add-250-to-300-new-stores-worldwide-over-next-five-years-nike-opens-new-nike-factory-store-in-citadel-outlets-los-ang.html, accessed on January 28, 2011.

ORTEGA, P. (1998): In Sam We Trust – The Untold Story of Sam Walton and Wal-Mart, the World's Most Powerful Retailer, New York.

OTTMANN, V. (2004a): Aufgedeckt: Die Media Markt Lüge, www.pcwelt.de, accessed on November 03, 2004.

OTTMANN, V. (2004b): Von wegen "Kaufen, Marsch, Marsch!": Mehrzahl der Media Markt- und Saturn-Angebote sind in Online-Shops billiger, www.presseportal.de, accessed on November 03, 2004.

OXENFELDT, A.; KELLY, A. (1969): Will Successful Franchise Systems Ultimately Become Wholly-Owned Chains?, in: Journal of Retailing, Vol. 44, No. 4, pp. 69-87.

OXYLANE (2010): Oxylane – The pleasure and the benefits of sports, company brochure, Villeneuve d'Ascq.

PACIFIC EPOCH (2010): 7-Eleven to Expand to 50 Shanghai Stores in 2010, http://pacificepoch.com/china-investment-research/articles/7-eleven-to-expand-to-50-shanghai-stores-in-2010, accessed on February 22, 2011.

PALMER, M. (2004): International Retail Restructuring and Divestment: The Experience of Tesco, in: Journal of Marketing Management, Vol. 20, No. 9/10, pp. 1075-1105.

PARDY, S.M. (2009): Convenience Rules_ 7-Eleven, Others in Convenience Category Proving Resilient Through Recession, in: www.CoStar.com, accessed on February 22, 2011.

PAYNE, A.; FROW, P. (2004): The role of multichannel integration in customer relationship management, Industrial Marketing Management, Vol. 33, No. 6, pp. 527-538.

PEDERZOLI, D. (2011): "En route" towards world leadership in the sports goods sector – Oxylane Group, in: Zentes, J.; Swoboda, B.; Morschett, D. (Eds.): Fallstudien zum Internationalen Management, 4th ed., Wiesbaden, pp. 535-560.

PETERS, R.-H. (2005): Media Markt - die Erfolgsstory von Europas größtem Händler für Haushalts- und Unterhaltungsgeräte, in: Stern, Vol. 57, No. 23, p. 118-121.

PFEIFFER, T. (2000): Good and Bad News for the Implementation of Shareholder-Value Concepts in Decentralized Organizations, in: Schmalenbach Business Review, Vol. 52, No. 1, pp. 68-91.

PIRK, K.-T.; TÜRKS, M.; MAYER, S. (1998): Leistungstiefenoptimierung in der Logistik, in: KRIEGER, W.; KLAUS, P. (Eds.): Gabler Lexikon Logistik, Wiesbaden, pp. 256-262.

PLANET RETAIL LTD. (Ed.) (2006a): Metro May Sell Remaining Stake in Praktiker/No Plans to Sell Real, http://www.planetretail.net/, 23 March 2006.

PLANET RETAIL LTD. (Ed.) (2006b): SWOT: Carrefour, Prepared by Planet Retail, www.planetretail.net.

POCSAY, S.; ZENTES, J. (2010): The Effects of Structural Bonds in Wholesaler's Customer Relationships, in: Marketing – Journal of Research and Management, Vol. 6, pp. 158-170.

PORTER, M. (1980) Competitive Strategy: Techniques for Analyzing Industries and Competitors, New York.

PRICEWATERHOUSE COOPERS (PwC); INSTITUT FÜR HANDEL & INTERNATIONALES MARKETING (H.I.MA.) (Eds.) (2010): Genug für alle da? – Wie gehen Händler und Konsumgüterhersteller mit Versorgungsrisiken um?, Frankfurt a.M.

PRIVATE LABEL MAGAZINE (Ed.) (2005): The Discount Wunderkind, http://www.privatelabelmag.com, accessed on March 01, 2006.

PROCTER & GAMBLE (Ed.) (2011a): Heritage, http://www.pg.com/en_US/media/media_kits.shtml, accessed on February 21, 2011.

PROCTER & GAMBLE (Ed.) (2011b): 2010 Annual Report, http://www.pg.com/en_US/media/media_kits.shtml, accessed on February 21, 2011.

PROCTER & GAMBLE (Ed.) (2011c): P&G eStore 2011, http://www.pgestore.com/, accessed on April 02, 2011.

PROMO MAGAZINE (Ed.) (2006): Wal-Mart and P&G Rank 'Best of the Best': PoweRanking, October 26, 2006.

PRÜMPER, W.; POHL, J.; THOMS, J. (2006): Beschaffungslogistik im Handel – Innovationen in Prozessen, Strukturen und Organisationen, in: ZENTES, J. (Ed.): Handbuch Handel, Wiesbaden, pp. 809-825.

PUBLIC BROADCASTING SERVICE (2006): Is Wal-Mart Good for America?, http://www.pbs.org/wgbh/pages/frontline/shows/walmart, 23 February 2006.

RAFIQ, M. (1997): Developing Customer Loyalty: the Saver Card Experience, in: HART, C.; KIRKUP, M.; PRESTON, D.; RAFIQ, M.; WALLEY, P. (Eds.): Cases in Retailing: Operational Perspectives, Oxford et al., pp. 43-61.

REICHHELD, F.; SASSER, W. (1990): Zero Defections: Quality Comes to Services, in: Harvard Business Review, Vol. 68, No. 5, pp. 105-113.

REILLY, W.J. (1929): Method for the Study of Retail Relationships, in: Research Monograph, No. 4, Austin, TX.

REINARTZ, W.J. (2010): Understanding Customer Loyalty Programs, in: KRAFFT, M.; MANTRALA, M. (Eds.): Retailing in the 21st Century: Current and Future Trends, 2. Ed. Berlin et al., pp. 409-429.

RETAILWEEK (2010): RetailWeek Knowledge Bank, Next plc – E-Commerce, http://rwkb.retail-week.com/DataRendering.aspx?dcid=7001&Company=17.

REYNOLDS, J. (1992): Generic Models of European Shopping Centre Development, in: European Journal of Marketing, Vol. 26, No. 8/9, pp. 48-60.

REYNOLDS, J. (2004a): An Exercise in Successful Retailing: The Case of Tesco, in: REYNOLDS, J.; CUTHBERTSON, C. (Eds.): Retail Strategy, Amsterdam et al., pp. 311-330.

REYNOLDS, J. (2004b): Introduction to retail strategy, in: REYNOLDS, J.; CUTHBERTSON, C. (Eds.): Retail Strategy, Amsterdam et al., pp. 3-22.

REYNOLDS, J.; CUTHBERTSON, C: (Eds.) (2004): Retail Strategy: The View from the Bridge, Amsterdam et al.

ROBERTI, M. (2003): Wal-Mart's Race for RFID, in: CIO Insight, 15 Septem-ber 2003, http://www.cioinsight.com/article2/0,1540,1780796,00.asp.

RODE, J. (2008): Bei Sainsbury's ersetzen Menschen Maschinen, http://www.lz.net/news/it-logistik/protected/Sainsbury-Wirft-High-Tech-aus-dem-Lager_63838.html?id=63838, accessed on March 01, 2011.

ROGERS, D. (1992): A Review of Sales Forecasting Models Most Commonly Applied in Retail Site Evaluation, in: International Journal of Retail & Distribution Management, Vol. 20, No. 4, pp. 3-11.

ROSA, T. (2004): Esprit Makes a Comeback in Puerto Rico, in: Caribbean Business, Vol. 32, No. 25, p. 30.

ROSENBLOOM, B. (2004): Marketing Channels: A Management View, 7th ed., Mason/OH.

ROSENBLOOM, B. (2007): The wholesaler's role in the marketing channel: Disintermediation vs. reintermediation, in: The International Review of Retail, Distribution and Consumer Research, Vol. 17, No. 4., pp. 327-339.

ROSENBLOOM, B.; LARSEN ANDRAS, T. (2008): Wholesalers as Global Marketers, in: Journal of Marketing Channels, Vol. 15, No. 4, pp. 235-252.

ROSSMANN (2011): Rossmann International, http://www.rossmann.de/unternehmen/rossmann-international.html, accessed on April 06, 2011.

ROULLEAU, M. (2006): Interview, in: Absatzwirtschaft, Vol. 49, No. 5, pp. 810.

ROWLEY, J. (2004): Loyalty and Reward Schemes: How Much is Your Loyalty Worth?, in: The Marketing Review, Vol. 4, No. 2, pp. 121-138.

RUDOLPH, T.; SCHRÖDER, T. (2006a): Länderbericht Dänemark, in: RUDOLPH, T.; SCHWEIZER, M. (Eds.): Das Discount-Phänomen, Zurich, pp. 247-255.

RUDOLPH, T.; SCHRÖDER, T. (2006b): Länderbericht Niederlande, in: RUDOLPH, T.; SCHWEIZER, M. (Eds.): Das Discount-Phänomen, Zurich, pp. 223-232.

RUDOLPH, T.; SCHRÖDER, T. (2006c): Länderbericht Österreich, in: RUDOLPH, T.; SCHWEIZER, M. (Eds.): Das Discount-Phänomen, Zurich, pp. 233-246.

RUDOLPH, T.; SCHRÖDER, T. (2006d): Länderbericht Vereinigtes Königreich, in: RDOLPH, T.; SCHWEIZER, M. (Eds.): Das Discount-Phänomen, Zurich, pp. 267-281.

RUDOLPH, T.; SCHWEIZER, M. (Eds.) (2006): Das Discount-Phänomen: Eine 360-Grad-Betrachtung, Zurich.

RUSS, C.; SCHWAIGER, A.; STAHMER, B. (2004): SimMarket, in: ZENTES, J.; BIESIADA, H.; SCHRAMM-KLEIN, H. (Eds.): Performance Leadership im Handel, Frankfurt, pp. 255-283.

RYAN, J. (2005): Galeries Lafayette – Four-Year Makeover – Was it Worth it?, http://www.visualstore.com/index.php/channel/10/id/9237.

SAINSBURY PLC (2006): Sainsbury's and Accenture successfully transition IT functions back to Sainsbury's, in: Company News, accessed on April 28, 2006.

SAINSBURY'S (2011a): Supply Chain Locations, http://www2.sainsburys.co.uk/sid/locations/locations.htm, accessed on April 06, 2011.

SAINSBURY'S (2011b): Primary Distribution, http://www2.sainsburys.co.uk/sid/info_sc_pd.htm, accessed on April 06, 2011.

SAINSBURY'S (2011c): Creating a world-class Supply Chain for Sainsbury's, http://www2.sainsburys.co.uk/sid/Documents/supplychainblueprint.pdf, accessed on April 06, 2011.

SANDERS, N.R.; PREMUS, R. (2005): Modelling the Relationship Between Firm IT Capability, Collaboration, and Performance, in: Journal of Business Logistics, Vol. 26, No. 1, pp. 1-23.

SAP; GFK PANEL SERVICES DEUTSCHLAND (2010): Preisoptimierung im deutschen Lebensmitteleinzelhandel, Walldorf – Nürnberg.

SAS Institute Inc. (Ed.) (2004): Kingfisher Asia Limited Uses SAS to Leverage Supplier Performance and Achieve Greater Profitability, Cary et al.

SCARDINO, E. (2004): As Esprit Relaunches, Spirit of Revival Reawakens in US, in: DSNRetailing Today, Vol. 43, No. 17, pp. 7-60.

SCHÄFER, M. (2006): Die Zukunft des Disocunt-Phänomens, in: RUDOLPH, T.; SCHWEIZER, M. (Eds.): Das Discount-Phänomen: Eine 360-Grad-Betrachtung, Zurich, pp. 109-119.

SCHLIEBE, K. (1998): Einkaufscenter-Management ist Marketing-Management, in: FALK, B. (Ed.): Das große Handbuch Shopping-Center, Landsberg/Lech, pp. 99-117.

SCHMITT, B. (1999): Experiential Marketing: How to Get Customers to Sense, Feel, Think, Act, New York.

SCHNERMANN, J. (1998): Projektentwicklung von Shopping-Centern – dargestellt an Entwicklungsphasen, in: FALK, B. (Ed.): Das große Handbuch Shopping-Center, Landsberg/Lech, pp. 139-163.

SCHOTANUS, F. (2007): Horizontal cooperative purchasing, dissertation, University of Twente.

SCHRAMM-KLEIN, H. (2003): Multi-Channel-Retailing – Verhaltenswissenschaftliche Analyse der Wirkung von Mehrkanalsysteme im Handel, Wiesbaden.

SCHRAMM-KLEIN, H.; MORSCHETT, D. (2006): The Relationship Between Marketing Performance, Logistics Performance and Company Performance for Retail Companies, in: International Review of Retail, Distribution and Consumer Research, Vol. 16, No. 2, pp. 277-296.

SCHUHMAYER, M. (2006): Das Hofer System brachte den Erfolg, in: Regal, Vol. 30, No. 1, pp. 31-34.

SEIFERT, D. (2001): ECR-Erfolgsfaktorenstudie Deutschland, in: Science Factory, 2/2001.

SEILER, M. (2005): High Performance, in: Marketing Management, Vol. 14, No. 6, pp. 18-23.

SHEFFI, Y. (2002): The value of CPFR, in: RIRL Conference Proceedings, Lisbon/Portugal, October 13 -16, 2002.

SHEPPARD, G. (2005): Fury at Sainsbury's Depot Control Move, in: Commercial Motor, Vol. 201, No. 5133, p. 18.

SHIUE, Y.C.; HORNG, D.J.; YEH, S.W. (2006): Carrefour's Global Reach: A Case Study of Its Strategy, in: The Journal of the American Academy of Business, Vol. 9, No. 1, pp. 171-175.

SHUGAN, S. (2005): Brand Loyalty Programs: Are They Shams?, in: Marketing Science, Vol. 24, No. 2, pp. 185-193.

SIGNORELLI, S.; HESKETT, J. (1984): Benetton, Harvard.

SIMCHI-LEVI, D., KAMINSKY, P.; SIMCHI-LEVI, E. (2000): Designing and Managing the Supply Chain: Concepts, Strategies, and Case Studies, New York.

SIMON, H.; GATHEN, A.; DAUS, P. (2008): Retail Pricing – Higher Profits Through Improved Pricing Processes, in: KRAFFT, M.; MANTRALA, M. (Eds.): Retailing in the 21st Century, 2nd ed., Berlin et al., pp. 319-336.

SLIWA, C. (2002): CPFR clamor persists, but adoption remains slow, http://www.computerworld.com/s/article/72360/CPFR_clamor_persists_but_adoption_rem ains_slow, , accessed on February 22, 2011.

SLOAN, C. (2004): Lafayette Maison Different From The Rest, in: Home Textiles Today, Vol. 26, No. 4, pp. 1-6.

SMITH, H. (2004): Who Calls the Shots in the Global Economy?, in: Public Broadcasting Service (2006): Is Wal-Mart Good for America?, http:// www.pbs.org/wgbh/pages/frontline/ shows/walmart/secrets/shots.html, accessed on February 23, 2006.

SMITH, D.; SPARKS, L. (2009): Temperature-Controlled Supply Chains, in: FERNIE, J.; SPARKS, L. (Eds.): Logistics & Retail Management, 3rd ed., London et al., pp. 172-188.

SOLIS, A.O. (2001): Some success stories in supply chain management, in: The Criterion, May 2001.

SOUSA, C.M.; BRADLEY, F. (2005): Global Markets: Does Psychic Distance Matter?, in: Journal of Strategic Marketing, Vol. 13 No. 1, pp. 43-59.

SPARKS, L. (1995): Reciprocal Retail Internationalisation: The Southland Corporation, Ito-Yokado and 7-Eleven Convenience Stores, in: Service Industries Journal, Oct95, Vol. 15, No. 4, pp. 57-96.

SPARKS, L. (2009): RFID: transforming technology?, in: FERNIE, J.; SPARKS, L. (Eds.): Logistics & Retail Management, 3rd ed., London et al., pp. 233-252.

SPARKS, L.; WAGNER, B. (2004): Transforming Technologies: Retail Exchanges and RFID, in: FERNIE, J.; SPARKS, L. (Eds.): Logistics and Retail Management, 2nd ed., London et al., pp. 188-208.

SPETHMAN, B. (2004): Loyalty's Royalty, in: Promo, Vol. 17, No. 4, pp. 32-41.

STANK, T.P.; DAVIS, B.R.; FUGATE, B.S. (2005): A Strategic Framework for Supply Chain Oriented Logistics, in: Journal of Business Logistics, Vol. 26, No. 2, pp. 27-45.

STATISTA (2010): Ranking der größten Sportartikelhersteller nach weltweitem Umsatz im Jahr 2009 in Milliarden Euro, http://de.statista.com/statistik/daten/studie/170718/umfrage/ groesste-sportartikelhersteller-weltweit-nach-umsatz/, accessed on February 16, 2011.

STEIN, F. (2005): Media Markt will Billigster sein, www.connect.de, accessed on October 24, 2005.

STERN, J.M.; SHIELY, J.S.; ROSS, I. (2001): The EVA Challenge: Implementing Value-Added Change in an Organization, New York et al.

STERNQUIST, B. (2007): International Retailing, 2nd ed., New York.

STEWART, G.B. (1990): The Quest for Value, New York.

STONE, M. (2003): Scoring Points: How Tesco is Winning Customer Loyalty, in: Database Marketing & Customer Strategy Management, Vol. 11, No. 2, p. 183-187.

STORES AND SHOPS (Ed.) (2004): Pariser Themenhaus, in: Stores and Shops, Vol. 7, No. 2, p. 8.

STRAUBE, F.; PFOHL, H.-C. (2008): Trends und Strategien in der Logistik 2008: Globale Netzwerke im Wandel, Bremen.

STÜHRENBERG, L.; STREICH, D.; HENKE, J. (2003): Wertorientierte Unternehmensführung, Wiesbaden.

SUNDHOFF, E. (1965): Handel, in: BECKERATH, E. et al. (Eds.): Handwörterbuch der Sozialwissenschaften, Vol. 4, Stuttgart, pp. 762-779.

SWOBODA, B. (1996): Interaktive Medien am Point of Sale, Wiesbaden.

SWOBODA, B.; JANZ, M. (2002): Einordnung des Pay on Scan-Konzeptes in die modernen Ansätze zur unternehmensübergreifenden Wertkettenoptimierung in der Konsumgüterwirtschaft, in: TROMMSDORFF, V. (Ed.): Handelsforschung 2001/02, Cologne, pp. 203-222.

SWOBODA, B.; SCHWARZ, S. (2006): Convenience-Stores – Internationale Entwicklung und Käuferverhalten in Deutschland, in: ZENTES, J. (Ed.): Handbuch Handel, Wiesbaden, pp. 395-421.

SWOBODA, B.; FOSCHT, T.; PENNEMANN, K. (2009): HandelsMonitor 2009: Internationalisierung des Handels, Frankfurt a.M.

SWOBODA, B.; SCHWARZ, S.; HÄLSIG, F. (2007): Towards a Conceptual Model of Country Market Selection: Selection Processes of Retailers and C&C Wholesalers, in: The International Review of Retail, Distribution and Consumer Research, Vol. 17, No. 3, pp. 253-282.

SWOBODA, B.; ZENTES, J.; ELSNER, S. (2009): Internationalisation of Retail Firms – State of the Art after 20 Years of Research, in: Marketing – Journal of Research and Management, Vol. 5, pp. 105-126.

TANGUY, G. (2009): Décathlon – Le colossi qui écrase tous ses rivaux, in: Capital, June 2009, No. 213, pp. 36-40.

TCHIBO (Ed.) 2010: Tchibo Corporate Website, http://www.tchibo.com, accessed on January 11, 2011.

TESCO (Ed.) (2006): Annual Review and Summary Financial Statement 2005, Hertfordshire.

TESCO (Ed.) (2010): Tesco PLC Annual Report and Financial Statements 2010.

TESCO (Ed.) (2011): Our Strategy, http://www.tescoplc.com/plc/about_us/strategy, accessed on March 3, 2011.

TAGESANZEIGER (Ed.) (2011): Denner-Chef Bamert geht nach nur einem Jahr, http://www.tagesanzeiger.ch/wirtschaft/unternehmen-und-konjunktur/DennerChef-Bamert-geht-nach-nur-einem-Jahr/story/20611194, accessed on February 27, 2011.

TEXTILWIRTSCHAFT (2001): Schweizer C&A-Dach – Brenninkmeijers ordnen ihre Interessen neu, http://www.textilwirtschaft.de/news/schlagzeilen/pages/Das-neue-Dach-von-C--A_12605.html?a=1, accessed on February 11, 2011.

TEXTILWIRTSCHAFT (Ed.) (2006): Galeries Lafayette plant neue Häuser – Auch im Ausland sollen Stores entstehen, in: Textilwirtschaft, Vol. 61, No. 2, p. 54.

TEXTILWIRTSCHAFT (Ed.) (2010): TK Maxx wächst weiter, No. 21, p. 7.

TEXTILWIRTSCHAFT (Ed.) (2011): TJX Companies, No. 9, p. 10.

THE ECONOMIST (Ed.) (2001): Wal Around the World, in: The Economist, Vol. 361, No. 8251, 6 December 2001, pp. 55-57.

THE ECONOMIST (Ed.) (2004): How Big Can it Grow?, in: The Economist, Vol. 371, No. 8371, 15 April 2004, pp. 67-69.

THE ECONOMIST (Ed.) (2006): Flat-Pack Accounting, in: The Economist, Vol. 379, No. 8477, 13 May 2006, pp. 69-70.

THE ECONOMIST INTELLIGENCE UNIT (EIU) (Ed.) (2005): Consumer Goods and Retail Forecast – World, London.

THE GUARDIAN (Ed.) (2004): The Miracle of Älmhult, http://www.guardian.co.uk/g2/story/0,3604,1240462,00.html.

THOMPSON, J. (2009): Discount fashion: Taking it to the Maxx, in: The Independent, http://www.independent.co.uk/news/business/analysis-and-features/discount-fashion-taking-it-to-the-maxx-1774064.html, accessed on February 25, 2011.

THORNDIKE, A.; WALTEMATH, A. (1999): Logistik bestimmt den Erfolg im Großhandel, in: Distribution, Vol. 30, No. 3, pp. 18-22.

T.J. MAXX (Ed.) (2011): T.J. Maxx, http://www.tjmaxx.com/, accessed on March 2, 2011.

TJX COMPANIES, INC. (Ed.) (2010): Background Information 2010, Company Brochure.

TJX COMPANIES, INC. (Ed.) (2011): Growing a Global, Off-Price Value Company, http://www.tjx.com/investor_3.asp, accessed on March 2, 2011.

TITUS (Ed.) (2011): Titus, http://www.titus.de, accessed on February 23, 2011.

TK MAXX (Ed.) (2011): TK Maxx, http://www.tkmaxx.de/, accessed on March 2, 2011.

TOELLER, T. (2005): Franchising im Handel – Die Erfolgsfaktoren der Fressnapf Tiernahrungs GmbH, in: Marketing- und Management-Transfer, April, pp. 3-8.

TORDJMAN, A. (1995): European Retailing: Convergences, Differences and Perspectives, in: McGOLDRICK, P.J.; DAVIES, G. (Eds.): International Retailing, London, pp. 17-50.

TRENDHUNTER (Ed.) (2011): Pop-up Roomvertising, http://www.trendhunter.com/trends/ ikea, accessed on April 02, 2011.

TRENZ, T. (2005): Online-Handel heizt Wettbewerb weiter an, www.lz-net.de, accessed on August 02, 2005.

TRENZ, T.; VOGEL, M. (2004): Media Markt lobt „Bestpreise" aus, in: Lebensmittel Zeitung, No. 14, April 02, 2004, p. 4.

TSAY, A.A.; AGRAWAL, N. (2004): Channel Conflict and Coordination in the E-Commerce Age, in: Production and Operations Management, Vol. 13, No. 1, pp. 93-110.

TULIP, S: (2003): The Logistics & Supply-Chain Forum 2003, in: Logistics & Transport Focus, Vol. 5, No. 10, pp. 50-53.

TWARDAWA, W. (2006): Die Rolle der Discounter im deutschen LEH, in: ZENTES, J. (Ed.): Handbuch Handel, Wiesbaden, pp. 377-393.

TWT (2010): TK Maxx und das Social Web, http://www.twt.de/news/blog/tk-maxx-setzt-auf-social-media-fur-mode-und-lifestyle.html, accessed on March 2, 2011.

UELLENDAHL, J. (2002): Secured Distribution as an Element in the Sales Strategy Based on the Example of Goodyear Dunlop in the European Union, in: SCHOLZ, C.; ZENTES, J. (Eds.): Strategic Management: A European Approach, Wiesbaden, pp. 201-219.

UNCLES, M. (2010): Understanding Retail Customers, in: KRAFFT, M.; MANTRALA, M. (Eds.): Retailing in the 21st Century – Current and Future Trends, Berlin et al., pp. 205-219.

UNCLES, M.; DOWLING, G.; HAMMOND, K. (2003): Customer Loyalty and Customer Loyalty programs, in: Journal of Consumer Marketing, Vol. 20, No. 4, pp. 294-316.

VARLEY, R. (2006): Retail Product Management, 2nd ed., London et al.

VEGA, R. (2004): Warehousing: Time to Think Outside the Box, in: Logistics & Transport Focus, Vol. 6, No. 2, pp. 16-21.

VERHAGEN, T.; VAN DOLEN, W. (2009): Online purchase intentions: A multichannel store image perspective, in: Information & Management, Vol. 46, No. 2, pp. 77-82.

VICKERS, J.; WATERSON, M. (1991): Vertical Relationships: An Introduction, in: The Journal of Industrial Economics, Vol. 39, No. 5, pp. 445-450.

VOGEL, M. (2004): Mediaonline gegen Media Markt, Kommentar, in: Lebensmittel Zeitung, No. 14, 02 April 2004, p. 4.

WALDEN, J. (2006): Best Buy: Customer-Centric Innovation, in: Human Resource Planning, Vol. 29, No. 3, pp. 34-36.

WALLACE, D.W.; GIESE, J.L.; JOHNSON, J.L. (2004): Customer retailer loyalty in the context of multiple channel strategies, in: Journal of Retailing, Vol. 80, No. 4, pp. 249-263.

WALLER, M.; DABHOLKAR, P.; GENTRY, J. (2000): Postponement, Product Customization, and Market-oriented Supply Chain Management, in: Journal of Business Logistics, Vol. 21, No. 2, pp. 133-159.

WALMART, INC. (Ed.) (2005): Annual Report 2005, Bentonville, AR.

WALMART, INC. (Ed.) (2006): Annual Report 2006, Bentonville, AR.

WALMART (2011a): Corporate Fact Sheet, http://walmartstores.com/pressroom/factsheets, accessed on February 21, 2011.

WALMART (2011b): Stores U.S. Fact Sheet, http://walmartstores.com/pressroom/factsheets, accessed on February 21, 2011.

WALMART (2011c): Logistics Fact Sheet, http://walmartstores.com/pressroom/factsheets, accessed on February 21, 2011.

WALTON, S. (1992): Made in America, New York.

WATERSCHOOT, W. VAN; KUMAR, S.P.; BURT, S., DE HAES, J.; FOSCHT, T.; LIEVENS, A. (2010): The classic conceptualisation and classification of distribution service outputs – Time for a revision?, in: MORSCHETT, D.; RUDOLPH, T.; SCHNEDLITZ, P.; SCHRAMM-KLEIN, H.; SWOBODA, B. (Eds.): European Retail Research, Vol. 24, No. II, pp. 1-32.

WATSON, E. (2005): Automation Left Sainsbury "'Buggered" When It Failed, in: Food Manufacture, Vol. 80, No. 11, p. 29.

Webster, M. (2010): Let the converged retailing evolution begin, in: Chain Store Age, March 2010, http://www.chainstoreage.com/article/let-converged-retailing-evolution-begin, accessed on January 1, 2011.

WEITZ, B.A.; WHITFIELD, M.B. (2010): Trends in US Retailing, in: KRAFFT, M.; MAN-TRALA, M. (Eds.): Retailing in the 21st Century – Current and Future Trends, 2nd ed., Berlin et al., pp. 83-99.

WELLMAN, D. (2005): IKEA Adds More Stores, More Food, in: Retail Merchandiser, Vol. 45, No. 8, p. 7.

WHEELER, P. (2010): UK: Next Retail Gets An iPhone App, http://appadvice.com/appnn/ 2010/03/uk-next-retail-gets-an-iphone-app/, accessed on February 11, 2011.

WHITEOAK, P. (2004): Rethinking Efficient Replenishment in the Grocery Sector, in: FERNIE, J.; SPARKS, L. (Eds.): Logistics and Retail Management, 2nd ed., London et al., pp. 138-163.

WILEMAN, A.; JARY, M. (1997): Retail Power Plays: From Trading to Brand Leadership, New York.

WILLIAMSON, O. E. (1985): The Economic Institutions of Capitalism, New York et. al.

WILSON, M. (2002): Shopping Esprit, in: Chain Store Age, Vol. 78, No. 5, pp. 51-52.

WINCOR NIXDORF (2005): Geschäftsbericht 2004/2005, http://www.wincor-nixdorf.com/static/finanzberichte/gb2004-2005/casestudies/aswatson.html, accessed on December 17, 2010.

WIRTSCHAFTSWOCHE (Ed.) (2004): Angebliche Billigriesen, in: Wirtschaftswoche, Vol. 58, No. 33, p. 37.

WIRTSCHAFTSWOCHE (2009): Versace, nur billiger, No. 48, p. 74.

WOLFSKEIL, J. (2005): Aldi und die Zeitfenster, in: Lebensmittel Zeitung, December 09, 2005, p. 2.

WOMEN'S WEAR DAILY (2004): Findings, in: WWD: Women's Wear Daily, Vol. 188, No. 104, p. 12.

WORLD BANK (Ed.) (2005): World Development Indicators 2005, Washington, DC.

WORLD FEDERATION OF DIRECT SELLING ASSOCIATIONS (Ed.) (2010): Publications – Statistical Information, www.wfdsa.org, accessed on November 17, 2010.

WORTZEL, L. (1987): Retailing Strategies for Today's Mature Marketplace, in: Journal of Business Strategy, Vol. 8, Spring, pp. 45-56.

WRIGLEY, N. (1988): Retail Restructuring and Retail Analysis, in: WRIGLEY, N. (Ed.): Store Choice, Store Location and Market Analysis, London, pp. 3 34.

WYLIE, D. (2005): Tesco Has Links with the Corner Shops of England's Past, http://www.loyalty.vg/pages/CRM/case_study_14_Tesco.htm.

YAHAGIA, T.; KAR, M. (2009): Seven-Eleven Group: US - Japan – China, in: Asia Pacific Business Review, Vol. 15, No. 1, pp. 41–58.

YEUNG, M. (2002): Esprit Faces Tougher Time in US, in: Asian Retail Headline News, http://www.siamfuture.com, 02 March 2002.

ZENTES, J. (2004): Performance Leadership im Handel – Stoßrichtungen und Konzepte, in: ZENTES, J., BIESIADA, H.; SCHRAMM-KLEIN, H. (Eds.): Performance-Leadership im Handel, Frankfurt, pp. 11-28.

ZENTES, J. (2005): Marketing, in: Vahlens Kompendium der Betriebswirtschaftslehre, Vol. 1, 5th ed., Munich, pp. 309-384.

ZENTES, J. (2006): Dynamik des Handels – Perspektiven und Zukunftsstra-tegien, in: ZENTES, J. (Ed.): Handbuch Handel, Wiesbaden, pp. 3-22.

ZENTES, J.; BARTSCH, A. (2002): Neuorientierung des Beschaffungsmanagements: Multi Channel Sourcing, Frankfurt.

ZENTES, J.; BASTIAN, J. (2010): Der Handel als Hersteller – Neuorientierungen der Wertschöpfungsarchitekturen, in: SCHÖNBERGER, R.; ELBERT, R. (Eds.): Dimensionen der Logistik - Funktionen, Institutionen und Handlungsebenen, Wiesbaden, pp. 975-991.

ZENTES, J.; MORSCHETT, D. (2002): Retail Branding – Concept, Effects and its Influence on the Internationalisation Process of Retail Companies in Europe, in: SCHOLZ, C.; ZENTES, J. (Eds.): Strategic Management – A European Approach, Wiesbaden, pp. 161-184.

ZENTES, J.; MORSCHETT, D. (2004a): Entwicklungstendenzen des Marken-artikels aus Handelsperspektive, in: BRUHN, M: (Ed.): Handbuch Markenartikel, 2nd ed., Wiesbaden, pp. 2719-2745.

ZENTES, J.; MORSCHETT, D. (2004b): Sortimentsdiversifikation im Handel – eine theoretische und empirische Analyse, in: GRÖPPEL-KLEIN, A. (Ed.): Konsumentenverhaltensforschung im 21. Jahrhundert, Wiesbaden, pp. 159-183.

ZENTES, J.; NEIDHART, M. (2006): Secured and Controlled Distribution – Die Industrie als Einzelhändler, in: ZENTES, J. (Ed.): Handbuch Handel, Wiesbaden, pp. 275-297.

ZENTES, J.; POCSAY, S. (2010): Value-Net-Integrator – ein Zukunftsmodell für kooperative Unternehmensnetzwerke, in: AHLERT, D.; AHLERT, M. (Eds.): Handbuch Franchising & Cooperation – Das Management kooperativer Unternehmensnetzwerke, Frankfurt a.M., pp. 13-230.

ZENTES, J.; RITTINGER, S. (2009): Retailing in Germany: Current Landscape and Future Trends, in: European Retail Research, Vol. 23, Issue I, pp. 153-182.

ZENTES, J.; SWOBODA, B. (1998): HandelsMonitor I/98: Wo wird im Jahre 2005 Handel gemacht?, Frankfurt a.M.

ZENTES, J.; BASTIAN, J.; LEHNERT, F. (2010): HandelsMonitor: Strategien der Nachhaltigkeit, Frankfurt a.M.

ZENTES, J.; HILT, C.; DOMMA, P. (2007): HandelsMonitor Spezial: Global Sourcing im Einzelhandel, Frankfurt a.M.

ZENTES, J.; JANZ, M.; KABUTH, P.(2002): Best Practice-Prozesse im Handel: Customer Relationship Management und Supply Chain Management, Frankfurt.

ZENTES, J.; MORSCHETT, D.; KREBS, J. (2008): HandelsMonitor 2008: Die Neue Mitte – Comeback eines Marktsegments, Frankfurt a.M.

ZENTES, J.; MORSCHETT, D.; NEIDHART, M. (2003): Vertikale Vertriebskooperationssysteme – Perspektiven und Strategien, in: IBB; H.I.MA. (Eds.): Die Zukunft der Kooperationen, Frankfurt, pp. 189-267.

ZENTES, J.; MORSCHETT, D.; SCHRAMM-KLEIN, H. (2006): Direktmarketing im Handel – Perspektiven und Beispiele aus dem internationalen Handel, in: WIRTZ, B.; BURMANN, C. (Eds.): Ganzheitliches Direktmarketing, Wiesbaden, pp. 593-621.

ZENTES, J.; MORSCHETT, D.; SCHRAMM-KLEIN, H. (2008): Brand personality of retailers – an analysis of its applicability and its effect on store loyalty, in: The International Review of Retail, Distribution and Consumer Research, Vol. 18, No. 2, pp. 167-184.

ZENTES, J.; NEIDHART, M.; SCHEER, L. (2005): HandelsMonitor Spezial: Vertikalisierung, Frankfurt.

ZENTES, J.; SCHRAMM-KLEIN, H.; NEIDHART, M. (2005): HandelsMonitor 2005/06: Expansion – Konsolidierung – Rückzug: Trends, Perspektiven und Optionen im Handel, Frankfurt a.M.

ZENTES, J.; SWOBODA, B.; MORSCHETT, D. (2005): Markt, Kooperation, Integration: Asymmetrische Entwicklungen in der Gestaltung der Wertschöpfungsprozesse am Beispiel der Konsumgüterindustrie, in: ZENTES, J.; SWOBODA, B.; MORSCHETT, D. (Eds.): Kooperationen, Allianzen und Netzwerke, 2nd ed., Wiesbaden, pp. 675-700.

ZENTES, J.; SWOBODA, B.; SCHRAMM-KLEIN, H. (2010): Internationales Marketing, 2nd ed., Munich.

ZENTES, J.; SCHRAMM-KLEIN, H.; MORSCHETT, D.; SWOBODA, B. (2009a): Does Corporate Social Responsibility Pay for Retailers?, in: REYNOLDS, K.; WHITE, J.C. (Eds.): Marketing Theory and Applications, Vol. 20, Proceedings of the American Marketing Association (AMA) 2009 Winter Educator's Conference, Tampa, pp. 433-434.

ZENTES, J.; SCHRAMM-KLEIN, H.; MORSCHETT, D.; SWOBODA, B. (2009b): The Impact of Retailers' Corporate Social Responsibility on Consumer Behaviour, in: KAMENS, M.; MARTIN, I.M. (Eds.): Enhancing Knowledge Development in Marketing, Vol. 20, Proceedings of the American Marketing Association (AMA) 2009 Summer Educator's Conference, Chicago.

ZHANG, J.; FARRIS, P.; KUSHWAHA, T.; IRVIN, J.; STEENBURGH, T.; WEITZ, B. (2010): Crafting Integrated Multichannel Retailing Strategies, Working Paper, Harvard Business School Division of Research, pp. 09-125.

ZILIANI, C.; BELLINI, S. (2004): Retail Micro-Marketing Strategies and Competition, in: The International Review of Retail, Distribution and Consumer Research, Vol. 14, No. 1, pp. 7-18.

Index

GABLER RESEARCH

GABLER

Mehr wissen – weiter kommen

↗

Global perspective and major aspects of international business strategies. This textbook introduces the complexity of international business based on the perspective of Multinational Corporations as inter-organisational and intra-organisational networks. The authors highlight the role of the external environment, discuss the major coordination mechanisms and organisational structures and examine various foreign operation modes. The book describes the particularities of international value chain activities and management functions and offers a thorough understanding of how Production & Sourcing, Research & Development, Marketing, Human Resource Management and Controlling have to be designed in an international company and what models are available to understand those activities in an international context.
In 20 lessons, a comprehensive overview of all key issues is given. Each lesson is accompanied by a case study from an international company to facilitate the understanding of all important factors involved in strategic international management.

In the second edition, all chapters have been updated, all case studies revised and recent data were integrated. The concept, though, remained unchanged.

Dirk Morschett / Hanna
Schramm-Klein / Joachim Zentes
**Strategic International
Management**
Text and Cases
2. ed. 2010.
x, 470 pp.
Softcover, EUR 42,00
ISBN 978-3-8349-2535-0

Änderungen vorbehalten. Stand: August 2011.
Erhältlich im Buchhandel oder beim Verlag

Gabler Verlag . Abraham-Lincoln-Str. 46 . 65189 Wiesbaden . www.gabler.de

GABLER